Nietzsche and the L

Nietzsche and the Divine

Editors
John Lippitt and Jim Urpeth

CLINAMEN PRESS

Copyright © Clinamen Press Ltd 2000
Introduction and selection of essays © John Lippitt and Jim Urpeth
Individual essays © contributors

First edition published Manchester 2000

'"Nietzsche and the Masters of Truth": the pre-Socratics and Christ', by Béatrice Han
first published in M. A. Wrathall and J. Malpas (eds): *Heidegger, Authenticity and
Modernity: Essays in Honour of Hubert L. Dreyfus, Vol. 1* (Cambridge, MA: MIT Press,
2000) pp. 165–186.

'Nietzsche as a Theological Resource', by Merold Westphal first published in *Modern
Theology* vol. 13 (1997, Blackwell), pp. 213–226.

Jim Urpeth would like to thank Susan Foale for all her support and advice

Published by Clinamen Press
Clinamen Press Limited
Enterprise House
Whitworth Street West
Manchester M1 5WG

www.clinamen.net

A catalogue record for this book is available from the British Library

ISBN 1903083 125

1 3 5 7 9 8 6 4 2

Typeset in Simoncini Garamond by
Northern Phototypesetting Co. Ltd, Bolton
Printed and bound in the UK by
Biddles Ltd, Guildford and King's Lynn
Printed on acid free paper

Contents

Reference key to Nietzsche's texts

Abbreviated titles of works by Nietzsche.
References to Nietzsche's texts are to part and section number, or title
and section number, not to page numbers.

AC	*The Anti-Christ*, (or *The Anti-Christian*)
AOM	'Assorted Opinions and Maxims' (incorporated into HH II)
ASC	'Attempt at a Self-Criticism' (Preface to the second edition of BT)
BGE	*Beyond Good and Evil*
BT	*The Birth of Tragedy*
CW	*The Case of Wagner*
D	*Dawn* (or *Daybreak* or *Dawn of Morning*)
EH	*Ecce Homo*
GM	*On the Genealogy of Morals* (or *On the Genealogy of Morality*)
GS	*The Gay Science* (or *The Joyful* [or *Joyous*] *Science* [or *Wisdom*])
HC	'Homer on Competition' (or 'Homer's Contest')
HH	*Human, All Too Human* (two volumes, I and II)
KGW	*Werke: Kritische Gesamtausgabe*
KSA	*Sämtliche Werke: Kritische Studienausgabe*
RWB	'Richard Wagner in Bayreuth'
SE	'Schopenhauer as Educator'
TI	*Twilight of the Idols*
UD	'On the Uses and Disadvantages of History for Life' (or On the Advantage and Disadvantage of History for Life)
UM	*Untimely Meditations* (or *Unfashionable Observations*)
WP	*The Will to Power*
WS	'The Wanderer and his Shadow' (incorporated into HH II)
Z	*Thus Spoke Zarathustra*

Notes on Contributors

Gary Banham is a lecturer in Philosophy at Manchester Metropolitan University. He is the author of *Kant and the Ends of Aesthetics* (2000) and co-editor of *Evil Spirits: Nihilism and the Fate of Modernity* (2000). He has also written numerous papers on Kant, Derrida, Lyotard and Duchamp, amongst others, and is Series Editor for the new Palgrave series of books 'Renewing Philosophy'.

Michael Bowles is currently head of the Philosophy and Theology subject group at the University of Greenwich. His main areas of interest are Kant, Nietzsche and Deleuze.

Thomas H. Brobjer is a lecturer in the Department of the History of Science and Ideas at the University of Uppsala, Sweden. He has published *Nietzsche's Ethics of Character: A Study of Nietzsche's Ethics and its Place in the History of Moral Thinking* (1995) and numerous papers on different aspects of Nietzsche's thinking. In recent years he has been working on a project entitled 'Nietzsche's Library and Reading and its Relevance for his Thinking'. His translation into Swedish of Nietzsche's *The Anti-Christ* is to appear in the coming year.

Richard S. G. Brown is Associate Professor of Philosophy at Brock University, Canada. He has published on Nietzsche, Kant, Heidegger, Irving Singer, and the *Bhagavad Gita,* and was guest editor for a special edition, on Nietzsche, of *Eidos: Canadian Graduate Journal of Philosophy*. He is currently working on a study entitled 'Nietzsche and the Physiology of Values'.

Jacob Golomb is Professor of Philosophy at the Hebrew University of Jerusalem. His books include *Nietzsche's Enticing Psychology of Power* (1989); *In Search of Authenticity: From Kierkegaard to Camus* (1995) and *Nietzsche in Zion* (forthcoming). He is also editor of *Nietzsche and Jewish*

Culture (1997) and co-editor of both *Nietzsche and Depth Psychology* (1999) and *Nietzsche: Godfather of Fascism?* (in press).

Ullrich Haase teaches at Manchester Metropolitan University. He has published on various authors in the phenomenological tradition and is currently finishing books on Blanchot and Nietzsche.

Béatrice Han is a lecturer in Philosophy at the University of Essex. Her *L'ontologie manquée de Michel Foucault* was published in 1997, and a translation is to be published in 2001. She is the author of numerous papers on Nietzsche, Heidegger and Foucault, as well as on themes in aesthetics. She is currently writing a book entitled 'Transcendence Without Religion', to be published by Routledge.

Christian Kerslake is a visiting lecturer at the University of North London. He has recently completed a doctoral thesis at Middlesex University on Deleuze, Spinoza and post-Kantianism.

John Lippitt is Senior Lecturer in Philosophy at the University of Hertfordshire. He is the author of *Humour and Irony in Kierkegaard's Thought* (2000), and editor of *Nietzsche's Futures* (1999), as well as numerous articles on Kierkegaard, Nietzsche and theories of humour and laughter. The Secretary of the Søren Kierkegaard Society of the UK, he is currently completing a study of Kierkegaard's *Fear and Trembling* for Routledge, and exploring various dimensions of the significance of narrative and fiction for ethics and the philosophy of religion.

Jill Marsden lectures in Philosophy at Bolton Institute of Higher Education. She writes in the fields of aesthetics and twentieth century continental philosophy and is currently completing a book for Palgrave's 'Renewing Philosophy' series on 'Nietzsche's philosophy of ecstasy'.

Graham Parkes is a Professor of Philosophy at the University of Hawaii. He is the editor of *Heidegger and Asian Thought* (1987) and *Nietzsche and Asian Thought* (1991); translator of Nishitani Keiji's *The Self-Overcoming of Nihilism* (1990), Reinhard May's *Heidegger's Hidden Sources: East-Asian Influences on His Work* (1996), and François Berthier's *Reading Zen in the Rocks: The Japanese Dry Landscape Garden* (2000); and author of *Composing the Soul: Reaches of Nietzsche's Psychology* (1994). He is currently working on a new translation of *Also sprach Zarathustra,* and a video project on the places in which Nietzsche did his best thinking.

Tyler T. Roberts is Assistant Professor of Religious Studies at Grinnell College, Iowa. He is the author of *Contesting Spirit: Nietzsche, Affirmation, Religion* (1998) as well as a number of articles on the intersections of religion and philosophy in Nietzsche and contemporary continental philosophy. His current research explores the concept of transcendence and its use in contemporary philosophy and theology for delineating the boundaries between the religious and the secular.

Jim Urpeth is Senior Lecturer in Philosophy at the University of Greenwich. He has published papers on themes in the thought of Kant, Nietzsche, Heidegger, Bataille, Foucault and Deleuze. He is currently writing a book on 'Transhuman Aesthetics' for Palgrave's 'Renewing Philosophy' series. He is the UK editor of the *Journal of Nietzsche Studies* and recently edited a special edition of the journal on 'Nietzsche and Religion'. His main research interests are in aesthetics and the philosophy of religion.

Paul J. M. van Tongeren is Professor of Philosophical Ethics at the Catholic University of Nijmegen, Netherlands. He is the author of *Die Moral von Nietzsches Moralkritik* (1989), *Reinterpreting Modern Culture: An Introduction to Nietzsche's Philosophy* (2000) and editor of *Eros and Eris: Contributions to a Hermeneutical Phenomenology* (1992).

Merold Westphal is Distinguished Professor of Philosophy at Fordham University. Past president of the Hegel Society of America and the North American Søren Kierkegaard Society, he has also served as Executive Co-Director of the Society for Phenomenology and Existential Philosophy. In addition to two books on Hegel and two on Kierkegaard, he is the author of *God, Guilt and Death* (1984) and *Suspicion and Faith: The Religious Uses of Modern Atheism* (1998) which includes a discussion of Nietzsche. His current research seeks to bring Levinas into conversation with Kierkegaard and to explore the relation of postmodern philosophy and religion.

Introduction

God is dead; but given the way of men, there may still be caves for thousands of years in which his shadow will be shown. – And we – we still have to vanquish his shadow, too (GS 108)

- And how many new gods are still possible! As for myself, in whom the religious, that is to say god-forming, instinct occasionally becomes active at impossible times – how differently, how variously the divine has revealed itself to me each time! (WP IV 1038)

Almost two millennia and not a single new God! (AC 19)

For many years a particular view of Nietzsche's relation to religion predominated. As a 'master of suspicion', Nietzsche was, along with Marx and Freud, taken to be one of the standard bearers of secularism and the proponent of uncompromising psycho-physiological insights into the origins of all 'other worldly' realms and aspirations. It was assumed that he rendered religion, without remainder, a merely 'human, all too human' affair. Not only this but, unlike for instance William James, Nietzsche seemed largely to reject the value religion might be thought still to have even when conceived entirely anthropologically. The key note of Nietzsche's relation to religion seemed to be univocally mordant, a relentless exposure of 'sickness', 'slavery', 'nihilism', 'reactive values' etc. However in recent years the received view that Nietzsche was unequivocally hostile to religion and that he sought only to 'unmask' the guises and ruses it adopted to conceal its psychological and sociological origins has been increasingly questioned. In large part, this collection belongs and contributes to this movement of complication and problematisation.[1]

Several developments in the interpretation of Nietzsche's thought have made possible a reassessment of his relation to religion. Arguably one of the most important of these has been the critique of the once predominant 'existentialist' and 'humanist' readings of Nietzsche. Many of the key twentieth century readings of Nietzsche, for all their differences, agreed that his thought, in addition to its well-known critique of all 'metaphysical', extra-historical sources of being and intelligibility, also developed a radical critique of the ontology and values of modern humanism. Nietzsche has long been acknowledged by many as the harbinger not only of the 'death of God' but also the 'death of Man'. After all, 'man is something which should be overcome' (Z 'Prologue' 3). Many of Nietzsche's readers have claimed that he, perhaps more thoroughly than any other thinker before or since, probed the multiple levels of implication linking God and Man beyond the simple opposition of theism and humanism, in relentlessly exploring the consequences for 'Man' of the 'death of God'.

However, even if now an interpretative commonplace, this view of Nietzsche's critique of the 'modern subject' hardly, in and of itself, points toward religion, however understood. Nonetheless, that for post-existentialist readings of Nietzsche, the 'human' is viewed as an 'effect', a product and site of contestation between forces and processes (i.e. the notions of 'will to power', 'eternal return', 'active' and 'reactive' etc.), not derived from, or under the control of, the human; that 'Man' is the product of a 'genealogy' of power relations and struggles far removed from its up-beat 'humanist' self-image, has provided many with a crucial leverage for rethinking the religious in this contemporary emphasis on the 'limits of the human'. The 'impersonalist' interpretations of many of Nietzsche's key themes (e.g. 'will to power' and 'eternal return') that characterise 'anti-humanist' readings of his texts tend to undermine the applicability to his thought of the well-worn religious/secular, theism/humanism oppositions. Indeed, Nietzsche's thought is taken to be a fundamental source of the move away from such time-honoured schemas that has occurred in a wide variety of disciplines in recent times. In addition, proponents of a 'religious' Nietzsche (including a number, but certainly not all, of the contributors to this volume) argue that the basic trajectory of his critique, as one of 'transvaluation', of necessity propels thought beyond such static oppositional structures. Heidegger famously termed this critical momentum in Nietzsche's thought a 'twisting free' from the oppositional structures of 'metaphysics'.[2]

Nonetheless, another important strand of contemporary reception of Nietzsche's thought would seem decisively to preclude a religious appropriation. Such readings stress the 'naturalistic', 'biologistic' and 'physiological' dimensions of Nietzsche's thought, his anti-idealist resolve to 'translate man back into nature' (BGE 230). Even accepting how contentious the interpretation of this aspect of Nietzsche's thought has proved to be, it would seem to preclude a positive 'religious' reading of his work.

For a number of contributors to this collection the way through this apparent *impasse* lies in what might be termed Nietzsche's 'divinization of life.' For example, Graham Parkes, following Nishitani, describes Nietzsche's thought as a 'Dionysian pantheism'. From this perspective, well-represented in our collection, Nietzsche's texts abound with a joy in, and celebration of, the irreducibility and intrinsic 'excess' of 'this world', an inherent sublimity without transcendent reference that can be reasonably described as 'religious' in character. Indeed Nietzsche's self-image as a 'disciple of Dionysus' provides the basis for those papers that detect a positively embraced 'religious' dimension in his texts. Perhaps the short answer to be given to those who might remain bemused by, or resistant to, the notion of such a positively conceived relation between Nietzsche and religion is, simply, Dionysus. For Tyler T. Roberts, Jim Urpeth and Jill Marsden amongst others in this collection, there is in Nietzsche's thought, alongside the better known project of critique, a gesture of 'affirmation' that, when identified with his perennial devotion to Dionysus, reveals a profoundly religious sensibility at the heart of his texts, albeit more in some than others.

But – it might well be asked – why the term 'divine' exactly in the title? This has been chosen, rather than 'religion', to indicate and reflect the cultural and historical range and reference of the collection. However, no assumption can be made as to any shared definition of the 'divine' among the contributors. Each paper implicitly clarifies its sense of the term. Also, this choice of terminology underlines how crucial it is to demarcate Nietzsche's predominantly hostile evaluation of Christianity (if not Christ) from his response to religion more widely. When the wide range of reference of the term 'religious' in Nietzsche's texts is appreciated, beyond his somewhat obsessive critical assault on the so-called 'Judaeo-Christian tradition', then the first step is taken toward a re-opening of the topic of Nietzsche and the divine in all its diversity.

In this collection, such a broadening of the usual confines of discussion in this area – which often implicitly identifies religion exclusively with Christianity – is signalled by those section headings that refer to the other religious traditions he addressed. That Nietzsche had much to say of a profound and provocative kind about not only Judaism and Christianity but also 'Eastern' religions and those of ancient Greece is now widely appreciated. The papers in sections II-IV reveal the complexity of debate in their respective areas and highlight the point that it is far too simplistic to assume that Nietzsche was completely hostile to the 'Judaeo-Christian' tradition and certain 'Eastern' religions and unproblematically enthusiastic about Greek religion. Contributors to these sections draw attention to the many nuances and complexities of Nietzsche's treatment of these traditions as well as, in the case of sections II and III, to their inter-relation. Indeed this issue is re-visited in various ways by other papers throughout the book.

The term 'divine' has also been chosen to indicate the range of theologico-philosophical perspectives found in the collection. Following Nietzsche's valorisation of multiplicity many of the contributors draw in diverse ways upon the manifold (in Merold Westphal's phrase) 'theological resources' Nietzsche provides to articulate the religious sensibility they find in Nietzsche's texts. In a sense this is to acknowledge those well-established strands of theology which, recognising the problems of anthropomorphism inherent in the notion of a 'personal deity', deploy the more neutral term 'divine' or 'godhead' instead of 'God'.

In addition to the three sections of the collection that address Nietzsche's relation to specific religious traditions there are three others that are more broadly defined. The collection begins cautiously and sceptically. Not every contributor to the collection finds Nietzsche to be so obviously 'god-intoxicated'! Before Westphal identifies the loosening of the assumptions of 'onto-theology' that has to occur before Nietzsche and religion can productively come into contact, Thomas Brobjer reminds us of the depth of Nietzsche's atheism. This reservation and hesitation about the relation between Nietzsche and religion is found, in different ways, elsewhere in the collection in the papers by John Lippitt, Michael Bowles and Ullrich Haase. Perhaps Lippitt's Kierkegaardian and Wittgensteinian concerns sound the most critical note in their suggestion that Nietzsche's critique of Christianity in the *Genealogy of Morals* may fail to connect with it on a fundamental level. Lippitt's paper stems from the school of Nietzsche interpretation which, its criticisms notwithstanding, sees him as a useful resource for those for whom philosophy is fundamentally a form of ethical practice: that is, which finds in Nietzsche a strongly 'moral perfectionist' dimension, to use Stanley Cavell's phrase.[3] Such an interpretation, of course, starts from a very different set of assumptions from those of the 'anti-humanists' – but it would be mistaken simply to assume that such readings can be unproblematically equated with those 'existentialist' or 'humanist' readings which the 'anti-humanists' seek to contest. In section VI Haase and Bowles develop distinct accounts of the ineliminable relation between the human and the divine that acknowledges the subtleties inherent in Nietzsche's most famous phrase – 'God is dead'. In this sense they contrast with the papers in section V in which – along with Parkes – the most positive alignments between Nietzsche and the divine are drawn.

The papers in section V explore the possibilities Nietzsche's thought offers for rethinking the divine given the 'death of God'. These papers argue that this extraordinary 'event' is responded to by Nietzsche and some of his notable successors as an opportunity of an historically unique kind to rethink transcendence without reference to a transcendent or suprasensuous order. It is to attempt to think the 'divine' beyond the traditional contrast of immanence and transcendence. It is to assume that Nietzsche's hostility was aimed not at religion *in toto* but at 'nihilistic' and 'reactive' or 'moral' forms of it. It is to reconnect religion affirmatively with the body, the senses, affectivity, desire – in short, with 'life' – but also to acknowledge the importance of *ascesis* therein.

Many of the papers in the collection acknowledge that the traditional ontological self-understanding of, in particular, the so-called 'Platonic-Christian' tradition is seriously undermined by Nietzsche's critique of it. It is also an assumption among many of the contributors that Nietzsche, perhaps implicitly acknowledging the thoroughness of Kant's critique in this regard, did not concern himself with the moribund field of the traditional 'proofs for the existence of God', but instead pursued the even more fundamental question of the *value* of the Christian God and of Christian values as well as those of other traditions. Of course, Nietzsche offered a range of ontological and epistemological critiques of the 'metaphysics' of, for instance, Christianity, often aligning this with reflections on the nature of language – 'I fear we are not getting rid of God because we still believe in grammar...' (TI '"Reason" in Philosophy' 5). Other features of his thought are equally significant here, not least his stress on the ontological primacy of 'becoming' and its challenge to what has become known as the 'metaphysics of presence' said to characterise the 'Platonic-Christian' tradition. Nonetheless it is the question of value, the *genealogical* character of Nietzsche's critique, that for many of the contributors to this collection is the most distinctive and radical aspect of his discussion of religion.

Having aimed to sketch some of the collection's major themes, let us next turn briefly to consider each individual paper.

I. Atheism and Theology

Many readers of Nietzsche will, no doubt, be uneasy about the tendency of a number of papers in this collection to complicate considerably and to render ambiguous Nietzsche's relation to the 'divine'. They will be even more nervous when, as in some cases, a 'religious' sensibility is said to underpin and pervade Nietzsche's thought. For many, such approaches blunt the challenge of Nietzsche's forensic exposure of the depth to which 'Platonic-Christian' values are ingrained in western culture, and threaten to jeopardise his critical evaluation of them as the source of 'nihilism'. In short, Nietzsche's atheism and rejection of all 'superterrestrial hopes' (Z 'Prologue' 3) are prematurely – and conveniently – forgotten.

Such reservations as these are clearly operative in Thomas Brobjer's paper. Brobjer argues that the mature Nietzsche espoused an unproblematic atheism. Drawing upon a wide range of sources, including letters and biographical material, Brobjer charts Nietzsche's progress from the devout Christianity of his childhood and youth to the uncompromising atheism that increasingly characterised his adult life. Nietzsche's unflinchingly courageous challenge to the values and beliefs of his family and contemporaries is clearly sketched by Brobjer, who identifies five stages in Nietzsche's voyage from 'pious Christian childhood' through a phase of 'passive atheism' to a culminating period of 'active' and 'explicit' atheism. In addition to a biographical focus Brobjer also offers a clear statement of a perspective endorsed by a number of other contributors in which Nietzsche's 'critique of Christianity is not so much based on the denial of the existence of God but on the questioning and denial of [Christianity's] value.' As an opening, Brobjer's paper provides a necessary statement of the well-established conception of Nietzsche's relation to the 'divine' as being one of unambiguous hostility.

If Brobjer is right, it would seem natural to ask: What use is Nietzsche to the theologian? This is the issue addressed by Merold Westphal, from a very different perspective. Westphal suggests that the God of ontology (the so-called 'onto-theo-logical project') has a 'twin' in the God of social theory (the 'socio-theo-logical project'). Both are gods created in a human image, mere means to human ends; both are instances of self-deceived human will to power simply putting 'God' to work as their 'man Friday'. However, Westphal suggests, theology can have another vocation, which includes vigilance against these two tendencies. One serious challenge to this tendency of human beings and societies to treat the world simply as means to their own flourishing, he argues, is monotheistic religion. Yet the Achilles' heel of monotheism is its tendency to commit the fallacy of 'cognitive transubstantiation': to slide from a view of God as absolute to viewing *its own thinking* of God as absolute. It is such onto- or socio- theologians for whom Nietzsche can be a 'prophylactic resource', protecting them from the theological equivalent of syphilis or aids: 'a deadly virus that kills theology by transforming what would be discourse about God into discourse about ourselves.' Westphal suggests two ways in which Nietzsche can help here. First, his perspectivism is a vital corrective to such *hubris*, reminding us as it does of that human finitude which the theologian, like Nietzsche, must accept. Second, allied to this hermeneutics of finitude is the hermeneutics of suspicion, which Westphal insists is an indispensable tool for the theologian. The reasons for this are threefold. The hermeneutics of suspicion reminds us of the difference between the truth of a belief and the shameful ways in which that belief can be held; it is a secular way of reminding the theologian of the sometimes forgotten centrality of sin for theology; and it helps, via its suspicion of human motives, to avoid the idolatry of worshipping as God an idol made in man's image.

Having introduced some of the issues from these two very different standpoints, our next three sections turn to considering 'Nietzsche and the divine' in the context of specific religious traditions and cultures.

II. Judaism and Christianity

Jacob Golomb, in a treatment of Nietzsche's relation to the Old Testament, aims to show that some of his key thoughts on matters such as power and authenticity could have been inspired by his reading of that collection of texts. Golomb maintains that the religion of the ancient Hebrews played as formative a role in the thought of the young Nietzsche as did the ancient Greeks. Central to Golomb's argument is a distinction he sketches between 'negative' and 'positive' conceptions and patterns of power, and, concomitantly, 'negative' and 'positive' religion. After an account of the defeat of 'positive' religion by its 'negative' correlate, Golomb draws a distinction seen as key to understanding Nietzsche's relation to Judaism. This distinction, basically akin to that proposed by Yirmiahu Yovel but somewhat different from that drawn by some other writers on this topic, is between the ancient Hebrews of the Old Testament, the 'second temple' Jews who instigated the 'slave revolt' which gave rise to Christianity, and the modern Jews of the dias-

pora. He also argues that the idea of authenticity or 'truthfulness' used
by Nietzsche, and incorporating 'endless self-affirmation and dynamic
openness', is rooted in the ancient Hebrews and their God.

Gary Banham further problematises Nietzsche's relation to Judaism.
Banham is concerned with the relation between that religion and Nietzsche's genealogical critique, in the process engaging with both Gillian
Rose and Yovel. He pays particular attention to the different 'voices' in
the *Genealogy of Morals*: voices which, he argues, highlight dimensions
of Nietzsche's deeply equivocal attitude towards Jews and Judaism.
Indicating that the voice of the first few sections of the first essay is interrupted by that of a 'free spirit' and 'democrat' (GM I 9), Banham considers, via Rose, the question of whether genealogical critique is a
'democratic' and – hence 'Jewish' – art. Drawing on Nietzsche's use of
the 'free spirit' figure in other texts, he draws out aspects of the complex
relation between morality and philosophy with which genealogy tries to
wrestle. Still further voices, and their significance for Judaism, are considered, before Banham turns to *The Anti-Christ* to challenge Yovel's
view of Nietzsche's relation to Judaism. In that late text, Banham
argues, Nietzsche traces a history of the Jewish people which has five,
rather than three, stages – a factor which he attempts to use further to
highlight the equivocations in Nietzsche's relation to Judaism, and their
significance.

John Lippitt is also concerned with dimensions of the *Genealogy*. But
whereas Banham's focus is on competing voices in Nietzsche's own text,
Lippitt considers a response to (at least one of) these Nietzschean
voices from another polyphonic *enfant terrible* of the nineteenth century,
Søren Kierkegaard. Lippitt contrasts two very different narratives of
faith: that found in the *Genealogy* and that in *Fear and Trembling*,
authored by the Kierkegaardian pseudonym Johannes de Silentio. He
focuses on two features of Nietzsche's portrait of the development of
'slave morality': the idea of undischarged instincts, 'denied appropriate
deeds' (GM I 10), turning inwards, and the transcendentalising phase of
slave morality's development, brought about under the direction of the
ascetic priest. Lippitt points out how the repression and internalisation
so central to Nietzsche's narrative contrast starkly with the joy and
absence of blame characteristic of the model of faith in *Fear and Trembling*. Moreover, against Nietzsche's suspicion that transcendentalising
moves devalue the finite, he shows how in *Fear and Trembling* the deval-
uation of the finite is precisely what Johannes warns against, such a
move being characteristic of mere 'infinite resignation', not 'faith'.

Indeed, absolutely integral to Johannes' portrait of faith is that its exemplars place a very high value on the finite. Lippitt further argues that the *Genealogy* violates the 'grammar' of certain key religious concepts, by blurring psychological, moral and religious uses of terms (such as 'sin') in such a way as to fail to respect the particularity of their context of use. It is in this respect that one might ask just how much Nietzsche genuinely engages with Christianity at all. Finally, Lippitt suggests it is important to take seriously the narrative dimensions of both these texts, as narrative is central to the kind of 'aspect-dawning' which both Kierkegaard and Nietzsche are aiming to bring about in their readers. But, drawing on James Conant's reading of Nietzsche on exemplarity, he concludes by suggesting that the *Genealogy* - a narrative, according to Lippitt, excessively reliant on types – is, *ceteris paribus*, less well-placed to bring about such aspect-dawning as is a text, such as *Fear and Trembling*, whose narrative deals with a specific exemplar.

III. Ancient Greek religion

In an article linking the third section of our collection with the second, Paul van Tongeren offers a detailed interpretation of an aphorism from *Human, All Too Human* entitled 'The non-Greek element in Christianity'. Here, Nietzsche discusses the opposition between Christianity and ancient Greek religion. Yet as van Tongeren points out, a close reading of this aphorism leaves one rather unclear as to exactly what Nietzsche opposes to what. In response to this problem, van Tongeren puts under the microscope the very idea of 'opposition' in Nietzsche, stressing the importance he places on related ideas such as 'struggle' and 'contest' after the fashion of the Greek *agon*. Van Tongeren argues that any opposition between *Griechentum* and *Christentum*, as two interpretations of culture or attitudes to life, must be understood within this agonistic context. Crucial here is the idea of measure (*Maß*). One needs a standard (*Maßtab*) in order to critique one's culture, and in many ways, for Nietzsche, Greek culture is that standard. However, this standard is neither undisputed nor fixed. Understanding Greek culture requires us to challenge, and allow ourselves to be challenged by, that culture. The latter dimension includes letting it challenge our prevailing understanding *of it*: an understanding which renders it powerless by making it consistent with contemporary – 'Christian' – culture, its alterity lost from view. But as well as this general point about mutual contestation, van Tongeren also argues that for Nietzsche, Christianity specifically is essential to our understanding of Greek religious culture. Christianity is a crucial bridge back to the Greeks: the opposition between Greek and Christian religion is 'a study in the conflict within the foundations of our common culture'; 'the two roots of our culture'. Among the crucial differences between them, he claims, is that Christianity makes a struggle resulting from tension impossible (not least because of its *absolute* subordination of humanity to God), whereas central to *Griechentum* is precisely the kind of 'measure' Nietzsche commends: 'a moderated moderation, a measure which is itself measured.'

Béatrice Han also explores Nietzsche's conception of the relation between the Greek and Christian worlds with reference to the crucial issue of the nature of truth. Han draws upon Marcel Détienne's important study, *Masters of Truth in Archaic Greece,* which identifies a shift in the Greeks' conception of truth. Han offers a clear re-statement of Détienne's account of a period in which, for the Greeks, truth was taken to reside in the personal authority of its author, the 'Master of Truth' in whom truth was existentially exemplified. However, this was, with the advent of 'metaphysics', supplanted by an image of truth in which it is conceived as an impersonal, theoretical affair concerning a relation of 'adequation' between a proposition and (a notion simultaneously introduced) its objective referent. This momentous change involves a transition from an essentially 'ethical' to an 'epistemological' conception of truth. For Détienne this fundamental shift in the conception of truth is the key to understanding the sea-change that occurred from the pre-Socratic to the Socratic-Platonic periods of Greek cultural history.

Han demonstrates throughout her paper Nietzsche's sustained valorisation of the pre-metaphysical conception of truth as described by Détienne. On this basis she develops an intriguing application of Détienne's claims to Nietzsche's thought suggesting a comparison between his accounts of, on the one hand, the contrast between the pre-Socratic and Socratic Greeks and, on the other, that between Jesus Christ and St. Paul. In this she implicitly links Nietzsche's *The Birth of Tragedy* and *The Anti-Christ* and thereby throws fresh light on Nietzsche's distinction, in the latter text, between the life of Christ and Pauline Christianity. Han proposes that Nietzsche's critique of Socrates and Paul can be interpreted as the identification of both as failed 'Masters of Truth' fuelled by *ressentiment* against such masters as the pre-Socratic tragedians and Christ respectively. Han's reading of Nietzsche's critique of Socrates and Paul illuminates very clearly the source of his condemnation of their imposition on to the 'Masters of Truth' of an 'adequationist' conception of truth that thereby neutralises the personal authority of the ancient poets and Christ. There are many fruitful possibilities that emerge from Han's approach, including her insightful reading of *The Anti-Christ* and the suggestion that Nietzsche's recovery of a non-epistemological conception of truth lies at the basis of his critique of the culture of his contemporaries who, apart from such exceptions as Goethe, lack the 'wholeness' that characterise a 'Master of Truth'.

Christian Kerslake considers the importance to Nietzsche of the role of 'forgetting'. He explores some of the nuances of such acts of forgetting in relation to our lack of power over the past, and the dimensions of the past's influx into the present which terrify Nietzsche's Zarathustra. This serves as a preliminary to the central feature of Kerslake's article, an attempt to explain why Pierre Klossowski considers eternal return to be 'a new version of *metempsychosis*'. Focusing on the ancient Greek, rather than oriental, origins of this doctrine – traditionally conceived, in Kerslake's words, as 'the preservation of the Person through different transcorporations'- he argues that the doctrine is not essentially related to that of the 'immortality of the soul'. Rather, Kerslake claims that the essential elements of metempsychosis are the far more Nietzsche-compatible ideas of memory and forgetting, and metamorphosis, the commonly associated ideas of disembodiment and immortality being relatively late additions.

IV. Hinduism and Buddhism

In this section, the papers by Richard Brown and Graham Parkes discuss Nietzsche's relation to Hinduism and Buddhism respectively. Both authors demonstrate, in different ways, the interesting possibilities that lie beyond Nietzsche's ostensibly derivative and limited knowledge of Eastern religious traditions as manifest in his use of notions such as the 'veil of *maya*' and criticism of others such as *nirvana*. Beyond the well-known mediated critiques of 'Eastern' religion found in Nietzsche's attack on Schopenhauer's 'buddhistic negation of the will', Brown and Parkes explore a more fruitful and nuanced exchange between Nietzsche and 'the East'. The similarities both find between Nietzsche's thought and different Eastern religions is, they suggest, especially manifest in *Thus Spoke Zarathustra*.

Brown both criticises aspects of Nietzsche's, Schopenhauerian derived, misconception of Hinduism and suggests a number of 'ironic affinities' between key aspects of Nietzsche's thought and aspects of the

Bhagavad Gita. Brown illustrates this claim through a comparative reading of the *Bhagavad Gita* and *Thus Spoke Zarathustra*. The central figures in both texts undertake, Brown claims, strikingly similar spiritual odysseys. Brown argues that there are surprising similarities between the central tenets of the *Bhagavad Gita* and such important themes in Nietzsche's thought as the 'body', the 'will to power' and 'fate'. Although Brown acknowledges the dangers of adopting an overly consensualist approach when undertaking such ambitious comparative exercises, he nonetheless insists that 'it never fails to be a fruitful exercise to reflect Nietzsche, the philosopher of perspectives, in as many mirrors as possible, and particularly so in mirrors which are cross-culturally framed and therefore usually not found within anyone's immediate focus.'

Graham Parkes argues that Nietzsche's thought is the expression of a profoundly religious conception of nature which he terms 'Dionysian pantheism', a formulation that resonates with aspects of a number of other papers in the collection. Parkes aims to illustrate how similar Nietzsche's religious sensibility so conceived is to Mahāyāna Buddhism with which Nietzsche was unfamiliar and to which, Parkes suggests, his generalised critiques of Buddhism do not apply. Enhancing the comparative dimension, Parkes acknowledges that the relation he discusses between Nietzsche's Dionysianism and a particular strand of Buddhism derives from the Japanese Nietzsche scholar Keiji Nishitani's pioneering study *The Self-Overcoming of Nihilism*. However, Parkes greatly extends this comparison through a detailed reading of *Thus Spoke Zarathustra* from a Mahāyāna perspective. He suggests some particularly intriguing affinities between 'eternal recurrence' and this form of Buddhism and explores its resonance with a number of other themes in Nietzsche's text.

Parkes insists that his claim that Nietzsche's thought can best be described in terms of 'Dionysian pantheism', particularly when this is linked to an attempt to demonstrate the 'ecological' as well as religious elements of Nietzsche's work, is not a mere 'naïve romanticism'. Indeed Parkes identifies, as the common element between Nietzsche's 'Dionysian pantheism' and Mahāyāna Buddhism, a shared critique of 'our death-anxiety-engendered desire to subjugate the natural world' and a mutual 'readiness for the absolutely sudden and thwarting,' that makes possible 'a way of being that verges on the divine through its fullness of sorrows and joys.'

V. Mysticism and Affectivity

Beyond Nietzsche's criticisms of specific religious traditions, the papers in this section address the extent to which Nietzsche also offers an alternative conception of the 'divine' that expresses a religious sensibility inherent to his thought. In pursuing this issue, Tyler T. Roberts, Jim Urpeth and Jill Marsden emphasise the importance for any 'Nietzschean' religion of mysticism and affectivity. The key philosophical issue they each discuss is Nietzsche's rethinking of transcendence as a 'this worldly' phenomenon intrinsic to temporality, desire and 'the body'. Roberts, Urpeth and Marsden also suggest how the reinterpretation of transcendence they find in Nietzsche's thought characterises, arguably more than he appreciated, some of the religious traditions he condemns.

To start with, Roberts explores what he describes as a 'mystical thematics' in Nietzsche's thought. Roberts notes the importance of mysticism in the young Nietzsche's engagement with Schopenhauer, and claims that certain mystical themes – chiefly 'an ecstatic union with the cosmos or ultimate reality' – are at the heart of *Zarathustra*. This complicates Nietzsche's famous claim, in his 'self-criticism' of *The Birth of Tragedy*, to have left behind the 'metaphysical comfort' of his first work and to now embrace a purely 'this-worldly comfort' (ASC 7). Yet in *Zarathustra*, Roberts argues, there remains a relation to transcendence 'not as escape, but as an expansion and reorientation of awareness in which one's life in the earthly and finite finds a new center "beyond" itself and "deeper" than itself.' Yet beyond all this, Roberts points out what is often not acknowledged in relation to discussions of 'mystical' elements in Nietzsche: namely, just what a contested term 'mysticism' has become in religious studies. Contrary to the traditional focus upon 'mystical experiences', Roberts argues that 'mystical thematics' need not focus upon private, individual experiences of selflessness or union with the divine. Instead, he commends a focus upon *disciplined practices* oriented to the divine. An important part of this change in orientation is a focus on mystical *writing* as a form of religious practice: a writing which is not so much 'about' the divine other, as itself the 'site and enactment of that otherness.' Drawing on Stanley Cavell, Cavell's hero Thoreau and the Christian apophactic tradition of 'negative theology', Roberts relates this discussion to Nietzsche's 'mature', post-*Zarathustra* writings. This is 'ecstatic philosophy': it embodies a deeply ambivalent attitude towards intoxication and excess, Nietzsche's enthusiasm for same being tempered by a suspicion echoing that of the Christian mystics to their 'mystical experiences'. Exploring the figure of Dionysus, the themes of departure and return, and various modes of 'unsaying' in Nietzsche's texts, Roberts concludes that for Nietzsche, as for such 'mystics' as Eckhart and Thoreau, there is something 'life-giving and divinizing' in 'the space of emptiness in which self is divided from self.'

Jim Urpeth also interprets Nietzsche as a fundamentally 'religious' thinker. In his paper Urpeth aims to clarify the nature of Nietzsche's religiosity and to consider his vehement critique of Christianity from this perspective. Nietzsche's critique of Christianity is then compared to two others, namely Rudolf Otto's critical defence and Georges Bataille's 'Nietzschean' critique of it. The organising theme throughout Urpeth's paper is these thinkers' respective accounts of religious affectivity insofar as each of them emphasises its primacy over the conceptual-doctrinal and moral aspects of religion. Two key issues are addressed by Urpeth throughout his comparison of Nietzsche, Otto and Bataille. These are, firstly, the task of rethinking the nature of religious affectivity in impersonalist, a-subjective terms. This is a crucial part of Urpeth's on-going project to outline a non-reductive 'religious materialism'. Secondly, the notion of immanence, and the role it plays in both rethinking transcendence and reconceiving the critique of specific religions.

These two themes provide the criteria Urpeth employs in his comparative evaluation of the three thinkers he considers. In the course of this analysis Urpeth highlights and reflects on the importance of the question of the autonomy of religion in relation not only to the moral domain but also, ultimately, to the 'human' itself. Urpeth's paper is animated by the credibility of a radically non-anthropomorphic religion and the search for 'traces' of such within Christianity (insofar as it affirms the 'sacred' at all).

Perhaps no other contributor makes such a bold and imaginative attempt to 'flesh out' a religious sensibility inherent in Nietzsche's thought as Jill Marsden. Although her paper pursues themes also addressed by Roberts and Urpeth, Marsden – employing but also extending Klossowski's reading of Nietzsche – ambitiously undertakes to describe a fully transvalued religiosity at work in Nietzsche. Marsden proposes that we find Nietzsche's positive religious voice in the themes of 'rapture', the 'lunar' and the 'nocturnal' in his texts. For Marsden there is a seam of intense and atheistic religious ecstasy at work in Nietzsche. Marsden's sensitivity to the metaphorics of Nietzsche's texts illustrates very effectively Roberts' notion of a 'mystics of metaphor' in

his thought. Apart from Klossowski, Marsden's interpretation of Nietzsche's religiosity is informed by such important commentators on his
thought as Bataille, Blanchot, Cioran and Irigaray. She also suggests
links between what she terms Nietzsche's 'religion of the night sun' and
aspects of the texts of writers such as Hölderlin and Dostoyevsky. This
is a religious sensibility – characterised by estrangement, alterity and
uncanniness – that resonates with aspects of Urpeth's paper. Marsden's
basic stance, also explored in other ways by other contributors, is the
'affirmation of eternal return as divine'. She, like Urpeth, reads Nietzsche as a thinker who emphasises the importance of the libidinal and
affective elements in religion. However, more than any other paper in
the collection, Marsden develops a reading of Nietzsche in terms of a
'sacred energetics of desire'.

VI. The return of the divine?

Our final section consists of two very different papers. Ullrich Haase
offers a critical discussion of the nature of the contemporary phenomenon of '*a return of God*, a new actuality of religion,' taking as his basis
recent texts on this topic by Derrida and Vattimo in which Nietzsche
figures prominently. Haase develops a multi-layered reflection on the
philosophical background and meaning of this religious turn and how its
post-Nietzschean context distinguishes it from earlier examples of the
absence and return of god. The specific phenomenon Haase emphasises
here is that of the 'secularisation of Christianity' and its paradoxical
effects on religion: a theme that Vattimo, taking his cue from Nietzsche,
analyses.

At the heart of Haase's paper is an interpretation, from a 'Heideggerian' perspective, of the meaning of the 'death of god' in Nietzsche's
thought. Indeed Haase draws to our attention the ontological and linguistic peculiarities of the notion of the 'death of god' and the fact that
these are all too often unaddressed in debates about it. Haase places his
discussion of these issues into a wider context in which he considers the
issue of the nature of the relation between philosophy and religion in the
contemporary epoch: taking as his example the modern incredulity with
the 'ontological argument'. Questioning the terms of engagement on
which questions of religion and the divine have been conducted over the
last two centuries, Haase argues that amongst its confusions is the inco-
herence of the idea of a private God. In stressing the importance of the
link between religion, language and community, Haase interestingly

rereads the 'madman' passage in *The Gay Science* in this light, reminding us that Nietzsche's German signifies one who has 'lost the boundary
and the bond of the community'. Haase also introduces a new voice,
rarely heard in this context, that of Bergson. Throughout his paper
Haase discusses the significance to the contemporary fate of religion of
Nietzsche's notions of both 'eternal return' and the 'overman'. Haase
draws together these diverse strands when he states: 'that we have difficulties with the question of the existence of Gods – and with Nietzsche's
philosophy generally – lies in the inability to unify thinking and thing
thought. Yet that brings us equally to the root of religion as to the difficulty of Nietzsche's text, for the experience of the unity of thinking and
thing thought is what we call mystic experience.'

Finally, Michael Bowles offers us a decidedly different take on the
topic of Nietzsche and the divine in a paper that develops a very distinctive interpretation of the fusion of life and the divine in Nietzsche's
thought. For Bowles, 'the return to life must be a divine act', and he
offers an intriguing reading of *Thus Spoke Zarathustra* to unfold this
claim. The key elements in Bowles's reading are an account of Nietzsche's notion of 'life' in *Zarathustra* in terms of the theme of 'eating' in
that text. In a sense this is reminiscent of Kerslake's, Urpeth's and Marsden's emphasis on a naturalistic or 'materialist' interpretation of Nietzsche. However, Bowles' conception of this is quite different from these
other papers in that he foregrounds the themes of 'codes', 'form' and
'styles' of life finding in their confrontation and interaction the play of
the divine.

This 'biological' perspective forms the basis of Bowles' interpretation
of the themes of tragedy, the 'death of god' and 'eternal recurrence' in
Zarathustra. In a subtle way Bowles criticises 'anti-humanist' readings of
Nietzsche, particularly on the topic of his relation to the divine. For
Bowles the divine is only to be found within the contestation of different styles of life, the digestion and incorporation of one 'code' by
another. The 'overcoming of man' is not, Bowles insists, a once and for
all event but, emphasising the role in Nietzsche's thought of the Greeks'
notion of *agon* (recall van Tongeren's claims here) he states: 'a god who
celebrates divinity does not want to obliterate the other players, for that
would be to destroy the game itself. The Nietzschean notion of divinity
is the celebration of the contest between codes: it is the act of throwing
against a god which is divine.'

As will be seen from the above, *Nietzsche and the Divine* is
unashamedly eclectic. It is important to emphasise perhaps the most

serious risk borne by many contributors to this collection. It couldn't be more explicitly stated by Nietzsche than when, in *Ecce Homo*, he writes:

> ...there is nothing in me of a founder of a religion – religions are affairs of the rabble, I have need of washing my hands after contact with religious people...I do not *want* 'believers',...I have a terrible fear that I will one day be pronounced *holy*: one will guess why I bring out this book *before-hand*; it is intended to prevent people from making mischief with me... (EH 'Why I am a Destiny' 1).

Whether some or all of the contributors are 'making mischief' with Nietzsche is an issue for our readers to decide. However, we hope that they will not feel the need to 'wash their hands' of this collection!

Jim Urpeth
John Lippitt
Universities of Greenwich and Hertfordshire
September 2000

Notes

1 Earlier versions of many of the papers in this collection were presented at the conference 'Nietzsche and Religion', held at the University of Greenwich in September 1998. This event was the eighth annual conference of the Friedrich Nietzsche Society. A selection of some of the other papers given at this conference have also been published (as a 'Nietzsche and Religion' themed edition, edited by Jim Urpeth) in the *Journal of Nietzsche Studies* 19 (Spring 1999).

2 M. Heidegger, *Nietzsche: Vol. 1* (New York: Harper and Row, 1979, trans. D. F. Krell) p. 210.

3 See S. Cavell, *Conditions Handsome and Unhandsome: the Constitution of Emersonian Perfectionism* (Chicago: University of Chicago Press, 1990).

1

Nietzsche's atheism

Thomas Brobjer

The whole of Nietzsche's thinking and philosophy can be seen as a response to Christianity. Nietzsche claimed that his first philosophical speculation at the age of thirteen concerned the 'problem of evil'. In general his childhood was characterized by profound piety and Christian sympathies. Nietzsche's real beginning as a philosopher, at the age of twenty-one, came about through his discovery of Schopenhauer, particularly his atheism which Nietzsche later explicitly claimed was that aspect of his thought which he found most attractive. Nietzsche's first book, *The Birth of Tragedy*, can reasonably be read as an attempt to construct an alternative world-view, a tragic *Weltanschauung,* to that of the Christian. In fact, from his school-days until his mental collapse in 1889, Nietzsche upheld a sharp dichotomy and hierarchy between the ancient world and Christianity. His break with Wagner and Schopenhauer around the year 1876, and thus his break with much of his own earlier philosophy, was caused by his realization that both of them were too influenced by Christianity. During his 'middle period' Nietzsche describes himself as a 'free spirit', praises Voltaire and proclaims the 'death of God'. In his magnum opus, *Thus Spoke Zarathustra*, Nietzsche emphasizes that Zarathustra is more 'godless' than any other man. Subsequently Nietzsche radicalises his critique of Christianity and makes it more explicit. *On the Genealogy of Morality* - which Nietzsche describes in *Ecce Homo,* as 'three decisive preliminary studies of a psychologist for a revaluation of all values' (EH 'Genealogy of Morals') and as containing 'the first psychology of the priest' (EH 'Genealogy of Morals') – includes a severe critique of Christianity and foreshadows *The Anti-Christ,* subtitled *'A Curse on Christianity'.* The main philosophical project of the last active years of Nietzsche's life was the 'revaluation of all values' which, as is made explicit, essentially means a revaluation of all Christian values.

Most of Nietzsche's philosophy can be seen as a critique of Christianity and as an attempt to construct an alternative to Christian views and values. His perspectivism and critique of the concept of truth is a critique of the Christian (and metaphysical) view of truth; his concept of the *Übermensch* can be seen as a contrast to the ongoing project of ever 'making man smaller' which Nietzsche identified with Christianity and modernity. Similarly the notion of 'eternal recurrence' can be seen as a cyclical alternative to the linear Christian conception of temporality, as an anti-teleological perspective in contrast to the teleology of Christianity.

I shall argue that Nietzsche's relation to Christianity passes through five phases moving from the devout Christianity of his childhood to the extreme atheism that marks his thinking from about 1880 onwards. I will review the evidence for each stage of this developing relation toward Christianity and briefly characterise each period. I shall then discuss how Nietzsche regarded his atheism, how he evaluated his godlessness and status as 'anti-christ'.

I
The pious Christian childhood (1844–1861)

Nietzsche was born and raised in a deeply religious family. His father was a pastor, his mother was the daughter of a pastor, both his grandparents were pastors (one of whom he often spent his school vacations with). Both of his aunts and his paternal grandmother, who for most of his upbringing lived with the family, were profoundly pious. His father, Ludwig Nietzsche, died when Friedrich was five years old, an event which seemed to have strengthened his faith and determination to emulate him. Hence Nietzsche's childhood and youth were very pious and Christian. When he began school, he was called 'the little pastor' due to the seriousness and sobriety of his comportment as well as his ability to cite from memory long passages from the *Bible*.

At the end of his early, long autobiography from 1858 written when Nietzsche was thirteen years old, he wrote, 'in everything God has safely guided me...I have firmly determined to serve him forever.'[1] The same attitude is expressed in many poems and letters from his childhood, and at both the Naumburg Domgymansium and Schulpforta Nietzsche's best subject was religion.[2]

At the time of his confirmation in March 1861 Nietzsche appears to have been profoundly pious and religious. At that time, he became close to Paul Deussen, also a pastor's son. Deussen later wrote of this period, 'I still very clearly remember the holy, otherworldly feelings, which filled us during the weeks before and after the confirmation. We would have been completely ready to, at once, leave this world for the purpose of being with Christ, and all our thinking, feeling and striving were filled with an otherworldly joy.'[3]

The period of loss of faith (1861–1865)

During the period following his confirmation Nietzsche's writing of pious religious poems and statements begin to decrease in number. He also began to read books that question the Christian faith. Most importantly, for his birthday in October 1861, he asked for two works by Ludwig Feuerbach, including *Das Wesen des Christenthum* which treats Christianity as merely the projection of human desires and illusions. In 1862 Nietzsche read and subscribed to the materialistically-oriented cultural journal *Anregung für Kunst, Leben und Wissenschaft* and became restless and less well-behaved. This change can be explained by puberty, but was possibly also caused by religious doubt and a loss of faith. Nietzsche's earliest sceptical and critical views of Christianity come from the early part of 1862. In a letter to Pinder and Krug from April 1862, which seems profoundly influenced by Feuerbach, Nietzsche wrote:

> we recognize that we are only responsible to ourselves, that a reproach over a failed direction in life only relates to us, not to any higher power…Christianity is essentially a question of the heart…The main teachings of Christianity only relate the fundamental truths of the human heart; they are symbols…To become blessed through faith means nothing other than the old truth, that only the heart, not knowledge, can make happy. That God became human only shows that humans should not seek their blessedness among eternity, but instead found their paradise on earth; the delusion of an otherworldly world has brought the human spirit into a false relation to this world: it was the product of a people's childhood.[4]

The same attitude is visible in the two important essays Nietzsche wrote for *Germania* in April 1862, '*Fatum und Geschichte*' and '*Willensfreiheit und Fatum*'.[5] In a note from 1879, Nietzsche claims that he was already an atheist at Pforta – implying that his loss of faith occurred between 1861-1864.[6] However, Nietzsche nonetheless wrote several religious poems during his last two years at Pforta and also elected the pastor Kletschke as his new tutor.

When Nietzsche left Schulpforta to study at the University of Bonn, he registered for both theology and philosophy, but his attendance and interest in the few (just two) theological courses he attended seems to suggest a growing disillusionment with Christianity. By the time of his second year at university in 1865, at the age of 21, Nietzsche's break with Christianity appears to have been decisive. He decided to discontinue the study of theology – and thus openly broke with the tradition, expectations and hopes of his family and particularly with his mother's wishes for his future path. This year he also intensively read and discussed David Friedrich Strauss' *Das Leben Jesu*, the closely allied author Daniel Schenkel's *Das Charakterbild Jesu* (third edition, 1864), and later in the year, the atheist Schopenhauer.[7] From June of this year we also have Nietzsche's telling letter to his sister Elisabeth in which he states,

> 'every true faith is thus infallible – it accomplishes what the respective faithful person hopes to gain from it. But it does not prepare a reference point whatsoever which could guarantee its objective truth. Here the paths of human beings part. If you prefer peace of mind and happiness, then better believe! But if you would like to be a disciple of truth, then search!' (KSB 2 61)

The following year, Nietzsche refused communion and criticized Christianity (from a Schopenhauerian perspective) in a letter to his friend Carl von Gersdorff.[8] We have too few sources and too little evidence to say, with certainty, what caused Nietzsche's break with Christianity. Historical criticism, the alternative *Weltanschauung* (which antiquity represented) and the influence of Feuerbach and Strauss constitute important sources. Possibly the method of historical criticism, that is, treating all texts historically by relating them to their historical context, was of the greatest importance. In *On the Genealogy of Morality* Nietzsche seems to suggest this – albeit with reference to his views on religion at the age of twelve – 'fortunately, I have since learnt to separate theology from morality and ceased looking for the origin of evil behind the world. Some schooling in history and philology, together with an innate sense of discrimination with respect to questions of psychology, quickly transformed my problem into another one' (GM 'Preface' 3).

Passive atheism – Nietzsche as non-believer (1866–1874).

After his break with Christianity, Nietzsche seems to have accepted atheism, but, on the whole, remained unconcerned and uninvolved with problems relating to Christianity. During the following ten years, until 1874, Nietzsche rarely discusses Christianity in letters, notebooks or published works. His relation to Christianity during this time can be described as 'Schopenhauerian' or 'metaphysical' variety of atheism, that is, although the truth of Christianity is rejected it, and other forms of metaphysics, are regarded as important ideals for human well-being.

Only twice in letters from this period does Nietzsche present what can be regarded as his own relation to Christianity. In a letter from the spring of 1868 religion is identified with metaphysics and regarded as of relevance to art and the construction of personality and culture, but as having nothing to do with truth.[9] In another letter, from 1870, Nietzsche refers to himself as among 'those who completely have left the Christian faith.'[10] These letters seem to be strongly influenced by Schopenhauer and Friedrich Albert Lange, whose *History of Materialism* Nietzsche read intensely in 1866, and several times again thereafter.

Nietzsche's only explicit critique of Christianity in his notes from this period was Schopenhauerian in nature and is directed at its indifference towards art.[11] At this time Nietzsche regarded Christianity as false but also as a movement which had been of crucial importance to the development of human culture. He also repeatedly emphasized the elements of antiquity within Christianity. Nietzsche's evaluation of Christianity during this period seems ambivalent, on the one hand it is exposed as false but, on the other hand it is acknowledged as a crucial example of man's need for metaphysics – a sign of the influence of Schopenhauer on his thought.

In the published works from this period, *The Birth of Tragedy* and the four *Untimely Meditations*, Christianity and related themes are almost completely absent. In the first of the *Untimely Meditations*, about the critic of Christianity David Strauss, Nietzsche actively avoids discussing Christianity.[12] In the second *Untimely Meditation*, about history, he seems, but with some regret, to accept the historicist critique of Christianity.[13] Hence, from a Schopenhauerian perspective, Nietzsche continued to see some advantages of certain aspects of Christianity even for the intellectual élite.

The Critique of Christianity: prepared, but not yet a major theme (1875–1879)

It is during the period 1875–1879 that Nietzsche moved from being a non-believer or passive atheist to being actively and explicitly atheist.

That Nietzsche's attitude to Christianity changed during this period is not surprising as he was moving toward a more 'positivistic' *Weltanschauung*.[14] In 1875, while working on notes for his planned *Untimely Meditation* entitled 'We Classicists' and while preparing and giving his university course 'Ancient Greek Religion' Nietzsche produced his first extensive critique of Christianity since the time of his initial break with it in 1861–1865.[15] These notes offer a severe cultural critique of Christianity in which it is negatively contrasted to the much 'healthier' ancient Greece, a theme already hinted at ten years earlier. Very few positive statements on Christianity are made during this period.

His first book, after the break with Schopenhauer and Wagner and a break in publications of several years, was *Human, All Too Human: A Book for Free Spirits* (1878). This is very different in style and content to his earlier books. Both its title and its motto proclaim a new, more anti-Christian attitude. Nietzsche now conceives himself as a 'free spirit' and the book is dedicated to Voltaire, 'one of the greatest liberators of the mind', on the centenary of his death. The book contains a chapter entitled, 'The Religious Life'.[16] Early in this section Nietzsche makes his atheism public when he states of Christianity that, 'what is certain...given the current state of knowledge, one can no longer have any association with it without incurably dirtying one's intellectual conscience and prostituting it before oneself and others' (HH 109). In 'Assorted Opinions and Maxims' (March 1879) and 'The Wanderer and his Shadow' (December 1879) discussions of Christianity are less prominent than in the first volume of *Human, All Too Human* and the critique of it is generally milder. It is with *Daybreak* (1881) that Nietzsche enters into the final, radical stage of atheism.

II

The late Nietzsche's critique of Christianity is not so much based on the denial of the existence of God but on the questioning and denial of its value. With this Nietzsche goes significantly further than most other proponents of secularism. As he states, 'what sets us apart is not that we recognize no God, either in history or in nature or behind nature – but that we find that which has been reverenced as God not 'godlike' but pitiable, absurd, harmful, not merely an error but a crime against life..We deny God as God...If this God of the Christians were proved to us to exist, we should know even less how to believe in him' (AC 47).

Nietzsche ended his philosophical career in 1888 with an intensive attack on Christianity and with a belief that the most important task for philosophy was the revaluation of all Christian values. This was the logical conclusion of a major *leitmotif* in Nietzsche's thinking since at least the writing of *Daybreak*. In this book, Nietzsche approvingly refers to the strength of the perspective of historical criticism, 'in former times, one sought to prove that there is no God – today one indicates how the belief that there is a God could arise and how this belief acquired its weight and importance: a counter-proof that there is no God thereby becomes superfluous' (D 95).[17] Around 1880 Nietzsche began to read a large number of studies and books about different aspects of Christianity, including works by Christian authors, and he incorporated much of this reading into his thinking and writing.[18]

In *The Gay Science* (1882) Nietzsche proclaims the 'death of God' (GS 125)[19] and calls himself 'godless', a self-description he then frequently repeats.[20] He even considered calling one of the books of *The Gay Science*, 'Thoughts of a Godless man'.[21] In this book Nietzsche claims that 'the decline of the faith in the Christian God, the triumph of scientific atheism, is a generally European event in which all races had their share and for which all deserve credit and honour' (GS 357). He continues and claims that 'Schopenhauer was the first admitted and inexorable atheist among us Germans,' (GS 357) and he emphasizes that Schopenhauer's atheism was a necessary consequence of his intellectual integrity and honesty, 'this is the locus of his whole integrity; unconditional and honest atheism is simply the presupposition of the way he poses his problem' (GS 357). It is clear that Nietzsche regarded a belief in God and in the values and truths of Christianity as a sign of intellectual cowardice and folly. In *On the Genealogy of Morality* (1887) he expresses this viewpoint thus, 'absolute, honest atheism (– and this is the only air which we more spiritual men of this age breathe!)' (GM III 27).

In *Thus Spoke Zarathustra* and the notes written during the years 1882-1885, the term 'Godless' constitutes a *leitmotif* in Nietzsche's writing, '"I am Zarathustra, the Godless!…Who is more godless than I, that I may rejoice in his teaching?' I am Zarathustra the Godless: where shall I find my equal? All those who give themselves their own will and renounce all submission, they are my equals….I am Zarathustra the Godless"' (Z 'Of the virtue that makes small' 3). This *leitmotif* continues to echo in Nietzsche's texts after *Thus Spoke Zarathustra*. In an early draft for *Beyond Good and Evil* (1886) Nietzsche planned to entitle a chapter 'We, the Godless', settling, in the end, for the more neutral 'The Religious Nature'.[22] Shortly thereafter, he thought of using the expression 'We, the Godless' as the title for a book.[23] Also, for the tentative continuation of *Beyond Good and Evil*, Nietzsche had a planned chapter with this title.[24] In another note from this time, he discusses what it means to be 'unbelieving and godless'.[25]

In *On the Genealogy of Morality* (1887) Nietzsche optimistically interprets the decreasing faith in God as possibly leading to new second innocence, 'indeed, the possibility cannot be rejected out of hand that the complete and definitive victory of atheism might release humanity from this whole feeling of being indebted towards its beginnings, its *causa prima*. Atheism and a sort of second innocence belong together' (GM II 20). Although rarely expressed so explicitly, the rejection of the Christian notions of guilt, shame and sin, is a major theme in Nietzsche's writings. In *Ecce Homo* (1888) he claims that, 'I have, for example, no experience of actual religious difficulties' (EH 'Why I am so Clever' 1) and claims that, 'I have absolutely no knowledge of atheism as an outcome of reasoning, still less as an event: with me it is obvious by instinct. I am too inquisitive... too high spirited to rest content with a crude answer. God is a crude answer, a piece of indelicacy against us thinkers – fundamentally even a crude prohibition to us: you shall not think!' (EH 'Why I am so Clever' 1). Later in the work Nietzsche makes the more general statement that it was atheism which attracted him to both Schopenhauer and Friedrich II.[26]

In Nietzsche's notebooks from this period his atheism is clearly expressed. In 1879 he explicitly calls himself an atheist for the first time.[27] In 1884–1885 Nietzsche emphasised that belief in God is less a question of truth or untruth but rather one of courage and integrity, 'the opposition of atheism and theism is *not*: 'truth' and 'untruth', but rather that we no longer allow ourselves to believe in a hypothesis which we, however, *gladly allow others* (still stronger!)' (KSA 11 31 28). He refers to 'our atheism' (KSA 11 31 29) and states with reference to himself and his equals that 'we are atheists' (KSA 11 35 9). In several notes Nietzsche claims that the Wagner he respected was an atheist and that his turn toward Christianity contributed to the decline of their relationship.[28] Nietzsche claims that atheism is the product of human development which can reach levels where the world can be viewed as it is rather than how we might wish it to be.[29] This is a major aspect of the passage which announces the 'death of God', 'is not the greatness of this deed too great for us? Must we ourselves not become gods simply to appear worthy of it? There has never been a greater deed; and whoever is born after us – for the sake of this deed he will belong to a higher history than all history hitherto' (GS 125). Nietzsche even had plans at this time to write a text entitled 'Atheism and its causes'.[30] In a letter to Overbeck from July 1888 he again refers to himself as an atheist.[31]

Nietzsche's affiliation to atheism does not, however, prevent him from criticizing certain atheists and 'free-thinkers'. He argues that many of them, especially 'English atheists', are often even less liberated from morality than religious thinkers.[32] The essence of Nietzsche's critique of these modern 'free-thinkers' and 'atheists' is that they are not radical enough. They deny the existence of God, but fail to draw the necessary conclusions from this – that modern values and the concept of truth itself need to be re-examined and revalued as well.[33]

For the late Nietzsche the evaluation of Christianity is not concerned with of the existence of God but with a question of one's relation to the *Weltanschauung* associated with it. For Nietzsche Christian values are 'life-denying' and reflect a mentality not strong enough to see the world as it is. Thus, when in *Ecce Homo* Nietzsche outlines the basis of the rank-order of humanity it is the virtues of courage and intellectual integrity which he emphasises above all else, 'how much truth can a spirit bear, how much truth can a spirit dare? that became for me more and more the real measure of value…error is cowardice … Every acquisition, every step forward in knowledge is the result of courage, of severity towards oneself, of cleanliness with respect to oneself' (EH 'Preface' 3).

More provocative and stronger than the terms 'godless' and 'atheist' is 'anti-christ'. Nietzsche did not only use this term as a title for one of his final texts but employed it regularly in the two years prior to its pub-lication in 1888, often as term of self-description. The first appearance of the term 'anti-christ' in Nietzsche's text is as early as 1873,[34] which is repeated in the *Untimely Meditations*.[35] He also uses the term in a note from 1882[36] and already, in a letter from 1883, Nietzsche begins to refer to himself as 'anti-christ'.[37] Shortly thereafter, he returns to the theme:

> Also the first review of the first book of *Zarathustra*, which has been sent to me (by a Christian and anti-semite, and, strangely enough, written in jail) gives me courage since also there the public position, the only one of mine which can be understood, precisely my relation to Christianity, is well and sharply understood. 'Either Christ or Zarathustra' Or more clearly, it deals with the old and long promised anti-Christ – thus feels the reader.[38]

From 1886 Nietzsche begins to use the term 'anti-christ' as a slogan sig-
nalling that for which he stands. In *Beyond Good and Evil* he asks, 'for
who among them would have been profound or primary enough for a
philosophy of anti-Christ?' (BGE 256). In the preface to the second edition of *The Birth of Tragedy* from August 1886, he writes,

> It was against morality that my instinct turned with this questionable
> book…it was an instinct that aligned itself with life and that discovered for
> itself a fundamentally opposite doctrine and valuation of life – purely artis-
> tic and anti-Christian. What to call it? As a philologist and man of words I
> baptized it, not without taking some liberty – for who could claim to know
> the rightful name of the Anti-christ? – in the name of a Greek god: I called
> it Dionysian (ASC 5).

In *On the Genealogy of Morality*, Nietzsche cries out:

> This man of the future will redeem us not just from the ideal held up till
> now, but also from the things which will have to arise from it, from the great
> nausea, the will to nothingness, from nihilism, that stroke of midday and of
> great decision which makes the will free again, which gives earth its purpose
> and man his hope again, this Anti-christ and anti-nihilist, this conqueror of
> God and of nothingness – he must come one day… (GM 2 24).

In *The Twilight of the Idols* Nietzsche refers to himself and his equals as
'we immoralists and anti-Christians' (TI 'Morality as Anti-Nature' 3). In
the epilogue to *The Anti-Christ*, he added a section called 'Law against
Christianity' which he signed 'The Anti-christ'. In December 1888 Nietzsche signed several letters in the same manner, and in *Ecce Homo* he
claims, 'I am, in Greek and not only in Greek, the Anti-Christ' (EH
'Why I Write such Excellent Books' 2). In early summer 1888 Nietzsche
returns to the figure of Zarathustra and says of him:

> Zarathustra goes so far as to claim about himself: 'I would only believe in a
> God who understood how to dance'

> To say it yet again, how many new gods are still possible!

> - Zarathustra, however, is merely an old atheist. One has to understand him
> correctly! Zarathustra to be sure, said he *would*;- but Zarathustra *will*
> not…(KSA 13 17 4)

In summary, the stages of Nietzsche's changing relation to Christianity
have been outlined and his use of the concepts 'atheism', 'godlessness'
and 'anti-christ' considered. We have seen that Nietzsche lost his faith
between 1861 and 1865 but that he avoided an explicit discussion

of Christianity until the mid-1870s. From this time, with increasing intensity, Nietzsche regarded himself as an atheist, and made the recognition of his atheism a necessary condition for understanding his philosophy. Nietzsche's atheism was, perhaps, more radical than that of any previous thinker. This can be seen by the force of his language and is due to the fact that, in relation to Christianity, he concentrated not on questions relating to epistemology and ontology, but on a critique of values.

Bibliography of cited works by Nietzsche

'Attempt at a Self-Criticism' in *The Birth of Tragedy and The Case of Wagner* (see below)

Beyond Good and Evil (Harmondsworth: Penguin, 1973, trans. R.J. Hollingdale)

Daybreak (Cambridge: Cambridge University Press, 1982, trans. R.J. Hollingdale)

Ecce Homo (Harmondsworth: Penguin, 1979, trans. R.J. Hollingdale)

Frühe Schriften (München: 1994, ed. H. J. Mette)

Human, All Too Human (Cambridge: Cambridge University Press, 1996, trans. R.J. Hollingdale)

Kritische Studienausgabe (München: Walter de Gruyter, 1988, eds: G. Colli, M. Montinari)

On the Genealogy of Morality (Cambridge: Cambridge University Press, 1994, trans. C. Diethe)

Sämtliche Briefe. Kritische Studienausgabe (Berlin: 1986, eds. G. Colli and M. Montinari)

The Birth of Tragedy and The Case of Wagner (New York: Random House, 1967, trans. W. Kaufmann)

The Gay Science (New York: Random House, 1974, trans. W. Kaufmann)

Twilight of the Idols and The Anti-Christ (Harmondsworth: Penguin, 1968, trans. R.J. Hollingdale)

Thus Spoke Zarathustra (Harmondsworth: Penguin, 1969, trans. R.J. Hollingdale)

Untimely Meditations (Cambridge: Cambridge University Press, 1983, trans. R.J. Hollingdale)

Werke: Kritische Gesamtausgabe (Berlin: Walter de Gruyter, 1995, eds. J. Figl and H. G. Hödl).

Notes

1   F. Nietzsche, '*Aus meinen Leben*' in *Frühe Schriften* (München: C.H. Beck, 1994, hrg. H. J. Mette) vol. 1 pp. 1–32 (see p. 31), hereafter BAW. This

text also appears in KGW vol. I, pp. 281–311. All translations from Nietzsche's *Nachlass* are my own. I am grateful to the Bank of Sweden Tercentenary Foundation for financial support that aided the writing of this paper.

2   Hence Nietzsche had from an early age both much practical involvement with, and theoretical knowledge of, Christianity. On this see J. Salaquarda, 'Nietzsche and the Judaeo-Christian Tradition' in B. Magnus and K.M. Higgins (eds.): *The Cambridge Companion to Nietzsche* (Cambridge: Cambridge University Press, 1996) pp. 90–118

3   P. Deussen, *Erinnerungen an Friedrich Nietzsche* (Leipzig, F.A. Brockhaus 1901) p.4

4   F. Nietzsche, *Sämtliche Briefe. Kritische Studienausgabe*, (Berlin: Walter de Gruyter, 1986, eds. G. Colli and M. Montinari) 1 202. Hereafter KSB. All translations from Nietzsche's letters are my own.

5   See BAW vol. 2 pp. 54–62. Both essays reveal the strong influence of Emerson whom Nietzsche was reading at this time.

6   'As an atheist I never said the table-prayer at Pforta and was never made a week-inspector by the teachers. Tact!' (KSA 8 42 68). This is an important but problematic statement for we know (as he refers to it in letters from the time) that he was, in fact, a week-inspector (a sort of teaching assistant) on a number of occasions!

7   Later Nietzsche claims that he was particularly impressed with Schopenhauer's atheism. See EH 'Untimely Meditations' 2.

8   KSB 2 119–123

9   KSB 2 267-271 (a letter to P. Deussen)

10 KSB 3 120 (a letter to Rohde).

11 KSA 7 5 26, 94; 8 58; 9 58.

12 In his notes for '*David Strauss: der Bekenner und der Schriftsteller*' Nietzsche seems more positive toward Christianity than is apparent from the published text – rather than the opposite as might be expected. See for example KSA 7, 27 1, 2, 3, 15. In the published book there is essentially no discussion of Christianity.

13 It may not be completely incorrect to see Nietzsche's lingering struggle with Christianity as an important motive for his writing the book. Later Nietzsche almost completely ignores it.

14 That Nietzsche regarded his development in this manner is clear from KSA 10 16 23 written in 1883.

15 Nietzsche gave these lectures in 1875 and in 1877-1878.

16 See HH 108–144.

17 Nietzsche's point here is that before such an understanding of Christianity one was forced to consider the proof or probability of the existence of God. However, with the insight into how Christianity arouse and to what needs it responded such arguments become superfluous.

18 For a chronological listing of Nietzsche's reading of 'religious' books see my 'Nietzsche's Changing Relation to Christianity' forthcoming in D. Santaniello (ed.): *Nietzsche and the Gods* (New York: State University of New York Press). For a more general discussion of Nietzsche's reading during his last four active years, see my 'Nietzsche's Reading and Private Library, 1885–1889', *Journal of the History of Ideas*, vol. 58 (1997) pp. 663–693.

19 The claim is also repeated at the beginning of *Thus Spoke Zarathustra*. Nietzsche's belief is, of course, not that God has actually died, since he does not believe in the existence of God, but that belief in God had become so undermined that it can no longer constitute the foundation of a *Weltanschauung*.

20 See GS IV 280, V 344, 346, 367. See also D 'Preface' 4 where Nietzsche also describes himself as 'godless'.

21 See KSA 9 19 12.

22 See KSA 12, 2 70, written in 1885/1886. In 'The Religious Nature' Nietzsche describes religion as a 'neurosis' (BGE 47).

23 See KSA 12 2 73, written in 1885–1886.

24 See KSA 12 2 82, written in 1885–1886.

25 See KSA 12 2 197, written in 1885–1886.

26 See also KSA 11 39 15.

27 See KSA 8 42 68, written in July to August 1879.

28 See KSA 11 34 205, 254 and 37 15, 41 2; 12, 9 65.

29 See KSA 11 31 14 and compare the contrast made between Plato and Thucydides in TI 'Ancients' 2.

30 See KSA 11 42 2, written in 1885.

31 KSB 8 361

32 Nietzsche refers to 'English atheists' in TI 'Expeditions of an Untimely Man' 5, 12; KSA 11 39 15; 12 5 50, 52 and 10 163; 13 11 45.

33 Nietzsche's critique is primarily directed at their belief in truth, 'they are far from being *free* spirits: for they *still have faith in truth*' (GM III 24).

34 See KSA 7 9 59.

35 See UM II 9. However, his use of it there is a direct quotation from Eduard von Hartmann's *Philosophy of the Unconscious* and is of less importance.

36 As Nietzsche states, '*Als Richtschwert der Religionen. Antichrist*' (KSA 9, 21 3).

37 Nietzsche to Malwida von Meysenbug in April 1883 'do you want a new name for me? The language of the church has one: I am…the anti-Christ' (KSB 6 357).

38 KSB 6 435 (a letter to Gast).

2
Nietzsche as a theological resource

Merold Westphal

Onto-theo-logy and its twin

Not every construal of the theological enterprise will be able to entertain
the possibility of Nietzsche as a resource, if not exactly an ally. For example, if theology interprets itself onto-theo-logically, it will be unable to
see any ambiguity or irony in his self-designations as immoralist and
anti-Christ. They will simply be the literal confessions of loathed enemy.
The possibility of Nietzsche as *ancilla theologiae* presupposes at least
an interruption of the interpretation of theology in onto-theo-logical
terms.

Heidegger himself suggests that there might be theological motives
for such an interruption. Speaking in a Pascalian tone of voice about the
god of philosophy, he writes, 'Man can neither pray nor sacrifice to this
god. Before the *causa sui*, man can neither fall to his knees in awe nor
can he play music and dance before this god.'[1] Metaphysics, when constituted onto-theo-logically, is a totalizing thinking that like its successor,
technological, calculative thinking 'reduce[s] everything down to man'
(ID 34). The 'god-less thinking' which abandons the god of the philosophers 'is thus perhaps closer to the divine God' (ID 72). This way of
looking at things obviously opens the door at least a crack to Nietzsche
and his death of God announcements. But how do we get to this point
of view?

Heidegger's account of the onto-theo-logical project takes its point of
departure from Aristotle's attempt to unite ontology, the study of being
as such, with theology, the study of the highest being. The particular
object of theology, according to Aristotle, belongs to the general concerns of the ontology because the unmovable substance he takes to be
the highest being would not be merely one being among others. In rela-

tion to all other beings it would be at once the *prima causa* and *ultima ratio*. Consequently, this science would be first philosophy 'and universal in this way, because it is first.'[2]

This notion that all being is to be understood from the highest being has a natural attractiveness to monotheists who hold that every being (as substance or as essence) is either God or created by God. So it is not surprising to find historical examples of theologies that interpret the God of Abraham in onto-theo-logical modes, with or without help from Aristotle.

But Heidegger's account of this metaphysical marriage of ontology and theology raises a red warning flag. It is obvious that in the onto-theo-logical project 'the deity enters into philosophy.' But Heidegger asks how this happens and on whose terms; he answers that in this project, 'the deity can come into philosophy only insofar as philosophy, of its own accord and by its own nature, requires and determines that and how the deity enters into it' (ID 55–56). And what is the task that philosophy assigns to the deity? It is the ontological task of gathering the whole of being into an intelligible totality. God has become a means to a human end. Philosophy's demand that the world should be entirely intelligible to human thought becomes the demand that God be philosophy's factotum in carrying out this project. This total intelligibility requires that 'Being manifests itself as thought,' the central theme of the *Logos* tradition in western metaphysics, if not in the Gospel of John. It is along this trajectory that we move, ever so quickly, from the book of Genesis to Hegel's *Science of Logic* (ID 57–60).

It may be worth our while to descend from these global descriptions to see onto-theo-logy at work in its everydayness. At a colloquium not long ago I heard a speaker defending a certain Thomism. Along the way she made two interesting moves that were picked up by a questioner during the discussion time. First, she presented Alasdair MacIntyre's critique of the secularization and impoverishment of theology from within in the attempt to address Christianity to the secular mind. She quoted MacIntyre's claim, 'nothing has been more startling than to note how much contemporary Christian theology is concerned with trying to perform Feuerbach's work all over again…' with the result that Christianity becomes 'a way of life in accordance with the liberal values and illiberal realities of the established order.'[3] With specific reference to Tillich's theology, MacIntyre was quoted as saying, 'when Feuerbach explained that he did not believe in the God of orthodoxy because God could at best only be a name for man's ultimate concerns, he was not regarded by theologians as being a particularly subtle defender of the Christian religion.'⁴

The second move was the portrayal of Protestant and Jansenist (and eventually nominalist) theologies as 'a deviated Christian tradition' because of their ethical views, especially in relation to the corruption of human nature by sin. Once again MacIntyre was quoted as finding the consequence of such views to be 'that from any human standpoint the divine commandments do become arbitrary fiats imposed on us externally; our nature does not summon us to obey them, because we cannot recognize them as being for our good.'⁵

The questioner asked whether the brand of Thomism being defended was not an instance of the Feuerbachianism whose denunciation prefaced the defence. According to the 'deviated' views in question, divine commands do not make sense to us humans; at least sometimes we find them to be 'arbitrary fiats imposed on us externally'. Our nature does not welcome them because at least sometimes 'we cannot recognize them as being for our good'. But how could this be an objection against the views in question unless there were already operative an *a priori* requirement of total intelligibility, the demand that God should always make sense to our human intellects in their present (finite and fallen) condition? Would not any God who accepted these ground rules be one created in our image rather than the other way around? Would not such a God be but a projection of what makes sense to our current fashion of thinking? Wouldn't we have here an historicized (Marxian) version of Feuerbach? Would the fact that the current fashions of thinking, however traditional or revolutionary, to which God would have to conform are those of religious rather than secular people make the project any less Feuerbachian?

It seems to me that the onto-theo-logical project has a shadow, a flip side, a cousin, a (fraternal) twin. If, in its presence, one looks for signs of a socio-theo-logical project, one is seldom disappointed. In this instance God enters into social theory rather than ontology, but on the same terms, as a means to human ends. In the first case the demand is to render the world (including God as its *Alpha* and *Omega*) fully intelligible. In this second case the demand is to render the world fully ours, to legitimate the political, economic, and technological hegemonies from which the faithful in any given case benefit, including compassionate, paternalistic hegemonies (which used to be called benevolent despotisms), from which the faithful benefit psychologically without having to pay too high a price in terms of power or wealth.

In both cases the will to power, carefully hidden from itself, puts God to work as its man Friday (or perhaps in these liberated days, as its girl Friday – for a female God is no less likely to be co-opted by human will to power). In either of these modes, theology has everything to fear and nothing to gain from Nietzsche. But if theology has another vocation, one that includes vigilance against its own onto-theo-logical and socio-theo-logical tendencies, the story might be different.

We can put it this way. If Nietzsche is right in his interpretation of Spinoza's *conatus* as the 'will to power', then everything tends to absolutize itself, to treat the world as its oyster, as the collective means to its own flourishing. In its content, monotheistic religion provides a powerful challenge to this tendency among human selves and societies. Thus Kierkegaard (as Anti-Climacus) can write:

> Every human being is to live in fear and trembling, and likewise no established order is to be exempted from fear and trembling . . . fear and trembling signify that there is a God—something every human being and every established order ought not to forget for a moment [6]

A fallacy and a prophylaxis

But monotheism also represents an all but irresistible temptation to slide (without noticing the *non sequitur* involved) from the confession that the object of the believer's thinking is absolute to the confusion that takes that thinking itself to be *ipso facto* absolute. If philosophical theology were to need a name for this sliding, we might call it cognitive transubstantiation; for what happens is that the intentional act, which remains to all appearances human, takes on the ontological perfections of its divine intentional object.

Of course this has all the cogency of assuming that to think of the Grand Canyon is to think deeply. But onto-theo-logians and socio-theologians who have more or less lost their footing on this slippery slope do not like to be reminded of this. It takes a certain perversity to want to be reminded of the fallacy of misplaced transubstantiation. It takes thinkers more committed to the truth, whatever it may be, than to the truth as we think we have discovered it so far. It takes thinkers caught up in what is for Nietzsche the last of the ascetic ideals. Ironically, it is just such theologians for whom Nietzsche can be a resource.

A prophylactic resource. A protection, not against the theological equivalent of unwanted pregnancy, but against the theological equivalent of syphilis or aids, a deadly virus that kills theology by transforming what would be discourse about God into discourse about ourselves and by transforming altruistic virtues into egoistic vices.

In other words, I am not suggesting that Nietzsche is a theological resource in the way in which scripture and tradition are. Still, there is something quasi-scriptural and quasi-traditional about his relation to the theologian. For he performs, if we will let him, the task of prophetic protest, the *ad hominem* critique of theology by its own professed standards. And for Jewish and Christian monotheism, if I am not mistaken, both scripture and tradition include important strands of prophetic protest. Amos and Jesus are quite different from Nietzsche, but all three managed to get very religious people angry at them in strikingly similar ways.

The first Nietzschean prophylaxis is his perspectivism. This is his version of the hermeneutics of finitude, and as such it should be of interest to theologians. For finitude is a theological theme that stands in intimate connection with the doctrine of creation. Just to the degree that Nietzsche's account of human finitude is compelling it can illumine the theologian's understanding of creation, even if it comes wrapped in the assurance that there is no Creator after all (or should we say 'before all'?).

Nietzsche's perspectivism is one of the negative footnotes to Plato in the history of philosophy. Both the Platonism of antiquity and the Cartesianism of modernity, along with all their legitimate children, have been the flight from perspective, the attempt to reflect oneself out of one's situation so as to see reality *sub specie aeternitatis*. Theology has often been a fellow traveller on these flights, tempted, in part, by the fallacious assumption mentioned above, that since it speaks of the Absolute it must speak absolutely. This is part of the reason, incidentally, that Nietzsche doesn't see much difference between Christianity and Platonism and describes the former as Platonism for the masses.

Against both the philosophical and the theological forms of this flight, Nietzsche is a constant reminder that we see the world from a particular historical, sociological, and even physiological perspective. In the presence of the metaphysics of presence that thinks it possible to reflect oneself out of perspective altogether and obtain 'the view from nowhere,' Nietzsche keeps quoting, as it were, from St. Paul. No matter how badly we want to see reality face to face, we can only see 'in a mirror, dimly', even 'in a riddle'.[7] So he speaks of truth as 'linguistic legislation,' as 'customary metaphors', and as 'illusions about which one has forgotten that this is what they are.'[8]

Perhaps there is an element of rhetorical overkill here. But perhaps very strong language is needed to remind us that our truth is human, all too human, and for that reason it is always meaningful to ask, Whose truth? There is a lot of sense in the claim that if God is real, in something like the traditional theistic sense, then reality is intelligible. But it does not follow that it is intelligible to us, since we are not God. As Kierkegaard's Climacus reminds us, 'existence itself is a system – for God, but it cannot be a system for any existing spirit.'[9]

Objection: 'This is your second reference to Kierkegaard. Perhaps by reminding us of the important affinities between these two, once the fathers of existentialism but now seen more often as proto-pomos, you hope to render more plausible your claim that Nietzsche might be useful to the theologian. But why not just turn to Kierkegaard, who, after all, is something of a theologian himself?'

Reply: A) By all means turn to Kierkegaard. I am the last one to discourage you. I myself spend more time reading and writing about Kierkegaard than Nietzsche. B) Nietzsche is also something of a theologian – of which more hereafter. C) I am making no claim for Nietzsche's indispensability. There are many thinkers from whom there is much to learn about the finitude of human knowledge. Hume and Sextus Empiricus, Kant and Kierkegaard, Marx and Freud, Peirce and Dewey, Heidegger and Wittgenstein, Rorty and Derrida – the list can be extended with ease. But Nietzsche (along with several others just mentioned) has this advantage. By virtue of his atheism he has built in a special protection against the fallacy of misplaced transubstantiation. Of course, he and his descendants need to be reminded that from the fact that we are not the absolute point of view it does not follow that there is no absolute point of view; and Kierkegaard's 'existence is a system for God' is important as such a reminder. But I believe there is real value in looking at human finitude in a landscape from which God has been entirely removed. Uncreated finitude is doubtless different from created finitude, so such a *mise en scène* cannot be ultimate from a theological standpoint. But it can be part of a much needed system of checks and balances for the theologian who seeks to claim divine origin but not divine nature for human thought, to remember that we are made, not begotten.

Objection: 'But there's a problem of self-referential consistency here. Is it not a performative contradiction to present as an absolute truth the claim that all human insight is relative to its perspective?'

Reply: No doubt. But that is to read Nietzsche in the worst possible light and to invite the suspicion that one is desperate to discredit him. There are at least two other possibilities. One more charitable reading would have him saying something like this: 'All human truth is relative to the believer's perspective, except the truth that this is so; this latter truth is the one insight we have that transcends perspective.' So far as I can see there is nothing self-contradictory about this claim. But while it has the virtue of being charitable, it does not strike me as plausible, either in itself or as a reading of Nietzsche.

An interpretation that is both charitable and plausible, at least as a reading of Nietzsche, would go like this: 'All human truth is relative to the believer's perspective, including the truth of perspectivism. While we may find perspectivism compelling, no formulation of it can claim to be final, certain, and beyond revision.' Perspectivism need not be presented as an absolute truth; it can be presented as an account of how reality looks from where one is situated. It does not thereby cease to be of value. The account of the game given by the winning coach cannot claim to be *the* truth about the game; other accounts must be taken into account, including those from the losing coach, the players, the referees, the radio and TV announcers, the fans, and the people selling hot dogs. But that does not mean that we do not listen with attention to what the winning coach has to say about the game.

Objection: 'That may all be OK for games and even for philosophical theories. But for the theologian to talk that way would be to abandon the kerygmatic mission of theology, to cut the gospel out of the gospel. Within the AAR is may be OK for the theologian to be no more than a purveyor of opinion (so long as that opinion is politically correct); but real theology needs to sustain a relation to the faithful and not just the curious, to church, synagogue, mosque, etc. We cannot ask the clergy to say, "This is how it looks from where I stand."'

Reply: But St. Paul talks that way, and he was not, to the best of my knowledge, a member of the AAR. He sought to relate to both synagogue and church. Yet he insists that our knowledge is partial, that we see as in a riddle. Speaking precisely of 'the light of the gospel of the glory of Christ, who is the image of God,' he insists that 'we have this treasure in clay jars, so that it may be made clear that this extraordinary power belongs to God and does not come from us.'[10] It was in reference to the epistemological dimension of the clay jar metaphor, I believe, that an evangelical Protestant theologian once described the Bible as 'the divinely revealed misinformation about God'. Coming from a staunch defender of biblical inerrancy, that is a profound, almost Nietzschean appreciation of our cognitive finitude. Not even in giving us a divinely inspired and inerrant biblical self-revelation could God transcend our finitude and enable us to see reality as it truly is, i.e., as God sees it.

Objection: 'Let me try again. Doesn't Nietzsche's perspectivism lead to theological silence, to a negative theology cut off from all positive theology. And isn't Feuerbach right in warning us against theologians of this sort. They affirm the existence of God. "But this existence does not affect or incommode [them]; it is a merely negative existence, an existence without existence, a self-contradictory existence,— a state of being which, as to its effects, is not distinguishable from non-being ... The alleged religious horror of limiting God by positive predicates is only the irreligious wish to know nothing more of God, to banish God from the mind.'"[11]

Reply: It was a deep appreciation of human finitude that generated negative theology in the first place. So it would not be surprising if one path out of Nietzschean meditations on human finitude leads in the direction of negative theology. I think it is on this path that Derrida has found himself discussing the relation of deconstruction to negative theology. But it does not follow that the negative theology for which one gains a new respect by the serious reading of Nietzsche needs to be cut off from positive theology. Nietzsche himself, was something of a positive theologian and prophet. He is quite kerygmatic about his Dionysian faith and about the metaphysics of eternal recurrence that undergirds it.

Is he inconsequent in this regard? I think not. What Nietzsche's positive theology suggests to me is that his perspectivism places no constraints on what we can say about the sacred, but only on how we say it. I want to suggest two things about that how. First, if we cannot have the absolute knowledge that philosophy has often demanded and professed, our theological discourse will have to embody the appropriate humility. But it is important that we not confuse humility with timidity (especially in the presence of Nietzsche, who sees through that fraud quicker than anyone else). Should we be tentative in our beliefs about God? Not if that means we should hold them without conviction, but only if it means we should hold them without arrogance, the arrogance that is willing to impose them on others but unwilling to learn from others.

The second adverbial constraint placed on theological discourse by perspectivism is a bit more complicated. It relates to the onto-theo-logical project. That project, it will be recalled, was to call upon God as the highest being to bring intelligibility to the totality of being. To this end God was presented as *prima causa* and as *ultima ratio*. I believe perspectivism requires us to abandon this project because it challenges the slide from claiming that reality is a system for God to claiming that it can be a system in and for our knowledge. If reality cannot be a system for us, then whether or not there is a God for whom it can be, it cannot be a system for us.

Does this mean we must give up speaking of God as creator? Not if I am right about the what and the how. What it requires us to give up is the assumption that when we speak of God as creator we have explained the world. A colleague of mine who is a very creative philosophical theologian once put it this way: 'the only thing you can get out of a cosmological argument is the conclusion that there is an explanation of the world. You haven't thereby given that explanation.' My suggestion is that this applies to creation talk whether its origin is in revealed or natural theology.

It is in the doctrine of analogy that Aquinas qualifies his positive theology with the radical finitism of his negative theology. Although Aquinas does not thematize his doctrine in this way, my suggestion is that its truth and his practice come down to the same thing, that negative theology places no constraints on what we can say about God but only on the how. When he insists, as he regularly does, that we do not know God through the divine essence, he says, in effect, 'philosophical theology gives us the rationally revealed misinformation about God, and *sacra doctrina* gives us the scripturally revealed misinformation about God. We can say whatever reason or scripture lead us to say about God, and we can hold the resultant beliefs with deep conviction. What we cannot say is that in them we know either God or the world as they truly are. Thus we cannot say that our beliefs are final or that they embody the intelligibility of reality. That finality and that intelligibility are only to be found in the mind of God.'

Final objection (for now – a nicely Nietzschean caveat – No?): 'You're preaching to the wrong congregation. To beat up on onto-theo-logy at the AAR is truly an exercise in carrying coals to Newcastle. We are not the Christian Coalition, dogmatically confident in a metaphysics and corresponding ethics to the point of being willing to impose it on everybody else. Our problem is, if anything, just the opposite. We are so sensitive to the situated character of thought that we have no gospel at all, unless it is the gospel of finitude. There is next to nothing we are willing to say about God with conviction, and we are the last place on earth to refer anyone with spiritual hunger. The only topic about which we are confident is the situated relativity of whatever we say.'

Final reply (for as long as you cease launching objections): A) There are fundamentalisms of the left as well as of the right, theologically, politically, and culturally speaking. Nor is the AAR free from the kind of dogmatisms of which Nietzschean perspectivism is a critique. Its dominant culture has an orthodoxy, or perhaps several orthodoxies, that are quite as intolerant of dissent as the orthodoxies they have replaced. One of these orthodoxies is a dogmatic Nietzscheanism that needs to be subjected to Nietzschean critique.

B) An important aspect of this latter point concerns the what and the how. Theologians within the dominant culture of the AAR are frequently perspectivists, whether they get this from Nietzsche or elsewhere. But they construe finitism to be a constraint on what may be said. Fully aware of the difficulty, if not impossibility, of providing unsituated warrant for this or that theological notion, they sometimes continue to assume that since they are in the university rather than the church only what is capable of universal warrant, untied to any particular community of belief and practice, is permitted. The result is the thinnest of theological soups. Or, perhaps, one of the new orthodoxies, whose universal warrant consists in being unchallenged by any but fringe groups in the AAR. To take seriously that universal warrant may be both impossible *and* unnecessary might be liberating in more places that one suspects on superficial view.

In short, my sense is that when Nietzsche's ox goes a-goring, there are more than enough oxes to go around.

A second prophylaxis

In addition to his hermeneutics of finitude, Nietzsche has an hermeneutics of suspicion. He believes that the philosopher 'has a *duty* to suspicion today, to squint maliciously out of every abyss of suspicion' (BGE 34). The reason is that 'the decisive value of an action lies precisely in what is *unintentional* in it, while everything about it that is intentional, everything about it that can be seen, known, "conscious", still belongs to its surface and skin – which, like every skin, betrays something but *conceals* even more. In short, we believe that the intention is merely a sign and symptom that still requires interpretation' (BGE 32).[13] Needless to say, the actions spoken of here include, but are not restricted to, cognitive acts: believings, presupposings, questionings, not questionings, and so forth.

Although Nietzschean suspicion operates in the epistemological as well as in the ethical realm (and belongs, in fact, to what we might today call the vice squad of virtue epistemology), he is careful to distinguish it from skepticism. 'In former times,' he writes, 'one sought to prove that there is no God – today one indicates how the belief that there is a God could *arise* and how this belief acquired its weight and importance: a counter-proof that there is no God thereby becomes superfluous' (D I 95).

Strong skepticism says, 'The evidence shows that God does not exist.'[14] Weak skepticism (agnosticism) says, 'the evidence for God's existence is insufficient to warrant belief. We do not know that God does not exist, but it would be irrational to believe so.' Suspicion does not ask about the evidence at all. The question is not whether the belief in question is true but how it has arisen and what gives it its survival value as a belief. In other words, it asks both what motives give rise to this belief and what functions it performs to pay, so to speak, for its upkeep. These two questions, of motive and of function, we can subsume under the concept of interest. Whereas skepticism asks about the evidence that supports a belief, suspicion asks about the interests that support a belief. N.B. In this shift the concept of support has changed. Evidence supports a belief epistemically; interests support a belief psychologically. One concerns the truth of a belief, the other its usefulness.

Here, as is often the case, skepticism gives rise to suspicion. If I am convinced that a belief is false or insufficiently warranted, I may become curious about how people come to hold and to sustain such a belief. But while the question of interest may presuppose a negative judgment about evidence psychologically, it does not do so logically; and Nietzsche is clear about this. He tells us explicitly that the discourse of suspicion is an alternative to the discourse of skepticism. It represents a different way of discrediting beliefs. Or, to speak more precisely, of discrediting believings. For, as Nietzsche clearly sees, suspicion as such is neutral with respect to objective questions about the truth of beliefs or the evidence supporting them. It is directed, subjectively, toward the believer's interests. It addresses the what only indirectly, the how directly.

Like the hermeneutics of suspicion to be found in Kierkegaard, Marx, and Freud (once again, no claim for utter uniqueness is made here), Nietzsche's rests on two important premises. The first is a distinction between latent and manifest content, a theory of the unconscious.

Because consciousness conceals, beliefs are signs and symptoms in need of interpretation.

Second, the theory of the unconscious is a theory of repression, bad faith, and self-deception. The fundamental project that gives rise to the interests in question is the will to power, and while Nietzsche wants to restore innocence rather than blame to this core of our being, he recognizes that it is at odds with currently prevailing moralities, with our operative super-egos. Self-deception occurs, not simply because there are interests at work in our believings, but because these interests so often are those we cannot acknowledge without shame.

Elsewhere I have compared Nietzsche to Marx and Freud in this way. What is religion most essentially according to these theories of bad faith?

For Freud – ontological weakness seeking consolation.

For Marx – sociological power seeking legitimation.

For Nietzsche – sociological weakness seeking revenge.[15]

For Freud what is shameful is not our weakness before the cruelty of nature (death) and society (guilt), but the dishonesty involved in allowing wish-fulfillment to provide consolation not supported by reason. Although Nietzsche does not share Freud's confidence in Reason, the dishonesty theme is central to his critique as well. In other words, for Nietzsche religious belief involves lapses from both moral and intellectual virtue.

It is now possible to see three ways in which the door is open to a religious appropriation of the hermeneutics of suspicion. They take us from seeing how it is a possible tool in the theologian's tool kit to seeing how it is a necessary tool.

First, because it is neutral with regard to the truth of the beliefs in question, the theologian's commitment to those beliefs is not a barrier. Asking questions about what motives lead to various beliefs and what role they play in the lives of the believing soul and the believing community (and Nietzsche moves easily back and forth between the I and the We, between psychology and sociology) does not presuppose either that the beliefs are false or that the one asking the questions takes them to be.

There is an important consequence to this. There is no *a priori* reason why the interests supporting a true belief should not be disreputable. Just as it is possible, as Aristotle and Kant have insisted so vigorously, to do the right thing for the wrong reason, so it is possible to believe the truth in ways that are shameful. It may be true that God will judge the wicked, but if I hold this belief in a spirit of hateful vengeance and use it to establish my (or our) moral superiority in ways that blind me to my (or our) own faults, my believing is discredited by what suspicion reveals.

There are two corollaries to this consequence. A) It would be to commit the genetic fallacy to assume that a belief is shown to be false by showing that believers (sometimes, often, always) employ shameful interests in the support of that belief. B) It would be to commit something like the same fallacy in reverse to defend oneself or one's community against a suspicion-generated critique by trying to show that the beliefs in question are in fact true, or that they haven't been shown to be false. Since truth is not the point, truth is not an adequate defense. Both sides need to be reminded, frequently and forcefully, what the logic of the situation is.

The second opening to a theological appropriation of the hermeneutics of suspicion derives from its parallel with the hermeneutics of finitude. Just as the finitude is a theological theme in relation to the doctrine of creation, suspicion is a theological theme in relation to the doctrine of the fall. In the theologian's language, it traces the noetic effects of human sinfulness. Nietzsche didn't intend his doctrine of the 'will to power' to be a secular, phenomenological account of original sin or his practice of suspicion to be an extension of the Pauline, Augustinian, and Lutheran employment of sin as an epistemological category; but he can be fruitfully read in that way. When he is, it begins to look as if suspicion is not simply an optional tool for the theologian but an indispensable one for any theologian who takes sin seriously.

We might note the following irony involved in the case of the theologian who does not take sin seriously. This usually happens out of the desire to take modern secular thought seriously, to avoid keeping theology in an ecclesiastical ghetto; but in the aftermath of secular suspicion, as developed by Marx, Freud, and Nietzsche, any theologian who does not take sin seriously loses touch thereby with some of the most powerful secular thinkers of the modern (and postmodern) world.

The third theological opening to suspicion is perhaps nothing but the flip side of the second. The theologian's work is in the service of the truth about the true God. For this reason the theologian shares, if in a somewhat more reflective mode, the prophet's abhorrence of idolatry. But just to the degree that human interests play a controlling role in the way we think and speak about God, that God becomes an idol, a God made with human hands. Conceptual and linguistic hands, to be sure; but since they are not less human than those that make graven images, the gods that result are no less idols. Of course, idols need not be new constructions out of whole cloth; they can be produced by editing, revising, taming.

A theology that wishes to be sensitive to such tendencies, not only in the work of its adversaries, but most importantly in its own work, will find the hermeneutics of suspicion an indispensable part of its methodology. Perhaps 'methodology' is not the right name for this practice, for we are not dealing here with the proper relation of a subject to its epistemic object. It is rather a question of the relation of the epistemic subject to itself, to its own shameful interests, which it does not always manage to keep unemployed. Seen in this light, suspicion is more nearly a spirituality than a methodology. So perhaps we should call it a practice and a posture rather than a tool. But it remains an obligatory and not an optional part of the theologian's art.

A final observation about Nietzschean suspicion. To this point I have spoken of it in relation to theology proper, beliefs about God. But we need to know very little about Nietzsche to realize that he is concerned with ethics at least as much as with metaphysics. He reverses the charge of Lactantius, that the virtues of the pagans are splendid vices, and argues that this is true of the altruistic virtues which the Jewish and Christian traditions sum up in the notion of neighbor love.

Now is not the time for a detailed tour of Nietzsche's moral inventory: a) of his discovery of the spirit of revenge behind ideals of justice; b) of his discovery of the desire for moral superiority behind ideals of pity or compassion; or c) of his discovery of laziness, timidity, cowardice – what Zarathustra calls the 'wretched contentment' of those 'weaklings who thought themselves good because they had no claws' (Z 'On those who are sublime') – behind all kinds of goodness. But such a tour, and it does take time, is an integral part of the spirituality mentioned above. Among its potential benefits to the theologian I mention but two. First, it counters the idealistic and existentialist withdrawals from metaphysics to ethics by suggesting that the latter is as problematic as the former. Second, it reminds the theologian that in ethics as well as in metaphysics, the how must never be rendered peripheral by the what. The heart of the matter is the heart.

Nietzsche wouldn't put it quite this way, but he shows us that whether it is a matter of metaphysics or of ethics, the theological project betrays itself when it abstracts the project of getting it right from the task of becoming righteous. Nor have we avoided this problem simply by abandoning dogmatic, objectivistic, foundationalist, totalizing conceptions of getting it right in favor of pluralistic and perspectival understandings of understanding. However necessary the hermeneutics of finitude may be, it remains in bad faith without an equally serious hermeneutics of suspicion.

Bibliography of cited works by Nietzsche

Beyond Good and Evil (New York: Random House, 1966, trans. W. Kaufmann)
Daybreak: Thoughts out of Season (New York: Cambridge University Press, 1982, trans. R.J. Hollingdale)
The Portable Nietzsche (New York: Viking Press, 1954, trans. W. Kaufmann).

Notes

1 Martin Heidegger, *Identity and Difference* (New York: Harper & Row, 1969, trans. J. Stambaugh) p. 72. Hereafter ID.
2 Aristotle *Metaphysics* 1026a30 in *The Complete Works of Aristotle* (Princeton: Princeton University Press, ed. J. Barnes).
3 Alasdair MacIntyre, *Marxism and Christianity* (Notre Dame: University of Notre Dame Press, 1968) p. 2.
4 Alasdair MacIntyre, *Secularism and Moral Change* (London: Oxford University Press, 1967) p. 69.
5 Alasdair MacIntyre, 'Atheism and Morals' in *The Religious Significance of Atheism* (New York: Columbia University Press, 1967) p. 39.
6 Søren Kierkegaard, *Practice in Christianity* (Princeton: Princeton University Press, 1991, trans. H.V. and E.H. Hong) p. 88.
7 See 1 *Corinthians* 13:12
8 See F. Nietzsche, 'On Truth and Lie in an Extra-Moral Sense' in *The Portable Nietzsche* (New York: Viking Press, 1954, trans. Walter Kaufmann) pp. 44–47.
9 Søren Kierkegaard, *Concluding Unscientific Postscript* (Princeton: Princeton University Press, 1992, trans. H.V. and E.H. Hong) I p.118.
10 See 2 *Corinthians* 4:4 and 7.
11 Ludwig Feuerbach, *The Essence of Christianity* (New York: Harper and Brothers, 1957, trans. George Eliot) p. 15.
12 The key texts by Derrida are '*Différance*' in *Margins of Philosophy* (Chicago: University of Chicago Press, 1982, trans. A. Bass) and the entire volume, H. Coward and T. Foshay (eds.): *Derrida and Negative Theology* (Albany: State University of New York Press, 1992) but especially, 'How to Avoid

Speaking: Denials' (pp. 73–142), and, more recently, '*Sauf le nom (Post-Scriptum)*' in T. Dutoit (ed.): *On the Name* (Stanford: Stanford University Press, 1995).

13 See M. Westphal, 'Nietzsche and the Phenomenological Ideal', *The Monist* 60:2 (1977), pp. 278–288.

14 The immediate issue here is the existence of God, but the distinctions here are quite general and can be applied to beliefs of all sorts. For nonreligious examples, see M. Westphal, 'Help From Gilbert and Sullivan' in my *Suspicion and Faith: The Religious Uses of Modern Atheism* (New York: Fordham University Press, 1998) chapter three.

15 *Ibid*, p. 229.

3
Nietzsche's positive religion and the Old Testament

Jacob Golomb

Contrary to the common view of Nietzsche as the unrelenting enemy of religion, I propose to bring out his more favourable views about faith and its adherents. I shall use Nietzsche's relation to the Old Testament in support of my thesis that Nietzsche did not totally repudiate the religious experience and even found some of its aspects congenial to one of the main objectives of his philosophy, viz., the reactivation of our creative powers. In Nietzsche's view, religious faith is not necessarily inherently nihilistic, and does not invariably undermine the value of our earthly life and our spontaneous creativity and vitality. Certain religious notions have served as conceptual resources and as emotional stimulants for the emergence of life patterns which Nietzsche ardently encouraged: the morality of positive power. Nietzsche implied that he borrowed his concepts of power and of the *übermensch* – among other things – from divinity as a model of an ideal Being. The case in point is the ancient Hebrew image of God as portrayed in the Old Testament, much admired by Nietzsche, who deployed it as an heuristic idea that inspired his late thought.

An explication of Nietzsche's positive view on religion will help us to understand that Nietzsche's celebration of the Old Testament was not simply a resentful act of a German philosopher who, out of hatred of the Germans and their nationalistic racial anti-Semitism,[1] wanted to annoy them with his 'untimely' and contrary preferences. Neither is it derived from capricious philo-Semitic sentiments, nor from his hatred of the negative elements of the Christian religion.[2] His favourable views regarding the ancient Hebrew faith relate to his pivotal notion of power (*Macht*) which he felt to be closely connected to certain elements of the Hebrew religion. It is even highly probable that the formation of this notion and of some other key ideas, like that of personal authenticity, were inspired by Nietzsche's reading of the Old Testament. From this point of view it becomes apparent that for the young Nietzsche, Hebrew religion played a formative role in his thought, no less than that of the ancient Greek gods and pagan culture.

Nietzsche's notion of positive as distinct from negative power

Nietzsche discerns two basic patterns of our moral behaviour: one deriving from the existence of positive power and another from its absence (allied with the will to achieve it). Hence he describes two distinct psychological types, which manifest their respective kinds of power in everyday patterns of life and in their intellectual creativity. The will to attain power always lies under the surface of all human expressions. This (at first) anthropological principle and its two diametrically opposed manifestations, the negative and the positive, are the ground for his various evaluations of cultural fields. A comprehensive elaboration of this distinction cannot be given here,[3] but to understand why Nietzsche admired the ancient Hebrew religion and rejected the early Christian faith we have to present it in a nutshell. In his main writings, Nietzsche deals extensively with these two types of power. Below, we can find most of the predicates that he used to characterize them:

Patterns of negative power	*Patterns of positive power*
1. lack or impoverishment of power;	fullness and plenitude of power;
2. depression, melancholy and suspension of action, reactivity;	elation, dynamic vitality; sheer activity and spontaneity;
3. heteronomous dependence upon external circumstances and resources;	autonomy and creation of values, self-sufficiency;
4. violence and cruel exploitation as means for enhancement of power and as a result of resentment;	violence as a spontaneous by-product of the direct manifestation of power;
5. castration and repression of instincts;	creative sublimation of instincts;
6. ascetic patterns of life;	aesthetic expressions of life;
7. dogmatism and extremism;	intellectual tolerance;
8. heaviness, passivity and *akrasia*;	lightness and gaiety;
9. vengefulness and *ressentiment*;	generosity and nobility;

10.	cowardice and pursuit of security;	heroism, courage and greatness;
11.	nihilism and decadence: preservation of life;	'strong instinct', 'will to life': enhancement of life;
12.	hatred out of fear;	refined contempt;
13.	resignation and submissiveness;	*amor-fati*, self-acceptance and affirmation;
14.	pessimism and 'thought of death';	'thought of life' and sober optimism;
15.	fear of natural inclinations;	sensuality and acceptance of one's inclinations;
16.	the need for system, logic and dialectics;	'the ability to accept contradiction';
17.	'internal distress and uncertainty', guilt feelings;	lack of guilt feelings, clear conscience;

As can be seen from these predicates, negative power is symptomatic of a weak personality, lacking in power but incessantly attempting to obtain it. In Nietzsche's view this pattern was characteristic of the early Christians, who formed their religion out of a desperate need for power:

> There are recipes for the feeling of power, firstly for those who can control themselves and who are thereby accustomed to a feeling of power; then for those in whom precisely this is *lacking*. Brahminism has catered for the men of the former sort, Christianity for men of the latter (D 65; KSA 3 63, my italics).

The early Christians, or what Nietzsche nicknamed the 'Jewish priests'[4] of the Second Temple, initiated the 'slaves' revolution in morality' and invented the concepts of sin, bad conscience and guilt as means for cruel revenge. These notions were often used to justify the abuse, even the torture, of others, thereby intensifying the early Christian's own feebleness:

> Oh, how much superfluous cruelty and vivisection have proceeded from those religions which invented sin! And from those people who desired by means of it to gain the highest enjoyment of their power! (D 53; KSA 3 57).

Negative power does not express itself spontaneously, but derivatively: it is fundamentally deficient and defective, striving to encourage and fortify itself, by – amongst other means – enjoyment and dominance obtained from abuse and cruelty. We can, Nietzsche says, acquire and intensify our power 'in two ways', by 'benefiting and hurting others' (GS 13; KSA 3 384). There are individuals who are so dependent upon others that they often enter into relationships which cause them pain or pleasure. This fact indicates that most of us do not yet have an inherent feeling of power, thereby relying on external relations as substitutes. The sense of the lack of power arouses our impulse to acquire it. For clearly, the need to hurt others is a sign that we still lack power, or of frustration in the face of such poverty. Time and again Nietzsche warns us of the misguided and perverse ways in which humans have sought to attain power – leading to a whole catalogue of nihilistic external cultural expressions. We are told, for example, how negative power causes one to wish to control and subdue another by an act of love, in which the lover 'desires unconditional and sole possession of the person for whom he longs … He alone wants to be loved and desires to live and rule in the other soul' (GS 14; KSA 3 387). Certain forms of morality derive from negative power, such as the instrumental morality of altruism: 'The neighbor,' Nietzsche says, 'praises selflessness because *it brings him advantages.*' In this context Nietzsche observes that 'the *motives* for this morality stand opposed to its principle' (GS 21; KSA 3 393), and asserts that it must be totally rejected. And thus he broadens his criticism to religion (especially to that of the Christians), which also exhibits an intricate network of *post factum* rationalization.

In any case, Nietzsche's philosophy of power is not an inductive theory or an empirical hypothesis, as Kaufmann claims.[5] Apart from its speculative ramifications it also contains an explicative and typological dimension – in contrast to the constructive and explanatory aspect of the empirical sciences. This dimension is vividly expressed in Nietzsche's descriptions of the different patterns of power and his distinction between its positive and negative manifestations. Explication, careful description and analysis of a given phenomenon do not require its rational justification and foundation, but the former may surely function as a necessary preparatory introduction for the latter. This is what Nietzsche has in mind when he says that all previous philosophers have 'wanted to supply a rational foundation' for the prevalent morality, but have completely ignored its vast variety and immense richness. Thus they were involved in providing a justifying philosophy, a 'science of morals' (namely, a rational ethics) and did not deal with the preliminary 'typology of morals' (BGE 186; KSA 5 105). Because of this exclusive preoccupation, the philosophers 'left in dust … the task of description,' and were not at all concerned 'to collect material, to conceptualize and arrange a vast realm of subtle feelings of value and differences of value which are alive, grow, beget, and perish.' (*ibid.*) They completely neglected 'attempts to present vividly some of the more frequent and recurring forms of such living crystallizations,' forgetting thereby that 'the real problems of morality…emerge only when we compare *many* moralities' (*ibid.*; KSA 5 105-106). In his main works, Nietzsche dealt extensively with such comparisons, and with descriptive typology and the 'subtle' distinctions between different ethical codes and religions, including the different stages of the Hebrew-Jewish religion.

This explicative dimension indicates that Nietzsche was not searching for new, esoteric values. Nor did he intend to establish a new ethics. His objective was to crystallize, to intensify, and to re-activate a number of values regarded for centuries by most as good and useful, securing the manifestations of positive power and fostering mental health. As can easily be seen from the above table, most of these values were already present in different religions and various cults. These positive aspects of religion were heuristic in Nietzsche's 're-evaluation' which was not conducted *ex nihilo* but in a culture saturated by positive notions (positive according to Nietzsche's evaluations) that were sanctified by the thousands of years of various religions and rites.

Positive versus negative religion

Nietzsche maintained that wherever there is a need for faith, will is weak and personality is frail. Paraphrasing Tertullian (*Credo quia absurdum*: 'I believe because it is absurd'), one can summarize Nietzsche's position as 'I believe because I do not will'. Active volition gives way to passive faith only out of weakness. This approach clearly suggests a criterion for positive power:

> How much one needs a faith (*einer Glauben*) in order to flourish … that is a measure of the degree of one's strength (or, to put the point more clearly, of one's weakness) . . . The demand that one wants by all means that something should be firm . . . that instinct of weakness … which, to be sure, does not create religious metaphysical systems, and convictions of all kinds, but – conserves them (GS 347; KSA 3 581–582).

This provides a concrete description of negative religion which stems from the absence of healthy, intrinsic and positive power. The need for faith as 'a support, a prop' is considered a symptom of weakness of will, or in Aristotle's terms, of *akrasia*. This analysis anticipates William

James' discussion of religious experience and its psychological function.[6] But while James advocates religion as an existential metaphysical crutch essential to survival, Nietzsche rejects this particular function of negative religion. In his view, it perpetuates weakness, endows it with a 'holy' transcendental legitimacy and thereby it checks the impulse to enhance our feeling of power through our own positive efforts and mental resources. Where crutches are provided for the cripples (in will and spirit), the incentive to overcome their handicap and walk independently will disappear. As a result they remain in a condition of psychological slavery:

> Faith is always coveted most and needed most urgently where will is lacking … the less one knows how to command, the more urgently one covets someone who commands, who commands severely — a god, prince, class, physician, father, confessor, dogma or party conscience (GS 347; KSA 3 582).

The consequences are not restricted to the arena of religion but permeate most of our social and political activities. Persons may flee from freedom, for example, towards totalitarian regimes and extreme forms of heteronomous rule, such as the dictatorship of an individual or a party. Negative religion is a *'disease of the will'* (*ibid.*) and as such it must be combatted and cured. This is the intention of Nietzsche's criticism of the negative religion. A healthy person does not need the therapy; a symptom of psychic health is that 'a freedom of the will .. [will] take leave of all faith.' One who does not require religion or faith is 'the *free spirit* par excellence' (*ibid*; KSA 3 583).

Nietzsche was not opposed to negative religion merely because it handicaps the free development of positive power; he regarded it as inimical to life itself. Negative religion in general, and ascetic religion in particular, do not merely weaken the will but directly repress the instinct to live altogether, glorifying death and abstinence. Wherever vital life is repressed, culture and spontaneous creativity are condemned to die. Negative religion is not only a passive symptom of sickness; it actively aggravates the disease and kills the patient. It is not merely one nihilistic symptom among others, but one that leads to a complete nihilism, the negation of creation (and life) itself, therefore it became for Nietzsche his arch-enemy.[7]

Nietzsche's opposition to negative religion was also related to his morality of positive power: 'I myself have now slain all gods … for the sake of morality' (GS 153; KSA 3 496). And thus Nietzsche sought to freeze or undermine our mental need for this kind of religious faith in order to prepare the human consciousness for a morality of genuine power. He recognized that behind the moral patterns of negative power loom the negative religions that justify and sanctify them.

Nonetheless, it must be pointed out that Nietzsche did not reject religion altogether as such. Indeed, he finds some of its characteristics most appropriate to the central aim of his philosophizing, viz., arousal to positive power. One could subsume such characteristics under the label 'positive religion', thereby indicating that they help to reactivate humanity's positive resources. This feature is especially emphasized in one of Nietzsche's comments on the origins of science:

> Do you really believe that the sciences would ever have originated and grown if the way had not been prepared by magicians, alchemists, astrologers, and witches whose promises and pretensions first had to create a thirst, a hunger, a taste for *hidden* and *forbidden* powers? . . . Even as these preludes and preliminary exercises of science were *not* by any means practiced and experienced as such, the whole of *religion* might yet appear as a prelude and exercise to some distant age. Perhaps religion could have been the strange means to make it possible for a few single individuals to enjoy the whole self-sufficiency of a god and his whole power of self-redemption . . . would man ever have learned without the benefit of such a religious training and pre-history to experience a hunger and thirst for *himself* and to find satisfaction and fullness in *himself*? (GS 300; KSA 3 538–539).

Nietzsche implies here and in the lines that follow that religion is not intrinsically nihilistic. It is not always directed at annihilating life and positive power. Parts of its conceptual arsenal, its values and practice have become stimulants of the human yearning for achievement, for self-perfection, integrity and for a morality of positive power. Some of God's attributes, especially those expressing his autonomy, his power and his ability to create might have become in Nietzsche's hands, as indeed they did, a divine and sublime paradigm for human beings endowed with creative and authentic powers.

Nietzsche was not, then, indiscriminately opposed to religion *per se*, but to its misuse and its negative components – just as the various types of historical consciousness are not good or bad in themselves, but find their value in the use made of them by various types of personalities.[8] Like other expressions of culture, religion exerts 'influence, always destructive, as well as creative and form-giving'. This 'selective and cultivating influence' is 'always multiple and different according to the sort of human beings who are placed under its spell and protection' (BGE 61; KSA 5 79).

Religion can be either negative or positive. It is first of all a function of the kind of power of the person who uses it; and secondly, of the use to which it is put. A positively powerful individual or people will use the positive elements of religion positively; a weak person or people will put religion to negative use. The same applies to independent philosophers and to the 'free spirits', who 'will make use of religion for their project of cultivation, and education.' (*ibid.*). This was frequently Nietzsche's own practice: he utilized the positive elements in religions for the purpose of educating and enticing others toward positive power. He believed such enticements were effective precisely because their goal, the realization of the positive power-pattern, was deeply rooted in the religious history of humankind and was imprinted in its religious rituals and myths.

It should be clear, however, that Nietzsche regarded even positive religion as a mere temporary means rather than an ultimate end. Once religion becomes an end in itself, it becomes *ipso facto* a negative religion *par excellence* and turns into a destructive element:

> One always pays dearly and terribly when religions do not want to be a means of education and cultivation in the philosopher's hand but insist on having their own sovereign way, when they themselves want to be ultimate ends and not means among other means (BGE 62; KSA 5 81).

It is very likely that Nietzsche himself had arrived at the concept of a positive power pattern from this godlike model of an ideal Being to whom people have attributed supreme qualities that in their view are worthy of pursuit. Nietzsche transferred several of these attributes from a transcendent God to his ideal *Übermensch*. He could not have convincingly done that had there not previously existed in our culture and collective consciousness a certain notion of God as absolutely free and creative; a Being endowed with perfect positive power, namely with most of the characteristics found on the side of the positive-power patterns in the above-drawn table.

Nietzsche understood this well and regarded the positive components of religions as the 'prelude' to his own morality and to his ideally authentic *Übermensch*. If negative religion annihilates life and will, and suppresses the expressions and cultivation of human power, positive religion (namely the positive components of religion as such) stimulates the renewal and reactivation of the morality of positive power. This insight into the positive and heuristic function of religion is implied in his statement that I take to be his rather ambivalent but crucial confession:

But you will have gathered what I am driving at, namely ... that even we
seekers after knowledge today, we godless anti-metaphysicians still take our
fire, too, from the flame lit by a faith that is thousands of years old, that
Christian faith which was also the faith of Plato, that God is the truth, that
truth is divine. – But what if this should become more and more incredible
... if God himself should prove to be our most enduring lie? (GS 344; KSA
3 577).

In section 24 of the third essay of the *Genealogy of Morals,* Nietzsche
repeats this passage *verbatim* from *The Gay Science,* but here with even
more emphasis on the 'faith in truth', and mentions the 'unconditional
will to truth'. At first glance it seems as if Nietzsche is suspicious of
(rather than endorsing) the connection with Christianity he uncovered
here and elsewhere.[9] However, a close inspection of his utterances discloses that Nietzsche is speaking here of a three stage transformation of
the concept of truth (*Wahrheit*): from the 'most enduring lie' of the
purely religious 'faith in truth' which stipulates that 'God is the truth'
and that 'truth is divine' (*ibid.*) to the 'convictions' of 'science' and the
'faith in truth' which are but 'a regulative fiction' to the existential ideal
of 'integrity' of 'unconditional and honest atheism' that paves the way to
the 'sublimated' 'concept of truthfulness' (*Begriff der Wahrhaftigkeit*)
(GS 357; KSA 3 600). In other words, Nietzsche directs our attention
to the fact that, were it not for the thirst for truth that was aroused by
the faith and will of a religious person (to use the language of
Kierkegaard, to 'have the truth on his or her side'[10]), then the thirst for
the cognitive truth that science might bring would not be aroused in the
first place. From this point of view, religious faith was really 'a prelude'
to the scientific, albeit mostly atheistic, attitude. At the last stage, the
existence of the notion of scientific truth, which again was but a 'regulative fiction', enabled Nietzsche to 'sublimate' it into his existential
ideal of a perfectly authentic *Übermensch,* who manifests the highest
quality of positive power, namely the personal 'integrity', authenticity or
'truthfulness' (*Wahrhaftigkeit*). This is how I read the following passage:

You see what it was that really triumphed over the Christian god: Christian
morality itself, the concept of truthfulness that was understood ever more
rigorously, the father confessor's refinement of the Christian conscience,
translated and sublimated into a scientific cleanliness at any price (GS 357;
KSA 3 600).

From the 'Christian conscience' and the truthfulness of confession in
the Christian ritual through to 'scientific cleanliness', Nietzsche arrived

at the existential cleanliness of personal authenticity and truthfulness of life ideally embodied in the fictitious person of Zarathustra. And thus, Nietzsche's transition from the creative and positive power of the Christian God to the creative, authentic and autonomous power of the *Übermensch*, is made possible due to the pre-existence of Christianity, or more exactly – due to the positive elements of the Christian faith (GS 377).[11] These elements of Christianity came to a sharp relief in the person of Jesus, as portrayed by Nietzsche in *The Anti-Christ*. Jesus, 'the first and the last Christian, exhibited unconditional generosity and many other traits of positive power. Moreover, he was completely devoid of feelings of vengefulness and *ressentiment* . But we should recall that for Nietzsche these very feelings are the epitome of the negative power as manifested in the 'morality of slaves'. And despite the fact that Nietzsche strongly objected to 'the religion of pity', his personal and intellectual integrity led him to stress the positive components of Christianity by admitting that:

> We are ... *good Europeans*, the heirs of Europe, the rich, oversupplied, but also overly obligated heirs of thousands of years of European spirit. As such we have outgrown Christianity and are averse to it – precisely because we have grown out of it, because our ancestors were Christians who in their Christianity were uncompromisingly upright: for their faith they willingly sacrificed possessions and position, blood and fatherland. We – do the same (GS 377; KSA 3 631).

This picture of the uncompromisingly sacrificing 'upright' Christian faith that goes all the way through is highly reminiscent of Kierkegaard's description of the 'existential sphere' of authentic faith (personified by the sacrificing Abraham in *Fear and Trembling).*[12] But unlike Kierkegaard, Nietzsche took a crucial further step: from the authenticity of the believer to authentic 'unbelief' (*ibid.*). His authentic atheism is the 'proof of strength' of one's authenticity, of the ability and personal courage to dance 'even near abysses' (GS 347; KSA 3).

However, this dialectical move from the *Christian* faith in truth to the *scientific* search for the cognitive truth that culminates in the *existential* search for personal truthfulness did not originate from Christianity alone. As Nietzsche puts it, one must grasp the Christian faith as springing 'from Jewish roots and comprehensible only as a growth on this soil' (TI 'The "improvers" of mankind' 4; KSA 6 101 and cf. GS 137). Hence it stands to reason that Nietzsche's morality of positive power, and many of his other positive ideas (like the primacy of life over the theoretical

preoccupation, his emphasis on the 'monumental' versus the 'antiquarian' historical consciousness) grew out of the culture of the ancient
Hebrews, as his concepts of the Apollonian and the Dionysian grew out
of the ancient Greeks.

I cannot fully discuss here Nietzsche's multifarious pronouncements
on religion and on Judaism[13] and will confine myself to illustrating the
foregoing theses by focusing on Nietzsche's image of the Old Testament
and the ancient Hebrew God. In this context, however, it is quite crucial to address ourselves to the question of why positive religion was historically defeated by negative religion.

Why has 'Rome ... bowed down' before
'*three Jews...* and *one Jewess*'?

> Wandering through the many subtler and coarser moralities which have so
> far been prevalent on earth, or still are prevalent, I found that certain fea-
> tures recurred regularly together and were closely associated – until I finally
> discovered two basic types and one basic difference.

> There are *master morality* and *slave morality* – I add immediately that in all
> the higher and more mixed cultures there also appear attempts at media-
> tion between these two moralities, and yet more often the interpenetration
> and mutual misunderstanding of both, and at times they occur directly
> alongside each other – even in the same human being, within a single soul.
> (BGE 260; KSA 5 208)[14]

Several central ideas occur here and in other related aphorisms. First,
Nietzsche describes his investigations of different moral patterns as a
search for 'certain features [that] recurred regularly together.' This
clearly is a description of the explicative method, which seeks to expose
the definitive and essential features of certain phenomena. The two
moral phenomena presented are actual cultural and religious patterns,
and not *a priori* constructions of our minds. 'Master morality' and its
derivatives (like the patterns of the *Übermensch*) are historical phenomena which Nietzsche defines more specifically to avoid confusion with
'slave morality'. They are not new conceptual constructs but pre-exist-
ing situations and personalities. In Nietzsche's own view, his originality
and innovative nature are not expressed by establishing novel moral precepts, but by elucidating antecedent moralities; by giving them new
names, he sheds new light on their essential features.[15] Unless the moral
phenomenon undergoes the most sustained explication, analysis and

classification, it cannot influence or move us. In other words: it cannot become an operative and significant ideal. This is how we should grasp Nietzsche's statement that 'Never yet has there been an overman' (Z, 'On Priests': KSA 4 119). There has never been a perfect empirical example of positive power. Such an archetype is given in the fictitious figure of Zarathustra, who consolidates the positive values scattered throughout human history and culture. An explicit moral ideal of positive power has been wanting. If we wish to be guided effectively by such an ideal we must bring it to a full and conscious explication. Once the explication of power has provided the necessary description of this implicit ideal, it will be transformed into an influential 'regulative' idea which, unlike the 'regulative fiction' of the 'convictions' of 'science' (GS 344), has none of the dimensions of construction but merely of instruction.

Secondly, while observing the cultural history of morality, Nietzsche uncovered 'the interpenetration and mutual misunderstanding of both '(BGE 260) and disclosed the slow, gradual progression from the 'morality of the herd' to a morality that increasingly stresses the value of the individual. The gradual emergence of the morality of positive power was already taking place in the history of humankind, Nietzsche claimed (GS 117-120), and hence the main goal of his explications was to speed up this process and to provide it with an operative and effective power. It follows that we must understand his 'transvaluation of all values' not as an abolition but as a gradual transfiguration of a negative power morality into a positive one. Clearly, this is not a radical change 'out of the blue'; in order that a significant change take place, the modifying element must already contain, at least implicitly, the seeds of this alteration. The process of transfiguration, therefore, is well established both in our cultural and religious history and also 'within a single soul' – fluctuating between the opposing vectors of constructive and destructive powers.

Thirdly, the explication of power reflects upon the 'single soul' of the individual. Nietzsche, like Freud, occasionally delineates parallels between phylogenesis and ontogenesis[16] – between the development of whole cultural patterns and their evolution in individual members of that culture. Thus, after claiming the interpenetration of the two moralities on the wider, historical level, Nietzsche went on to make an onto-genetic statement, namely that such processes 'occur directly alongside each other – even in the same human being.' It is difficult to speak about morality, which requires a social context, with reference to the 'single soul'. Hence Nietzsche was describing here a more transitory, fluctuating emotional and mental state of the individual: 'the true pathos of every period of our life' (GS 317). Such an individual 'pathos of life' crystallizes into a social formation of moral patterns and positive/negative ways of life.

The view that positive and negative powers can be found even in the same person and to a different degree and proportion within one 'soul' (the exclusivity of one or the other type of power is only given in the theoretical descriptions of the ideal and 'pure' type of a person) helped Nietzsche to explain the main paradox that seems to overshadow this exposition. The empirical supremacy of negative power challenges the results of Nietzsche's descriptive analyses, from which it follows that the positive power is power *par excellence*, the power bearing the authentic moral capacity. Thus it is reasonable to expect that it should dominate our culture. Nietzsche declared that he wrote *On the Genealogy of Morals* precisely to deal with this issue. The third essay of this work addresses 'the question whence the ascetic ideal, the priests' ideal, derives its tremendous *power* although it is the *harmful* ideal *par excellence*, a will to the end, an ideal of decadence.' (EH-GM; KSA 6 353)[17] In other words: if the morality of positive power is so sublime and good, how is it that our contemporary social-ethical circumstances are so remote from manifesting its high qualities? In Nietzsche's terms, how is it possible to explain the 'very remarkable' historical fact that 'Rome has been defeated beyond all doubt'? (GM I 16; KSA 5 286). And, in our present context, one may ask how come the positive religion of the ancient and mentally powerful Hebrews was defeated by the negative religion of the meek 'Jewish priests' and the first Christian 'slaves' who lacked the spiritual resources of positive power? How did it happen that despite the qualitative superiority of positive power and its impressive appearances in the history and the religion of the ancient Hebrews and, for that matter, also of the pagan cults of the ancient Greeks, it has been pushed aside by a weaker and negative religion?

Nietzsche's rather extensive response may be summarized as follows: it was not some inherent flaw in positive religion that prevented its enduring predominance but rather a weakening from within. This happened because the negative elements that co-existed within the culture and religion of the ancient Hebrews, gained the upper hand by means of the dubious manipulative tactics of the Jewish priests who succeeded in mobilizing *more* 'slaves' who were weak enough to become the victims to these various manipulations.[18] Thus sheer numbers ensured their historical victory and the qualitatively superior spiritual and positive *Macht* of the 'masters' was overpowered by the quantitative physical-military force (*Kraft*) of the 'slaves'.[19]

To understand this argument we have to remember that the distinction between the negative and positive modes of power is an idealized generalization of the various power vectors active within the single individual. Humanity is not regulated by a relatively stable configuration of positive and negative powers. The two opposite vectors of power constitute *temporally alternating* sentiments and different types of pathos in constant conflict within the human character. Thus any morality, religion and society necessarily manifest both the negative aspects of repression, violence, weakness and cowardice as well as the positive dimensions of sublimation, creativity and greatness (*BGE* 188). Every individual living within the social and moral framework is necessarily a slave who represses part (or most) of his drives; yet he is also a master, creating values and sublimating force. This perpetual conflict between the two power components, together with the repressive aspect of social nature, renders the human species '*the* sick animal' (GM III 13; KSA 5 367). However, this sickness is necessary for restoring creative health: 'The bad conscience is an illness … but an illness as pregnancy is an illness' (GM II 19; KSA 5 327). Without partial repression and restraint of drives, sublimated activity would be impossible. Similarly, without repressive morality, social conscience, and imposition of Apollonian forms upon our chaotic instincts, a stable society would not be possible. The route to superior culture leads through the repressive processes of its originators. Humanity, however, can halt at the stage of repressive negative power and cease its progress toward the more advanced stage. It is then detained at the stage of self-aggression, hatred, resentment and guilt-feelings. And thus Christianity is, according to Nietzsche, founded upon *repressive* asceticism, turning it into its very ideal and end, fixating humanity within the stage of 'pregnancy', which becomes a permanent *sickness* never giving new birth to creation. The objective of Nietzsche's philosophy is to free us from this fixation, from the stage of the 'camel' (as in 'The Three Metamorphoses' of *Zarathustra*), and to help us recover. He believes that the enticing elements of his anthropological philosophy will undo our repression and bring us to the stage of the 'lion', in which both negative power and its moral implications will be overcome. Nietzsche's ultimate purpose is to assist us in attaining the stage of the 'innocent' and newborn 'child', free of the oppressive 'camel load' of guilt feelings and unhealthy repression. Nietzsche therefore repeatedly emphasizes the motif of self-overcoming, of vanquishing the 'heavy camel spirit' in all of us. However, this self-overcoming needs as its antecedent condition the very repressive social morality and its various manifestations of positive religions that extricated us from the barbarian animal state and helped us redirect our drives and form our souls and spirits (GM II 16). This morality which occurs 'directly alongside' patterns of positive religion has thus actually prepared the way for the morality of positive power. In every individual there is a constant struggle between positive and negative powers that renders self-conquest possible.

Now, to return more concretely to our subject of religions, how was it that the dominating 'masters' with their positive religion were defeated by the 'slaves', and were seduced by the negative and ascetic religions and moral patterns of guilt and bad conscience? In a phrase: '*Why do the weak conquer?*' (WP 864). The answer briefly is: the 'masters', i.e., the mentally powerful individuals, operating within a social context, necessarily underwent the process of internalization and repression of drives. Therefore, they possessed in some degree the potential for 'guilt, bad conscience and the like,' and the seductive and 'clever' manipulations of the sophisticated slaves (the 'Jewish priests' and the early Christians) were directed at the vulnerable part of their mental constitution. These negative seductions (*Verführungen* in Nietzsche's language[20]) of the negative religion that have seduced people into accepting and justifying their negative, feeble power can succeed only if they contrive to evoke our inherent negative elements. The powerful persons and their positive religion were thus betrayed, among other things, by their internal 'fifth column'.

Nietzsche also uses this explanation to account for the fact that positive religion fell prey to the most influential missionaries of the negative religion, foremost among them in his eyes being '*The first Christian ... the apostle Paul*'. 'That the ship of Christianity threw overboard a good part of the Jewish ballast ... that is a consequence of the history of this one man' (D 68; KSA 3 64–68). Because of his teachings, many of the positively powerful aspects of the ancient Hebrews as expressed in the Old Testament were obliterated. And thus, following the introduction of the concepts of 'sin', 'guilt', and 'bad conscience' by Paul and his followers , their strong sensuality underwent a process of 'the annihilation of the passions' (GS 139) and 'denaturing of natural values' (AC 25). All that (according to items 5, 6, 15 and 17 in the table earlier) put them clearly in the domain of the negative power and religion.

It was, therefore, Paul who out of feelings of *ressentiment* and venge-fulness (see items 4 and 9) set the Hebrews on the destructive path of repression. 'With the logician's cynicism of a rabbi' (see item 16), Paul started among the Jewish people 'that process of decay which had begun with the death of the Redeemer' (AC 44). Thus as Socrates diverted the ancient Greeks from positive to negative patterns of power, so did Paul to the ancient Hebrews. He succeeded because he 'directed himself to the lowest class of Jewish society and intelligence' (WP 198) – in other words to those of the Jewish people who lacked positive power and therefore were easily tempted by these 'books of seduction by means of *morality*' (AC 44). However, the Hebrew *élite* – and here Nietzsche is not interested in the sociological-political meaning of the word but in the sublime mental patterns of a soul endowed with positive power – was not tempted by Paul and the New Testament, and despite political exile continued to manifest positive qualities.[21]

However, before the 'Jewish priests' (AC 26) of the second temple and prior to the onset of the second exile and the Pauline Christian Bible, there was a golden period of the Old Testament which fully (though never optimally because of the presence of the 'moralistic' prophets of the late period of the ancient Israeli kingdom like Isaiah) expressed the positive powers of the ancient Hebrews. Let us now look more closely into this epitome of positive religion.

The positive religion of the Old Testament

Many positive components of religion as such which inspired Niet-zsche's philosophy were concentrated in the rites and religion of the ancient Hebrews in the land of Israel. His conscious affinity for the expressions of positive power on the part of the Hebrews, is manifest in his warm attitude toward the 'Jewish Old Testament, the book of divine justice', where 'there are human beings, things, and speeches in so grand a style that Greek and Indian literature have nothing to compare with it. With terror and reverence one stands before these tremendous rem-nants of what once man was.' (BGE 52; KSA 5 72)

In this context it is important to realize that Nietzsche distinguished between the ancient Hebrews of the Old Testament, the 'Christian' Jews of the second temple who instigated the 'revolt of the slaves' and thus gave birth to Christianity, and the modern Jews in the Diaspora.[22] This wide range of distinctions embraces his discrimination between the Old and the New Testaments and, like the latter, is also derived from his basic juxtaposition of positive and negative power. While Jews in the Diaspora were fluctuating between negative and positive patterns,[23] and the New Testament expressed (exclusively if we ignore the figure of Jesus) the patterns of negative power, the dominant element of the ancient Hebrews' Old Testament was the positive power-pattern:

> The *Old* Testament – that is something else again: all honor to the Old Testament! I find in it great human beings, a heroic landscape, and something of the very rarest quality in the world, the incomparable naïvete of the *strong heart*; what is more, I find a people (GM III- 22; KSA 5 393).

The Old Testament was not an expression or result of *akrasia* but of the plenitude of power and positive resources of the people who created it. Its heroes were powerful persons: noble, courageous and adventurous; they had 'strong instincts' and behaved spontaneously, directly and impulsively. They manifested the Dionysian character of ecstatic vitality and affirmation of life and even their vices were the by-products of their will to live a full life and were not the expression of malice and evil. In this respect the great heroes of the Old Testament were living 'beyond good and evil', which were the moral parameters created and fostered by the New Testament and the Christian ethos.[24] According to Nietzsche such heroic persons endowed with positive powers were absent from the New Testament.

Another theme that runs through *The Anti-Christ* and other writings where Nietzsche presents the ancient Hebrews and their rites in a rather positive light is his implicit maxim 'show me who your God is and I'll tell you who you are.' For instance, he maintained that the ancient Hebrew God and his followers were 'the expression of a consciousness of power (*des Macht-Bewusstseins*), of joy in oneself … of the self-confidence of the people.' (AC 25; KSA 6 193). The Hebrew God was the 'God of Israel, the god of a people … strong, brave, masterful and proud' (AC 17), of 'people of an inflexible self-will' (WP 199). All these predicates can be found in the positive power column of the table delineated earlier.

Clearly, it is not the Hebrew religion as such that was of interest to Nietzsche, but its relation to the key concept of his mature thought – *Macht* – which he derived in part also from this religious context. The religion of the ancient Hebrews becomes in Nietzsche's 'hand' a means of 'education and cultivation' (BGE 62). In contrast to the early Christians who used the 'negative' elements of the ancient Hebrew faith for their own purposes (especially the spiritualization and the moralization of the God of Israel by the late prophets like Isaiah (AC 25)), Nietzsche used the positive aspects of the Old Testament, for fostering his own ideal human image which is diametrically opposed to the 'ascetic ideals' of Christianity. He picked up its positive ingredients for the sake of enticement, cultivation and enhancement of positive power. Nietzsche reckoned that such an enticement might work since its object, namely the phenomenon of positive power, was deeply rooted in the history of mankind and its original religions, especially in 'the history of Israel' and the image of the Hebrew God:

> Originally, especially at the time of the kings, Israel also stood in the right, that is, the natural, relationship to all things. Its Yahweh was the expression of a consciousness of power, of joy in oneself, of hope for oneself: through him victory and welfare were expected; through him nature was trusted to give what the people needed – above all, rain. Yahweh is the god of Israel and therefore the god of justice: the logic of every people that is in power and has a good conscience. In the festival cult these two sides of the self-affirmation of a people find expression: they are grateful for the great destinies which raised them to the top ....The people ... clung to the vision ... of a king who is a good soldier and severe judge: above all, that typical prophet (that is, critic and satirist of the moment), Isaiah ...

> What happened: they changed his concept, they denatured his concept: at this price they held on to him. Yahweh the god of 'justice' no longer one with Israel, an expression of the self-confidence of the people: now a god only under certain conditions. The concept of God becomes a tool in the hands of priestly agitators, who now interpret all happiness as a reward, all unhappiness as punishment for disobeying God, as 'sin': that most mendacious device of interpretation, the alleged 'moral world order'...

> *Morality* – no longer the expression of the conditions for the life and growth of a people, no longer its most basic instinct of life, but become abstract, become the antithesis of life. (AC 25; KSA 6 193-194).

I quote this passage at length because it exemplifies most of the theses presented here, especially the distinction between the positive and negative religion, the distinction between the ancient Hebrew image of Yahweh and the Jewish-Christian God, and the basic distinction between the positive versus negative power-patterns of worship.

First of all, the ancient Hebrew concept of God was the direct expression of affirmation of life, and a projection of the healthy, spontaneous, naive and harmonious relation to nature before it become de-naturalized by Jewish-Christian theology that moralized it by introducing into it the 'moral world order'. The positive religion of the ancient Hebrew, described by Nietzsche in almost Dionysian terms that remind one of his description of the pre-Socratic period of ancient Greece in *The Birth of Tragedy*, was a direct 'expression' and affirmation of life struggling with nature, enjoying its victories and accepting in the *amor fati* fashion its failures and disasters. The use in this instance of the proper name of the divinity, 'Yahweh' rather than the 'abstract' and plain 'God' indicates that it embodied the concrete reality of a living people and the expression of their natural life-needs, of their saying 'yes' to life and to happiness. Whereas the ancient Hebrew religion was an expression of plenitude of power and thirst for life, the Jewish-Christian religion became a 'tool in the hands of priestly agitators' who were afraid of life, of their instincts and of the nature within them and in front of them; it became an instrument for overcoming of their negative and feeble powers and a means for the subjugation of others by the manipulative introduction of devious concepts like guilt and 'sin'.

The second point has to do with the appearance of the early Jewish-Christians. With their emergence, the positive, creative and natural balance between people and nature, people and their God, people and their natural morality, was shattered. The persons who conceived this theology had already lost their positive powers and were trying, by means of religious manipulations, to overcome their feebleness and fear of life and death. It is not a coincidence that in the above-quoted passage, Nietzsche described the prophet Isaiah as a 'critic and satirist of the moment', that is, in terms that he used in describing Socrates in *The Birth of Tragedy*. Socrates, by introducing rationality 'at any cost' to the ancient Greek culture, destroyed the delicate balance and highly creative synthesis between the Dionysian-instinctual elements and the logical Appollonian drives in the souls of the Greeks, and thus brought about the decline of the youthful, naive , powerful and healthy creations of the Homeric period. Thus as Socrates and Plato were the turning point in the 'Greek Dionysian' early culture, so were the prophets who stood up to the kings, against spontaneous vitality, and brought about the moralization of nature and the 'gloomy religious-moral pathos'. Therefore in several of his writings Nietzsche draws the parallels between the 'appearance of the Greek philosophers from Socrates onwards' which was a 'symptom of decadence' and 'decline' with the appearance of 'the prophets'. Thus as the 'Platonic slander of the senses ... was preparation of the soil for Christianity' (WP 427), so the late prophets' negation of life prepared the ground for 'morality'. However, just as Nietzsche's relation to Socrates was highly ambivalent, so was his attitude toward the prophets of the Old Testament. Nietzsche criticized Socrates for bringing about an exaggerated Apollonization of culture which encouraged repression of one's Dionysian-vital instincts (BT 2 and TI 'The Problem of Socrates'). Nevertheless, he admired Socrates as a person whose intellectual integrity, stamina and courageous way of incurring and facing his own death were expressions of an heroic personality.[25] The greatness of the 'damage' Socrates had inflicted upon the whole western culture bespoke his greatness as a person. Despite the fact that Nietzsche deplored the deeds of Socrates and, for that matter Jesus too, he admired them for the greatness of their impact. Nietzsche exhibited this sort of ambivalence also toward the figures of the great prophets, like that of Moses, the first of the prophets and the lawgiver who formulated a completely new 'table of values' which is 'the tablet of their [Hebrews'] overcomings' which became a turning point in the history of human morals. In the first part of *Thus Spoke Zarathustra* Nietzsche refers implicitly to Moses and his ten commandments: ' "To honor father and mother and to follow their will to the root of one's soul" – this was the tablet of overcoming that another people hung up over themselves and became powerful and eternal thereby' (Z 'On the thousand and one goals'). The processes of overcoming one's nature and the performance of a re-evaluation of all values belong in Nietzsche's view to patterns of positive and creative power and hence Moses and other great prophets in the Old Testament merit his highest admiration. As long as the prophets struggled heroically against the political establishment (the kings) and sought to promote natural and common-sense morality and decency also against the corrupted clerks of the temple, Nietzsche admires them unreservedly. This admiration for the prophets of Israel is typically expressed by Nietzsche in a comparison with their Christian heirs. For example, he quotes from Luke 6: 23 and sarcastically adds: '*Impertinent* rabble! They compare themselves with the prophets, no less' (AC 45).

Why, then, was Nietzsche ambivalent toward 'the typical prophet' Isaiah who seems to be a kind of a Jewish Socrates? We can only speculate here, for Nietzsche is not at all explicit on this point. Thus as the well being and the creative abilities of a people and a culture require the synthesis of the Dionysian and Appollonian drives, namely the sublimation of the Dionysian raw instincts with the Appollonian rational and logical forms, so also it requires the balance between the natural-sensual inclination and the spiritual and moral values. These two elements were represented by the kings of ancient Israel and the prophets who faced and restricted them by a morality of restraint and justice. The values of those prophets served life; it protected and even sanctified it. However with the appearance of Isaiah that balance was shattered by his excessive moralization of nature and of history, by his prophecy of salvation, by his valorization of the other-worldly domain at the expense of the earthly life. In this respect he prepared the appearance and victory of the Christian values which were nihilistic in Nietzsche's view since they negated and denied life no less than did the 'Platonization of Nature' according to the Socratic paradigm.

The pronouncements of such Hebrew prophets as Isaiah was rejected by Nietzsche but their style and manner were much admired. These prophets were prophets of wrath, and by their example the people of Israel fashioned their God: 'they modeled their angry holy Jehovah on their angry holy prophets' (D 38), Nietzsche claimed, admiring their 'grand style in morality' (BGE 250), their 'sense for the sublime' (GS 135) and the Hebrew landscape 'over which the gloomy and sublime thunder cloud of the wrathful Jehovah was brooding continually' (GS 137). This dark and angry Israel's Yahweh was dialectically necessary for the revelation of the religion of love and grace, just as the repressive European Christian culture of Nietzsche's day was necessary for his own prophecy of the new 'Dionysian Europe' that would re-emerge after the re-valuation of all values. This line of thought explains his exclamation that:

> A Jesus Christ was possible only in a Jewish landscape… Only here was the rare and sudden piercing of the gruesome and perpetual general day-night by a single ray of the sun experienced as if it were a miracle of 'love' and the ray of unmerited 'grace'. Only here could Jesus dream of his rainbow and his ladder to heaven on which God descended to man (GS 137).

However, Paul quickly ruined the purity of the love and grace of the 'single ray of the sun' Jesus, and Christianity had lost its only genuine Christian. Due to Paul's destructive impact, the positive religion of the Old Testament deteriorated into the negative religion of the New Testament: 'What a *negative* Semitic religion, the product of an *oppressed* class, looks like: the New Testament (- in Indian-Aryan terms: a chandala religion)' (WP 145).

The Hebrew God and Nietzsche's ideal of authenticity

The main positive function of the ancient Hebrews' faith was rooted in the fact that their projected image of God strengthened their positive powers by crystallizing and sanctifying their vitality and affirmation of life and by making these values into explicit and stimulating ideals. Their personal God, by showing them what he is, urged them to become what they are, and hence his other function was to call them to embrace what Nietzsche cherished mostly – the ideal of authentic life.

In the Old Testament, the Hebrew God reveals himself to Moses out of the bush and to Moses' query on behalf of 'the children of Israel', 'What is his name?', 'God said unto Moses, I AM THAT I AM' (Exodus 3: 14). Martin Luther's German translation of the Bible, very familiar to Nietzsche from his religious upbringing, says: '*Ich werde sein, der ich sein werde*'. Now is it sheer coincidence that the subtitle of Nietzsche's intellectual autobiography, *Ecce Homo* is also called: '*Wie man wird, was man ist*'? Before I attempt to answer this speculative but fascinating question, I have to remind the reader of Nietzsche's teaching on authentic life for which this subtitle serves as a concise formula.

Nietzsche did not use the term 'authenticity' explicitly, but we can locate its origin in his recurrent distinctions between *Wahrheit* (truth) and *Wahrhaftigkeit* (truthfulness): 'a proof of truth is not the same thing as a proof of truthfulness … the latter is in no way an argument for the former' (D 73).[26] This notion of *Wahraftigkeit* is virtually a synonym of the Heideggerian term *eigentlich* and of what in the later existentialist literature was described as *authentic*[27]. Since there is no necessary logical connection between truth and truthfulness, Nietzsche could admire Schopenhauer, Socrates and Jesus while rejecting their teachings. The shift from philosophy to philosophers and that from the traditional meaning of truth to personal authenticity occurs repeatedly in Nietzsche's treatment of the history of philosophy. In his lectures on the pre-Socratics he declares: 'The only thing of interest in a refuted system is the personal element. It alone is what is forever irrefutable.'[28]

One of the basic intuitions of Nietzsche's thought is the concept of complete immanence, formulated in sections 108-125 of *The Gay Science*. Transcendental entities or supra-natural powers do not exist; there is no 'pure reason', no other world, no domain different from or superior to our own. After the 'death of God' one has to adopt the God-like role of being the originator of truth and of one's own self. The absence of a 'pre-established harmony' between our cognition and reality permits us to shift our emphasis to the creation of our own genuine selves. Thus there is a natural connection between our faith in the Almighty and our modern need for creating our own selves. Here the ancient Hebrews' faith in a personal Yahweh and their intimate and natural relations to him rather than to some 'abstract' ontological deity based on theological rationalizations and justifications did not obstruct their ability to create their own selves, and perhaps this is another reason why Nietzsche admired this kind of religion so much and preferred it to the Christian-theological version.

It appears that there are two seemingly contradictory models of authenticity in Nietzsche's thought. The first model (traceable perhaps to Rousseau) derives its inspiration from the biological metaphor of a plant actualizing the potential of the seed. It assumes the individualistic thesis, namely, that 'every man is a unique miracle' (SE 1), a unique aggregate of drives and wishes. One becomes authentic, according to this model, if one manages fully to realize this complexity in one's lifetime. The second model employs the metaphor of art and artistic creation. The search for authenticity is seen as the wish to reflect one's own indeterminacy by spontaneous choice of one out of the many possible ways of life. The individual is a kind of an artist who freely shapes his self as a work of art.

It would be a mistake, however, to suppose that Nietzsche embraced these two models equally. The second conception, that of artistic creation, has clear precedence. Nietzsche rejected crude naturalism and determinism and did not believe that one's inherent nature completely determines one's self. Nietzsche was less concerned with biological nature and more with cultural conditioning and formative influences which blindly shape one's character. To become 'what we are' is not to live according to our so-called 'innate nature', but to create ourselves freely. To that end we need to know ourselves so as to distinguish what we can change in ourselves, and in the external circumstances that have shaped us; we must recognize what we have to accept as inevitable, and must do so in the heroic manner of *amor fati*.[29] The concept of self-overcoming (*Selbstüberwindung*), which is central to Nietzsche's thought,[30] would become meaningless were the biological model really dominant.

We are relatively free to shape our identity and ideals. This freedom makes us responsible for our characters just as artists are responsible for their creations. Hence, Nietzsche is not propounding an 'ethics of self-realization.'[31] This ill-chosen term distorts Nietzsche's view since it presupposes a given personal self and rests on the biological model of authenticity. Nietzsche, however, makes it clear that becoming one's true self is a perpetual movement of self-overcoming; it is a process of a free creation of one's own perspectives and ways of life.[32] His ideal of authentic life includes a denial of any kind of permanent, *a priori* fixed essences or definitions of human beings. We are what we are by creating ourselves and by what we are doing and thinking in our life. But exactly this flexibility as to our essence which is an open-ended enterprise of becoming what we are, a creative life-process without any definitive name is the very meaning of God's answer to Moses: '*Ich werde sein, der ich sein werde*'. Here we find no definitive name or essence thus the sheer dynamism of the present and the emphasis on what one is.

This endless self-affirmation and dynamic openness characterized the Hebrew God and also Nietzsche's ideal of personal authenticity. The connections between them can be further cemented by the following considerations: in the first chapter of the Bible we read: 'And God said, let us make man in our image, after our likeness ... So God created man in his own image, in the image of God created he him' (*Genesis* 1: 26–27). And hence, if the image of God is the indefinable 'I AM THAT I AM' this should be also the image of man as created by God. These are the divine roots of human authenticity and perhaps also the Biblical roots of the key moral ideal of Nietzsche's philosophy. If so, Nietzsche's indebtedness to the Old Testament (be it even on the implicit or unconscious level) is far greater than most commentators care to admit, and the formative influence of this 'Book of Books' is far deeper than is commonly assumed. All these, I believe, are the grounds of Nietzsche's attraction to the Bible of the ancient Hebrews of Israel and to its people.

Bibliography of cited works by Nietzsche

Unless specified the following translations of Nietzsche's works have been used:

The Anti-Christ, in W. Kaufmann (ed. and trans.) *The Portable Nietzsche* (New York: Viking, 1954)

Beyond Good and Evil (New York: Vintage, 1966, trans. W. Kaufmann)

Daybreak (Cambridge: Cambridge University Press, 1982, trans. R. J. Hollingdale).

The Gay Science (New York: Vintage, 1974, trans. W. Kaufmann)

On the Genealogy of Morals (New York: Vintage, 1967, trans. W. Kaufmann and R. J. Hollingdale)

Human, All Too Human (Cambridge: Cambridge University Press, 1986, trans. R. J. Hollingdale).

Philosophy in the Tragic Age of the Greeks (Chicago: Henry Regnery, 1962, trans. M. Cowan).

"Schopenhauer as Educator", in *Untimely Meditations* (Cambridge: Cambridge University Press, 1983, trans. R. J. Hollingdale)

Thus Spoke Zarathustra, in Kaufmann, *The Portable Nietzsche*.
Twilight of the Idols, in Kaufmann, *The Portable Nietzsche*.

Notes

1   Cf. some of the articles in J. Golomb (ed.) *Nietzsche and Jewish Culture*
    (London and New York: Routledge, 1997) and J. Golomb and R. S.
    Wistrich (eds.) *Nietzsche the Godfather of Fascism? On the Uses and Abuses
    of a Philosophy* (Princeton: Princeton University Press, forthcoming).

2   As is implied by I. Eldad in his article 'Nietzsche and the Old Testament',
    in J. C. O'Flaherty, T. F. Sellner and R. M. Helm (eds.) *Studies in Nietzsche
    and the Judaeo-Christian Tradition* (Chapel Hill and London: University of
    North Carolina Press, 1985) pp. 47–68.

3   It can be found in my *Nietzsche's Enticing Psychology of Power* (Jerusalem
    and Ames: Hebrew University Magnes Press and Iowa State University
    Press, 1989).

4   See especially GM. The anachronistic use of the term 'priest' (*Priester*,
    which does not belong to the history of Jewish religion) indicates that Niet-
    zsche had in mind the Christian priest as the prototype of his Jewish coun-
    terparts and anticipators such as the prophets, Pharisees and rabbis.

5   W. Kaufmann, *Nietzsche: Philosopher, Psychologist, Antichrist* (Princeton:
    Princeton University Press, 1968), pp. 92 and 183.

6   W. James, *The Will to Believe and Other Essays in Popular Philosophy* (New
    York: Longmans, Green, 1897); *The Varieties of Religious Experience: A
    Study in Human Nature* (New York: Longmans, Green, 1902).

7   Nietzsche deals with these nihilistic ramifications of negative religion in an
    aphorism entitled 'Christianity and Suicide' (GS 131), amongst other
    places.

8   See Nietzsche's second *Untimely Meditation* 'On the uses and disadvan-
    tages of history for life' and cf. Golomb, *Nietzsche's Enticing Psychology of
    Power*, ch. 2.

9   Here I am indebted to the critical comments of John Lippitt and Jim
    Urpeth who pointed to a possible inconsistency between my interpretation
    and the above-quoted passages from Nietzsche. Their editorial scrupu-
    lousness forced me to be more clear on this point.

10 Cf. my 'Kierkegaard's Ironic Ladder to Authentic Faith', *International Jour-
    nal for Philosophy of Religion* vol. 32 (1991) pp. 65–81.

11 See also Nietzsche's letter to Gast (July 21, 1881), where he confesses his
    personal and intellectual proximity to Christianity.

12 See my *In Search of Authenticity* (London and New York: Routledge, 1995),
    ch. 3.

13 Comprehensively discussed by K. Jaspers, *Nietzsche and Christianity*
    (Chicago: Henry Regnery, 1961). Cf. also my 'Nietzsche on Jews and

Judaism', *Archiv für Geschichte der Philosophie*, vol. 67 (1985) pp. 139–161 and 'Nietzschs Judaism of Power', *Revue des études juives*, vol. CXLVII (1988) pp. 353–385. Finally, see also W. Santaniello, *Nietzsche, God, and the Jews: His Critique of Judeo-Christianity in Relation to the Nazi Myth* (Albany: State University of New York Press, 1994).

14 See also GM I 16 and BGE 200.

15 'What is originality? To *see* something that has no name as yet and hence cannot be mentioned although it stares us all in the face . The way men usually are, it takes a name to make something visible for them. – Those with originality have for the most part also assigned names' (GS 261; KSA 3 517).

16 On many other similarities between Nietzsche's philosophical psychology and Freud's psychoanalysis see Golomb, *Nietzsche's Enticing Psychology of Power.*

17 See also GM III 13.

18 The same structure of argument can be applied also to Socratic dialectics which was working as a 'gadfly' on the minds and not so much on the hearts and emotions (as in the religious domain) of his puzzled audience.

19 Nietzsche is uncharacteristically consistent in his recurring distinction between *Kraft* and *Macht*. This distinction is quite crucial to a sound understanding of Nietzsche's mature philosophy of power because it represents his emphasis on the transition from physical force (and violence (*Gewalt*)) to mental power. See Golomb, *Nietzsche's Enticing Psychology of Power*, ch. 5, and my 'How to De-Nazify Nietzsche's Philosophical Anthropology' in Golomb and Wistrich (eds.), *Nietzsche: Godfather of Fascism?*

20 Nietzsche consistently distinguishes this from his tactic of positive enticement (*Versuchung*). See the concluding chapter of Golomb, *Nietzsche's Enticing Psychology of Power.*

21 See, e.g.: BGE 248; 251; WP 832; GS 136; D 205.

22 There are some scholars who made a slightly different threefold distinction between 'pre-prophetic, prophetic, and modern Jewry' (see M. F. Duffy and W. Mittelman, 'Nietzsche's Attitudes Toward the Jews', *Journal of the History of Ideas*, vol. 49 (1988) pp. 301–317). However, as I will show below, this distinction is somewhat misleading, as many of the Hebrew prophets (especially during the periods of the great kings of ancient Israel) manifested, according to Nietzsche's evaluations, a great deal of positive power and hence belonged to the glorious and heroic period of the Old Testament in distinction to those prophets of the late first kingdom and the second temple who undermined the kings' powers and were instrumental in fostering the emergence of Christianity. Elaboration of the positive attitude that Nietzsche showed toward modern Jewry lies beyond the scope of the present paper and can be found in the author's articles mentioned in note 13 and in Y. Yovel, *Dark Riddle: Hegel, Nietzsche and the Jews* (Cambridge: Polity Press, 1998).

23   For the positive patterns see BGE 248; 251; WP 832; GS 136; D 205, but
     for the more negative ones see HH 475; A 27; A 24; A 46; WP 864.

24   On the almost exact congruence between Nietzsche's distinction of 'good
     and evil' versus 'good and bad' and negative versus positive powers see the
     last two chapters of Golomb, *Nietzsche's Enticing Psychology of Power*.

25   Cf. W. Kaufmann, *Nietzsche* pp. 391–411; W. J. Danhauser, *Nietzsche's View
     of Socrates* (Ithaca and London: Cornell University Press, 1974).

26   See also GS 357; BGE 1.

27   For elaboration of this and other points made here in connection with Niet-
     zsche's teaching on authenticity, consult my *In Search of Authenticity from
     Kierkegaard to Camus* (London and New York: Routledge, 1995) ch. 4, 5
     and 6, and 'Nietzsche on Authenticity', *Philosophy Today* vol. 34 (1990) pp.
     243–258.

28   'Philosophy in the Tragic Age of the Greeks, "A later Preface".'

29   One Apollonian principle, expressed in the command 'know thyself', is
     self-consciousness. This means knowing one's own instinctual desires,
     being aware of one's hidden wishes and of one's genuine, Dionysian char-
     acter. At the same time it recommends coming to terms and living with
     them in a well-functioning and authentic manner. The really authentic or
     powerful person, though cognizant of sickness, affirms life and health.

30   This notion is the key to the meaning of the will to power, as illustrated in
     Thus Spoke Zarathustra, where Nietzsche discusses the will to power in
     terms of the unceasing will to overcome oneself. The will to be rid of the
     superfluous elements of one's character and culture indicates spiritual
     maturity. If one were to ask Nietzsche the purpose of this self-overcoming,
     his answer would be, to attain maturity, authenticity and power. In this
     respect the will to power is of a piece with the quest for authenticity — the
     will to become the free author of one's own self. The optimal will to power
     is expressed by the ideally authentic *Übermensch*. If this will is diminished
     in quality, the inclination to evade the task of creating one's self and to
     identify with the 'herd' will strengthen.

31   W. Kaufmann, *Nietzsche* p. 158.

32   This does not mean that Nietzsche was unaware of the strong pressure
     exerted by social convention and educational systems. Hence the road to
     authenticity and spontaneous creativity requires the two stages described
     by Nietzsche's Zarathustra: 'the spirit becomes a camel; and the camel, a
     lion; and the lion, finally, a child.' (*Z,* 'On the three metamorphoses'). The
     individual ('the lion') must liberate himself from 'the camel', i.e., from all
     the external layers imposed on him by institutional conditioning. Only
     then, after attaining a childlike state of 'innocence' (*ibid*), can he proceed
     to the second stage, in which he consciously adopts and assimilates moral
     norms. These norms may well reflect the traditional values discarded in the
     first stage; it is not their content that matters, but the unconstrained *manner*
     in which they are adopted.

4
Jews, Judaism and the 'free spirit'

Gary Banham

This piece will retrace the complexity of relation between Nietzsche's genealogical critique and Judaism. In the process it will negotiate with the revisionist reading of Gillian Rose and suggest a complexification of a schema proposed by Yirmiahu Yovel. It will be the burden of the argument that understanding the nature of Nietzsche's use of the figure of the 'free spirit' is integral to grasping the role of equivocation in Nietzsche's genealogical analysis. It will be further suggested that whilst Nietzsche's genealogical analysis has immense power that tracing the role played by the figure of the 'free spirit' within it will help us to locate the political and spiritual limitations of the project of genealogical critique.

Genealogy, priests and Jews

In the second section of the preface of *On the Genealogy of Morals* Nietzsche defines the inquiry in the work as being concerned with 'the *origin* of our moral prejudices' which is further defined in the third section of the preface as the problem of discovering 'under what conditions did man devise these value judgments good and evil?'. These enquiries are said to have begun in a more tentative manner in *Daybreak* and *Human, All Too Human*. The latter of these was, he now writes, specifically directed against Schopenhauer who glorified 'the instincts of pity, self-abnegation, self-sacrifice' so that such instincts became for him 'value-in-itself' (GM Preface 5). Having uncovered the connection of the genealogical analysis to a critical engagement we are led to a clear statement of what Nietzsche takes to be in question: 'the *value* of pity and of the morality of pity' (GM Preface 6). Whilst this seems clear enough it is necessary to remember that the type of 'pity' that Nietzsche is questioning is connected to 'self-sacrifice'. Nietzsche indicates in *Beyond Good and Evil* that this is not the only type of pity as there is also pity for 'creator, sculptor, the hardness of the hammer' (BGE 225) which teaches not self-sacrifice but rather sacrifice of 'matter, fragment, excess, clay....that which has to *suffer* and *should* suffer' (BGE 225). So if genealogy is comprehended by Nietzsche as involving critique then what it is engaged in is not critique of all morality or even all morality based upon pity. It is the type of morality that is grounded in the promotion of feelings of renunciation that is in question.

The inquiry undertaken is into how this form of evaluation came to exist and to determine on what soil it grew. The first essay is based on contrasting the morality of good and evil with a morality of good and bad. In the process of presenting this contrast the transformations in language which led from one of these evaluations to the other are uncovered. The highest caste originally designates itself as good and the lower caste as bad. Over time this vocabulary became subtle so that 'a concept denoting political superiority always resolves itself into a concept denoting superiority of soul' (GM I 3). Whilst the ruling group being composed of priests does not necessarily violate this rule (as we can tell from the case provided by the Laws of Manu discussed in *The Anti-Christ* §56–7) it does provide occasions for exceptions to it to arise. With the ruling caste a priestly caste, the designation of 'good' and 'bad' becomes overlaid by the distinction between 'pure' and 'impure'. These terms originally referred to a distinction between types of hygienic habits.

> The 'pure one' is from the beginning merely a man who washes himself, who forbids certain foods that produce skin ailments, who does not sleep with the dirty women of the lower strata, who has an aversion to blood – no more, hardly more! (GM I 6)

This 'purity' is essentially physical in origin and based upon rules of guidance for diet and sexual behaviour. But whilst the origin of this evaluation is based upon an extension of the primary form of difference between 'good' and 'bad' as affecting the modes of intercourse between those of one caste and another this extension comes in time to take on a new meaning as the 'symbolical' notion of purity crystallizes around the physical sense of it.

This leads to Nietzsche's caution about the priestly mode of evaluation.

> There is from the first something *unhealthy* in such priestly aristocracies and in the habits ruling in them which turn them away from action and alter-

nate between brooding and emotional explosions, habits which seem to
have as their almost invariable consequence that intestinal morbidity and
neurasthenia which has afflicted priests at all times; but as to that which
they themselves devised as a remedy for this morbidity – must one not
assert that it has ultimately proved itself a hundred times more dangerous
in its effects than the sickness it was supposed to cure? (GM I 6)

The habits of physical cleanliness turn the priest from action. The con-
centration on ensuring that contact with other orders of men is regulated by rules of diet and abstinence produces a fixation on the inner
effects of external action which ensures that emotional states are given
new attention. The effects of priestly regimes are to make men 'indolent
and overrefined' (GM I 6). But it becomes possible due to the new
depth which is attached to everything for humanity to become evil. The
priest is not *physically* powerful. Whilst warrior aristocracies required
physical health which finds expression in war, with the priests a new type
of *agon* arises: one of spirit.

Nietzsche now proceeds to provide his foremost example of the new
form of morality which diverges from the original equation of 'good'
with 'physically strong'.

> Human history would be altogether too stupid a thing without the spirit
> that the impotent have introduced into it – let us take at once the most
> notable example. All that has been done on earth against 'the noble', 'the
> powerful', 'the masters', 'the rulers', fades into nothing compared with
> what the *Jews* have done against them; the Jews, that priestly people, who
> in opposing their enemies and conquerors were ultimately satisfied with
> nothing less than a radical revaluation of their enemies' values, that is to say,
> an act of the *most spiritual revenge*. (GM I 7)

The Jews are said to have created out of hatred a morality of reaction
which depends upon the impossibility of action. The inversion of values
which the Jews are said to have carried out was stated in *Beyond Good
and Evil* to be the work of the prophets who, according to Nietzsche,
'fused "rich", "godless", "evil", "violent", "sensual", into one and were
the first to coin the term "world" as a term of infamy' (BGE 195). This
revaluation of values, this 'spiritual revenge', is termed by Nietzsche, *the
slave revolt in morals*.

The revolt consists in seeing success in the world as 'evil' and thus
branding physical prowess, conquest, sexual attraction as 'evil'. Nietzsche
understands the motive actuating this evaluation to be 'hatred' but derives
from its slow historical maturation the arrival of the religion of love.

> That love grew out of it as its crown, as its triumphant crown spreading
> itself farther and farther into the purest brightness and sunlight, driven as
> it were into the domain of light and the heights in pursuit of the goals of
> that hatred – victory, spoil, and seduction – deeper and more and more cov-
> etously into all that was profound and evil. (GM I 8)

This type of war is still based on a quest for victory and conquest and is
not without access to arts of seduction but in relation both to ends
and means there is a transvaluation. Seduction must thus also take
place in capturing the mode of evaluation in order to change the focus
of love itself. From this Jewish inversion of moral judgments grows
Christianity.

But before Nietzsche proceeds with his analysis of the revaluation of
values said to have taken place in the 'slave revolt' led by the Jews his
text is interrupted by a 'free spirit' and democrat. One of the effects of
this interruption is to make the arguments of the first essay equivocal in
a sense in which they have not yet appeared to be. The 'free spirit's'
words are said to be an 'epilogue' to what is now termed (retroactively)
'my speech'. This 'free spirit' declares that if the Jews are responsible for
the successful 'slave revolt' it follows that 'in that case no people ever
had a more world-historic mission' (GM I 9). Democrat that it is, this
voice welcomes the progressive emancipation of the human race from
the 'masters' and states that the Church seems rather to hinder than
hasten this development. The voice concludes that the 'poison' of emancipation is something that it loves: 'It is the church, and not its poison,
that repels us. – Apart from the church, we, too, love the poison. – ' (GM
I 9). This 'free spirit' provokes a response from the authorial 'speaker'
who says this interruption has occurred because the 'free spirit': 'had
been listening to me till then and could not endure to listen to my
silence. For at this point I have much to be silent about' (GM I 9).

The original 'speech' suggested that the priest made humanity more
'evil' and saved history from stupidity but indicated the cost of this to
consist in a form of hatred more dangerous to the species as a medicine
than the illness of stupidity that it suffered from. Hence the Jews
appeared to be a form of *pharmakon*. Whilst this picture is already difficult in indicating that if the Jews operated as a means for saving us from
a danger they did so by posing a greater danger, it now appears that there
is a further tension within the work between voices and between types
of silence. Here is how Gillian Rose interprets the tension between
voices and silences:

This inner dialogue between the ignoble voice and the noble voice lies at the heart of what Nietzsche means by 'genealogy': it is the 'conscience of method'; the art of compassion of his own – and our – riven integrity. Formed by both Christianity and morality, the second, noble voice is honest about loving his poison – his redemption from the master, from power as such – and thus he is truly democratic – prepared to overcome his *ressentiment* and to form his power with the power of others; the first, ignoble voice, by refusing to forget, cherishes in silence his lack of power; in *ressentiment* he invents his evil enemy, and thereby affirms a division of impotence between imagined demonic powers and righteous indignation which preserves his own innocence and indignity.[1]

Rose's interpretation of the interlocutor's relation to the authorial voice considerably complicates the question of what is occurring in Nietzsche's genealogical critique. This complication consists firstly in the suggestion that the differential modes of valuation which genealogical critique is tracing are also operative within it. This is what is meant by referring to the notion of Nietzsche's 'riven integrity'. The further complexification introduced by Rose however is to suggest that Nietzsche's 'riven integrity' is also our own and that the reception of genealogical critique is marked by the same equivocations which inform its making. The readers of *On the Genealogy of Morals* contain within them a duality of evaluation which is related to the history which is recounted as having produced them. That Nietzsche was well aware of the duality in question in his own case is clear enough from his self-assessment in *Ecce Homo* where he describes precisely his 'dual descent' from 'both the highest and the lowest rung on the ladder of life, at the same time a *décadent* and a *beginning*' (EH, 'Why I Am So Wise' 1). In support of Rose's discovery of this duality within the *Genealogy* we also have Nietzsche's statement about *On the Genealogy of Morals* in *Ecce Homo* as being a work that contains in each of its three parts 'a beginning that is *calculated* to mislead' (EH, '*Genealogy of Morals*: A Polemic'). What is surprising however, and of the utmost interest in interpreting the relation between the 'free spirit's' interruption and the rest of the work is the suggestion made by Rose that the 'noble' voice of the dialogue (and, by implication, the noble silence contained within it) is given through the 'free spirit'. What makes this surprising is that the authorial silence and authorial comment after the 'free spirit's' interruption certainly appears to distance itself from the 'free spirit', not least in describing the 'free spirit' as a democrat. The suggestion that the 'free spirit' represents the noble voice of the dialogue is, however, given able support in Rose's indication that the ability of this voice to relate itself to the 'poison' of emancipation indicates a more subtle art of engagement with a *pharmakon* than the casting of the latter (in priestly mode) as 'evil'. Despite the reason this gives for supporting Rose's interpretation of the interruption of the first essay by the 'free spirit' this interpretation requires further investigation, not least because it would tend to make genealogical critique a 'democratic' art. Since the 'free spirit's' intervention connects the 'poison' of emancipation with precisely the revaluation of values the argument of the first essay has attributed to the Jews, to indicate as Rose would do that genealogical critique is a 'democratic' art is also to suggest that it is a Jewish art. In order to begin investigating the possibilities of this reading it will be necessary to depart for a time from the interpretation of the *Genealogy* in order to investigate some of Nietzsche's uses of the figure of the 'free spirit'.

Nietzsche and the 'Free Spirit'

The term 'free spirit' has a history within Nietzsche's *oeuvre*. *Human, All Too Human* is subtitled 'a book for free spirits' and *Beyond Good and Evil* contains a whole part containing twenty sections entitled 'The Free Spirit'. Furthermore, in the preface to the second edition of the *Genealogy*, Nietzsche stated that his ideas on the origins of morality were given first expression in *Human, All Too Human* and adds:

> *That* I still cleave to them today, however, that they have become in the meantime more and more firmly intertwined and interlaced with one another, strengthens my joyful assurance that they might have arisen in me from the first not as isolated, capricious, or sporadic things but from a common root, from a *fundamental will* of knowledge, pointing imperiously into the depths, speaking more and more precisely, demanding greater and greater precision. (GM 'Preface' 2)

The thoughts which were presented 'for free spirits' are still held to when writing the *Genealogy* which indicates that these thoughts belong together in some type of integral unity. It is still the case, despite this, that the thoughts expressed in the *Genealogy* differ from those in *Human, All Too Human* because of the fact that they have now become more 'firmly intertwined and interlaced with one another', thus more deeply connected, which is stated in the very same section of the preface to indicate philosophical development of the thoughts as philosophers 'may not make isolated errors or hit upon isolated truths' (GM 'Preface' 2).

The suggestion of the intertwined nature of the thoughts in question in the essays that make up the *Genealogy* seems to give oblique support to Rose's interpretation of the 'free spirit''s utterance. If it is part of the philosopher's development to intertwine his thoughts together then a certain acceptance of his mixed descent seems to be a necessary part of Nietzsche's essay which would lead to the view that the projection on to the Jews of responsibility for the revaluation of values should involve an agreement that the Jews are a 'world-historical' group who it is vitally necessary to relate oneself to. Further support for this account of the 'free spirit's' interruption is given when we see how Nietzsche explains the character of the 'free spirit' in his *Ecce Homo* treatment of *Human, All Too Human*. Nietzsche states:

> The term 'free spirit' here…means a spirit that has *become free*, that has again taken possession of itself. The tone, the voice, is completely changed: you will find the book clever, cool, perhaps hard and mocking. A certain spirituality of noble *taste* seems to be fighting continually against a more passionate current in order to stay afloat. (EH, *'Human, All Too Human With Two Sequels'* 1)

The conflict between a spirit which has a noble taste and a more passionate current is precisely what Rose suggests is at work in the *Genealogy*. If the spirit which has a noble taste is taken to be the 'free spirit' itself then there would seem here to be extremely good evidence for Rose's claim.

Given Nietzsche's later caution about *Human, All Too Human* these comments about the role of the 'free spirit' within it have perhaps more interest for a reader of the *Genealogy* than an interpretation of *Human, All Too Human* itself. Since *Beyond Good and Evil* is the work nearest in time of publication to the *Genealogy* the sections within it concerned with 'the free spirit' are here of the greatest interest. Significantly, *Beyond Good and evil* is described in *Ecce Homo* in the following manner: 'The refinement in form, in intention, in the art of *silence* is in the foreground' (EH, *'Beyond Good and Evil* Prelude to a Philosophy of the Future' 2). Since the interruption of the *Genealogy* by the voice of the 'free spirit' provoked a response about the art of silence it would seem that a look at a work in which the 'art of silence' is foregrounded would be precisely necessary.

The second part of *Beyond Good and Evil* is entitled 'The Free Spirit' which ensures that it is interposed between a part entitled 'On the Prejudices of Philosophers' and one entitled 'On the Religious Nature'.

Each section of the part devoted to 'the free spirit' contains a point of advice. After an exordium in which Nietzsche informs us that 'the best knowledge' wants to hold us in a simplified world as it is 'in love with life' (BGE 24), which indicates a relationship between life and simplicity, Nietzsche proceeds to suggest that philosophers should beware of being defenders of truth and rather adopt 'masks and subtlety, so that you may be misunderstood!' (BGE 25). After these cautionary tales told to philosophers which point in many directions (towards simplicity from love of life and away from truth for defence of the type of the philosopher) Nietzsche moves on to suggesting the way in which morality should be approached:

> we believe that the intention is only a sign and a symptom that needs interpreting, and a sign, moreover, that signifies too many things and which thus taken by itself signifies practically nothing – that morality in the sense in which it has been understood hitherto, that is to say the morality of intentions, has been a prejudice, a precipitancy…but in any event something that must be overcome. (BGE, 32)

If morality is not to be approached through a reference to intentions it would follow that is has appeared in history masked as Nietzsche suggests the philosopher should appear. Thus there is in fact an intimate connection between morality and philosophy which points to the rationale behind Rose's account of genealogical critique. Philosophy has of necessity to appear in a form which requires deciphering, as does morality. Therefore a philosophical inquiry into morality is doubly deceptive in the way it presents itself to us. The caution in reading which it would be necessary to learn from such indications must affect even the hypothesis presented in this part of *Beyond Good and Evil* of the notion of 'will to power' once we note that Nietzsche writes that 'a noble posterity could once again misunderstand the entire past' and adds: 'have we ourselves not been this "noble posterity"? And, in so far as we comprehend this, is it not at this moment – done with?' (BGE, 38).

The final section of this part of *Beyond Good and Evil* brings together these cautionary elements of the work and tells us that the philosophers of the future are those who will be 'free, *very* free spirits' – although Nietzsche identifies himself here as a precursor of such philosophers he also describes himself here with an enigmatic 'we' as a free spirit himself. The freedom of the spirit to which Nietzsche attaches himself is precisely of the type mentioned later in *Beyond Good and Evil* as belonging to he who has pity not for the 'creature' man but rather for the 'creator' man (BGE, 225). This spirit is 'full of malice towards the lures of dependence which reside in honours, or money, or offices, or raptures of the senses' (BGE, 44). This description of a 'malice' towards the 'world' connects the 'spirit' in question with precisely the Jews seemingly deprecated in the *Genealogy*.

That Nietzsche relates both himself and the future possibilities of philosophy to the character of the 'free spirit' is indubitable from this survey. That the appearance of the character of the 'free spirit' is also connected to the necessity of duplicity, that philosophy cannot be based on a 'truthful' self-presentation and that morality is itself a sign-language which requires deciphering but which is done by someone who further requires deciphering, all this is also clear from this survey. That Rose's suggestive account of the place of the 'free spirit's' interruption is thereby proved to be correct would be saying too much. However, in addition to evidence we might encounter within the works of genealogical critique themselves, we do have some clear grounds now for supporting her *suspicion*.

Genealogy, *ressentiment* and Judaism

The citation from Rose contained a reference to *ressentiment* although it is not until the section which begins immediately after the interruption of the first essay by the 'free spirit' that this notion is introduced. In introducing this notion the revaluation of values from the type of the master to that of the slave is indicated to reside precisely in a new development in *ressentiment* itself.

> The slave revolt in morality begins when *ressentiment* itself becomes creative and gives birth to values: the *ressentiment* of natures that are denied the true reaction, that of deeds, and compensate themselves with imaginary revenge. While every noble morality develops from a triumphant affirmation of itself, slave morality from the outset says No to what is 'outside', what is 'different', what is 'not itself'; and *this* No is its creative deed. This inversion of the value-positing eye – this *need* to direct one's view outward instead of back to oneself – is of the essence of *ressentiment*: in order to exist, slave morality always first needs a hostile external world; it needs, physiologically speaking, external stimuli in order to act at all – its action is fundamentally reaction. (GM I 10)

The notion of a creative turning being given to *ressentiment* is not clear without a prior account of why this might seem innovative. To this extent at least Gillian Rose is right in another of her contentions about this work, namely that the first essay 'is best understood in the light of the third'.[2] For it is in the third essay of the *Genealogy* that a clear definition is provided of what *ressentiment* consists in. It is given in a physiological form as being 'a desire to *deaden pain by means of affects*' (GM III 15). It is thus a type of nervous illness which is characterizable as a 'tormenting, secret pain' which 'requires an affect, as savage an affect as possible' (GM III 15). Thus the body of the sufferer will be attended by a medicine which concentrates only on certain superficial aspects of the illness and directs the response of the sufferer to their illness in a new direction. Here the priest is introduced as an *ascetic* and Nietzsche enumerates the forms this asceticism can take (with lengthy accounts of Buddhism and Brahmanism). Ascetic prescriptions range from starving the body, mechanical activity and inculcation of habits, provision of petty pleasures (through charity and the cultivation of pity) through to the '*formation of a herd*' (GM III 18). This last which organizes all those suffering into a group (a Church) enables continuous and expert application of technique to the mass of a people. But even here we are only confronted with an 'innocent' treatment of *ressentiment*: the 'creative' treatment of this illness by one who is himself sick turns on a relation to feeling.

> Man, suffering from himself in some way or other but in any case physiologically like an animal shut up in a cage, uncertain why or wherefore, thirsting for reasons – reasons relieve – thirsting, too, for remedies and narcotics, at last takes counsel with one who knows hidden things, too – and behold! he receives a hint, receives from this sorcerer, the ascetic priest, the *first* hint as to the cause of his suffering: he must seek it in *himself*, in some *guilt*, in a piece of the past, he must understand his suffering as a *punishment*. (GM III 20)

The creative use of *ressentiment* is twofold: first, force the one suffering to believe they are responsible for it themselves and, second, lead them to locate the cause of their suffering in past deeds so that their present is concentrated on the remembrance of the past. This second aspect of the ascetic discipline is what enables the priest to take real hold of the believer as the latter now is given constant cause for regurgitating their experience, for never having done with anything.

The distinction between the evaluations 'good and evil' and 'good and bad' can now be clearly told. Whilst the latter originates in a self-affirmation, with the denegated concept a mere shadow of the affirmed one, the former takes the opposite form. For the man of *ressentiment* evil is the greatest power and 'good' a mere after-effect. The struggle between these forms of evaluation is, for a spiritual nature, conducted within the self. But it is also one of world-historical proportions:

> The symbol of this struggle, inscribed in letters legible across all human history is 'Rome against Judea, Judea against Rome': – there has hitherto been no greater event than *this* struggle, *this* question, *this* deadly contradiction. Rome felt the Jew to be something like anti-nature itself...(GM I 16)

The alignment of the two forms of moral evaluation with two historical types marks an extreme moment of condensation in the essay. Forces treated with great care in relation to types of voice and types of silence are suddenly and univocally determined. At this point also the understanding of nobility is altered so that the so – delicately recovered notion that the noble is a 'free spirit' is endangered as Nietzsche describes the Roman as 'noble' and this evaluation seems to mark everything Jewish in opposition to nobility (despite the earlier indication that 'spirit' arose here and everything equivocal that clustered around the intervention of the 'free spirit').

The extraordinary tension of this closure of the first essay contrasts markedly also with the care and attention given to the account of asceticism in the third essay. After expounding the notion that philosophers of asceticism understand such a life as good because they are themselves anti-life one of the personae within the *Genealogy* provides a transvaluation of the notion of asceticism:

> *the ascetic ideal springs from the protective instinct of a degenerating life* which tries by all means to sustain itself and to fight for its existence; it indicates a partial physiological obstruction and exhaustion against which the deepest instincts of life, which have remained intact, continually struggle with new expedients and devices. The ascetic ideal is such an expedient; the case is therefore the opposite of what those who reverence this ideal believe: life wrestles in it and through it with death and *against* death; the ascetic ideal is an artifice for the *preservation* of life. (GM III 13)

The ascetic ideal persists as a means of life protecting itself in conditions which are the most perilous. The adoption of this ideal is the means a type of humanity has of surviving under emergency conditions. This is the true sense of Nietzsche's suggestion that ascetic morality is slave morality: the slave must divorce thought from action as his realm of action is systematically circumscribed for him and thus he lives more fully in imagination than in fact. Thus, the ascetic priest is 'among the greatest *conserving* and yes-creating forces of life' (GM III 13).

The ascetic priest must be understood as an artist of world-historical proportions – he builds the finest and most lasting bulwarks against the depression which comes naturally to the vast majority of humanity – he makes the slaves important in a way in which strictly speaking they are not and cannot become. But if asceticism is thus approached from the 'noble' standpoint of the 'free spirit' within the third essay what effect does this have on the understanding of Jews and Judaism? Within this third essay Nietzsche confesses admiration for the Old Testament as opposed to the New and here indicates that the 'mawkishness' that characterizes the latter is 'not so much Jewish as Hellenistic' (GM III 22). The tension of the equivocations within the work finally explode when the 'free spirit' is reintroduced towards the close of the work. Here Nietzsche follows the logic of his account of the 'free spirit' very much in the manner of Rose's suggestion but *not* with her result. Whereas the effect of her suggestion was that the 'free spirit' should be understood to have a democratic inflection which permitted the possibility of understanding Jews as related kindred to the 'free spirits' and hence to be affirmed, Nietzsche now suggests that the relation between these types points to quite a different conclusion. The 'free spirits' are introduced as the latest, most subtle form of the priest. As the latter arose on the basis of a concern with physical cleanliness so the former has a concern with intellectual cleanliness. This entails that the 'free spirits' are precisely not free because: *'they still have faith in truth'* (GM III 24). Nietzsche now opposes to these 'free spirits' the 'comedians' of the ascetic ideal, parodists who launch the best undermining of the ascetic way of life *precisely through their adherence to it* (GM III 27). This final twist in the inquiry turns a self-reflexive question upon it again.

If the third essay's culmination with questioning the whole position of the 'free spirit' might be thought to have disqualified in principle the whole rationale of Rose's reading it is worth turning in conclusion to one of the 'voices' of the second essay, the only part of the work which contains no direct reflections on Jews or Judaism at all. Within it we can locate a 'voice' whose statements would seem to give renewed credence to Rose's reading and whose 'voice', appearing as it does in the 'middle' essay might be thought to add a note of moderation to the 'voices' which conclude the first and the third essays:

> As power increases, a community ceases to take the individual's transgressions so seriously, because they can no longer be considered as dangerous

and destructive to the whole as they were formerly....As the power and self-confidence of a community increase, the penal law always becomes more moderate...It is not unthinkable that a society might attain such a *consciousness of power* that it could allow the noblest luxury possible to it – letting those who harm it go *unpunished*....This self-overcoming of justice: one knows the beautiful name it has given itself – *mercy*; it goes without saying that mercy remains the privilege of the most powerful man, or better, his – beyond the law. (GM II 10)

If the 'noblest luxury' is a form of self-overcoming of the law by the relinquishment of punishment, would this not be to follow the logic of the 'free spirit' and to 'democratically' achieve emancipation from the master by allowing the new formation of 'power with the power of others' that Rose precisely defined as the stance of the 'noble' and 'free' voice of the *Genealogy*?[3]

Jews and Judaism in *The Anti-Christ*

Nietzsche's positions on Jews and Judaism in the *Genealogy* can be seen to be marked by an equivocation and this equivocation is itself related to the personae within Nietzsche's works. In considering *The Anti-Christ* we will be given the opportunity to further visit Rose's revisionist reading of Nietzsche. *The Anti-Christ* also provides us with an opportunity for correcting an aspect of the influential account of Nietzsche's encounter between Jews and Judaism provided by Yirmiahu Yovel. Yovel states that Nietzsche's account of Jews and Judaism can be summarized as containing three phases. The first phase consists in the interpretation Nietzsche provides of the Old Testament. Yovel describes Nietzsche as affirmative of the Old Testament because it contains a 'vital, natural, this-worldly' life which is built on 'self-affirmation rather than self-recrimination'.[4] We have seen an example of this type of evaluation in the third essay of the *Genealogy* and we will see a repetition of it in *The Anti-Christ*. This is distinguished by Yovel from Nietzsche's account of the Judaism of the Exile in which Nietzsche is said to find the origin of the revaluation of values that permits the rise of Christianity. Finally, both of these phases are distinguished by Yovel from the account of Diaspora Jews who are depicted as the object of Nietzsche's praise because they 'have the merit of having rejected Christ and served as a constant critic and counter-balance to Christianity'.[5] In support of this third positive evaluation of post-Biblical Jews Yovel cites both *Human, All Too Human* and *Beyond Good and Evil* (which sources also consolidate the suggestion we have pursued of a connection between Jews and the 'free spirit').

Whilst Yovel's account is suggestive and its influence certainly assists in counteracting earlier presentations of Nietzsche as allied with the anti-semites whom he attacked for the majority of his life, this tripartite picture is not sufficient to capture the role of Jews and Judaism in *The Anti-Christ*. We will see that in fact in this work Nietzsche distinguishes not three but five stages in the history of the Jews. Whilst the picture given here is thus more complicated than suggested by Yovel it is also an extreme case of compression of themes which introduces again the extraordinary tension we discovered at the closure of the *Genealogy*.

In Section 24 of *The Anti-Christ* Nietzsche presents a wide overview of the history of the Jews immediately after asserting that Christianity grew from Judaism.

> The Jews are the most remarkable nation of world history because, faced with the question of being or not being, they preferred, with a perfectly uncanny conviction, being *at any price*: the price they had to pay was the radical *falsification* of all nature, all naturalness, all reality, the entire inner world as well as the outer. (AC 24)

This account corresponds with the statement in the third essay of the *Genealogy* that the ascetic ideal arose as a way of affirming life *under emergency conditions*. The peculiarity of precisely what this means is further accentuated later in the same section of *The Anti-Christ*:

> Considered psychologically, the Jewish nation is a nation of the toughest vital energy which, placed in impossible circumstances, voluntarily, from the profoundest shrewdness in self-preservation, took the side of all *décadence* instincts – *not* as being dominated by them but because it divined in them a power by means of which one can prevail *against* 'the world'. The Jews are the counterparts of *décadents*: they have been compelled to *act* as *décadents* to the point of illusion, they have known, with a *non plus ultra* of histrionic genius, how to place themselves at the head of all *décadence* movements (-as the Christianity of *Paul*-) so as to make of them something stronger than any party *affirmative* of life. (AC 24)

The Jewish nation is thus interpreted not as a group characterized by the type of nervous indisposition which Nietzsche indicated to be of a piece with the humanity of *ressentiment* in the *Genealogy* but rather to be composed of the 'toughest vital energy' which aligns them not with the slavish nature but rather with the type of human Nietzsche elsewhere describes as being formed by instincts of ruling: the masters. Under extreme conditions they have been compelled to utilise the instincts of *ressentiment* despite not being creatures of *ressentiment* themselves. They have thus been compelled to be 'the counterparts of *décadents*' up 'to the point of illusion' and this is now compressed into a formula for understanding the mode of life of the ascetic priest in general.

> For the kind of man who desires to attain power through Judaism and Christianity, the *priestly* kind, *décadence* is only a *means*: this kind of man has a life-interest in making mankind *sick* and in inverting the concepts 'good' and 'evil', 'true' and 'false' in a mortally dangerous and world-calumniating sense. (AC 24)

Whereas in the *Genealogy* it was precisely the contention that the role of the ascetic priest can be captured in the formula that there is a need at the stage of development at which this figure arises for 'doctors and nurses *who are themselves sick*' (GM III 15) the voice speaking at this point of *The Anti-Christ* specifically separates the human type who wields power through asceticism from those over whom this power is wielded in comprehending the former as having an interest in promoting sickness whilst precisely not being dominated by the instincts of sickness.

There now follows the indication of 'five stages' in the process of the '*denaturalizing* of natural values' in the exemplary history of Israel (AC 25). This five stage account opens with a stage at which Israel is said to be in a '*correct*, that is to say natural relationship to all things' (AC 25). At this point the God of Israel is identified with justice as a simple self-affirmation of the people. This first stage is identifiable as the first stage as described by Yovel. It is retained as the picture of Israel even after it has ceased to describe the reality and 'the people retained as its supreme desideratum that vision of a king who is a good soldier and an upright judge: as did above all the typical prophet (that is to say critic and satirist of the hour) Isaiah' (AC 25). Whilst in *Beyond Good and Evil* Nietzsche referred to the prophets as those who were responsible for the revaluation of values (BGE, 195) here he instead aligns the prophets with criticism and satire and implicitly praises Isaiah for the enunciation of the Messianic promise. This change of stance with regard to the prophets coinciding with a view that the notion of the Messiah is of an accord with the earlier '*correct*' relationship of Israel to the world indicates a suggestion that it may be precisely in the figure of the conquering king who is holy and warlike that Nietzsche finds a sign of the 'nobility' of Ancient Israel.

The second phase in Israel's history is marked by the descent into Babylon as suggested by Yovel. At this point, says Nietzsche, the old God should have been surrendered. Instead the revaluation of values takes place through the becoming abstract of morals:

> *Morality* no longer the expression of the conditions under which a nation lives and grows, no longer a nation's deepest instinct of life, but become abstract, become the antithesis of life – morality as a fundamental degradation of the imagination, as an 'evil eye' for all things. (AC 25)

Sensuous things become degraded in favour of imaginary ones: the movement of *ressentiment* become creative as the *Genealogy* expressed it. This second phase is described as in the concluding sections of the *Genealogy* in the voice of one who describes something from which they dissociate themselves, as if uninvolved in what is described.

The third phase in the development is a consequence of the second. It touches the relation of Israel to its history:

> These priests perpetrated that miracle of falsification the documentation of which lies before us in a good part of the Bible: with unparalleled disdain of every tradition, every historical reality, they translated their own national past *into religious terms*, that is to say they made of it a stupid salvation-mechanism of guilt towards Yahweh and punishment, piety towards Yahweh and reward. (AC 26)

This is the stage at which the revaluation of values leads to the arrival of the priest as one who dominates the life of the people and inserts himself everywhere and not least into the past. The turning of the attention of the people towards the past as if towards a future, this indicates the destruction of the Messianic hope (and the arrival of apocalypse). Thus according to this interpretation 'the *great* epoch in the history of Israel became an epoch of decay, the Exile, the long years of misfortune, was transformed into an eternal *punishment* for the great epoch' (AC 26).

The fourth stage is, like the third, undiscussed in Yovel's enumeration. This is the point at which the reinterpretation of history undertaken by the priest is given its licensed form as 'a "sacred book" is discovered – it is made public with all hieratic pomp, with days of repentance and with lamentation over the long years of "sinfulness"' (AC 26). Through the Book comes the Law and with this comes the legislative kingdom of the priest. Finally, the fifth stage is said to be the arrival of Christianity from the preceding development. The possibility of this is understood to be based upon a further accentuation of abstraction: 'the invention of an even *more abstract* form of existence, an even *more unreal* vision' which can be expressed as:

> a revolt against 'the good and the just', against the 'saints of Israel', against the social hierarchy – *not* against a corruption of these but against caste, privilege, the order, the social form; it was *disbelief* in 'higher men', a *No* uttered towards everything that was priest and theologian. (AC 27)

At this point the crux of Nietzsche's equivocation about Judaism comes to the fore. The arrival of Christianity is said to be possible because of the abstraction of a religion which asserted the power of a people even in captivity yet the religion of Christianity which grows out of this soil is also in its basic principle a *negation* of this soil. Whilst the Jewish life was possible as the life of a people precisely through the plastic energy of the priestly caste that came to power in the Exile this life contains within itself the seeds of the power through which it will be transmuted. The 'spiritual revenge' over every Babylon will originate then through a war against the strict necessity of a higher life which is embodied within the form of the priest and the theologian.

This is the equivocation at the heart of the fifth stage of Israel's history as Nietzsche tells it and which makes possible the praise of the Diaspora described by Yovel. There are two crucial moments in the staging of the history of Christianity in *The Anti-Christ* which connect to the types of voice and the types of silence we have uncovered in the genealogical critique of Judaism. Firstly, the depiction of Jesus himself which is separated from the account of Paul and the later history of Christianity by isolating Jesus as a type of 'idiot' or, 'with some freedom of expression', a 'free spirit' as: 'he cares nothing for what is fixed: the word *killeth*, everything fixed *killeth*' and the whole of life 'possesses for him merely the value of a sign, a metaphor' (AC 32). If, even in extremely free expression, it is possible to describe Jesus as a 'free spirit' then it becomes more comprehensible what the equivocations attaching to this expression are in Nietzsche's vocabulary. For Jesus' idiocy consists precisely in his *extreme* freedom where the force of law lacks any force at all and 'love' becomes a supreme power *precisely through its abstraction*. If this form of life of Jesus is concentrated for Nietzsche in the inability to take seriously the forceful necessities of political life (the life of peoples) then one side of Nietzsche's own *décadence* can be located precisely in this kinship with Jesus, a kinship however which also disconnects the *extremely* free spirit from Judaism precisely due to an attachment of this spirit to a 'truth' understood abstractly.

After later demonstrating that the Church emerges from the antithesis to Jesus by the Apostle Paul who shifted the centre of gravity away from forms of life entirely towards the 'Beyond' Nietzsche mightily complicates his whole suggestion of Christianity arising from Judaism when he confesses that it outbid all the cults of the Roman Empire by using their (non-Jewish, Hellenistic) techniques (AC 58), and yet persists in contrasting the 'Jewish' Christian religion with the Empire itself. The conclusion of the whole work, however, points to the understanding of the origin of Christianity in a revolt against the law which bound Judaism together. Furthermore, this original revolt against law is related to the comprehension of the German Reformation which latter produced in Protestantism another mode of living which is grounded on 'faith alone'. Luther's revolt is, however, connected by Nietzsche, not to the overturning of the rich hierarchies of Catholicism, but to a rejection of the return to antiquity that is the Renaissance. The great sorrow over the loss marked by the replacement of the Renaissance by the Reformation leads to the pronouncement by Nietzsche of his own eschatological commandment:

> And one calculates *time* from the *dies nefarus* on which this fatality arose – from the *first* day of Christianity! – *Why not rather from its last? – From today?* – Revaluation of all values! (AC 62)[6]

The final assault on Christianity which would found a new calendar and usher in a new earth is interpreted by Gillian Rose as a repetition of the very illness it diagnoses as *The Anti-Christ* 'has been composed by a great, resentful genius, who would force these intense fictional rememberings of evil deeds.'[7]

The movement of *The Anti-Christ* is far from being as clear as this summation from Rose suggests but its forceful conclusion does reproduce the tension noted in the *Genealogy*, the difference being that there is here no sudden self-reflexive move which questions the mode of questioning, no reference to the 'comedian' of the ideal as being its best opponent. The lack of this at the close of *The Anti-Christ* does suggest that the *personae* who is operative as authorial within it has here created a work which partakes very fully of that which it analyses so that the motif of revenge is taken to conclude a work which uncovers the abstract attachment to revenge at the origin of Christianity.

At the point of central equivocation in both works we find two figures: the 'free spirit' and alongside it, as its supposed noble progenitor, Rome. Whilst Rome is set against Judea in 'letters legible across human history' in the *Genealogy* (GM I 16), in *The Anti-Christ* we are given the opposition between Paul said to be 'the *eternal* Jew *par excellence*' against 'Rome, the world' (AC 58). In the *Genealogy* the figure of the 'free spirit' is introduced to indicate a love for the 'poison' which Christianity introduced, so long as this poison is separated from the Church and in *The Anti-Christ* we are given the form of such a poison separated from the Church in the 'free spirit' called Jesus. Nietzsche's self-reflexive move with regard to the 'free spirit' in the earlier work suggests that belief in truth is still a faith whilst the later work presents a reconstruction of Jewish history which indicates that the Jews as being the 'counterparts of *décadents*' are closer to the 'comedians' of the ideal described at the close of the *Genealogy* than any other figures. The relationship between Jew and 'free spirit' as given in the mode of life of Jesus also indicates the equivocations around all three of these figures to have a central political/spiritual sense.

The equivocations of Nietzsche's relation to Judaism are based on an *agon* which rends modernity itself and which Nietzsche acknowledged to be enacted in his own deepest recesses. The relation to Rome as a centre of political power and formation of culture is one which is as riven for Nietzsche as the relation to Judaism as if the latter is a powerful 'counterpart' of *décadence* the former is a counterpart of Greece with the replacement of the artistic man by the political (BT 21). The formation of an art of ruling to replace the rule of art: this is the split trajectory of religion and politics, Judea and Rome. Unless there is a negotiation of spirit with law which captures a relation to time which is not grounded in either repetition of the past or fixation on the present, there can be no eternal return which transvalues love and overcomes revenge. This remains the task of a Nietzschean politics.

Bibliography of cited works by Nietzsche

The Anti-Christ (Harmondsworth and New York: Penguin, 1968, trans. R. J. Hollingdale).

Beyond Good and Evil (Harmondsworth and New York: Penguin, 1972, trans. R. J. Hollingdale).

The Birth of Tragedy (Cambridge and New York: Cambridge University Press, 1999, trans. R. Spiers).

On the Genealogy of Morals (New York: Vintage, 1969, trans. W. Kaufmann).

Notes

1   Gillian Rose 'Nietzsche's *Judaica*' in G. Rose *Judaism and Modernity: Philo-sophical Essays* (Oxford and Cambridge, MA: Blackwell, 1993), pp. 104–5.
2   *Ibid*, p. 103.
3   *Ibid*, p. 105.
4   Yirmiahu Yovel 'Nietzsche and the Jews: the Structure of An Ambivalence' in J. Golomb (ed.) *Nietzsche and Jewish Culture* (London and New York: Routledge, 1997), p. 127. This article is a compression of a much more detailed analysis Yovel undertakes elsewhere which involves a comparison of Nietzsche's and Hegel's writings on Judaism. (See Y. Yovel, *Dark Riddle: Hegel, Nietzsche and the Jews* (Cambridge: Polity Press, 1998).) This would require a much more extensive response than is possible here where I have merely attempted to correct a false impression produced by Yovel's compression of his own analysis.
5   *Ibid*, p. 128.
6   For the full text of the decree see vol. 6 of Colli-Montinari, translation available in Gary Shapiro *Nietzschean Narratives* (Bloomington: Indiana University Press, 1989), p. 146.
7   G. Rose, *Judaism* p. 108.

5
Nietzsche, Kierkegaard and the narratives of faith

John Lippitt

The aim of this article is to compare key dimensions of the content and methodology of two seminal texts on religious faith: Nietzsche's *On the Genealogy of Morals* and Kierkegaard's *Fear and Trembling*. Against the background of the *Genealogy*, I offer a reading of the two forms of religious life – 'infinite resignation' and 'faith' – discussed by Kierkegaard's pseudonym Johannes de Silentio in *Fear and Trembling*. In the first section, I shall argue that precisely what distinguishes 'faith' from 'infinite resignation' is the ability of the former to encompass a mode of being and self-relation which the latter lacks: a mode of being and self-relation which is able to dwell in 'the finite', to 'hold fast to the temporal'. The significance of this is twofold. First, what has struck both sympathetic and unsympathetic readers of Nietzsche as one of the most interesting aspects of the *Genealogy* is his account of how, 'denied appropriate deeds' (GM I 10), undischarged instincts turn inwards with disastrous consequences, the denial of an active outlet resulting in repression and rancorous *ressentiment*. Yet such repression and internalisation contrasts starkly with the joy and absence of blame characteristic of faith as portrayed in *Fear and Trembling*. Second, the transcendentalising move that devalues the finite, to which Nietzsche also objects, and which he (and large numbers of his commentators) sometimes take to be the identifying mark of religiousness in its 'Platonic-Christian' manifestations, is again, for Johannes, less a feature of 'faith' than of its 'lower' religious cousin, 'infinite resignation'. *Fear and Trembling* thus presents us with a form of religious life which is exempt from two of the *Genealogy*'s main accusations.

Following on from this, in the second section I suggest that, its astute psychological insights into certain corrupted forms of religiosity notwithstanding, the *Genealogy* is a text significantly aspect-blind to

many religious possibilities. Taking my cue from Wittgenstein and his
followers in the philosophy of religion, I suggest that part of the reason
for this is Nietzsche's tendency to violate the 'grammar' of certain religious concepts. Nietzsche does this, I shall suggest, by failing to recognise key differences between psychological or moral uses of particular
terms, on the one hand, and the distinct uses of those terms made within
specific *religious* traditions on the other. In the third section, I turn to an
often unnoticed dimension of the respective methodologies of our two
texts. I agree with Martha Nussbaum and D.Z. Phillips, amongst others,
that there is a particular role to be played by literature, or more generally narrative, in bringing about the kind of aspect-dawning at which
both Kierkegaard and Nietzsche are aiming. *Prima facie*, it would seem
that both the *Genealogy* and *Fear and Trembling* score highly in this
regard: both tackle their subject matter via narratives, and their seductive power (or lack of it) is to a large extent a function of whether a
reader gets 'caught up' in the narratives which they recount. But there is
an important difference nonetheless. As Aaron Ridley has recently
pointed out, the *Genealogy* proceeds predominantly with reference to
certain human types (most prominently the slave, the priest, the
philosopher, the artist, the scientist and the noble).[1] I suggest that an
approach which relies excessively on types is less well-placed to bring
out the kind of aspect-dawning at which both texts aim than is an
approach which relates – as does *Fear and Trembling* – to a specific *exemplar*. Ironically, it is by combining Ridley's work on R.G. Collingwood
with James Conant's reading of Nietzsche on exemplars that puts us in
a position to see this.

The *Genealogy* and *Fear and Trembling*

To begin, I shall focus on two dimensions of Nietzsche's portrait of the
development of 'slave morality': the dangers of undischarged instincts,
and the transcendentalising phase of its development brought about
under the direction of the 'ascetic priest'. As is well-known, the 'revolt'
of the oppressed 'slave' against the more powerful 'noble' occurs,
according to Nietzsche, when '*ressentiment* itself becomes creative and
gives birth to values: the *ressentiment* of natures that are denied the true
reaction, that of deeds, and compensate themselves with an imaginary
revenge' (GM I 10). In other words, denied any natural outlet for his
frustrations – chiefly those that arise from his, largely unconscious, self-
loathing – the slave, whose chief virtue is his 'cleverness' (GM I 10),

brings about an alternative set of values to the triumphant self-affirmation of the less 'clever' nobles. This set of values enables the slave to label the noble 'evil', and himself, in contrast, 'good'. The mechanisms of this extraordinarily important event in human history are complex and intricate – so much so that Nietzsche himself sometimes appears confused about exactly what gives rise to what.[2] But what matters for our purposes here is that the slave's 'imaginary revenge' ultimately depends upon his enforced repression and internalisation: 'All instincts that do not discharge themselves outwardly *turn inward* – this is what I call the *internalization* of man: thus it was that man first developed what was later called his "soul"' (GM II 16). And here is the problem: the mere fact that an instinct needs to be repressed owing to the lack of a natural outlet does not disempower it; it remains, potentially, 'the most dangerous of all explosives' (GM III 15). So the slave's non-creative *ressentiment*, and all that arises from it, results from his feeling 'on the receiving end of life'.[3] The problems of *ressentiment* and bad conscience,[4] together with the picture of guilt which is built up on them,[5] are ultimately a form of enforced passivity – or, more accurately, of the disastrous consequences of what happens to an instinct which, deprived of its 'natural' outlet, is repressed.

The next main character in Nietzsche's story is the priest, under whose direction the crucial transcendentalising step is made. So far, the slave has begun to make sense of his suffering by blaming it on the nobles. But the danger of stopping here is that this might appear to be an argument against life. A pessimism, Schopenhauerian or otherwise, might ensue. The priest's tactic for addressing this is to retain the idea of blame, but to ditch the idea of focusing that blame on an external agent. Instead, he manages to persuade the slave that he *himself* is to blame for his suffering. (Could any external agent *really* be to blame for the *whole* of your suffering?) But as Ridley points out, what is needed here is a story which 'will make it not just logically possible and existentially desirable for the slave to blame all of his suffering on himself, but psychologically plausible as well.'[6] This is where the crucial transcendentalising move is made. The slave, accustomed to associating punishment with having broken a custom or law – of being guilty in a legal or at least quasi-legal sense – is a prime target for the subtle transformation of this into a *moral-religious* kind of guilt: guilt before God, or sin. The slave's suffering is a punishment: a punishment for being a sinner. Yet tied up with this – and, presumably, a vital part of its appeal to the slave – goes the possibility of one's sins being *forgiven*: Christianity's 'whole mysterious machinery of salvation' prevents suffering from being 'sense-less' (GM II 7). Add to this the pleasure which Nietzsche – aided by some highly selective quotations from Aquinas and Tertullian[7] – claims Christianity takes in the imminent suffering of the 'unsaved' (such as the 'evil' nobles) and we start to see how this transcendental story could be very appealing to the resentful slaves of Nietzsche's narrative.

Another crucial dimension of the priest needs to be discussed, namely the description of him as 'ascetic'. Like his account of bad conscience, Nietzsche's view of asceticism is complex and multifarious. Neverthe-less, what he is opposed to is at least one dimension of what he calls 'the ascetic ideal': the view, as Ridley puts it, that 'existence is just one big procedure to be engaged in ascetically'.[8] One may deny oneself some-thing – sex or alcohol, say – for some 'higher' purpose which is purely immanent. But for some, the *whole* of existence is to be viewed asceti-cally. What could *this* self-denial be for? No immanent purpose is left to serve as an answer. Instead, such *ascesis* must be 'inevitably deferred elsewhere, outside of life, to another realm.'[9] This is a crucial part of the transcendental consolation which the priest is required to posit if the slave is to buy into his story. And despite the 'fresh suffering' (GM III 28) which the ascetic ideal brings, nevertheless 'man was *saved* thereby, he possessed a meaning…he could now *will* something; no matter at first to what end, why, with what he willed: *the will itself was saved*' (*ibid.*)

As we might expect from its author's status as one of the great 'mas-ters of suspicion', the *Genealogy* posits thoroughly scurrilous motives for the development of such a religious consciousness. Yet Nietzsche's is an intriguing and in many respects plausible story, and even many of his opponents far more sympathetic to the religious traditions he attacks have judged him as someone worth taking seriously and deserving of some kind of response. In the all too brief summary above, I have high-lighted the dangers of enforced passivity and the priest's transcenden-talising move as particularly important features of Nietzsche's narrative. But if we now turn to our second text, *Fear and Trembling*, we come across an account of faith some of the distinguishing features of which avoid these Nietzschean accusations. Moreover, we come across an account of something less than 'faith' – 'infinite resignation' – which does seem to share some of the features for which Nietzsche condemns Christianity *qua* 'slave morality'. What is significant about this is Johannes's determination that the reader should not confuse faith with something it is not. The question, then, is whether that is what Niet-zsche, in the *Genealogy*, has done.

What, according to *Fear and Trembling*, is 'faith'? First, an important preliminary point. It would be mistaken to take any view expounded in *Fear and Trembling* as being unequivocally that of 'Kierkegaard'. The secondary literature increasingly recognises the importance of taking seriously what Kierkegaard, writing under his own name in an appendix to his pseudonymous authorship in the *Concluding Unscientific Post-script*, describes as 'my wish, my prayer'[10] to keep the pseudonyms apart: to attribute the views of the author of any given pseudonymous text to that pseudonym, rather than simply assuming that it represents the view of Kierkegaard himself. The failure to take this request seriously can lead to egregious errors, such as noting that, for instance, something 'Kierkegaard' says in *The Sickness Unto Death* (written by the Christian pseudonym Anti-Climacus) 'contradicts' something 'Kierkegaard' says in the *Postscript* (written by the 'humorist' Johannes Climacus, who repeatedly denies being a Christian). So in what follows, I shall take the views of *Fear and Trembling* to be those of the text's pseudonymous author, Johannes de Silentio. Whether, and if so to what degree, they represent the view of Kierkegaard himself, is another question, beyond the scope of the present article.

Amongst the first things that a reader of *Fear and Trembling* is likely to notice is that a book centrally concerned with the nature of faith proceeds by looking at Abraham as a – perhaps the – paradigm exemplar of faith, rather than by any attempt to *define* faith. Faith is approached *negatively*, by a series of contrasts with what faith is not. I do not have space here to discuss the full range of these contrasts, but shall focus on the best-known and most important: the contrast Johannes draws between the 'knight of faith' and the 'knight of infinite resignation'. The main point of introducing the latter is as probably the fullest and most memorable concrete illustration of what faith is not. I shall try to show that it is the knight of infinite resignation, not the knight of faith, who bears a striking resemblance to the mode of being and self-relation characteristic of Nietzsche's slave under the influence of the priest.

Johannes' most vivid contrast of infinite resignation and faith occurs in the story he tells of a young lad who falls in love with a princess.[11] His primary question is how the attitude of a lad who was a knight of faith would differ from one who was a mere knight of infinite resignation. However, we need first to understand the difference between the attitude of infinite resignation and that of a certain kind of stoicism, represented by characters Johannes describes as the 'slaves of misery, the frogs in life's swamp' (FT p.71). The latter are 'realists', in the sense that they try to persuade the lad that nothing can come of such a love. Why not settle for someone of his own station in life? The lad considers such an attitude beneath contempt ('Let them croak away undisturbed in life's swamp' (FT p.71)), relying as it does on a mode of valuation which thinks in terms of minimising risk. Johannes contrasts the knight of infinite resignation with 'those capitalists who invest their capital in every kind of security so as to gain on the one what they lose on the other' (FT p.72). The point of the economic imagery is that it appears as if life too requires us to make certain 'investments': what is worth our attention and dedication, and what is not? According to the 'slaves of misery', a humble lad's negligible chances with a princess make the lad's love a 'bad risk'. But the lad's attitude makes it clear that for him, issues of love, care and commitment should not be approached from the perspective of risk-minimisation. Instead, he seems to embody the central Kierkegaardian thought that 'purity of heart is to will one thing': once he has determined that this love really is 'the content of his life' (that is, it is no mere infatuation), we are told that he concentrates 'the whole of his life's content and the meaning of reality in a single wish' (FT p.72). His love for her is unconditional, and to a large extent his sense of self is determined by it; it is an identity-conferring commitment. Such an unconditional commitment is a necessary prerequisite to the movement of infinite resignation.

Sadly, Kierkegaard's contemporaneity with Hans Christian Andersen notwithstanding, this is no fairy tale: our lad and his princess do not live 'happily ever after'. The lad recognises that he will not 'get the girl', and here is where the movement of infinite resignation itself enters the picture. Despite the fact that this love is central to the lad's sense of himself, he renounces it in 'resignation'. In this way, a vital part of his identity is lost. Yet in doing so, Johannes claims, he gains an 'eternal consciousness' (FT p.72): in renouncing something finite, he gains something infinite. The following passage is crucial for our purposes:

> His love for the princess would take on for him the expression of an eternal love, would acquire a religious character, be transfigured into a love for the eternal being which, although it denied fulfillment, still reconciled him once more in the eternal consciousness of his love's validity in an eternal form that no reality can take from him. (FT p.72)

In other words, the love becomes 'eternalised': transformed and channelled into love for 'an eternal being' – God. (Johannes leaves mysterious the mechanism by which this is supposed to happen, but various theories of sublimation would appear to be strong *prima facie* candidates.) Note that this parallels the transcendentalising move made by the slave under the manipulative direction of the priest, under several aspects. First, and most fundamentally, something finite or immanent (the slave's suffering, explicable in purely immanent terms; the lad's love for the princess) becomes transcendentalised (suffering as the result of guilt before God, or sin; the lad's love for 'an eternal being'). Moreover, the effects of these transcendentalising moves bring with them analogous comforts and (self-deceptive?) alterations in the slave's and lad's self-relations. The 'machinery of salvation' enables the slave to feel better about himself: though both are sinners, he will be saved whereas the noble will be damned. Likewise, a consolation becomes available to the lad: 'in infinite resignation there is peace and repose and consolation in the pain' (FT p.74). This consolation is, I suspect, a function of the lad's coming to think of the existence he has once he has 'resigned' as 'higher' – more 'spiritual' – than his pre-resignation existence. As Edward Mooney puts it, his life 'is no longer focused by concern for a finite individual. His standpoint is now *outside* the flux of petty, worldly things.'[12] This leads to our third, related, point. The lad – like the slave – *devalues the finite* (or immanent) *in favour of the infinite* (or transcendental). We are told that: 'He pays no further finite attention to what the princess does, and just this proves that he has made the movement infinitely' (FT p.73). So much so that Johannes implies that the lad, once he has made the movement of resignation, would actually be *embarrassed* if the princess were to become 'available' to him. As Mooney suggests, the price that the lad has paid for his diminished hurt is diminished *care*.[13] The knight of infinite resignation manifests *diminished care for the finite*. This is not to say that his viewpoint is indistinguishable from the kind of stoicism which preaches total non-attachment. There is a certain kind of 'stoic hardening of the self to disappointment'[14] which would, at the outset, counsel the lad not to get attached to anything: that way he will not be disappointed when it is taken from him. As we have seen, this is not the attitude of the knight of infinite resignation. His attachment is central to his mode of being and self-relation, is an identity-conferring commitment. Nevertheless, he is prepared to 'resign' – renounce – that which is most important to him. And what distinguishes him from the stoic is that in doing so, his attachment is *transformed* - infinitised; eternalised; transcendentalised. Yet this – Johannes and Nietzsche would agree – entails a kind of loss.

So far, then, we have seen that there are important parallels between the change in self-relation brought about in the slave under the manipulation of the priest, and the lad in the movement of infinite resignation. But the religious form of life which Johannes really admires is something which is 'higher' than infinite resignation: the form of life which he calls 'faith'.

The crucial difference, for our purposes, between infinite resignation and faith is that the knight of faith's care for the finite, and ability to dwell in it, is undiminished. Not for him the kind of transcendentalising move made by both slave and lad which devalues the finite in relation to the infinite. This is what amazes Johannes about Abraham: faced with the divine command to sacrifice Isaac, Abraham – while prepared if need be to carry out the sacrifice – trusts in God so that 'on the strength of the absurd' he believes that he will 'get Isaac back' – and not in an afterlife, but in *this* life. If the lad were a knight of faith, Johannes tells us, he would do

> exactly the same as the other knight, he infinitely renounces the claim to the love which is the content of his life; he is reconciled in pain; but then comes the marvel, he makes one more movement, more wonderful than anything else, for he says: 'I nevertheless believe that I shall get her, namely on the strength of the absurd, on the strength of the fact that for God all things are possible' (FT p.75).

Exactly what Johannes means by 'belief on the strength of the absurd' is a notorious question. For instance, debate has raged as to whether the knight of faith is supposed to believe the logically impossible, or rather – as Johannes's text actually says – in what appears to be 'impossible, humanly speaking' (FT p.75). But this is not our concern here. For present purposes, I want merely to note that the relation of the knight of faith to the finite is utterly different to that of his 'resigned' counterpart. The knight of faith's 'greatness' lies in large part in his ability 'to stick to the temporal after having given it up' (FT p.52). While a full account of the meaning of this phrase is beyond the scope of this paper, such an account would turn upon the Kierkegaardian idea of 'repetition' [*Gjentagelse*], central to which is the idea of giving something up and yet getting it back in some transformed and transfigured sense.[15] But what matters for our purposes is that the knight of faith's care for and commitment to the finite; the temporal; the immanent, is in no way diminished by whatever 'movements' he makes. *This* is where he differs from the knight of infinite resignation, and it is *this*, Johannes insists, which makes Abraham, *qua* knight of faith, so 'great'.

Relatedly, one recent commentator has argued that one of the knight of faith's main features is his joy;[16] and again, a joy taken *in the finite*. A particularly good example here is Johannes's image of a far more mundane knight of faith than Abraham: a man who fantasises about a delicious meal that his wife might have prepared for him, yet who is just as joyous when he returns home to much plainer fare than he had imagined.[17] To clarify further the idea of joy in the finite, it is useful to consider another Kierkegaardian pseudonym, Johannes Climacus, author of the *Concluding Unscientific Postscript*, and his famous discussion of whether a religious person could legitimately enjoy a trip to the Deer Park, a Copenhagen amusement park. What is significant about this for us is that, like Johannes, Climacus also talks of the 'movement of infinity', and insists that a religious person must find a way of combining his 'God-relationship' with the finite ends and trivial activities of human existence, such as visits to the Deer Park. (It is significant here that the Deer Park was considered 'the epitome of noisy, stupid vulgarity'.[18]) Climacus is suspicious of 'the monastic movement', the religious attitude which valorises withdrawal from the world in order to pursue closeness to God. Such withdrawal is neither necessary nor even desirable: if made, Climacus insists, it should be done with 'a certain sense of shame'.[19] (Climacus compares the person who can only pursue a God-relationship by withdrawal from the world with a woman who, unable to use the thought of her beloved to give her strength to go about her work, instead needs to go to *his* place of work and be with him continually.) Thus Climacus goes further than Johannes, in describing as an 'illness' the inability to bring one's God-relationship into a further relationship with the finite.[20] Yet it is basically this of which Johannes's lad as knight of infinite resignation is incapable. We can thus assume that Climacus would pass the same verdict on such knights as he would on those heading for the cloister.

My overall point here is that this stress on the importance of finding joy in the finite seems the very antithesis of the slave's rancorous repression. As part of his discussion of 'The Religious Nature' in *Beyond Good and Evil*, Nietzsche claims of religious 'nay-sayers' that 'the degree to which life has been spoiled for them might be inferred from the degree to which they wish to see its image falsified, thinned down, transcendentalized, deified' (BGE 59). Johannes would not be unsympathetic to such a sentiment. Yet nothing could be further from the knight of faith, with the joy that he takes in the finite.

A second key feature of the knight of faith's joy – again in stark contrast to the slave and the priest – is the *absence of blame and accountability* which feature in his view of the world. Abraham never asks who is to blame for the call to sacrifice Isaac; the hungry 'mundane' knight of faith never blames his wife for the absence of a banquet. (Neither, unlike the priest-influenced slave, does Abraham see his suffering – his anguish over his dilemma – as any kind of *punishment*.) Indeed, in the 'Attunement', Johannes portrays four 'sub-Abrahams': more examples of what faith is not, to be contrasted with the Abraham who deserves the title knight of faith. Each of these imagined Abrahams is prepared to obey God's command, but none, Johannes insists, is a knight of faith.[21] It is significant that in all of the first three cases, blame is present as a central factor. The first Abraham pretends to be a heartless monster, thinking it better that Isaac blame his father rather than God. The second – even after the appearance of the ram has made the human sacrifice unnecessary – 'saw joy no more' (FT p.46), and blames God for the whole ordeal. The third 'begged God to forgive his sin at having been willing to sacrifice Isaac, at the father's having forgotten his duty to his son' (FT p.47). In other words, he considers the ethical to be the highest duty, and insofar as his willingness to sacrifice Isaac amounts to a momentary willingness to violate this highest duty, he thinks in terms of his *own* sin, guilt and blameworthiness. Yet in the Abraham who truly deserves the title knight of faith, blame has dropped out of the picture, to be replaced by joy.

In summary, then, the repression and internalisation of which the *Genealogy* paints such an unedifying portrait contrasts with the joy and absence of blame characteristic of the *Fear and Trembling* picture of faith. If there is repression and internalisation here at all, it exists in infinite resignation, not faith. Moreover, Johannes's paradigm exemplar of faith, Abraham, does *not* make the kind of move to which Nietzsche so strongly objects: the kind of transcendentalising move which devalues the finite. Indeed, the value placed on the finite is precisely what distinguishes faith from infinite resignation. *Fear and Trembling* thus presents us with a form of religious life which is exempt from two of the *Genealogy*'s main accusations.

The 'grammar' of the religious

It can hardly be denied that the *Genealogy* offers a psychologically penetrating insight into certain sorts of religious consciousness. Nevertheless, as I suggested at the outset, it is a text significantly aspect-blind to some important religious possibilities, not least the model of faith described above. What are the reasons for such aspect-blindness? I want in this section to draw on both Kierkegaard and Wittgenstein to suggest that one such reason, and a significant weakness of the *Genealogy,* is Nietzsche's failure there to pay adequate attention to differences between the 'surface' and 'depth' grammars of certain religious concepts and utterances. Nietzsche tends to blur crucial grammatical differences between religious, moral and psychological concepts. We have already seen the ease with which he slides from an essentially *psychological* discussion of guilt and bad conscience to a discussion of *religious* concepts: sin understood simply as guilt before God. But both Kierkegaard and Wittgenstein would be deeply suspicious of the assumption that any distinctively *religious* meaning of guilt could be understood by simply extrapolating from a *psychological* view of guilt. This seems to take insufficiently seriously the Wittgensteinian insight that the meaning of a term is largely provided by the context of its use.[22] Compare this to Kierkegaard's idea that picturing religious faith as continuous with 'ordinary' – epistemic – forms of belief involves 'dialectical confusion'. Such confusion arises precisely from the failure to pay attention to the differences in meaning that result from the different contexts of use of terms such as 'belief' or 'faith'. Specifically *religious* uses of certain terms only have sense within certain kinds of life.

Up to a point, of course, the *Genealogy* recognizes this latter point: hence Nietzsche's treatment of the religious in terms of characters such as the slave and the ascetic priest. But to see the significance of the point, consider the idea that sin is not merely a sub-category of guilt, but a central pivot of an entire world-view: what Wittgenstein, in the 'Lectures on Religious Belief', describes as a picture which 'regulat[es] for all'[23] in a certain kind of life. Religious notions such as sin and redemption are notions which ground entire ways of seeing the world, and unless one understands the way these terms function in specific, concrete religious contexts, one will seriously misunderstand them. It is here, I suggest, that Nietzsche falls short. Consider the following, from Rudolf Otto:

> Sin is a religious, not a moral concept … if sin, expiation, lostness, salvation from the state of being lost, the fall and original guilt, are drawn into the moralistic, not to say the juridical sphere, they must lose their original meaning which lies entirely within the ancient numinous sphere of the Old and New Testament … sin remains primarily that which lies purely within the realm of religious relationships: it is primarily the failure, inhibition, or atrophy of the purely religious spiritual functions themselves, of reverence and awe … it is made up not of moral order … the religious conscience …

transcends all morality and makes profanity, that is to say our estrangement from God and our natural resistance against possessing God, itself into guilt.[24]

In other words, as a *religious* term within Judaism and Christianity, sin is primarily an *ontological*, not a psychological category: a state of being, rather than a state of consciousness. The way in which this rebounds on Nietzsche is that to try to understand sin, *qua* religious category, in moral-psychological terms, is to pay insufficient attention to its natural context. Wittgensteinian philosophers who have written on religion, from Peter Winch to Norman Malcolm to D. Z. Phillips, have all taken seriously the idea that 'religious beliefs have certain *unique* features that have to be addressed in responsible descriptions of religious beliefs'.[25] Yet the *Genealogy* is not above conflating the sphere of the religious with that of the moral. To take another example, consider the second essay's discussion of guilt as indebtedness to a creditor eventually sliding into the idea of debt to God as the ultimate creditor. But this raises the question as to whether what Nietzsche is attacking is Christianity (or the so-called 'Judaeo-Christian tradition'), or some fundamental misunderstanding of these religious forms of life. To say this is not to rule out the possibility that this might partly be a function of Christianity's misunderstanding of itself: perhaps when, to come to an issue close to Kierkegaard's heart, Christianity *qua* 'state religion' comes to act as if it were nothing more than a socially respectable 'moral code'.[26] Hence my overall point: the result of Nietzsche's inattention to context is that the *Genealogy* remains aspect-blind to some important religious possibilities.

Johannes *contra* Nietzsche:
exemplar-narratives and type-narratives

What is the significance of aspect-blindness and aspect-dawning to our wider discussion? Clearly, both Nietzsche and Kierkegaard can be seen as trying to bring about a change of aspect in the view of religious faith held by their readers. This is one reason why neither logically deductive nor empirically inductive arguments for or against the existence of God will serve the purposes of either of them. Whatever else they may be, religious beliefs are particular kinds of 'seeing as'. A necessary condition for the alteration of such a belief, therefore, is that a person come to see things under a different aspect. As one commentator puts it, speaking of attempts by (Christian) religious believers to persuade non-believers,

'All that the believer can do is to attempt to seduce the non-believer to see things differently, to shut the eyes and open them up again to a new world in which coincidence is replaced by design, anomalies by miracles and surprise by wonder.'[27] A contrary shift of aspect would be part of what a *loss* of faith consisted in. In this final section, I want to suggest, following Martha Nussbaum and D. Z. Phillips, that literature and narrative have a particularly important role to play in bringing about such aspect-dawning.[28] This enables us to see one important dimension of why the *Genealogy* and *Fear and Trembling* are the kind of text that they are – but also, I suggest, why the *Genealogy* is at a disadvantage to *Fear and Trembling* as a potentially self-transformatory text.

The use of narrative and literature in philosophy (especially moral philosophy) has a chequered history. One common view is that the moral philosopher's use of literature should not obscure the fact that moral philosophy should be about how people *in general* ought to act. On this view literature, if it is to be used at all, can be used only as a source of ethically (or, in the philosophy of religion, religiously) salient examples which could just as easily come from alternative sources. Both Nussbaum and Phillips, in different ways, oppose this view. What their responses have in common is a stress upon the importance of the *concrete particularity* with which good literature presents us. Phillips argues that literature offers a useful corrective to the inappropriate tendency of moral theory towards over-generalisation. Literature is 'a source of reminders (not examples) from which philosophy can benefit in wrestling with issues concerning the firm or slackening hold of various perspectives in human life.'[29] The concrete particularity of these 'reminders' is a vital part of their importance, and 'the detail and particularity displayed in literature' are not 'options which philosophy can dispense with.'[30] The failure to appreciate this can lead to both 'an obscuring generality in philosophical theories about morality' and 'blindness with regard to certain perspectives on human life.'[31]

Prima facie, it would seem that both the *Genealogy* and *Fear and Trembling* are exempt from Phillips' charge of theoretical over-generalisation. After all, both tackle their subject matter via narratives which are full of intriguing *dramatis personae*: nobles, slaves and priests; lads and princesses; Abraham and Isaac. The seductive power – or lack of it – of these texts is to a large extent a function of whether a reader gets 'caught up' in the narratives which they recount. But, I want to argue, there is an important difference nonetheless. As Ridley has recently pointed out, one significant feature of the *Genealogy* is that it proceeds with reference to certain human *types*: most prominently, the slave, the priest, the philosopher, the artist, the scientist and the noble. I want to suggest that an approach such as this, which relies predominantly on types, is less well-placed to bring about the dawning of an aspect than is an approach which relates to a specific *exemplar*, such as the treatment of Abraham in *Fear and Trembling*.

I should make clear that this is not intended as a criticism of Nietzsche's work (or a commendation of Kierkegaard's) as a whole, but rather only of what I take to be the overly heavy reliance on types in the *Genealogy*. Elsewhere, of course, Nietzsche deals with the positive, negative and – more commonly – deeply multi-facted and ambivalent dimensions of some important and complex exemplars, such as Socrates, Goethe, Schopenhauer and Wagner. To repeat: I am not aiming to draw any general conclusion about Nietzsche and Kierkegaard here, but am concerned only with comparing the predominantly type-based methodology of the Genealogy with *Fear and Trembling*'s sustained focus on a specific concrete exemplar.

My basic argument is as follows. Central to my interest in the thought of both Nietzsche and Kierkegaard is the importance they both place on self-transformation. I follow Nietzsche in suggesting that an especially important role in self-transformation is played by relating oneself to an exemplary other.[32] But a crucial part of this relationship, I suggest, is the fact that what one relates oneself to is that exemplary other *in their concrete particularity*. Relating oneself to an exemplar, therefore, is importantly different from relating oneself to a type. Central to the reasons for this is that, if Nietzsche is right, exemplars disclose to us a higher *self*, not just a higher type. The reason types cannot do this (at least, nowhere near as effectively) is their *lack* of concrete particularity. The *Genealogy*'s reliance on types is thus a serious drawback as regards its potential to bring about the kind of aspect-dawning needed in self-transformation.

Let us expand upon this. In the introduction to his fine book on the *Genealogy*, Ridley points out that Nietzsche 'thinks through particular *types* of person … he uses these personalities as arguments. For him, these types function as magnets for issues or for aspects of issues which are then pursued, psychobiographically, through a disquisition on the personality types that exemplify them.'[33] This basic observation lies behind the structure of Ridley's book, which takes the *Genealogy*'s six key types – listed earlier – as the heading for each of its chapters. As Ridley acknowledges, each character type serves to focus some particular set of issues: for instance, the slave 'acts as a focal point for the investigation of *ressentiment*, bad conscience, and self-aggrandizement'; the priest 'to focus issues about asceticism, transcendentalism, and power'[34]; and so on. This treatment of issues via character types contrasts with Johannes' method in *Fear and Trembling*, where – subsidiary walk-on characters like the lad and his princess notwithstanding – the theme of faith is approached by focusing upon the concrete particularity of a specific exemplar of faith, namely Abraham. Elsewhere, Ridley has persuasively drawn upon a distinction made by R. G. Collingwood which is, I suggest, important in considering the difference between relating to an exemplar and relating to a type. Collingwood distinguishes between 'description' – bringing a thing under a particular conception; presenting it as a certain *type* of thing – and 'expression' – which 'individualises'; shows the thing in question to be not a certain *type* of thing, but *this* thing. What matters about this for our purposes is that, on Collingwood's distinction, Nietzsche's approach in the *Genealogy* – dealing predominantly in types – amounts to description, whereas Johannes' approach more fully recognises 'expression': that we need to dwell on Abraham in his concrete particularity in order to have any hope of coming to terms with that 'faith' of which he is an exemplar. But why is this significant? Its significance inheres in our related argument, about the difference between relating oneself to an exemplar and relating oneself to a type. As we have already mentioned, Conant argues that for Nietzsche, what is significant about the former is that in such a process of relating, a 'higher self' is disclosed. However, I suggest that the same is not the case in the latter: because relating oneself to a type can all too easily amount to having what Collingwood calls a 'corrupt consciousness'. To unpack this idea, let us first turn to Conant's argument.

What does an exemplar disclose? This is one of the key questions which Conant elicits from Nietzsche's discussion of exemplarity in 'Schopenhauer as Educator'.[35] As a preliminary, we can say that a 'positive' exemplar offers 'a concrete representation of who one seeks to become – one which enables one to focus one's conception of what it is to which one aspires.'[36] But additionally, Conant relates this to Nietzsche's discussion of the soul's 'desire to look beyond itself and to seek with all its might for a higher self as yet still concealed from it' (SE 6). The basic answer to our question, then, is that an exemplar discloses to me my 'higher self'. Not merely a higher *type*, but my *own* higher self (albeit one 'as yet still concealed' from me). This fits with a key theme introduced in the first section of Nietzsche's essay, when he claims that 'your true nature lies, not concealed deep within you, but immeasurably high above you, or at least above that which you usually take yourself to be' (SE 1). Conant points out that Nietzsche deliberately lets the significantion of the term 'exemplar' slide between two meanings: the exemplar as *other* (and thus not *me*), and the exemplar as 'higher self' (that is, some eventual state *of myself*). The point inherent in this deliberate creative tension is that what the exemplary other discloses is something which *I* have the potential to be.

Why cannot types, like exemplars, disclose 'higher selves'? Up to a point, doubtless they can. I would not for a moment wish to deny that a person might benefit from coming to see aspects of himself as 'slavish', for instance, as a result of an encounter with the *Genealogy*. But if we return to Collingwood, we can see an additional and significant hurdle which any text dealing in types has to clear. This is the problem which Collingwood labels the 'corrupt consciousness'.

The 'corruption of consciousness', stigmatised by Collingwood as 'the worst disease of mind',[37] is essentially a sense of alienation from one's own experience such that one fails to experience that experience *as* one's own. As Ridley puts it, a corrupt consciousness 'is one which, because it fails to clarify its own thoughts and feelings, refuses to acknowledge its own experiences as its own: it says about them "That ... is not mine."'[38] In other words, it fails to 'own' its experience. What such a consciousness fails to pay attention to is what David Owen, offering a Collingwoodian interpretation of Stanley Cavell, has called the expressive dimension of moral judgement: 'that dimension of the moral life which involves the self's understanding of itself from an expressive point of view, i.e. the self's understanding of itself in its individuality.'[39] The danger of forms of self-relation which rely excessively upon types is that the reader is encouraged to think of himself as a particular *type* of self, rather than as *this* self. Like Nietzsche's 'herd' person, or Kierkegaard's member of the 'crowd', Collingwood's 'corrupt consciousness' 'does not have experiences which are his own ... [he] can only recognise his experiences as the experiences of a certain type of self rather than the experiences of this, his own, self.'[40] Such a failure to 'own' one's experience can all too easily encourage various forms of ethical and religious evasion – not least that involved in evading responsibility for one's judgements because, in a key sense, they are not one's own.[41] This is the worry that lies behind Kierkegaard's frequent condemnation of being concerned with 'what the age demands', and the tendency to want to answer questions such as what it means to be a human being in general terms, rather than in the first person.[42]

It is regrettable that the *Genealogy* does not utilise the insight of 'Schopenhauer as Educator' about the functioning of exemplars. A major problem with the *Genealogy*'s methodology of dealing predominantly in types rather than exemplars is that it does not forestall the way of thinking outlined above, and the concomitant dangers of evasion. What is significant about this is that, if the above suggestions are on the mark, the *Genealogy*'s dealing in types can diminish its effectiveness as a self-transformatory, 'moral perfectionist', text. Its focus upon types is an instance of the generality which Phillips and Nussbaum are worried about, and from which certain types of literature and narrative can rescue us. Whereas both the *Genealogy* and *Fear and Trembling* contain and embody narrative approaches to the issue of faith, it is the latter text, by focusing on an exemplar rather than on types, that is, *ceteris paribus*, better placed to bring about in a reader the kind of self-transformatory aspect-dawning at which both authors are aiming. Much more could be said here, of course. Further investigation may well show that Johannes' narrative portrait of Abraham comes off rather badly in comparison with the richness of the portraits of religious exemplars painted by Dostoevsky or Tolstoy.[43] Nevertheless, in his tacit recognition of the importance of the concrete particularity of exemplars in philosophy as narrative, Johannes has one key advantage over the Nietzsche of the *Genealogy*. It is ironic that what *Fear and Trembling* recognizes and the *Genealogy* greatly underplays is a Nietzschean insight.[44]

Bibliography of cited works by Nietzsche

Beyond Good and Evil (New York: Vintage Books, 1966, trans. Walter Kaufmann).

On the Genealogy of Morals (New York: Vintage Books, 1967, trans. W. Kaufmann and R. J. Hollingdale).

'Schopenhauer as Educator', in *Untimely Meditations* (Cambridge: Cambridge University Press, 1983, trans. R. J. Hollingdale).

Notes

1   See A. Ridley, *Nietzsche's Conscience: Six Character Studies from the Genealogy* (Ithaca: Cornell University Press, 1998)

2   Aaron Ridley explores some of the tensions and downright confusions in the *Genealogy* with impressive care and in illuminating detail in *Nietzsche's Conscience.*

3   Ridley, *Nietzsche's Conscience*, p. 24.

4   Or 'bad bad conscience', as Ridley calls it: a 'slave-moralised' form of bad conscience. What Ridley calls 'good bad conscience' is a raw, not-yet-slave-moralised form which, Ridley argues, the nobles would also have to have had. See Ridley, *Nietzsche's Conscience*, chapter 1.

5   On this point, see especially GM II.

6   Ridley, *Nietzsche's Conscience*, p. 54.

7   See GM I 15.

8   Ridley, *Nietzsche's Conscience*, p. 60.

9   Ridley, *Nietzsche's Conscience*, p. 61.

10 S. Kierkegaard, 'A First and Last Explanation', appended to *Concluding Unscientific Postscript to the Philosophical Fragments*, (Princeton: Princeton University Press, 1992 ed. and trans. H. V. and E. H. Hong), p. 627.

11 S. Kierkegaard, *Fear and Trembling* (Harmondsworth: Penguin, 1985, trans. A. Hannay), pp. 70ff. Hereafter FT.

12 E. F. Mooney, *Knights of Faith and Resignation: Reading Kierkegaard's Fear and Trembling* (Albany: State University of New York Press, 1991), p. 49.

13 Mooney, *Knights of Faith and Resignation*, p. 53.

14 *Ibid*.

15 For an illuminating account of this in relation to Kierkegaard's discourse on the book of Job, see E. F. Mooney, *Selves in Discord and Resolve: Kierkegaard's Moral-Religious Psychology from* Either/Or *to* Sickness Unto Death (London: Routledge, 1996), chapter 3.

16 This point is central to the reading of *Fear and Trembling* advanced by J. Kellenberger in *Kierkegaard and Nietzsche: Faith and Eternal Acceptance* (London: Macmillan, 1997).

17 See FT, p. 69.

18 See G. Pattison, *'Poor Paris!' Kierkegaard's Critique of the Spectacular City* (Berlin and New York: Walter de Gruyter, 1999), p. 99.

19 Kierkegaard, *Postscript*, p. 414.

20 Kierkegaard, *Postscript*, p. 486.

21 This in itself shows that the widespread popular view of *Fear and Trembling* – that its message is 'If God's command contrasts the demands of the ethical, always obey God!' – is a great misunderstanding.

22 For some applications of this famous Wittgensteinian idea to the sphere of religious belief and practice, see the 'Lectures on Religious Belief' section of L. Wittgenstein, *Lectures and Conversations on Aesthetics, Psychology and Religious Belief*, (Oxford: Basil Blackwell, 1966 trans. and ed. C. Barrett).

23 Wittgenstein, *Lectures and Conversations*, p.54

24 R. Otto, *Religious Essays: a Supplement to 'The Idea of the Holy'* (London: Oxford University Press, 1931, trans. B. Lunn), pp. v, 7, 14, 27, 28–9. I am grateful to Jim Urpeth for bringing these passages to my attention: see Urpeth's essay in this volume.

25 N. K. Verbin, 'Religious Beliefs and Aspect Seeing', *Religious Studies*, Vol. 36 no. 1 (2000), p. 2, my emphasis.

26 This is one important dimension of what Kierkegaard calls 'Christendom', for which he reserves much of his most savage polemical ire. See, in particular, the articles brought together as *Kierkegaard's Attack Upon 'Christendom'* (Princeton: Princeton University Press, 1944, trans. W. Lowrie).

27 Verbin, 'Religious beliefs', p. 21.

28 See M. C. Nussbaum, *The Fragility of Goodness: Luck and Ethics in Greek Tragedy and Philosophy* (Cambridge: Cambridge University Press, 1986), and especially *Love's Knowledge: Essays on Philosophy and Literature* (Oxford: Oxford University Press, 1990); D. Z. Phillips, *Through a Darkening Glass: Philosophy, Literature and Cultural Change* (Oxford: Basil Blackwell, 1982). Nussbaum and Phillips are not of course alone in making such claims, but they are, in my view, two of the most interesting writers on the interrelationship between philosophy and literature. For present purposes, I prefer the more inclusive term 'narrative' to 'literature' because texts such as the *Genealogy* and *Fear and Trembling* would probably fall between the descriptive stools of 'literature' and 'philosophical treatise'.

29 Phillips, *Through a Darkening Glass*, p. 1.

30 *Ibid.*, p. 4.

31 *Ibid.*

32 For a brilliant account of this, see J. Conant, 'Nietzsche's perfectionism: a reading of "Schopenhauer as Educator"', in R. Schacht (ed.), *Nietzsche's postmoralism* (Cambridge: Cambridge University Press, forthcoming). My citations are from page numbers in unpublished manuscript form.

33 Ridley, *Nietzsche's Conscience*, p. 14: my emphasis.

34 *Ibid.*

35 Some of the following material is adapted from my *Humour and Irony in Kierkegaard's Thought* (London: Macmillan, 2000), p. 34.

36 Conant, 'Nietzsche's perfectionism', p. 19.

37 R. G. Collingwood, *The Principles of Art* (Oxford: Clarendon Press, 1938), p. 336.

38 A. Ridley, *R. G. Collingwood: a Philosophy of Art* (London: Phoenix, 1998), p. 7.

39 D. Owen, 'Cultural diversity and the conversation of justice: reading Cavell on political voice and the expression of consent', *Political Theory*, vol. 27 no. 5 (1999), p. 581.

40 Owen, 'Cultural diversity', p. 582.

41 *Ibid.*

42 See Lippitt, *Humour and Irony*, especially chapter 2.

43 This suggestion was put to me by George Pattison.

44 I am grateful to Jim Urpeth for his astute and helpful comments on an earlier version of this article.

6
The non-Greek element in Christianity
Contest and measure in Nietzsche's understanding of Christianity[1]

Paul J.M. van Tongeren

The non-Greek element in Christianity – The Greeks did not see the Homeric Gods above them as masters and themselves beneath them as slaves, as
did the Jews. They saw, as it were, only the mirror image of the most successful specimens of their own caste, hence an ideal, not an antithesis of
their own being. They feel related to each other; there exists a reciprocal
interest, a sort of *symmachia*. A human being thinks nobly of himself when
he gives himself such gods and puts himself in a relationship like that of the
lesser nobility to the higher; whereas the Italic peoples have a real peasant
religion, continually fearful of evil and capricious despots and tormentors.
Wherever the Olympian gods withdrew, Greek life was also more dismal
and fearful. – By contrast, Christianity crushed and shattered human
beings completely and sank them as if into slimy depths: in the feeling of
complete dejection, the gleam of a divine pity could then suddenly shine
forth, so that someone surprised and stunned by grace let out a cry of rapture and for a moment believed that he bore the whole of Heaven within
him. All the psychological discoveries of Christianity work upon this pathological excess of feeling, upon the deep corruption of head and heart necessary for it: it wants to destroy, shatter, stun, intoxicate; there is only one
thing it does not want: *measure*, and hence it is, when understood most profoundly, barbaric, Asiatic, ignoble, non-Greek. (HH 114)[2]

In this article I will present an elaborate discussion of this aphorism,
concentrating on the role of the opposition between ancient Greek
culture and Christianity. In this introductory section I will gather
together some of the questions that are raised by the text.

The title of the aphorism indicates that the opposition between Greek
and Christian is its main theme. But that impression is altered already
by the first sentence. For there it is not the Christians but the Jews who
are presented as opposed to the Greek. One might be inclined to think
that Nietzsche identifies Judaism with Christianity (as many contempo-

rary Christians do, when they speak of the Judaeo-Christian tradition, even if Nietzsche would identify the two in a rather critical way). But he certainly does not, apart from a few cases where 'Judaic' has a very specific meaning. A few lines further in our text, the opposition changes once more. Now the 'Italic peoples' are the ones being opposed to the Greek. And with the 'Italic peoples' he does not refer to Christians, as is clear from an earlier version of this same text (which we find in the *Nachlass*) in which he speaks of 'the Romans'.[3]

We may already conclude this: Nietzsche's text is about oppositions and it re-emphasizes a tension in what are usually called – in a very conciliatory tone – 'the roots of European culture'. This aphorism is about these roots, that is, about things that have a vital significance for our culture. And Nietzsche's main concern seems to be the relation between these different roots, a relation which he seems to interpret as an opposition, or even a bundle of oppositions. The first cluster of questions to be raised concerns this opposition or these oppositions. If there is one opposition, what exactly are its poles? Are the Romans on the same side as Jews and Christians? Or, if there are oppositions – in the plural – how are they related to each other?

In the second place, the opposition(s) must be determined with respect to content. If, for the moment, we restrict ourselves to the opposition as it is suggested by the title, we will have to determine the characteristics of Christianity and of ancient Greek culture. What does 'Greek' mean to Nietzsche, such that Christianity can be called 'non-Greek'? (For we should not overlook that this word 'non-Greek' is both the first word of the title, and the last word of the aphorism.) Or should we avoid saying that Christianity as such *is* non-Greek, and look instead for something non-Greek in it? Has it some Greek elements as well, these being non-Greek only when 'understood most profoundly' (*im tiefsten Verstande*)?

And what does 'Greek' mean in the context of religion? Does anything like Greek religiosity exist in a way that could be compared to Christianity? Especially in his early writings (although the term occurs once more in the *Twilight of the Idols*) Nietzsche speaks more often about *Griechentum*, suggesting that this is as such already a kind of counterpart to *Christentum*. In this aphorism, however, Nietzsche seems to refer to a specific feature of religion: the relation to the gods. What is the Greek relation to the gods? And if – as is usually the case in Nietzsche – Greek also means 'healthy' and 'strong', and religions are the symptoms of the quality of life of its adherents, we will have to address the question, what a healthy or strong religion could be in the framework of Nietzsche's work, and especially his critique of religion.

After all: these kinds of questions can and must be asked in relation to other aspects or topics of Nietzsche's philosophy as well, whether we speak about religion or about morality, or about philosophy or science. It always seems to be the same kind of question that presses to the forefront: what exactly is being criticized by Nietzsche, and what stays beyond the reach of his critique; what exactly does he oppose to what; and is there, properly speaking, anything beyond the criticized at all?

The aphorism on what is 'non-Greek in Christianity' is taken from the first volume of *Human, All Too Human*. That book was published in 1878, about the time when Nietzsche decided definitively to quit his job as a professor of classical philology at the University of Basel. But what he published in 1878 was to a great extent thought and written, at least in its first version, in the years before; in those years when he was compelled to banish his free thinking to the margins of his life as a philologist and a university professor.

G. Colli and M. Montinari found an earlier version of this text in a notebook with notes from the spring of 1875. At that time Nietzsche was preparing a course on 'The Religion of the Greeks'. He taught this course twice, in the winter of 1875/76 and two years later, in the winter of 1877/78. For my discussion of the questions I have raised, I will make use of this text and other notes from the time in which *Human, All Too Human* emerged, next to the published writings that should always be the first point of reference.

Different oppositions

Let us start by looking once more, and more carefully, at the different oppositions that seem to be (more or less hidden) in the text. After the title suggests the opposition between the Greek and the Christian, it turns out that the Jews and the 'Italic peoples' are on the same side as Christianity, i.e. opposed to the Greek. This is remarkable and unexpected. For in another famous text where Nietzsche criticizes Christianity in a similar vein (that is, as being mean and slavish as opposed to the superior and noble), we find Rome on exactly the opposite side. I am referring to the well-known penultimate section of the first essay of the *Genealogy of Morals*. In this section (GM I 16) Nietzsche distinguishes primarily between two types of morality, and he symbolizes the struggle between these two ultimately as 'Rome against Judea, Judea against Rome'. Here Judea refers to Christianity, as is obvious from all three examples that Nietzsche gives: the first example is the Revelation to St. John; the second is what he calls the three Jews and one Jewess before whom everybody nowadays bows down (Jesus, Peter, Paul and Mary); and the third example is the Reformation as a revival of Judea after the preceding revival of the noble ideal in the Renaissance. We are not surprised to find Judea and Christianity together on one side of the opposition, but here as in many other places,[5] Rome is definitely on the other side, opposed to where we found it in our section from *Human, All Too Human*.

But the identification or at least association of Judaism and Christianity at the other pole of the opposition is by no means constant in Nietzsche's thought. In other texts we find these two opposed to each other. In *Human, All Too Human* (second volume, first part [i.e. AOM] 95) we find Christianity as lyrical being opposed to the 'two other creations the Semites have given the world', which are 'Homeric-epic religions'. Even more explicit is *Daybreak* 72, where the 'Jews, as a people firmly attached to life – like the Greeks and more than the Greeks – are opposed to' the Christians. One more example: at some places Nietzsche constructs an opposition between the Jewish Old Testament on the one side and the Christian New Testament on the other side (cf. BGE 52; GM III 22); in *Beyond Good and Evil* 52 he states that neither the New Testament nor anything in Greek or Indian (religious) literature could be compared to the grand style of the Old Testament; from which it appears that the opposition here is between Greek, Indian *and* Christian on the one side, against Jewish on the other.

We have to conclude that although Nietzsche often does present Greece and classical antiquity as opposed to Christianity or Judaeo-Christianity,[6] he nevertheless often stresses their relationship and affinity. In his course on the 'Religion of the Greeks' he deals extensively with 'the different elements on which the Greek cult was based'; and as the first of these elements he discusses the Semitic elements in great detail (pp. 338-345). From which we have to conclude that even Greece (or *Griechentum*) has Semitic roots, according to what Nietzsche writes at the very time in which he composes our text on the opposition between *Griechentum* and *Christentum*. The least we can say is that there are many different oppositions, or that Christianity and the other religions occupy quite different places within a variety of oppositional determinations.

One last example will serve to highlight an element in our text that was not mentioned before. Nietzsche calls Christianity not only barbaric, ignoble and non-Greek, but also Asiatic. We do find this association between the Christian and the Asiatic more often (e.g. D 169), but also in this respect we find opposed examples as well, where Christianity is opposed to Greek, Indian, Persian and Scandinavian religiosity (D 130).

Although our overview is limited, we cannot but conclude that when Nietzsche writes about Christianity, he does so preferably and almost without exception in the form of some kind of opposition to one or more other religion; but the interpretation of this opposition and the relations in which Christianity appears are multifarious. How should we understand this?

The opposition as such

In my presentation of the examples so far, I already excluded one possible interpretation of the problem: the chronological one. We find the differing oppositions all over Nietzsche's writings, without there being a kind of development from one conception to another.

Another possible interpretation is the one suggested by Lou Salomé (albeit not specifically in relation to Nietzsche's critique of religion, but more generally), and that was also held by Karl Jaspers. Both conclude from this multifariousness and variability that Nietzsche was inconsistent. Lou Salomé stated that Nietzsche was not able to sustain one and the same line of thought longer than the length of one aphorism.[7] And Jaspers claimed that there is nothing in Nietzsche's writings which is not contradicted by himself in other places.[8]

Although this might be a slight exaggeration, it does nevertheless hit upon an important characteristic of Nietzsche's writings. With this characteristic in mind we should in my view speak not of contradictions in Nietzsche's philosophy, as Jaspers does, but rather of Nietzsche's 'philosophy of oppositions'.[9] The survey that I gave of Nietzsche's different oppositional determinations of Christianity shows (in my opinion) that he is not primarily interested in establishing this or that particular opposition, but that the most important thing to him is that there *is* some kind of opposition. Nietzsche here is *creating* oppositions as if that is his way to save the phenomena. This is exactly what he does very often and what may be called a basic feature of his writing: to establish opposition and struggle wherever there is or threatens to be only uniformity and unanimity. This is one of the most basic characteristics of his 'method', it is what he later on will call his 'genealogy', and for which his 'metaphysics of the will to power' will be a kind of ground-work; it is also what gives his writing its unmistakable polemical tone.[10]

One of his reasons for opposing the Greek and the Christian, or for stressing this very opposition, might be that Nietzsche hereby is polemically contradicting contemporary philology. Being a classical philologist living in a Christian world, Nietzsche has mainly to do with these two religious cultures. But for him it also means that he has to establish the tension between them. And in any case he wants to counter their amalgamation (*Verquickung* KSA 8 5 39) in contemporary philology. We find this protest against the submission of antiquity to Christianity by philology in many of the notes from the time in which Nietzsche prepared his course on the religion of the Greeks. Classical antiquity has according to Nietzsche been used (or abused, as he would put it) successively as a seduction to Christianity and as its defence. And as soon as it no longer served these goals, philology was invented in order to make antiquity harmless for Christianity (KSA 8 5 107).

My point is that in all this, the opposition as such is more important than its particular content. Let us explore this point a little further. The emphasis on opposition might remind us of Nietzsche's critique of the typical metaphysical prejudice. He calls 'the faith in opposite values' the 'fundamental faith of the metaphysicians' (BGE 2). Both *Human, All Too Human* (HH 1) and *Beyond Good and Evil* (BGE 2) begin with a critique of this faith or prejudice. Should we say that Nietzsche is subject to this same prejudice that he is criticizing so strongly?

What exactly is this prejudicial faith of metaphysics? The metaphysicians are convinced, according to Nietzsche, that the good cannot originate in the bad, nor truth in falsehood, nor beauty in ugliness. Therefore they assume that all these sublime qualities have their own, metaphysical, origin. The oppositions in which the metaphysicians believe are fixed and determined. They divide reality into two separate domains for all eternity. Or, as Nietzsche would put it, they devalue reality by opposing it to a true reality elsewhere. What Nietzsche is doing is quite the opposite: instead of devaluing reality through this metaphysical kind of opposition, he is trying to re-invest reality with value by interpreting it as a continuously changing struggle between possibilities. In *Human, All Too Human* he opposes to metaphysics his 'chemistry of concepts and sensations' (HH I 1); in *Beyond Good and Evil* he calls it his 'philosophy of the dangerous maybe' (BGE 2). These are his ways to save the phenomena – to save them from over-simplification – to re-invest reality with value, by using the opposition in a way that is completely opposed to the metaphysical faith in oppositions.

Maybe we should say that Nietzsche is trapped, at least partly, within the metaphysical framework that he is criticizing (just as his thinking is often caught up in the resentment that he is questioning). For this struggle between possibilities through which he tries to re-invest reality with value is often conceived of in terms of oppositions, i.e. dual relations between mutually exclusive poles. It would be more radical if he would speak in terms of plurality instead of dual oppositions; or – better – if he would do so more often; for he does so sometimes, as we shall see. But more often, the dual opposition dominates. The reason for this, however, lies in Nietzsche's understanding of this plurality. Nietzsche conceives of it in terms of a struggle or fight. Reality only exists in a plurality of interpretations, but these interpretations are in conflict with each other. It is conflict in this sense that seduces him to this dual, oppositional interpretation of plurality.

This oppositional interpretation is, however, not as such a sufficient reason for saying that Nietzsche remains trapped in the metaphysics that he is criticizing. Quite the contrary: he tries to think conflict in a non-metaphysical way. Let me try to explain this.

The significance of the conflict between different interpretations also determines the nature of this conflict. Precisely because there always has to be this relation of conflict, the struggle may not dissolve itself in the conclusive victory of one of the conflicting parties. In reality the continuation of conflict is secured by the multiplicity of the will to power: the conqueror in one fight will find another opponent elsewhere. In Nietzsche's normative understanding of reality (that is, an understanding which is oriented towards affirmation), however, this characteristic demands a further definition of the struggle. *This struggle not only divides but also binds: by fighting each other the conflicting parties keep the struggle alive.* Here we find a very important distinction between the oppositions in which the metaphysicians believe, and the oppositions we find in Nietzsche. The former are oriented towards their own dissolution: the true is opposed to, and condemns, the untrue, as something that ought not to exist. The metaphysical opposition was – according to Nietzsche – invented precisely for that reason: so that truth should not become dependent on falsehood. In Nietzsche's oppositions, however, the poles remain bound to each other, without the tension in their relation being in any way mitigated. This means that the struggle we are dealing with here has a very particular form: it is the struggle as contest in which the competing parties are bound to a certain measure: the measure that guarantees the continuation of the struggle.

It is clear: the model of the struggle that Nietzsche envisages is the model of the Greek *agon*, which particularly in his early writings is a very important concept.[11]

The opposition between *Griechentum* and *Christentum* must – in my opinion – be understood within this framework. What is most important is that there is opposition; but in order to have opposition, one needs opponents. 'Greek' and 'Christian' are names for two forms of culture, two interpretations of culture, that are in conflict with each other, or that are brought back in conflict with each other by Nietzsche, or whose conflicting relation is brought to the forefront by him.

In what follows I shall try to elaborate this point. I shall try to show that what is being said about the opponents, must indeed be understood from within the framework of the contest and its importance for Nietzsche. The particular characteristic qualities of each of the opponents must be understood from within the framework of their conflict, and not the other way around.

In the present context I shall restrict myself mainly to the religious features of these two poles, *Griechentum* and *Christentum*, although these names stand for more than just that; they indicate forms of culture, attitudes towards life, ways of life, qualities of life.

Before entering into the description of these opponents, however, I first want to consider once more Nietzsche's motivation for establishing this particular opposition between the Greek and the Christian. As we have already seen, we shall encounter the theme of struggle in his motivation as well.

Christentum versus *Griechentum*

It is very clear that from the beginning Nietzsche put his classical philology in the service of a philosophical critique of his own contemporary culture. There are many indications of this, including his inaugural address (*Antrittsrede*), the public lectures that are his first public appearance in Basel outside the classroom (the lectures 'On the Future of our Educational Institutions'), and his first official publication as a professor of classical philology, *The Birth of Tragedy out of the Spirit of Music*. The courses he teaches are purely philological and archaeological, but in the notes from the time when he is preparing his courses, it becomes very clear what is inspiring him in his philological work. In one of those notes we read that the correct starting point for the philologist is not to try to recognize in antiquity what is esteemed in one's own culture, but precisely the opposite: 'to start out from the insight into modern perversity, and to look back from there.'[12]

These notes were partly worked out in the *Untimely Observations*, in which Nietzsche's interest in the critique of contemporary culture is prominent. Others remained unpublished or were used for aphorisms in his later writings, especially his *Human, All Too Human*. The first version of the aphorism that I took as starting point was written in 1875, the year in which Nietzsche was making plans for still more *Untimely Observations*. He made an outline for one in which the prevailing philology would be criticized for its efforts to kill its own critical capacity. The title was to be 'We Philologists'. At this same time he was also preparing an essay on religion. It is clear that his choice to teach a course on the 'Religion of the Greeks' also had this culture-critical background and framework. We find a lot of evidence for that in the notes from this time. My reason for dwelling on this culture-critical effort, is that it explains why Nietzsche's interest in Greek religion should be moulded in the form of the opposition between the Greek and the Christian. Let's explore this relation in more detail now.

For a critique of one's culture, one needs a standard. (It is important to know that the German word for standard or criterion, *Maßstab*, contains the word *Maß* which is 'measure'). The philologist disposes of such a standard in his knowledge of antiquity, and especially of Greek culture. Philology is, just as Nietzsche says in his second *Untimely Observation* on history, not the collecting of antiquities (the 'antiquarian' mode of history), but a mixture of an antiquarian collecting and preserving, the erection of monuments in honour of those who are to be held up as an example, and a critical evaluation. This means that Greek culture is not only a standard for the evaluation of contemporary culture, but that it has to be evaluated itself as well.

That Greek culture functions for Nietzsche as a standard for evaluation is clear from the outset. I refer again to the aphorism that I took as a starting point: the judgement that is ultimately passed on Christianity, is that it is 'non-Greek', or – what is the same – 'barbaric'. The Greeks called everybody who did not speak Greek 'barbaric'. To call something 'barbaric' shows therefore that one's perspective is Greek. This perspective is also very obvious in the opening section of Nietzsche's introduction to his course on the 'Religion of the Greeks':

Never since, has there been a religion like the Greek one: by virtue of its beauty, its splendour, its plurality (*Vielfalt*) and coherence, this religion is unique in the world, and one of the highest products of the Greek spirit. (…) One has to make the greatest efforts to call to mind such a phenomenon clearly; only then can one obtain a standard for what is barbaric in religious cultures (p. 323)

Nevertheless, Greek culture is not an undisputed standard. Quite the contrary. In a note, Nietzsche writes: 'The task would be, to overcome Greece (*das Griechentum*) by deeds. But for that one would first have to know it!'[13] The only adequate attitude for someone studying antiquity is, according to Nietzsche, an attitude of contest – this contest, or *agon*, being itself a very Greek characteristic. That is even a general rule: 'Only in contestation does one get to know the good.'[14] The great examples for the study of antiquity are the leading figures of the Renaissance and Goethe. They were able to compete.[15] The contemporary philologists, however, no longer understand this art of the contest (KSA 8 5 167).

But not only do we have to study Greek culture through contestation in the sense that we – from our standpoint – have to compete with antiquity. It is also the other way around: we will only be able to get to know Greek culture if we challenge the prevalent interpretation of antiquity, through which it has been made powerless, dissolving its critical capacity by making it consistent with our contemporary culture. The prevalent interpretation is the interpretation as put forward in the prevalent or dominant culture, which is Christian through and through. Nietzsche says of contemporary philology here, what he says about many other aspects of our culture elsewhere: however unbelievingly or irreligiously it may behave, it still is Christian through and through – based on a Christian metaphysics, and mirroring itself in a Christian morality.

Nietzsche takes this prevalence very seriously: without Christianity there is hardly any antiquity left for us. This brings him to the unexpected claim, which we nevertheless find several times in his early writings, that the disappearance of Christianity will also make our knowledge and our understanding of antiquity disappear.[16] Christianity is in fact the bridge between antiquity and our contemporary culture. And although it has obscured our view of antiquity through its distorting interpretations, it remains the only link between antiquity and us. Only by bringing these two together, over and against each other, only by linking them in a relation of contest, can antiquity be studied in an appropriate way. Without Christianity we will lose antiquity; without opposing antiquity to Christianity, we will misunderstand it.

This oppositional relation between antiquity and Christianity is even more important because of what Nietzsche calls 'the whole religious basis of life'.[17] Greek culture, Greek life has, according to Nietzsche, a religious foundation; the religious cult is even 'the oldest thing we know of the Greeks.'[18] We will not be able to know the Greeks, let alone be able to take their culture as a standard for critical contestation, without any insight in this religious foundation. And, again quite unexpectedly, this religious foundation is, according to Nietzsche, the same in Greek and Christian culture, in *Griechentum* and *Christentum*! (KSA 8 5 156)

I understand this as follows: there is a common basis for Greek and Christian culture, which is however elaborated and realized in different, even oppositional ways in each. The religious foundation is – so to say – a battleground, a place which is common to oppositional parties. When we study the religious foundations of Greek culture, we study a particular realization of a common ground, and one that can only be studied appropriately if we conceive it as one pole in a conflict, that is, if we see it in the framework of that conflict.

The study of the opposition between Greek religion and Christianity is – or should be – a study of the conflict within the foundations of our common culture. Nietzsche is interested in the conflict between the two roots of our culture because each one of them can only be understood appropriately as in conflict, because only in conflict do they show something of the foundations of culture. And because he is interested in the conflict between *Griechentum* and *Christentum*, he has to be in conflict himself with the prevalent philological interest in Greek antiquity. For, whereas contemporary (philological) culture attempts to reconcile the two poles of the conflict, or remains indifferent or ignorant of the tension between them, Nietzsche tries to revive their conflict and, by doing so, to revitalize contemporary culture.

We may conclude that the theme of conflict and struggle is patently obvious in Nietzsche's interest in Greek religion as opposed to Christianity. Let us now turn to what he says about both poles as such.

Christianity

I take it that only now do we have the right context to understand what Nietzsche says about Christianity and (in the next section) about Greek religious culture. Only after grasping that Greek and Christian culture are parties in a struggle, can we understand what they are, or why Nietzsche conceives them as he does. We will see that this theme of struggle or conflict runs deep into Nietzsche's understanding of both parties. Both are described in terms that indicate a particular attitude towards struggle or conflict.

Central to Nietzsche's interpretation of Christianity is the concept of sin. 'It was Christianity which first brought sin into the world' (HH WS 78).[19] Sin is characteristic of Christianity for several reasons. First, because sin is a representation of evil as being something without any positive value, something which ought not to be there at all – we are reminded of the metaphysical oppositions mentioned earlier. The Greeks on the other hand did not talk about sin, but about a breach of the rules, a transgression, an offence, a sacrilege (*Frevel*); and they *did* attribute value to this offence: 'The Greeks (…) were rather closer to the notion that sacrilege, too, might have some nobility (…) and in their desire to invent some dignity for sacrilege and to incorporate nobility in it, they invented *tragedy*' (GS 135). But the evil of sin is, for Christians and Jews, absolute. Evil is not something to be moderated, but something to be eradicated. And it should be eradicated radically, so that even the passions that motivate sin are not to be mastered but rooted out.[20] The founder of Christianity is therefore, according to Nietzsche, like 'a dentist, whose sole cure for pain is to pull out the teeth' (HH WS 83).

Connected to this absolutization of sin is the fact that sin can ultimately only be directed against God (*ibid.* and 81), which implies that man, as a sinner, is completely lost. With his absolute concept of sin the Christian condemns himself absolutely. For it is impossible to fight against the Christian God. He is elevated above every contest (*ibid.*) In *Daybreak* 130, Nietzsche distinguishes Christianity in this respect not only from Greek, but also from Indian, Persian and Scandinavian religiosity: except in Christianity, some limits are always placed on the power of the gods, be it through fortune, or because they themselves are sensitive to offerings, or because they will at some point go under in some kind of twilight of the gods (*Götter-Dämmerung*). This absolute opposition between God and the human being characterizes Christianity, and makes any relation of tension between the two impossible. For that reason Christianity must lead to self-hatred as we find it in Pascal (D 79), or to an unconditional surrender to the arbitrariness of grace.

Moreover this absolute opposition also precludes struggle between human beings: the *absolute* subordination to the omnipotent God relativizes any difference and inequality between people. Nietzsche writes that this emphasis on equality as the effect of absolute subordination was Jesus' way to abolish secular justice (HH WS 81). It must be said that, according to Nietzsche in *Homer's Contest*, there could be no contest between gods and humans even for the Greeks. He calls the human being and god 'two powers that are never allowed to fight with each other'; and he even calls it the very meaning of the gods 'that the human being is never be allowed to risk a contest with them' (KSA 1 787). This very proscription indicates, however, the ever-present temptation to hubristic contest with the gods and its acknowledgement by Greek religion.[21] *Ought not* presupposes *can*.

It would be easy to give many more examples of the presence of this figure of struggle in Nietzsche's description of Christianity. To me it seems to be a key to a correct understanding of his interpretation of Christianity. Even where Nietzsche speaks about the Christian religion in a more positive sense, it can be understood from this same perspective. Nietzsche values Christianity to the extent to which it introduces oppositions (e.g. in the character of the saint, who commands distance). Also the blind spots in Nietzsche's understanding of Christianity should be understood from within this framework: it is at least significant that he never speaks about the central doctrine of incarnation, in which this absolute opposition between God and human being seems to be broken down.

But instead of elaborating on this, I shall conclude this section by turning back to the aphorism from *Human, All Too Human* which I took as my starting point. Between God and the human being there is as little contest as there is between absolute masters and completely submissive servants; they are of a different nature. The Christian God is, according to Nietzsche, a capricious ruler. Although he does not mention sin explicitly in this text, the effects of sin as described are very obvious in the second half of the text: through sin the human being is immersed in complete dejection (sunk 'into slimy depths'), from which he can only be saved through absolute grace. Both dejection and grace are without any measure or moderation. 'Depravity' (*Verworfenheit*) and 'rapture' (*Entzücken*) are states in which the human being is passive, stupefied, intoxicated. God and human beings are not well matched in Christianity; and for that reason it is, 'when understood most profoundly (…) non-Greek.'

Griechentum

The figure of struggle is even more obvious in Nietzsche's understanding of Greek religiosity than in his interpretation of Christianity. The opposition in which they are caught is affirmed by Greek religiosity, because it is in itself characterized through and through by plurality and tension. The following passage from section 4 in Nietzsche's introduction to his course on the 'Religion of the Greeks' will clarify what I mean:

> We wish to concentrate on the means by which a cult now develops itself further; for the stable element in a cult is so powerful that it comes all too easily to a standstill. All further development is bound to the struggle, to the clash of different ritual claims, and to the efforts to mediate them. The extraordinary multifariousness of the Greek cult is a proof of the struggles that gave rise to it. The settling of accounts between piety and piety towards what was long honored; (…) the violent imposition of foreign elements by force in the political process of tribes and cities; the gradual spreading of cults from abroad, (…) the introduction of completely new cults due to sudden natural events and the helplessness of all existing gods; the mutual demarcation of the rights of gods that were honored in common; (…) the struggle amongst the predicates ascribed to one single deity and the breaking loose of some of them, giving rise to new deities (through division, as is the case with many animals) – these are the most important means. (p. 337)

The principle of development of Greek religion, as well as its greatness, consists in this plurality which it harbours. Nietzsche not only points to the polytheism of the Greeks (which is, according to him, a sign of their abundance of spirit (KSA 8 5 103)), but he also shows that every one of these many Greek gods is itself again a collection of many gods: 'Almost all Greek deities are collections'.[22] Nietzsche's course on Greek religion is for the most part an analysis of these many different elements that were gathered in the Greek gods.

There are gods which are concrescents from a long history and which may dissolve at any moment. Moreover, according to Nietzsche, one and the same god is a different one at each different place where it is worshiped: 'a Greek god actually is at every place a particular being, something different, something that does not exist somewhere else, something with its own cult and legend, its own ritual; it is strictly localized; the Zeus here is in terms of the cult not the same one as the Zeus over there.' (p. 416) Because of this there also have to be many priests all of whom stand for their own god or even for their own cultic instants of the god (*ibid.*). There is no central power, there are no priestly representatives of the whole religion; nor is there any holy charter (KSA 8 5 104). The opposition between priests and sooth-sayers (Greek: *manteis*) is, according to Nietzsche, 'a salutary opposition between the representatives of the religious.'[23] Everything which could lead to uniformity is banished; 'No obligation to believe, no obligation to visit the temple, no Orthodoxy, they tolerated all possible opinions about the gods.'[24] Greek religion appears to be a bundle of contradictions. And what is true of Greek religion is true for Greek culture in general as well: 'For a long time Greece is a chaos of all possible influences and styles.'[25]

The term chaos however points to a problem which is implied by this – pure – plurality. Pure plurality without any order does not produce a culture, nor a cult, nor a religion. On the other hand, however, every organization of plurality threatens the conflict, and with that, it threatens the dynamic which is – at least potentially – implied by plurality. Nietzsche recognizes this problem. He speaks of 'the overloading giving rise to unintelligibility as its result'[26] as the danger of every later phase of the cult. He searches for 'the *organizing powers* of the cult': 'What created ever new unities out of such multifarious elements?'[27] This latter expression indicates already a solution to the problem: there has to be some order and therefore some unity must be created, but Nietzsche speaks about 'ever new unities' in order to maintain plurality. He admires the Greeks because of their sense of order (*'Order*, articulation, beauty, cosmos' (*ibid.*)), he speaks of their 'talent for order'. One might think that with this judgement on the Greeks Nietzsche does an injustice to the Romans who after all are pre-eminent organizers. Nietzsche acknowledges some relationship, but according to him, the Greeks are much more admirable than the Romans, because they even knew how to moderate their sense of order: 'Even their sense of order is moderated, it does not fall victim to the pedantry and the legality like the Roman sense of order does.'[28]

This idea of a moderated moderation, a measure which is itself measured, is to my mind the central characteristic of Greek culture according to Nietzsche. Its cultural form is the *agon* or contest. Nietzsche calls this contest the '*Klugheit der Griechen*' ('the prudence of the Greeks' (HH WS 226)). There he writes that the decline of the musical and gymnastic contest also made the Greek state disintegrate. Similarly in *The Birth of Tragedy* he showed that tragic Greek culture died with the disappearance of the contest between Apollo and Dionysos: 'because you had abandoned Dionysus, Apollo abandoned you' (BT 10). The 'new opposition: the Dionysian and the Socratic' was of a different kind, a conflict of annihilation, not an *agon*, and therefore 'the art of Greek tragedy was wrecked on this.' (BT 12) The psychological root of the *agon* is the contest (e.g. KSA 8 3 49) and with that envy (KSA 8 5 70). According to Nietzsche, contest and envy characterize the Greek: Greek men among each other, Greek gods among each other (cf. e.g. KSA 8 5 120) as well the relation between gods and human beings. In the text that I took as my starting point Nietzsche mentions the relation between higher and lower nobles as his model for the Greek relation between gods and human beings. In Greek religion they are matched with each other, whereas in Christianity they are not. According to the Greeks, gods and human beings are not equal, but they are unequal in a productive manner; they are bound to each other in contest. Contest is the measure of their difference in both senses: as the measure that limits their difference, and as the standard for measuring their difference.

In our aphorism from *Human, All Too Human* one word is emphasised: *measure*. This measure is not the measure of modesty, even less the measure of ascetic moderation. It is the measure of contest; the measure that binds plurality in a way which makes this plurality productive and saves it from indifference on the one hand and rigid uniformity on the other.

Conclusion: measure, Dionysos versus the crucified

I conclude by summing up in terms of this measure what we saw before regarding Nietzsche's opposition between Christian and Greek culture and regarding his critique of Christianity. When Nietzsche opposes *Christentum* and *Griechentum* he tries to reinsert Christianity into a relation of contest. Christianity is criticized first because as a religion it withdrew through its pathological excess of feeling the relation between gods and humans from the measure of contest, as well as the relation among humans; but also because in European culture it became the one and only religion so that there cannot be a serious religious contest any longer. Christianity as the religion of excess, succeeded in becoming the only religion.

In this paper I have argued mainly from Nietzsche's early writings. But in this respect as in many others the early writings point to what in the later writings is said in a more explicit and excessive way. The excessiveness of Christianity may be part of the explanation for the apparent excessiveness of Nietzsche's critique of Christianity, his 'curse on Christianity' (*Fluch auf das Christentum*), as the subtitle of *The Anti-Christ* reads. The excessive religion that reigns without any competition, demands an excessive attack.

At the same time as he wrote his *Anti-Christ*, Nietzsche worked on his last autobiography, *Ecce Homo*. As is well known, this book ends with a very short last section: 'Have I been understood? – *Dionysus versus the Crucified. ...*' ('*Hat man mich verstanden?* – Dionysos gegen den Gekreuzigten...') This '*gegen*' ('versus') with which Nietzsche links Greek and Christian religion, does not refer to a substitution or succession; it is not an 'instead of' or 'either/or', but it refers to the measure of the struggle. This excessive cry is an expression of an agonistic measure.[29]

Bibliography of cited works of Nietzsche

Sämtliche Werke: Kritische Studienausgabe. (Munich: Walter de Gruyter, 1980, eds. G. Colli, M. Montinari).

Notes

1   A slightly different version of this paper was published in Dutch in the *Tijdschrift voor Filosofie* vol. 61: 1 (1999), pp. 3–26. For their comments on a previous version of this text, I am grateful to the members of the Nijmegen 'Nietzsche-werkgroep' and especially to Dr. Herman Siemens.

2   My translation. Both the Stanford translation (*Human, All Too Human I* The Complete Works of Fr. Nietzsche, Vol. III. Stanford: Stanford University Press, 1995 trans. G. Handwerk) and R. J. Hollingdale's translation (Cambridge: Cambridge University Press, 1986) contain some mistakes, some of which are more serious than others. Nietzsche writes '*italische Völker*'. The Stanford translation of this – 'Italian peoples' – is rather dubious, because it blurs the distinction with the German '*italienisch*', and because Nietzsche certainly has not the later (Christian) Italians in mind, but the Romans, or even the pre-Roman population of Italy (see also below and note 3). Hollingdale translates '*Ungriechisch*' with 'un-Hellenic', which is dubious because of Nietzsche's habit (especially in his early years) of distinguishing '*Griechisch*' from '*Hellenisch*'. More serious are his patently wrong translations of '*Symmachie*' as 'symmetry' and of '*Erfindungen*' as 'sensations'. Because of these problems with the available translations, I quote the German text as well:
    Das Ungriechische im Christenthum. – Die Griechen sahen über sich die homerischen Götter nicht als Herren und sich unter ihnen nicht als Knechte, wie die Juden. Sie sahen gleichsam nur das Spiegelbild der gelungensten Exemplare ihrer eigenen Kaste, also ein Ideal, keinen Gegensatz des eigenen Wesens. Man fühlt sich mit einander verwandt, es besteht ein gegenseitiges Interesse, eine Art Sym-

machie. Der Mensch denkt vornehm von sich, wenn er sich solche Götter giebt, und stellt sich in ein Verhältniss, wie das des niedrigeren Adels zum höheren ist; während die italischen Völker eine rechte Bauern-Religion haben, mit fortwährender Aengstlichkeit gegen böse und launische Machtinhaber und Quälgeister. Wo die olympischen Götter zurücktraten, da war auch das griechische Leben düsterer und ängstlicher. – Das Christenthum dagegen zerdrückte und zerbrach den Menschen vollständig und versenkte ihn wie in tiefen Schlamm: in das Gefühl völliger Verworfenheit liess es dann mit Einem Male den Glanz eines göttlichen Erbarmens hineinleuchten, so dass der Ueberraschte, durch Gnade Betäubte, einen Schrei des Entzückens ausstiess und für einen Augenblick den ganzen Himmel in sich zu tragen glaubte. Auf diesen krankhaften Excess des Gefühls, auf die dazu nöthige tiefe Kopf- und Herz-Corruption wirken alle psychologischen Erfindungen des Christenthums hin: es will vernichten, zerbrechen, betäuben, berauschen, es will nur Eins nicht: das Maass, und desshalb ist es im tiefsten Verstande barbarisch-, asiatisch, unvornehm, ungriechisch.

3 Other places where the term *'Italisch'* appears are: UM 3 (*'den antiken italischen Genius'*); GM I 5 (*'vorarische Insasse des italischen Bodens'*); KSA 7 9[143]: (*'antiken italischen Genius'*), and KSA 7 16[28] (*'das graeko-italische Volk'*).

4 The German title reads: 'Der Gottesdienst der Griechen', which is again difficult to translate: *'Gottesdienst'* is religion, but with an emphasis on the practice of worship. As far as I know this text is not translated in English, but it is published in the critical edition by Colli and Montinari, in KGW II 5, pp. 355–520. I will refer, however, to the Musarion-edition: Fr. Nietzsche, *Gesammelte Werke*, Band V, (München: Musarion Verlag, 1922) pp. 323–463.

5 Cf. e.g.: D 71, where Nietzsche speaks of the 'Christian revenge on Rome'.

6 Other examples are D 29, 69 and 78 and BGE 46 and 49.

7 See: Lou Andreas-Salomé, *Looking back: Memoirs.* (New York, Paragon House, 1991); English translation of *Lebensrückblick* (Zürich: Verlag Max Niehans, 1951), p. 49 and Lou Andreas-Salomé; *Nietzsche* (edited, translated, and with an introduction by Siegfried Mandel, English translation of *Friedrich Nietzsche in seinen Werken*, Wien: Verlag Karl Konegen, 1894: Redding Ridge: Black Swan Books, 1988), p. 91f. For a different appraisal of Nietzsche's earlier aphoristic writings, see: Lou Andreas-Salomé, *Nietzsche* p. 77ff.

8 K. Jaspers, *Nietzsche. Einführung in das Verständnis seines Philosophierens.* (Berlin: Walter de Gruyter, 1946, 2nd edition), p. 17.

9 I am referring to the very important book of W. Müller-Lauter, *Nietzsche. Seine Philosophie der Gegensätze und die Gegensätze seiner Philosophie* (Berlin and New York: Walter de Gruyter, 1971). The title of the recently published English translation is misleading: *Nietzsche. His Philosophy of Contradictions*

and the Contradictions of his Philosophy (Urbana/Chicago: University of Illinois Press, 1999).

10   I have elaborated this in my *Reinterpreting Modern Culture. An Introduction to Fr. Nietzsche's Philosophy* (West Lafayette: Purdue University Press, 2000). See especially chapters III and IV.

11   Cf. H. Siemens, 'Nietzsche's Hammer: Philosophy, Destruction, or the Art of Limited Warfare', *Tijdschrift voor Filosofie*, vol. 60: 2 (1998), pp. 321–347.

12   *'nämlich von der Einsicht in die moderne Verkehrtheit auszugehn und zurückzusehn –'* (KSA 8 3 52).

13   *'Das Griechenthum durch die That zu überwinden wäre die Aufgabe. Aber dazu müßte man es erst kennen! –'* (KSA 8 5 167).

14   *'Nur im Wetteifer lernt man das Gute kennen'* (KSA 8 23 132).

15   In the threefold slogan of the Renaissance, *translatio, imitatio, aemulatio* we recognize the contest mainly in the third part, even if for many Renaissance figures this *aemulatio* referred rather to a Christianizing of antiquity!

16   Cf. e.g. UM 2.

17   *'die ganze religiöse Basis des Lebens'* (KSA 8 5 15).

18   *'das älteste, was wir von den Griechen wissen'* (KSA 8 5 155).

19   *'Erst das Christenthum hat die Sünde in die Welt gebracht.'* See also D 92, where Nietzsche regards the mild modern form of Christianity, Christianity in the form of moralism without the strict concept of sin, as the euthanasia of Christianity.

20   Cf. GS 139; also TI part V, 1: *'il faut tuer les passions'*.

21   Cf. KSA 1 787; KSA 7 16 31.

22   *'Fast alle griechischen Gottheiten sind angesammelte'* (KSA 8 5 113).

23   *'Ein heilsamer Widerspruch zwischen den Vertretern der/s Religiösen'* (p. 431).

24   *'Keinen Glaubenszwang, keinen Tempelbesuchszwang, keine Orthodoxie, man duldete über die Götter alle möglichen Meinungen.'* (p. 375)

25   *'Für eine lange Zeit ist Griechenland ein Chaos aller möglichen Einflüsse und Stilarten'* (p. 404).

26   *'die Überladung und dadurch hervorgerufene Unverständlichkeit'* (p.338).

27   *'die organisierenden Gewalten des Cultus'; 'Was schuf aus so vielspältigen Elementen immer wieder neue Einheiten?'* (p. 364).

28   *'Auch ihr Ordnungssinn hat ein Mass, er verfällt nicht in das Pedantischen und Juristischen, wie der der Römer.'* (p. 338).

29   G. Schank, *Dionysos gegen den Gekreuzigten. Eine philologische und philosophische Studie zu Nietzsches 'Ecce Homo'* (Bern: P. Lang, 1993).

7
Nietzsche and the 'Masters of Truth': the pre-Socratics and Christ

Béatrice Han

Among the major themes of Nietzsche's philosophy, his criticism of truth is one of the most ubiquitous and best known. Just as well known is the paradox that derives from its radicality. Unless one accepts the (essentially non-Nietzschean) idea that all statements should be treated as equivalent, this criticism seems to cancel itself insofar as it presupposes an implicit claim to truth.[1] Therefore, Nietzsche's position would be threatened either by a nihilistic and generalised levelling of all values, or by the ancient argument against the sceptics to the effect that any proposition that denies the existence of truth reasserts by definition the reality of what is negated by it. Either a universal relativism, or a contradiction between the propositional content and the very existence of the proposition. If so, how could Nietzsche justify his own claim to truth?

The usual strategy used to save Nietzsche from this quandary consists in distinguishing between different understandings of truth . It is clear that among the three traditional conceptions of truth namely, internal consistency, *adequatio rei et intellectus* and efficiency, the first cannot be held to, since Nietzsche praised contradiction and rejected the primacy of logic in thought. However, the status of the two remaining possibilities, metaphysical (*adequatio*) and pragmatist (efficiency) is more complicated. Heidegger is the only commentator that, instead of seeing in Nietzsche the self-declared adversary of metaphysics, understands his work as its hidden point of completion. Yet the Heideggerian thesis agrees *a contrario* with those of other exegetes insofar as it confirms indirectly the existence of an unbreakable bond between metaphysics and the adequationist conception of truth. For Heidegger, the ultimate reason why Nietzsche still belongs to the horizon of metaphysics is that he implicitly reactivates the traditional definition of truth as *homoiosis*.[2]

Although they oppose Heidegger on the question of Nietzsche's relationship to metaphysics, most commentators accept this connection and
agree that Nietzsche's criticism of traditional, metaphysical concepts is
accompanied by the rejection of the notion of *adequatio* itself.[3] From this
perspective the denial of the 'in-itself' developed in *Human, All too
Human* and evenmore so in *The Gay Science* indicates the impossibility
to regard as an ideal the notion of a correspondence with reality.[4] As
Nietzsche states, 'what is "appearance" for me now? Certainly not the
opposite of some essence!.. Certainly not a mask that one could place
on an unknown X or remove from it' (GS I 54). The reason why our
truths are 'false' is not, as in *Truth and Lies in an Exra-Moral Sense,* that
they do not encapsulate the essence of things, but that the latter should
be thought of as fictitious; we have to renounce the very possibility of
correspondence. According to well-known claims, our truths must be
understood as schematising fictions which crystallise the flux of reality in
the logical categories (such as identity) that allow us to orient ourselves
within the world.[5] A 'true' proposition would thus be one which is useful
to life. However, it is essential to note that this pragmatist definition has
a mostly *polemic* purpose. In fact, the real meaning of genealogy is to
denounce the unconscious pragmatism of science and of metaphysics,
precisely by unveiling its original occultation by the adequationist understanding of truth. What we see as (adequationally) true is, to take up
William James' favourite expression, what 'works'. But the fact that a
proposition works is no guarantee of its veracity, 'a belief, however necessary it may be for the preservation of a species, has nothing to do with
truth' (WP III 487). The possibility of playing a proposition's efficiency
against its truth value being in itself proof of the distance that separates
Nietzsche from a pragmatism which remains for him merely a critical
tool.[6] Yet if – contrary to what Danto or Rorty think[7] – the pragmatist
understanding of truth cannot be taken to replace its much criticised
metaphysical counterpart in Nietzsche's thought, how will Nietzsche
ever be able to justify his claim to speak the truth?

The hypothesis explored here is that the answer to this question lies
in the Nietzschean analysis of the birth of metaphysics and of the adequationist conception of truth. The texts that Nietzsche wrote about the
pre-Socratics and the advent of Platonism have been studied many
times, but usually with regards to their 'downstream' effects, in order to
identify the consequences of the beginning of Western nihilism.[8] By contrast, my aim here is go 'upstream', from the history of metaphysics to
what might be called its *pre*-history. Such a journey seeks to uncover the

archaic understanding of truth that was buried by the joint invention of the intelligible world as ultimate reality and truth as *adequatio*. What did speaking the truth mean to the thinkers of the 'epoch of Greek tragedy'? How different from its metaphysical counterpart was the understanding of truth presupposed by their discourse? The first part of this paper establishes that the latter question rests upon two assumptions. Firstly, the idea that the truth content of a proposition does not depend on its adequation with an objective referent (the notion of which had not appeared yet), but on its link to the living singularity of its author as expressed by the notion of an archaic 'tyranny of truth' (HH V 261). A true claim is one that is asserted by someone truthful (the Master). The second assumption is that truth must not be understood from an epistemological, but an *ethical* perspective, a point which I shall elucidate by using Marcel Détienne's famous analysis in *The Masters of Truth in Archaic Greece.*[9]

These points will be used to reinterpret the two major turning points in Nietzsche's genealogy of the West – the birth of metaphysics and of Christianity, the common thread being that both cases are instances of the archaic understanding of truth being overthrown by an impersonal and highly abstract conception of it. Finally it will be argued that Nietzsche's own existential practice of philosophy seeks to revive the magisterial understanding of truth. As we shall see, 'becoming what one is' remains the only way left for us Moderns to recover, *via* the artistic stylisation of the self, the integrity that was immediately granted by nature to the pre-Socratics. Having lost the (Schillerian) *naïveté* of the Greek 'Golden Age', we must first create ourselves in order to regain the authority to speak the truth.

I

The late preface of 1879 to Nietzsche's writings on the pre-Socratics takes as its guiding principle the impossibility to understand 'early Greek philosophy' without referring it to the individuals in whom it originates. As Nietzsche states, 'I have selected those doctrines which sound most clearly the personality of the individual philosopher, whereas the complete enumeration of all the transmitted doctrines, as it is the custom of the ordinary handbooks to give, has but one sure result: the complete silencing of personality.'[10] Nietzsche original intuition is that any true philosophical doctrine owes its authenticity to the singularity of its author (the 'personality of the individual philosopher') rather than to its objective content. The correct hermeneutic principle will therefore consist in restoring the organic link that tied the archaic Greek philosopher to his own thought. Viewed in this light, the current depersonalisation operated by our 'ordinary handbooks' is not only a moral flaw, but also an epistemological mistake. As specified later by the text, each philosophical system is a 'tribute' to the 'great human individualities', and must be seen from their point of view.[11] Contrary to the positivist dogmas that were prominent at his time, Nietzsche regards objectivity as an enemy to truth. Just as 'the worth of an action depends on who accomplishes it and on whether it stems from the depth or the surface of the individual, i.e. on its *individuality*'[12] the truth value of a discourse will vary with the speaker's identity – it does not depend on gnoseological, but on ethical criteria. Thus, Nietzsche describes Heraclitus' doctrine as the philosophical transposition of the thinker's virtues – solitude and independence, strength, courage, breadth of view – that allow him to identify justice and harmony behind the universal struggle of life. The reason why the 'doctrine of becoming is true' is that the Ephesian 'has the truth'[13] because of what he *is*. There is no impersonal access to truth : *aletheia* depends on *ethos*.

In the case of the pre-Socratics, this deep-rootedness of thought in the thinker is seen as *apodictic* : it is caused by the existence of a '*severe necessity between their thinking and their character*',[14] this internal necessity being explained by the fact that 'the early Greek masters ... all those men are *integral, entire and self-contained*, and hewn out of stone.'[15] This integrity itself is accounted for by Nietzsche's analysis of the body and its instincts. Like the Homeric Greeks described in the first chapters of *The Birth of Tragedy*, the pre-Socratics are still governed by an instinctual hierarchy through which the multiple forces that compose the individual are harmonised.[16] This process results in the emergence and stabilisation of a dominant tendency (the 'character'), from which the individual's words and deeds will naturally stem. Whereas the hallmark of modernity is reflection – the 'sentimental' as described by Schiller in *Naïve and Sentimental Poetry*[17] – the pre-Socratics' most distinctive feature is the *naïveté* through which an indissoluble continuity is naturally established between what a man is on the one hand, and his ability to speak the truth on the other. This contrasts starkly with the contemporary 'scholar' (*der Gelehrte*), whose loss of unity results in an inconsistent and arbitrary relationship between his being and his thinking, 'whatever remains to him of his "own person" seems to him *accidental*, often *capricious*, more often disturbing ... He finds it an effort to think about "himself", and not infrequently he thinks about himself mistakenly : he can easily confuse himself with another, he fails to understand his own needs and is in this respect alone unsubtle and negligent' (BGE VI 207).

'"*Je*" *est un autre*' as Rimbaud said. Concave, almost eviscerated, the modern subject is nothing but a 'passage way, the *reflection* of foreign beings and events.' Having lost all sense of selfhood, he is unable to distinguish between interiority and exteriority, and therefore to establish a coherent perspective. In this, he is the very antithesis of the strong individual described in *The Genealogy of Morals* whose multiplication of identities is voluntary, plurality being always controlled by a care for synthesis that enriches his understanding of himself and of the world. Yet the deepest meaning of this modern shattering of the self is not merely psychological: its most fundamental consequence is the impossibility for the Moderns to ground in truth their own discourse, a point to which I shall come back.

By contrast, the distinctive feature of the 'real philosophers' is that they achieve a perfect isomorphism between their word and their nature, they are the incarnation of their thought and this thought, the necessary expression of character. As Nietzsche states, 'the real philosophers of Greece are those before Socrates (with Socrates something changes). They are all noble persons ... They anticipate all the great conceptions of things : *they themselves represent these conceptions, they bring themselves into a system* (WP II 437). The notion of 'representation' is not to be taken here in its classical, Cartesian sense and does not refer to the conscious thematisation of a perceptual or imaginary content. On the contrary, it indicates the symbolical movement through which the individual's *ethos* naturally transposes his thought – it is an embodied representation, just as the Dionysian man is said to become the incarnation of the dithyramb in *The Birth of Tragedy*. Correlatively, the system loses its metaphysical meaning and ceases to be seen as the theoretical web in which ideas can be caught and fixed (as expressed by Nietzsche's criticism of Spinoza, the 'spider' – a pun on the German word *Spinne*). Far from being abstract, the systematisation now becomes organic, its totalising aspect being referred to the individual as a living, concrete totality (they 'bring themselves into a system'). The pre-Socratics achieved the 'individual system' that the Jena Romantics longed for – 'aren't all systems individuals, just as individuals are systems at least in embryo and tendency'[18] – an ideal the existential possibility of which has been lost by Modernity, to Nietzsche's own regret, 'let us confess how utterly our Modern world lacks the whole type of a Heraclitus ... Empedocles, and whatever other names these royal and magnificent hermits of the spirit had' (BGE VI 204).

Having systematised themselves, the original Greek Masters will be '*tyrants of truth*'. Nietzsche, citing as examples Parmenides, Pythagoras, Empedocles and Anaximander, states that, 'each great thinker with the belief that he was possessor of absolute truth, became a tyrant' (HH V 261). Because of its immediacy, the natural balance of the pre-Socratics' instincts prevents the appearance of the reflective element that doubt thrives upon – hence the possibility of the 'belief' in oneself and the '*involuntary*' way to build all the possibilities of the philosophical ideal'.[19] The same process begets that 'joy' that Winckelmann deemed characteristic of pre-Platonic Greece, 'perhaps happiness in the belief that one was in possession of the truth has never been greater in the history of the world'(HH V 261). The presence of this unconditional faith in one's 'personal excellence' (WP II 430) is precisely what defines the noble spirit: 'what is noble?..It is the *faith* which is decisive here … some fundamental certainty which a noble soul possesses in regard to itself, something which may not be sought or found and perhaps may not be lost either' (BGE IX 287). This is why, contrary to that which Socrates will establish, the archaic tyranny of truth is not nefarious. In this case, the imposition of truth is not a reactive phenomenon, but a purely active one, the natural consequence of the 'severity' and 'arrogance' of the pre-Socratics.[20]

Conversely, Nietzsche attributes the decadence of Ancient Greece to the progressive decline of these great tyrants, suddenly overcome by the 'quarrelsome and talkative hordes of the Socratic schools' (HH V 261). In a highly significant manner, Plato is then described as a *failed* tyrant, 'the incarnate desire to become the supreme philosophical lawgiver and founder of states: he appears to have suffered terribly from the non- fulfilment of his nature, and towards the end of his life his soul became full of the blackest gall' (HH V 261). Plato is the living proof of the disappearance of the archaic structure. The impossibility for him to 'fulfil his nature' by imposing his truth outward turns the violence of his instincts against him and causes *a contrario* the dissolution of his internal unity – 'the tyrannical element now raged as poison through [his] own body' (HH V 261).

Significantly enough, there is a striking similarity between Nietzschean analyses and those elaborated by Marcel Détienne almost a century later in *The Masters of Truth in Archaic Greece.* For Détienne too, the leading question is to know 'how the passage … was operated to a new intellectual regimen, that of argumentation and of the principle of contradiction, along with the transition to a dialogue with the object and the referent of a statement'(MTAG p.7). Like Nietzsche, Détienne is interested in the birth of the adequationist conception of truth, accordingly defined by 'conformity with logical principles on the one hand, and with reality on the other', and thus 'impossible to dissociate from the notions of demonstration and verification'(MTAG p. 41). Détienne's most interesting point, in this regard, is that the pre-metaphysical understanding of truth is characterised by its *non*-adequationist aspect: it is a magisterial form of truth, the specificity of which is the impossibility to dissociate it from the one who speaks it. For Détienne the archaic Greek 'Masters of Truth' have 'the privilege of dispensing the truth simply because they are endowed with the qualities that make them special' (MTAG p.6). Thus, 'when a poet praises someone, he does so in his own name, through aletheia: his word is *alethes*, like his mind. The poet is … a Master of Truth' (MTAG p. 66, emphasis added). In the same way, the only reason why Nereus, the 'Old Man from the Sea', can prophetise is that he himself is *alethes*, truthful.

As Nietzsche had already pointed out, archaic thought does not view the truth of a discourse as an objective feature rather it depends on the personal ability of the speaker to speak truly. Thus, the King of Justice's[21] sentence cannot be verified by its relationship to reality, nor by the search for 'objective' proofs.[22] On the contrary, it is because it is the *King of Justice's* sentence that it can transform reality by freeing the accused from guilt, "*Aletheia* states an assertoric truth : it is an efficient power, it *creates being*" (MTAG p. 6). It is only fair to add, however, that according to Détienne the possibility of speaking the truth depends as much on the (socio-institutional) function of the speaker (as a poet, a seer or a King) as on his personal capacities. Yet notwithstanding this (non-negligible) divergence, it is clear that the notion that the possibility of speaking the truth cannot be 'severed' from 'the qualities … of a certain type of man' like the idea that the word of the Master of Truth is '*the privilege of an exceptional man*' (MTAG p. 132, emphasis added) both follow the same logic as the Nietzschean interpretation, which thus derives from Détienne's study an unexpected confirmation.

II

This account of the structures of pre-Platonic thought sheds a new light on the Nietzschean analysis of the birth of metaphysics. At the beginning of the IVth century BC, the archaic understanding of truth was brought down by the combination of two major events: on the one hand, the creation of a new object (the intelligible world), and on the other, the emergence of the impersonal subject of knowledge (the theoretical man). Because of this dual modification, the very horizon of truth changed: 'the great concepts "good" and "just" are severed from the presuppositions to which they belong and, as liberated ideas, become objects of dialectics. One looks for truth in them, one takes them for entities, or signs of entities. One invents a world where they are at home, where they originate' (WP II 430).

What takes place is a three stage falsification process. Firstly, the 'great concepts' seem to benefit from the metaphysical turn in that they are freed from the magisterial relationship (they become 'liberated ideas'). But as in the case of the emancipation of women (and as Derrida pointed out, is not truth, too, 'woman'?)[24] such a liberation is nothing but an illusion.[25] Just as the 'emancipated' woman loses her femininity through the voluntary adoption of virile features, in the same way thought, severed from the living singularity of the individual, acquires a false universality by forgetting its local source (the 'presuppositions' of the concepts, which are not theoretical but refer to the particularities of the 'Greek soil' in which they are rooted). In the second stage of this metaphysical trickery these concepts become in themselves the *loci* of truth ('one looks for truth in them'). This phony autonomy is explicitly aimed at the archaic necessity that required that truth should be grounded in the speaker's integrity – an indirect proof of the *reactive* character of Platonic nihilism. The final stage of this logic of ever-increasing isolation consists in substantiating these abstractions by 'inventing a world' for the ideas, an intelligible and distinct world that will retrospectively be identified as their 'true' origin. This dynamic insensibly transforms the concrete deep-rootedness of values in the contingency of a spatio-temporal set of conditions (the 'soil') into a transcendent foundation. It is the hallmark of the slow emergence of metaphysics. Interestingly, Détienne describes the same phenomenon in fairly similar terms to Nietzsche: '*Aletheia* become a power more strictly defined and more abstractedly understood : it symbolises ... a plane of reality that takes the form of an atemporal reality, that asserts itself as immutable and stable Being' (MTAG p. 194).

This degeneration of the archaic model is accompanied by the birth of a new type of man, the 'abstractly perfect man', who is the ethical counterpart of the 'theoretical man' already exemplified by Socrates in *The*

Birth of Tragedy.[26] As Nietzsche states, 'one had need to invent the abstractly perfect man as well – good, just, wise, a dialectician. In short, the *scarecrow of the Ancient philosopher*: a plant removed from all soil ... The perfectly absurd *"individuum"* in itself!' (WP II 430, emphasis added). The absurdity of the concept of an 'individuum in itself' is due to the impossibility of universalising specific characteristics without denaturing them: as shown by Kierkegaard, what really defines individuality is *singularity*.[27] To try to generalise it, or worse to substantiate it as an in-itself, denotes a fundamental mistake that deprives the magisterial relationship from its idiosyncratic conditions of possibility – the Pre-Socratic philosopher is superseded by the 'scarecrow'. This movement is amplified with the emergence of Socratic dialectics as a new discursive mode. Beyond depriving the strong the use of their strength – Deleuze's main point in his famous exegesis[28] – the true aim of dialectics is to ruin the archaic understanding of truth by claiming that the dissociation of the speech from its author is a necessary precondition of truth. In this regard, the way Nietzsche describes the *pre*-dialectical period is particularly significant: 'before Socrates, the dialectical manner was repudiated in good society ... Why this display of reasons? Why should one demonstrate? *Against others one possessed authority*' (WP II 431).

The archaic understanding of truth could account for this 'authority' by rooting it in the speaker's personal 'excellence'. As indicated by Détienne, 'the truth [of the Master] is an assertoric truth: no one discusses it, no one demonstrates it. Fundamentally different from our traditional conception, *aletheia* is neither conformity between a proposition and its object, nor between a judgment and the judgments of others' (MTAG p. 69) – in Nietzschean terms: *'one commanded: that sufficed'* (WP II 431). Yet this noble structure (it is typical of 'good society') is replaced by the *'cold knife thrust of the syllogism'* (WP II 431), a mode of discourse the objectivity of which severs the organic link between the pre-Socratics and their discourse and, by turning the latter into a reasoning articulated through logical strictures, emphasises the depersonalisation of the philosopher and makes him *'the embodiment of cool, triumphant reasonableness'* (WP II 431). As indicated by Plato himself in the *Cratylus* to speak the truth will hereafter mean to 'say things as they are'.[29]

Set within this wider context, the psychology of Socratism finds its true function: to genealogically reveal the way the metaphysical conception of truth has been able to supersede its archaic counterpart. Socrates is identified as a catalyst.[30] As we know, he is depicted by the later Nietzschean texts as a being endowed with 'depraved and anarchic instincts', as a 'monster' whose physical aspect is the (un)aesthetic reflection of internal disorders. According to the Pre-Socratic logic of truth, however, his ugliness would have been in itself the refutation of his thought – not a theoretical proof, to be sure, but a judgment from nature that would have revealed Socrates' utter lack of the harmonious *ethos* necessary to found the truth of his discourse.[31] Being prevented by his unbalanced nature from being a Master, Socrates was forced to develop a hyper-rationalist attitude: 'shrewdness, clarity, severity and logicality as weapons against *the ferocity of the drives*. These must be dangerous and threaten destruction: otherwise there would be no sense in developing shrewdness to the point of making it into a tyrant'(WP II 433). The original 'tyranny of truth', which stemmed from the Master's power to impose his own truth on others and was the immediate consequence of his faith in himself, was therefore reversed into a 'counter-tyranny'(TI, 'The Problem of Socrates' 9).Tyrant in spite of himself, Socrates was mostly tyrannised, 'to make a tyrant of shrewdness: but for that the drives must be tyrants' (WP II 433). He became moral *not from choice, it was* de rigueur' (WP II 432), and thus succumbed to the 'greatest seduction'— 'to make oneself abstract, ie to detach oneself' (WP II 428). Now impersonal, truth can be objectively proven so that everyone can agree on it – it has become a commonplace: just like the Athenian democracy itself, it is nothing but a public matter.[32]

III

Interestingly, this conflict between two understandings of truth – archaic and metaphysical – is also operative in another famous oppositionin Nietzsche's thought, that of Christ and Paul. The analogy bears on three points. Firstly, one of the Messiah's most prominent characteristics is the impossibility of dissociating the content of his teaching from his person and from his life, 'Christ has *demonstrated and lived* a new way of life' (WP II 166). The syncope is explicit: demonstrating does not mean giving theoretical reasons – it is, simply enough, living. Messianic truth is proven neither by nor in discourse , 'he no longer required any formulas, any rites for his intercourse with God – not even prayer ... He knows that it is only in the *practice* of life that one feels "divine"'(AC 33). Conversely, 'the life of the Redeemer was *nothing other than his practice*, and this is what makes it a real life, *a life in truth*' (WP II 166). Secondly, Christ is endowed, like the ancient Masters, with the internal harmony that allows him to ground in his personal *ethos* the truthfulness of his words. He possesses 'the deep *instinct* for the way one must live in order to feel oneself in heavens, to feel oneself "eternal"'(AC 33). Echoing the 'severe necessity' characteristic of the pre-Socratics, the intuitive 'depth' of this instinct unifies his life and his works. As suggested by the predominance of 'feeling' and by the absence of any reflective element (one *'feels* in Heaven', one *'feels* eternal', or again one *'has the feeling* of being divine') Jesus – like the archaic Greeks – is thus defined by a *naïveté*,[33] the Christian equivalent of which reveals itself as the Messianic 'innocence'. Finally, he is no more a dialectician than the pre-Socratics: *'dialectic is equally lacking : the very idea is lacking that a faith, a "truth", might be proved by reasons'* (AC 32). Christ does not try to convince through objective proofs, neither does he seek to elicit beliefs that are deemed too intellectual: 'Christ's faith is not set in formulas – it *lives*, it is diffident of formulas … The *experience of "life"*, as he alone knows it, it adverse to any kind of letter, formula, law, faith, tenet' (AC 32). Ultimately, Christ's teaching is not theoretical: it is embodied by his life.

In fact, the Messiah is the very archetype of the 'Master of Truth' in that he gives the notion of an adequation between the man and his word, which is the very core of the magisterial relationship, its strongest meaning. Christ is *by definition* the incarnated Word. The reason why he 'does not require any formulas, any rites in his intercourse with God'(AC 33) is that he is the 'glad tiding' (AC 35) become human. In this, he reveals himself as the absolute singularity, the very incarnation of the singular – *'there was only one Christian, and he died on the Cross'* (AC 39), a fact which in turn has two major consequences. Firstly, Christ's incommensurability to anyone but himself gives his discourse absolute credence: spoken by the one who is above all men, the Messianic word will be truer than any other. Secondly, this singularity is an 'exemplar' (WP II 169) insofar as what it demands from the disciples is not a merely intellectual comprehension, but practice: *'Christianity is a way of life, not a system of beliefs'* (WP II 212). Christ does not convince, but converts. He shows us *'how to act, not what we ought to believe'* (WP II 212). For this reason, the *imitatio Christi* reveals itself as the hidden horizon and the extreme limit of the magisterial relationship. By imitating Jesus, the disciples will directly partake, through an effect of quasi-magical contagion, of the Messianic *ethos* itself. Thus, 'only Christian *practice*, a life such as he lived who died on the cross, is Christian' (AC 39).

While the figure of Christ functions as the religious transposition of the Pre-Socratic 'Master of Truth', Paul can be interpreted as the Christian analogon of Socrates. Just like the latter, Paul is 'passionate' and 'violent' (D 68). He is a 'very tormented, very pitiable, very unpleasant man who also found himself unpleasant' (D 68). The very existence of this torment and the lack of serenity that results from it are in themselves proofs of the loss of the original 'innocence' or naïveté: Paul is a Modern in that he is a man of reflection preyed upon by internal divisions that create a succession of anarchic cycles, in which exhilarated moments alternate with depressive fits. Moreover, the reason why Paul is incapable of truth is that, like Socrates himself, he is fighting against his own disorganised nature, 'general problem ... what will become of the man who defames the natural, and denies and degrades its practice?' (WP II 228). Identical problems call for analogous solutions: 'in fact, the Christian proves himself to be an *exaggerated form of self control*: in order to restrain his desires he seems to find it necessary to extirpate and crucify them' (WP II 228). Mirroring the Socratic cure, the Paulinian remedy against the 'natural instincts reinterpreted as vices'[34] will lie in setting up a tyranny whose reactive character is expressed by the fact that – just like in Platonic times – it stems from need, not strength, 'he understood what the pagan world *had the greatest need of*' (WP II 167).[35]

Incapable of being a 'Master of Truth', Paul follows in Socrates' steps by turning against the magisterial relationship itself. In this regard, the form of his 'torment' is highly significant: he 'suffered from a fixed idea, or more clearly from a fixed question ... what is the Jewish *law* really concerned with? And in particular, what is the fulfillment of this *law*?' (D 68). Here again, the presence of an 'obsession' denotes the loss of immediacy; but the fact that it has the *law* as its focus, i.e. a theoretical object, a command which is by definition both abstract and universalising, shows how far Paul has come from the original paradigm of the *imitatio Christi* (that was not grounded in precepts but in the setting of an exemplary model of life). As Socrates did before him, Paul wants to replace facts by interpretations: 'psychology of Saint Paul: the given fact is the death of Jesus. This has to be *explained*' (WP II 171, emphasis added). Since he does not find any explanations in Christ's life, Paul makes them up: 'from the facts of Christ's life and death [Paul] made a quite arbitrary selection, *giving everything a new accentuation*' (WP II 167). This is particularly clear in the case of the Messiah's death. According to the mimetic logic of the magisterial relationship, Jesus' death was nothing more than 'one more sign of how one ought to behave ... Not to resist: this was the *example*' (WP II 170). As the martyrs perfectly understood, this death had to be imitated, not explained:

'salvation through faith (namely, that there is no means of becoming a son of God *except by following the way of life taught by Christ*)' (WP II 170). Yet Paul gave a formal meaning to the Messiah's ending by rein-terpreting it in a transcendent way, as a promise of redemption through which the sensible world is deprecated a second time.[36] The essentially immanent notion of *imitatio Christi* was thus reversed, 'into the faith that one is to believe in some sort of miraculous subtraction of sins' (WP II 170), whereas in fact, 'it is false to the point of nonsense to find the mark of the Christian in a "faith", for instance in the faith in redemption through Christ' (AC 39).

By giving Christ's death a theoretical meaning, Paul is not only mis-taken he caused others to break away from the magisterial relationship. Like Socrates before him, he proceeds by inventing 'counterfeits of true Christianity',[37] *formal* counterfeits that are best characterised by their impoverished existential content. Thus, 'the teaching that the son of man is the son of God, the *living relationship between God and man* : this is made into the "second person of the divinity"'(WP II 170, emphasis added). The concrete, living individual is reinterpreted as an abstract person, a move which in itself is symbolical of the passage from the Greek emphasis on singularity to the formalism of the Roman world.[38] In the same way, 'brotherhood on the basis of sharing food and drink together after the Hebrew-Arabic custom, [is seen] as the "miracle of transubstantiation"' (WP II 170). An ordinary practice (the sharing of food) is torn from its local origin (the 'Hebrew-Arabic custom') and turned into a dogma, the dramatic consequences of which (during the Reformation) Nietzsche, as a Pastor's son, could not but be aware of. The common point between these examples is that they use the same decontextualising and depersonalising logic: 'consider with what degree of freedom Paul treats, indeed almost juggles with, the problem of the person of Jesus: someone who died, who was seen again after his death … a mere "*motif*": *he then wrote the music to it*' (WP II 177, emphasis added).

Thus, Paul is the 'inventor of Christianism' (D 68) precisely in that he *betrayed* Christ by turning the embodied 'person of Jesus' into a 'motif', i.e. a decorative element destined to be merged within a wider context (Christianity itself) in which its singularity will disappear. By reversing the former priority of the practical over the theoretical, or more precisely by abolishing the necessity of grounding an individual's ability to speak the truth on his *ethos,* Paul – ironically enough – 'annulled primitive Christianity *as a matter of principle*' (WP II 167, emphasis added).

IV

Yet the most interesting feature of Nietzsche's analyses of the pre-meta-physical understanding of truth and its decline may be that they allow us to identify the deep reason for his condemnation of his contemporaries, 'lack of respect for individual philosophers has involuntarily generalised itself into lack of respect for philosophy' (BGE VI 204). The main evil that Modernity suffers from is *the loss of the magisterial relationship.* Severed from its deep-rootedness in the singularity of the thinker, philosophy has been objectified, 'reduced to a theory of knowledge' (BGE VI 204). The circle of nihilism is now completed: at the very opposite of the positive domination of the 'tyrants of truth', philosophy lives 'its last throes, an end, an agony, something inspiring pity. How could such a philosophy – *dominate!*' (BGE VI 204). As could be anticipated from the disappearance of the magisterial structure, such an agony comes from 'the exaggerated manner in which *the "unselfing" and depersonalisation of the spirit* is being celebrated nowadays as if it were the goal itself and redemption and transfiguration' (BGE VI 207).[39] Attuned to the general – 'already his thoughts roam *to a more general* case' (BGE VI 207) – the German has lost any sense of his own singularity, and reveals himself unable to systematise his being and his thought: 'his habit of meeting everything and experience halfway, the sunny and impartial hospitality with which he accepts everything that comes his way, his type of unscrupulous benevolence, of dangerous concern about Yes and No ... And as a human being he becomes all too easily the *caput mortuum* of these virtues!' (BGE VI 207). In this reversal of the archaic logic, the individual, instead of being the living proof of the virtues expressed by his discourse, becomes the point in which these virtues, unable to root themselves in his ethical substance, degenerate and perish.[40] The Nietzschean practice of philosophy can be interpreted as a desperate attempt to revive the ancient understanding of truth. Thus, the philosophers of the future, these 'new friends of truth', reject the idea that 'their truth [should be] supposed to be a truth for every man, which has hitherto been the secret desire and hidden sense of all dogmatic endeavours' (BGE II 43). Against the universalising assumptions of metaphysics, one must restore the singularity of the magisterial relationship: 'in the end it must be as it is and has always been: great things for the great, abysses for the profound, shudders and delicacies for the refined, and, in sum, all rare things for the rare' (BGE II 44).

This ideal of a scarcity of truth ('all rare things for the rare') is the only way truth can recover its value: the greatness of philosophical conceptions must become again the reflection of the achievements of the individual. Thought has to recover its non-theoretical meaning by being linked anew to the life of the thinker, 'philosophy, *as I have so far understood and lived it*, means living voluntarily among ice and high mountains – seeking out everything strange and questionable in existence' (EH 'Preface' 3). Theoretical comprehension must be rooted in existential experience: understanding something means living it, 'I have always written my writings with my whole body and life. *I do not know what purely intellectual problems are*'.[41] In this existential context it is hardly surprising that Nietzsche should take up the magisterial admonition to honesty originally betrayed by Socrates, then by Paul: 'will to truth does not mean: "I will not allow myself to be deceived" but – there is no alternative – "*I will not deceive, not even myself*"; and with this, we stand on moral ground' (GS V 344). After the collapse of the metaphysical '*Hinterwelten*', the foundation for a cognitive content can only be ethical: truth is not proven, but endured. Conversely, only the philosopher's capacity to endure truth can serve as a criterion to discriminate between philosophies: 'how much truth does a spirit endure, how much truth does it dare? More and more that became for me the *real measure of value*. Error (faith in the ideal) is not blindness, error is cowardice' (EH 'Preface' 3, emphasis added). One must reverse the Socratic principle and the idealist tradition that supports it (the 'faith in the ideal'): contrary to Socrates' famous claim, it is not 'enough' to judge well in order to behave well. One must behave well *prior* to judging well. What really matters, in the formation of knowledge, is the relationship to the self: 'every attainment, every step forward in knowledge, follows from courage, from hardness against oneself, from *cleanliness* in relation to oneself.'[42]

In this endeavour, however, the major difficulty remains the identification of a *modern* criterion for veracity. The scission characteristic of the post-Socratic times makes it impossible for us 'sentimentals' to resurrect the archaic ideal of a natural balance between our instincts. As Schlegel put it, 'the Greek ideal of humanity was perfect concord and symmetry of all powers, natural harmony, but the Moderns show an awareness of inner dissension which makes such an ideal impossible.' The Hellenic 'Golden Age' has vanished, and even Göethe, the greatest of all the Europeans, was unable to retrieve it: 'he felt the profoundest desire to regain the traditional ways of art and to bestow upon the ruins and colonnades of the temple that still remained their ancient wholeness and perfection ... His demands were, to be sure, having regards to the powers possessed by the Modern age, unfulfillable' (HH IV 221).[43] Therefore, the only possibility for us Moderns to tell the truth will depend on the greatest individuals' ability to shape themselves and their lives. Once reflection has settled in, the pre-Socratic integrity can only be recovered *via* a work on the self which aims at restoring the internal unity of character, and consequently the possibility of a necessary connection between the individual's *ethos* and the truth he speaks.

In this regard, Pindar's famous admonition, 'becoming what one is', can be seen as a testimony to the Nietzschean desire to revive the magisterial relationship. One must become *worthy of truth* in order to be able to found it *as* true. This is the deep purport of the 'grand style', of the well-known admonition to 'master the chaos that one is ... to become simple' (WP III 842). The artist has to conquer through art what was freely given by nature to the pre-Socratics – the integrity of an harmonious *ethos*. Thus, he is haunted by an obligation which is the exact transposition of the archaic ideal – to 'turn things into the reflection of our inner plenitude and perfection' (WP III 842). Deprived of the instinctive unity of his archaic forerunners, the modern artist must create himself so as to be able to create. One may therefore apply to him, although in a very different sense, the famous imperative initially expressed in *De Profundis* — 'to turn one's life into a work of art'. Yet, contrary to what Wilde intended in his apology of dandyism, this does not mean that the artist's life might substitute itself for his works as the ultimate, embodied artwork. The true reason why we must turn our lives into works of art is that one's life is the existential condition of possibility of any claim to authenticity, while conversely, the value of an individual's art can only be measured by his capacity for style: 'the greatness of an artist is not measured by the "beautiful feelings" that he elicits ... but by his aptitude to grand style' (WP III 842).

In this regard, Göethe's paradigmatic status and claim to greatness is precisely that he has been able to recover the archaic ideal by satisfying its demand for integrity: 'what he wanted was *totality* ... he *created himself*' (TI 'Raids of an Untimely Man' 49, emphasis added). The 'man', however, was the product of his epoch insofar as he had internalised even its worst characteristics – 'sentimentality, idolatry for nature, the idealistic, unrealistic instincts' (TI 'Raids of an Untimely Man' 49). Yet unlike his contemporaries, Göethe also possessed the ethical stance necessary to the harmonisation of these contradictory qualities – 'he was not fainthearted and took as much as possible upon himself, above himself, *into himself '* (TI 'Raids of an Untimely Man' 49). Thus, Göethe managed to overcome the dissensions typical of the Christian age: 'he fought against the separation of reason, sensation, emotion and will (preached with the most horrifying scholasticism by Kant, the antipodes of Göethe); *he disciplined himself into wholeness'* (TI 'Raids of an Untimely Man' 49).

By disciplining himself, Göethe *stylised* himself: he re-established the archaic harmony between being, doing and speaking, which is the reason why he can be said 'strong enough for freedom' (TI 'Raids of an Untimely Man' 49). Seeing beyond the chimeras of German idealism, that identified freedom with an autonomous faculty the legitimate use of which was to be grounded in rational deliberation, Göethe recovered the *instinctive* sense of freedom, 'the *feeling* of freedom, subtlety, full power, of creative placing, disposing, and forming reaches its peak: in short, *necessity and "freedom of will" then become one"* (BGE VI 213, emphasis added). Contrary to what Spinoza thought, freedom is not necessity well understood: it is necessity well perceived, i.e. the subjective feeling of strength that results from the perfect harmonisation of character achieved either by nature (the pre-Socratics) or *via* art (Göethe himself). In this heroic endeaviour, Göethe reached the paradoxical point 'when we no longer do something "voluntarily" but do everything out of necessity' (BGE VI 213). Freedom unveils itself as compatible with destiny, and bestows on the newly unified individual the 'faith' – another pre-Socratic theme *par excellence* – that is required to 'stand with a glad and trusting fatalism in the midst of the universe' (TI 'Raids of an Untimely Man' 49). Now able to ground the truth of his word in the newly formed integrity of his character, Göethe can claim as his own the highest of all truths, i.e. the 'eternal return', he can endure the knowledge that, 'as a whole, everything affirms and redeems itself' (TI 'Raids of an Untimely Man' 49).

Thus, Nietzsche's reconstruction of the pre-Socratic understanding of truth plays an architectonic part in the Nietzschean corpus: going back to the very origins of our history, it enables us to grasp the common point between such diverse events as the invention of metaphysics and of adequationist truth by Socrates and the reformulation and betrayal of Christ's teaching by Paul. In both cases, the truth-speaking power that the 'Master of Truth' derived from his personal excellence is brought down. In both cases, the principal cause of this fall is *ressentiment*: because they were by definition unable to enter the magisterial relationship, Socrates and Paul turned against it and replaced it by an abstract, impersonal understanding of truth. Moreover, the ideal horizon outlined by the possibility of recovering the archaic conception of truth allows for a better understanding of the importance devoted by Nietzsche to the theme of self-creation and to such heroic figures as Göethe or Zarathustra. For each of these modern heroes of truth, the ultimate stake of the metamorphosis of the self is to recover the unified *ethos* in which the archaic 'tyrant' could ground his own truth, and thus to revive the magisterial relationship.

Finally, this prospect sheds a new light on Nietzsche's relationship to his own thought. Most commentators have underlined the highly personal character of Nietzsche's writings, and the necessity – explicitly expressed in *Ecce Homo* – to take into account the author's psychology in the interpretation of his work. In this regard Nehamas and Thiele have defended apparently opposed theses. According to Nehamas Nietzsche created himself as a literary character through his writings, while for Thiele he used his writings to shape his own life.[44] Both interpretations obviously share the same assumption, namely that it is impossible to read Nietzsche's texts without linking them to the self-creating work done by the author on himself.[45] As Nietzsche states, 'my judgment is *my* judgment: no one else is so easily entitled to it – that is what such philosophers of the future may perhaps say of themselves' (BGE II 43). It is hardly difficult to recognise, in this deep continuity between speaker and spoken word, the main characteristic of the magisterial relationship, i.e. the necessary rooting of philosophical truth in the *ethos* of the philosopher. In the light of this, it does not come as a surprise to see Zarathustra, Nietzsche's spokesman, defined by his truthfulness: 'his doctrine, and his alone, has truthfulness (*Wahrhaftigkeit*) as the highest virtue' (EH Why I am a Destiny 3). The 'Last Men', because of their lack of ethical substance (they suffer from the 'cowardice of the idealist who flees from reality'), can only triumph '*at the expense of truth* and at the expense of the future' (EH Why I am a Destiny 3), by renouncing the magisterial relationship and by taking refuge in the intelligible world, a move that also provides them with a criterion for (adequationist) truth. In contrast Zarathustra is the living synthesis of the three figures of mastery analysed by Détienne: at the same time Poet, Seer and Legislator, and 'more truthful *(wahrhaftiger)* than any other thinker'(EH Why I am a Destiny 3) he will be the 'Master of Truth' of the future.

Bibliography of cited works by Nietzsche

Beyond Good and Evil (New York: Vintage Books, 1989, trans. W. Kaufmann)
Daybreak (Cambridge: Cambridge Uuniversity Press, 1982, trans. R. J. Hollingdale)
Ecce Homo (New York: Vintage Books, 1967, trans. Kaufmann)
Human, All Too Human (Cambridge: Cambridge UP, 1986, trans. R. Schacht)
The Antichrist in *The Portable Nietzsche* (New York: Penguin Books, 1968, trans. W. Kaufmann)
The Gay Science (New York: Vintage Books edition, 1974, trans. W. Kaufmann)
The Will to Power, trans. W. Kaufmann (New York: Vintage Books, 1967, trans. W. Kaufmann and
R.J. Hollingdale)
Twilight of the Idols (Indianapolis: Hackett Publishing Company, 1997, trans. R. Polt)

Notes

1 See Maudemarie Clark on the 'problem of self-reference' in *Nietzsche on Truth and Philosophy* (Cambridge : Cambridge University Press, 1990) p. 3 and A. Nehamas on the 'paradox ofinterpretation' in *Nietzsche: Life as Literature,* (Cambridge Mass. : Harvard University Press, 1985) p. 66.

2 See M. Heidegger, *Nietzsche*, vol. III, (San Francisco : Harper and Row, 1979, trans. D.F.Krell) pp. 123–149.

3 See for example, Walter Kaufmann *Nietzsche: Philosopher, Psychologist, Antichrist* (Princeton: Princeton University Press, 1974); Jean Granier: *Le problème de la vérité dans la philosophie de Nietzsche* (Paris: Presses Universitaires de France, 1966) and Arthur Danto: *Nietzsche As Philosopher* (New York, MacMillan, 1965).

4 One should note, however, that the question is more complex than it seems. Admittedly, the first text that Nietzsche explicitly devoted to truth ('On Truth and Lie in the Extra-Moral Sense') is already strongly critical in that it stipulates that our truths are 'illusions we have forgotten are illusions', they are linguistic transpositions of reality born from the needs intrinsic to communication itself, and whose metaphoric character has been covered-up by their repeated use. See D. Breazeale (ed.): *Philosophy and Truth: Selections from Nietzsche's Notebooks of the Early 1870's* (New Jersey: Humanities Press, 1979, trans. D. Breazeale) p. 84. Yet, as Clark has shown, the early Nietzsche's attacks against language-borne truth remain metaphysical: the metaphorical character that condemns our truths to falsity stems from the impossibility for language to be a faithful reflection of the 'in-itself'. Thus, 'we believe we know something about the things themselves when we speak of trees, colors, snow, and flowers; and yet we possess nothing but

metaphors for things, *metaphors which in no way correspond to the original essences'* (D. Breazeale: *Philosophy and Truth* p. 83, emphasis added). Therefore, Nietzsche's early claims about truth implicitly rest upon the (Kantian) infra-structure of Schopenhauer's *World as Will and Representation*, which presupposes both a noumenal essence for phenomena (the 'things themselves', their 'original essence') and an adequationist conception of truth (the reason why linguistic metaphors are false is that they do not 'correspond' to the 'things in themselves'). Although he recognises the impossibility of any correspondence with the noumenal, the young Nietzsche remains enough of a metaphysician to deplore its lack.

5 The relationship between truth, schematisation and falsification of reality is one of the major contributions of Heidegger's analysis of Nietzsche in *Nietzsche,* vol. III. See pp. 68–76. On the Nietzschean critique of categories, see Michel Haar: *Nietzsche et la métaphysique* (Paris: Gallimard) chap. 1, 'La subversion des catégories logiques et des identités'.

6 Thus, truth is defined as 'the sort of *error* without which a certain type of being could not live' (WP II 493), a statement which in itself presupposes that efficiency cannot be the determining criterion for thinking truth. For criticism of Nietzsche's supposed 'pragmatism' see A. Nehamas, *Life as Literature* pp. 52–55; M. Clark, *Nietzsche and Truth* pp. 12–13, 31; John Wilcox: *Truth and Value in Nietzsche,* (Ann Arbor: University of Michigan Press, 1974) and especially 'Nietzsche Scholarship and the "Correspondence Theory of Truth": the Danto case', *Nietzsche-Studien* 15 (1986) p. 337–357.

7 See R. Rorty: *Consequences of Pragmatism* (Minneapolis: University of Minnesota Press, 1982).

8 See. Michel Haar, *Nietzsche* chapter 3, 'Le renversement du Platonisme et le nouveau sens de l'apparence'.

9 Marcel Détienne: *Les Maîtres de vérité dans la Grèce archaïque* (Paris, Pocket, 1994). All translations are my own. Hereafter MTAG.

10 Cited by L. Thiele: *Nietzsche and the Politics of the Soul: A Study of Heroic Individualism* (Princeton: Princeton University Press, 1990) p. 25.

11 See F. Nietzsche: *Philosophy in the Tragic Age of the Greeks* (Chicago: Regnary Gateway, 1962, trans. M. Cowan) p. 24.

12 *Ibid,* (emphasis added).

13 *Ibid,* p. 66

14 *Ibid,* later preface (1879) p. 79 (my emphasis).

15 *Ibid.*

16 On this question see Tracy Strong's excellent analyses in *Friedrich Nietzsche and the Politics of Transfiguration* (Berkeley: University of California, 1975) pp. 135–185.

17 'Naïve' art is that which is achieved through unconscious harmony with nature and instinct, the (irretrievable) model of which is the Greeks of the classical age. By contrast, 'sentimental' poetry is born from reflection on the

creative process itself, its aims and its relation to its past. The distinction is taken up by Nietzsche in BT 4 where Homer is described as the epitome of the naïve poet.

18 F. Schlegel: *Philosophical Fragments* (Minneapolis:University of Minnesota Press, 1991, trans. P. Firchow) p. 51.

19 F. Nietzsche: *Volonté de Puissance: essai d'une transmutation de toutes les valeurs* (Paris: Gallimard, 1913) I 76 (emphasis added)

20 See HH 262. The theme of 'severity' is recurrent in BGE (see 210) in which Nietzsche closes the circle of Western history by describing the 'philosophers of the future' as 'severe spirits'.

21 According to Détienne: the king as the head of political power, considered in his judicial capacity.

22 Such as an alibi, for example.

23 According to the same logic, the Seer's truth cannot be tested against reality because it *shapes* it. By predicting the future, the seer transforms it (see Oedipus).

24 See TI 'History of an Error' 2. See Jacques Derrida: *Eperons* (Paris: Flammarion, 1978) p. 37.

25 See for example BGE 239.

26 See BT 15.

27 As opposed to the sheer numerical particularity that results from the possibility of enumerating many distinct but essentially identical units within a given set of entities.

28 See G. Deleuze: *Nietzsche et la philosophie* (Paris: Presses Universitaires de France, 1966) pp. 183–189.

29 Plato: *Cratylus, Parmenides, Greater Hippias, Lesser Hippias* (London: Heinemann, 1926, trans. H.N. Fowler) 385b

30 As Nietzsche states, 'with the Greeks everything goes quickly forwards, but it likewise goes quickly downwards; the movement of the whole machine is so accelerated that a single stone thrown into its wheels makes it fly to pieces. Socrates, for example, was such a stone' (HH 261).

31 In fact, this is a reversed form of Hegelianism. In the *Aesthetics*, the beauty of the Greek God's statue was construed by Hegel as the plastic expression of the harmony between spirit and matter itself symbolised by the uninterrupted line of the God's nose, that link his brow (spirit) to his lower face (matter). According to a similar reasoning, Socrates' ugliness appears as a testimony to the fundamentally disharmony to governs him.

32 It is worth mentioning that Détienne too sees in the birth of Greek democracy the major cause of the decline of the magisterial understanding of truth. Thus, 'the hoplitic reform signifies the end of the warrior as a particular individual, and the extension of his privileges to the citizen' (MTAG p. 132). The disappearance of the Homeric hero's aura is accompanied by the apparition of a 'common space' (*meson*) in which the right to speak and the goods are

shared. The '*es meson*' speech is related to the interest of the group, and must be addressed to all the members of the assembly (*ibid*, p. 143). It is mostly a 'dialogue-speech, mostly egalitarian' (*ibid*, p. 145), which 'is mostly grounded in the social group's agreement, itself manifested by approbation or disapprobation' (*ibid*, p. 146).

33 Christ is said to be a 'naïve' and a 'great symbolist' (AC 34). On this point, see M. Haar: *Pardela le nihilisme: Nouveaux essais sur Nietzsche* (Paris, Presses Universitaires de France 1998) pp. 65–122.

34 *Volonté de puissance* I 387

35 As Nietzsche states, 'people like St Paul have an evil eye for the passions...hence their idealistic tendency aims at the annihilation of the passions, and they find perfect purity in the divine. Very differently from St Paul and the Jews, the Greeks directed their idealistic tendency precisely toward the passions and loved, elevated, gilded, and deified them' (GS 139).

36 See AC 40. Nietzsche indicates clearly the link between Plato's invention of the intelligible world and the way it was taken up (under a moralising form) by Christianity in TI 'History of an Error'.

37 Nietzsche gives the following examples: 'a God who died for our sins; redemption through faith; resurrection after death' (*Volonté de puissance* I 366).

38 Consider the invention by Roman Law of the notion of the juridical person as opposed to that of the individual.

39 One will recognise in this vocabulary Paul's 'counterfeits'.

40 Because this blind acceptance of the real is the very opposite of a virtue: see Z 'Of the Three Metamorphoses'.

41 Cited in L. Thiele: *Nietzsche and the Politics of the Soul: A Study of Heroic Individualism* (Princeton: Princeton University Press, 1990) p. 131.

42 *ibid* (emphasis added).

43 The rest of the passage, however, shows the same optimism as in the last chapters of *The Birth of Tragedy* in that it concludes on the possibility of a renewal of the 'Golden Age': 'the sorrow he feels was widely compensated by the joy from knowing that they had been realised in the past and that we can still partake of this achievement' (HH 221). Later Nietzsche will give up this hope, along with the faith in a renewal of Dionysism through Wagner's opera.

44 A. Nehamas, *Life as Literature*, chap. 1 and L. Thiele: *Nietzsche and the Politics of the Soul*.

45 See also T. Sadler's interpretation, for whom Nietzsche has a 'heroic' conception of writing, *Nietzsche: Truth and Redemption* (London: Athlone Press, 1995) pp. 116–174.

8
Nietzsche and the doctrine of metempsychosis

Christian Kerslake

An ambivalence concerning the past and memory runs like a faultline through Nietzsche's work[1]. In *Assorted Opinions and Maxims* 223, criticising the practice of direct self-observation in the pursuit of self-knowledge, he argues that 'we require history, for the past continues to flow in us in a hundred waves; we ourselves are, indeed, nothing but that which at every moment we experience of this continued flowing.' The notion of interiority is unravelled here by means of an image of the preservation and action of the past in the present. Compare *Daybreak* 441, entitled 'Why what is closest grows more and more distant':

> The more we think about all that has been and will be, the paler grows that which is. If we live with the dead and die with them in their death, what are our 'neighbours' to us then? We grow more solitary – and we do so because the whole flood of humanity is surging about us. The fire within us, which is for all that is human, grows brighter and brighter – and that is why we gaze upon that which immediately surrounds us as though it had grown more shadowy and we had grown more indifferent to it.

In both these texts, the past is conceived as the body of a flood, a massive, ongoing surge that issues in the present but whose force and weight dwarf the fragile line of foam that is left on the shore, marking the extent of the thrust. In both texts humanity is identified with the body of the waves; the waves form our *substance*. As late as *Beyond Good and Evil*, we hear the same idea, in the following aphorism: 'the past of every form and way of life, of cultures that formerly lay right next to or on top of each other, now, thanks to this mixture, flows into us "modern souls"' (BGE 224). In a note from the mid-1880's, the notion appears in its starkest form: 'in the mental realm there is no annihilation' (WP 588).

But there is already a sense that the past can overwhelm the present in these aphorisms. To return to the other metaphor in the aphorism from *Daybreak*: 'the fire within us, which is for all that is human, grows brighter and brighter – and *that* is why we gaze upon that which immediately surrounds us as though it had grown more shadowy and we had grown more indifferent to it.' The *flood* that we are is now *aflame*, and the increasing glow lighting up our own bodies makes dim shadows of the things around us.

This image is reminiscent of several elements that circulate in the Platonic idea of reminiscence: having descended from the radiance of the truth, bearing a recollection, an *anamnesis*, of the truth that was first unveiled in the past, the sensible world becomes a dim realm to the dazzled initiate of truth. His surroundings can only be lit up by beauty, which creates a vortex in the sensible world, through which the immortal past can be glimpsed. The difference between Plato and Nietzsche here seems to be that Nietzsche emphasises the *intensity* of memory, the potentially dangerous quantity of light assumed by the initiate, whereas Plato rarely questions the benefits of recollection to life.[2]

In the second *Untimely Meditation*, Nietzsche proposes that the intensity of the past be counteracted by an *act* of forgetting. 'Forgetting is essential to action of any kind, just as not only light but darkness too is essential for the life of everything organic... There is a degree of sleeplessness ... which is ultimately harmful to the living thing' (UD 1). There is an implication here that the dark intestines that support organic activity are not simply unknown – they are also *forgotten* at a certain level. Natural history is still history, and a part of the past, of inheritance. However, the 'degree of sleeplessness' that marks how much of themselves human organisms can afford to bring to consciousness varies according to 'how great the *plastic power* of a man, a people, a culture, is' (ibid). A strong organism will be able to *incorporate* the things of history and the past into itself without allowing them to intrude upon the activity of the present; 'the most powerful and tremendous nature would ... [be able to] draw to itself and incorporate into itself all the past, its own and that most foreign to it, and as it were transform it into blood. That which such a nature cannot subdue it knows how to forget' (UD 1).

Nietzsche's ambivalence towards the past becomes particularly telling here: if a strong nature can transform *all* the past into blood, even what is most foreign, firstly why does Nietzsche say that 'forgetting is essential to action of *any* kind' (italics added), and secondly, why the need for the concluding sentence of the quotation? What would be left that is resistant to being subdued?

Moreover, Nietzsche says that it is the ability to act *unhistorically*, or in an *untimely* way, that allows for the possibility of victory in a crisis: 'He who cannot sink down on the threshold of the moment and forget all the past, who cannot stand balanced like a goddess of victory without growing dizzy and afraid, will never know what happiness is' (*ibid.*). However, this forgetting does not appear to yield utterly undetermined action, but rather the smooth operating of the incorporated wisdom of the past – such would be the 'balance' that is the condition of victory. But surely this would amount precisely to a 'transform[ation of the past] into blood'? Is there a confusion in Nietzsche at this point, or is he trying to gesture towards something interesting and perhaps only half-grasped? If we read carefully, it can be seen that Nietzsche does not intend the act of forgetting to obliterate the past, but rather to allow it to come to the surface more smoothly, unhindered by self-consciousness. It is the consciousness of the past, or the ability of the conscious part of ourselves to cope with and channel the past, that is criticised. But if forgetting then acts *in the service of* the past, as a faculty that appears to condition the flow of a more profound power of bodily memory, then we need to criticise our ordinary notions of forgetting and memory.

In *Daybreak* 126, written about six years later, we find the claim that 'it has not yet been proved that there is *any such thing* as forgetting; all we know is that the act of recollection does not lie within our power.' The question of memory and forgetting, and of the past in general, is intimately bound up with the question of our power, or lack of it, over the past; in fact it puts in question the notion of power itself. For example, the more one *tries* to repeat a past event, the more the past event retreats from our capabilities. Thus to interrogate memory as a faculty runs the risk of actually obscuring the question of the influence of the past; and to this day, memory remains one of the obscurest parts of mental functioning. To continue *Daybreak* 126: 'We have provisionally set into this gap in our power that word "forgetting", as if it were one more addition to our faculties. But what, after all, does lie within our power! – if that word stands in a gap in our power, ought the other words not to stand in a gap in our *knowledge of our power*?'

Concepts of memory are therefore often as elusive as memory itself. For Plato, *anamnesis* is clearly something different from recollection as the faculty of retrieval. For Nietzsche, the fact that the power of our faculty of memory not only does not exhaust the power of the past, but confuses it, produces on the one hand a suspicion, sometimes even a paranoia, concerning the powers of the past, and on the other hand a desire to approach these powers. After all, 'we ourselves are indeed nothing but that which at every moment we experience of this continued flowing' of the past.

In *Human, All too Human* (12–13), Nietzsche describes dreaming as the return of the brain to its pre-historic habits; sleep lets us fall through layers of the past into what is most archaic. The incorporated errors of cultivated humanity are thus superficial; in dreaming, we experience the conflicts that gave rise to these incorporations and their valuations, and alongside them the drives in their primitive form. Dreams are, in a sense, a recollection of the most distant past; not recollection of an actual event, but of the psychic life of the past. This occurs in the manner of an *anamnesis* of something we forget in the light of day. As in Platonic *anamnesis*, we cannot say that we *recognise* the events that are recalled in this kind of 'memory'; what is recalled is not a memory of something that has been lived in this life. For Plato and the mystical tradition such memories can only be of *past lives*.

In *Thus Spoke Zarathustra*, it is not a dream, but a nightmare that precipitates Nietzsche's account of the Eternal Return. In Book Two, the chapter entitled 'The Prophet' starts by telling how nihilism is creeping upon the present; the prophet of nihilism declaims that 'we have grown too weary even to die; now we are still awake and we live on – in sepulchres!' Zarathustra is plunged into a depression at this because it closes off the beautiful future he has been envisaging with and for his disciples. For three days he doesn't eat, and he goes into a sleep or trance. Finally he awakes and tells of his dream. He is sitting among coffins, guarding the dead. 'Life overcome regarded me from glass coffins.' The past lies before him, cut off from the activity of the present. The past is dead, just as a memory is a sterile image, visible through the glass coffin of a memory-image. Time passes listlessly, without event, until three crashing bangs on the gate shake Zarathustra from his torpor. He tries his key to the door, but it no longer fits.

> Then a wind tore the door asunder: whistling, shrilling and piercing it threw to me a black coffin:
>
> And in the roaring and whistling and shrilling, the coffin burst asunder and vomited forth a thousand peals of laughter.
>
> And from a thousand masks of children, angels, owls, fools, and child-sized butterflies it laughed and mocked and roared at me.

This terrified me dreadfully: it prostrated me. And I shrieked with horror as I had never shrieked before.

But my own shrieking awoke me – and I came to myself.

What is the meaning of this nightmare? Zarathustra shakes his head to the optimistic interpretation of his disciples, who say that Zarathustra himself is the wind stirring up the sepulchres and introducing into them the gaiety of children's laughter. The laughter of these masks of children seems demonic and choking. But Zarathustra offers no interpretation. Instead, we glean from the following chapter, 'On Redemption', what was at stake. The past itself, in some way, must be willed. If it is not to become a countermovement to the present, the will must be taught to *will backwards*.

Does this simply mean that we must recognise that will to power was at work in the past as much as it is now? No – it is the form of the past itself that is the problem, not its contents. The macabre images of the coffin are *masks* of children, owls and fools; they have a strangely static quality while a shrieking issues from the writhing, indeterminate creature underneath. They are like the souls of the dead in Hades as described by Homer. The dead Patroclus emerges from the Underworld to visit Achilles in a dream; his deathly presence can only be admitted into the phenomenon of the dream. When Achilles wakes and tries to grasp the spirit, it vanishes in a wisp of smoke and goes gibbering underground.[3] When Odysseus tries to grasp his dead mother in his journey to the Underworld, 'three times she fluttered out of my hands like a shadow or a dream.' His mother tells how, when the body dies, the *psyche* 'flitters out like a dream and flies away.'[4] These *psychai* are insubstantial yet not disembodied: they are like dream and memory images in more than one respect. Dead souls are found in Hades carrying out the most celebrated activities from their lives: thus Orion still hunts in Hades.

There is a horror of this insubstantiality in Nietzsche's invocation of the contents of the coffin. If the chapter 'Of Redemption' reveals these images to be the souls of the past, a multiplicity of shrill ghosts who suddenly overwhelm the possibilities of the present, then given Nietzsche's previous affirmation of the presence of the whole of the past in the life of the present, why does *this* episode spark the chain of parables that lead to the Eternal Return? What is it about this influx of the past into the present, that is so terrifying to Zarathustra?

For Nietzsche, the past *lives* in us, yet is obviously excluded from our willing. Not only are memory-images like ghosts, but the life of the past itself is really only a half life in that it cannot *change*, nor can it be affected by anything else, although it has a peculiarly powerful insistence of its own. But it is this paradox that generates the metamorphosis of the concept of will in Nietzsche. The will can only learn to control the influx of the past by learning to 'will backwards'. The will cannot just reconcile itself with the past, as the past itself is a permanent feature of existence, a permanent realm of ghosts untouchable by will; there is no way of sublating the past *itself*. 'The will that is will to power must will something higher than any reconciliation – but how shall that happen? Who has taught it to will backwards, too?' (Z, 'Of Redemption'). Nietzsche recognises that the will cannot *overcome* the past either – the past cannot be commanded, or 'willed over'. He is instead proposing another option under the slogan 'willing liberates': precisely through the principle of the permanence of the past, Nietzsche proposes the idea that the past is *still acting in the present*. Thus, in a sense the past and present merge, the coffins break open again, and the liberation of the willing of the past in the present 'redeems' the ghosts from their insubstantial existence. Whereas the notion of will was previously conceived as present activity geared towards dealing with the environment, now it is admitted that the notion of willing, as present activity, does not exclude a plurality of wills. Hence the past actually does live in us, and continues to live *and will* in us. The past becomes present. The archaic influx thus constitutes us as willing.

A new problem emerges. The masked, spectral inhabitants of the black coffin are presumably resuscitated; blood is poured back into their veins, and they thereby lose their nightmarish character. But if the ghosts have returned to life through the destruction of the distinction between present and past, then our cohabitation of this reborn, eternal world with the inhabitants of the past gains a new uncanniness. *We* seem to have become lost in this plurality of willing. A plurality of willing runs through *us*. Our status as present beings granted the prerogative of looking back at the past no longer holds, because the life of the past has invaded the present.

To recall again *Beyond Good and Evil* 224: for us 'modern souls', 'our drives now run back everywhere; we ourselves are a kind of chaos – : in the end [however] … 'the spirit' perceives its advantage in all this. Through our semi-barbarism in body and desires we have secret access everywhere, as no noble epoch has ever had, and above all access to the unfinished cultures and to every semi-barbarism that has ever existed on earth'. But how can such a 'spirit' that can perceive its advantage be granted a special role in the plurality of willing?

A clue lies in the notion of 'semi-barbarism'; i.e. never complete barbarism. These notions of access to the past should be placed alongside the intertwined notions of incorporation and truth as error from *The Gay Science* onward. For Nietzsche the abbreviations and errors of organisms, such as the cognitive framing of the perceptual world so that it yields stable substances and can select causal patterns, are necessary tools for the survival of that organism, whose first 'error' is to believe that it itself is necessary. These errors are incorporated into the body, brain and culture of that organism.

Bearing in mind these qualifications, we may now discern a 'who', a spirit, in the midst of this plurality of willing. It is none other than the voice of the species, the presiding set of errors that must be incorporated into the species if it is to become powerful. The universe refigured under the sign of the will to power brings us back to ourselves as *herd mentality*. The spirit is herd mind.

However, as power relations are still current in us, the congregation of impulses preserving herd mentality are always at the mercy of other continuing impulses. Numerous drives still act through us. Hence the incorporations of error still coexist with older, archaic drives that have preserved themselves in the emergent unity of the mind. Thus only a 'semi-barbarism' is possible for a living creature, because a *proportion* of archaic and incorporated error is necessary for the minimum of life.

Now, we need to briefly comment on how Nietzsche manages to see through the lures of his own herd-mind. This is a subject in itself, but because it is important for what follows, I shall mention six ways out of the herd mind that are found by Nietzsche. Firstly, the continuing presence of affects that counter-attack consciousness, thus opening different possibilities for life, different pleasures. This, secondly, promotes a suspicion concerning one's servitude to *particular* goals and habits. Thirdly, on an historical scale, the dialectic of truth best described by Nietzsche in *On the Genealogy of Morals* (III 27), shows how the drive for truth ends up sabotaging its moral and religious presuppositions, and then itself.

Then there are three affective patterns that happen to be incarnated together in Nietzsche: firstly the phenomenon of pain experienced as joy that had been an avowed personal obsession of Nietzsche's from *The Birth of Tragedy* onwards; the breaching of the limits of the individuated body gives off a mysterious scent of joy, as if there is something in it crying to get out. Then, on the other hand, there is illness and consequent retreat because of it. Among the numerous parallels with shamanism in Nietzsche's thought, this is particularly strong. A shaman is often considered chosen after the occurrence of a protracted psychosomatic illness. The corresponding retreat turns his or her mind back upon their body in a mutually destabilising way; accordingly, shamanic initiation will often exacerbate this process through the ritual dismemberment of the novice's body, and its surrendering up to demons. Finally, there is the experience of ecstacy, such as it appears in the vision of the eternal return at Sils-Maria, in which a high tension of the body issues in a loss of personal self and a feeling of timelessness.

These experiences show the body to be not just the incorporation of the past, but the play of incorporations and drives. They lead Nietzsche to start to distrust the Person the body supports – the 'who' that we saw with horror was none other than the voice of the species. As Pierre Klossowski puts it, '[Nietzsche] began to distrust his own brain.'[5] As Klossowski also remarks in his essay 'Nietzsche, Polytheism and Parody', the question of aphorism 110 in *The Gay Science*, 'to what extent can truth endure incorporation?', with its final remark 'That is the question; that is the experiment', assumes a disturbing quality.[6] Truth, as error by which certain creatures live, will obviously 'endure' incorporation – they are identical. But truth, as adequacy to the growing multiplication of affective perspectives unleashed by Nietzsche, will not – it goes against the grain of incorporation. Nietzsche does not envisage a future incorporation of truth, not foremost because of his scepticism about truth, but because he does not believe that the body will be able to stand it. Truth will entail the dismemberment of the body; whether 'truth' could retain its usual meaning in such an event is another question. Here Nietzsche is gesturing towards a New Body.

But this threat does not just concern a specifically Nietzschean physiology with a concomitant paranoia about the inheritance of 'error'. In the notion of archaic inheritance in its pre-eternal return form, especially in the aforequoted aphorism 223 from *Assorted Opinions and Maxims*, Nietzsche is concerned with the real activity of the past in the present, whether it be in different geographical areas where ways of life are conserved, or in bursts of passion that issue from oneself. There are elements of ourselves that are ancient, and have been lived for generations, whether it be fear of snakes, or the silent helmsman that takes control in moments of crisis. To recall our earlier discussion, if I must forget myself sometimes when I act, how can I say that this is me who is acting? Or is it rather all the more me in that I don't have to think about it? But the question is: can we say this quite so simply if this occult activity has no consciousness? The idea that the multiplicity implicated in the past still acts in the present would seem to unground personal identity more than it might ground it, through its being 'my' past.

The spectres in the coffin terrify Zarathustra because he, as an individual, who has been planning a great future for his *Übermenschen*, not only cannot tolerate the forces of the past without being dismembered in some degree, but he knows that the individuality that underwrites his sense of self-consciousness and preserves him from this dismemberment is a God-blessed, herd creation. This has all the real trappings of a nightmare. The idea of willing backwards entails the fragmentation of the body, through the invocation of a plurality of wills all struggling in the foam of each moment, as the monstrous wave of past and present pushes forward. It is this nightmare double bind, that truth will only be able to be pursued through the fragmentation of the body of inherited errors that in the first place has made something like the concept of truth possible, that finally precipitates Nietzsche's new vision of the idea of eternal return. How can the framing of this great chaotic wave in terms of eternity help the problem? Klossowski calls the eternal return 'a new version of metempsychosis,'[7] and the rest of this essay is devoted to understanding why.

II

The eternal return can be conceived as a grand formulation in absolute terms of the question of the multiplicity of the self. When the vision of return comes to me, I realise that if what it says is true, I must have *forgotten* it, because I have supposedly lived this moment before. I am thus apparently remembering what I had previously forgotten infinitely many times before. And if this moment is to return again, then I am fated to forget the revelation of the eternal return again, in order to remember it again. Klossowski has brought out these notions of remembering and forgetting as essential to Nietzsche's idea. There is an essential likeness between Nietzsche's version of the eternal return and the Platonic myths of *anamnesis*, or recollection, and forgetting. Furthermore, if we now look at the influences at work in Plato's ideas of *anamnesis*, we find further clues as to how to understand the return. The guiding idea that we will trace briefly through Pythagoras, Orphic doctrine, Empedocles and Plato is that of metempsychosis, otherwise known as the transmigration of souls, which concerns the passage of the soul after death into a new body. I will leave aside the Oriental origins of this idea to focus on its role in Greek mystical life. The doctrine attempts to cultivate the experience of a reminiscence, an *anamnesis*, an *un-forgetting*, that one has lived before in a different body, whether it be animal, vegetable, or human. In the reminiscence, one's identity becomes part of a chain of others. The adherent of the doctrine must attempt to avoid forgetting this memory and becoming oblivious to their greater Self. We will investigate whether this is possible in the terms supplied by the doctrine of metempsychosis.

But first Nietzsche's own version of metempsychosis must be described. Klossowski tells how the experience of eternal return must first appear as an experience of the occult communion of all things, a feeling of necessity leading to here and now, a necessity which moreover I have no control over.[8] This feeling becomes a thought, via the dynamic of affective forces that gives rise to thought. But the experience seems to exclude definition in terms of coherent language. Nietzsche's awareness that *this* moment will return, *this* spider's web on *this* rock-face, bears with it the corollary that the next moment will contain a different *this*. His quest to flee the errors of the herd-mind revolves around his desire to set free the configurations of affects that resist the herd-mind. Hence this moment is singular, and not to be connected to the next by means of false connections. Instead we must affirm its secret necessity.

Now, each configuration of affects that I attempt to *know*, I bring into the light of consciousness; but the affect then retreats into darkness.[9] But when an affect takes me by surprise, such as laughter or tears, the light of consciousness recedes. This is a consequence of the fact that 'we simply lack any organ of knowledge' (GS 354); each 'truth' depends on the configuration of errors that gave rise to it, which in turn depend on the configuration of affects at play and giving rise to these errors. All knowing is subject to determination by the affects, even this knowing. Each item of knowledge will be eclipsed by another affective perspective. The hermeneutic circle thus has a concomitant *experience* in the to-ing and fro-ing of the affects determining the perspective of knowledge. It is here that Klossowski locates the birth of the image of the circle: 'there is here a profound necessity inscribed in the law of being which is explicated in terms of the universal wheel, in the image of eternity; that ultimately the inversion of night into day and sleep into the waking state of consciousness results from this law, we see too late. It remains that conscious thought only constitutes itself in the ignorance of this law of return.'[10] To submit to this law is to enter a ceaselessly turning circle; but to *will* this law is something entirely different. It is to see one's own place in the movement of the hermeneutic circle as determined by a larger circle of which one is part. To accept it as a circle, but to accept that one will always be stationed in an epicycle somewhere along the circumference. Thus Klossowski writes that 'vehement oscillations [will] overwhelm an individual so long as he seeks only his own centre and is incapable of seeing the circle of which he is himself a part; for if these oscillations overwhelm him, it is because each one of them corresponds to an individual *other* than the one he believes himself to be, from the point of view of the unfindable centre.'[11]

The revelation that I am many, that *my name is legion*, coincides with the death of God. If there is no one God to whom I am responsible, no basis in totality for the allotment of my continuous identity, then I become abandoned to a fortuitous passage through many apparent identities,[12] this only being obscured by my willed forgetting of this essential openness in myself.

For Klossowski, what is essential in Nietzsche's experience of the return is the transformation involved in its affirmation. If I affirm that this moment will return eternally, then 'at the same time I learn that I was *other* than I am *now* for having forgotten this truth, and thus that I have become other by learning it.'[13] If I am to return eternally, then I must forget the revelation again to come back again as one who has the revelation revealed to me anew in the next cycle. This much is 'logical'. However, Klossowski avers that this forgetting and remembering will continue to happen in *this* life by the economy of the return. If I become other through the return, then I am no longer able to will myself as I have been up until now, because my past becomes detached from me. But I still must will the entire chain that brings me back to now, as that chain led fortuitously to this moment. I re-will all experiences, and all my acts, 'but not as *mine.*'[14] But if I accept that I will forget this moment too, I am really affirming the wider coherence to which I belong – the entire series – at the cost of forgetting this moment too. 'I deactualise my present self in order to will myself *in all the other selves whose entire series must be passed through* so that, in accordance with the circular movement, I once again become what I am at the moment I discover the law of the Eternal Return.'[15] But this series cannot be integrated into a *coherent* totality from *my* point of view; I am excluded from the coherence to which I belong. This is so moreover because 'my present consciousness will be established only in the forgetting of my other possible identities' (*ibid*). Really I must consider my past as having been lived *once and for all*, in order to have a coherent picture of myself at all. So the vision of myself as a mere part of a chain of other possible selves, each with their own affective potentiality, must be forgotten. To will myself as part of this circle, I must forget it in any case, so as to fulfil its movement, and enter into a new phase of the cycle. We then reach the bizarre conclusion that 'it was therefore necessary for me to forget this revelation in order for it *to be true!*'[16] This is ultimately why Klossowski sees the eternal return as 'a simulacrum of a doctrine.'[17] However, this by no means diminishes the insidious power of the thought; it increases it, as if a new insubstantial demon has been set free in the web of thought. The *possibility* of this thought, combined with my suffering of the hermeneutic circle of affective knowledge, is enough to suggest that I renounce being myself *once and for all*. It creates the possibility that different versions of myself coexist, or subsist, with the present one.

Let us descend now for a while from Klossowski's spiralling insinuations, and reflect upon the traditional idea of metempsychosis. One thing strikes us first of all: surely the idea of metempsychosis is precisely meant to concern the preservation of the Person through different transcorporations?[18] It can be considered to be the very first notion of continuous personal identity, simply taking the necessity for a continuity of the Person through the changing states of one body slightly too far – and applying it to many bodies. *If* there is an identity of consciousness throughout different bodily incarnations, then we can say that the same person is involved. Thus Locke argues that if we remember some action of the past as being ours, then we were the person who committed that action, despite the fact that the material of the body has changed in the meantime. He suggests in the *Essay* that metempsychosis does make sense in principle *if* we are conscious of the lives we lived before.[19]

However, while the juridical idea of the immortality of the soul is undoubtedly lurking behind Locke's account of the separability of the Person from the material man,[20] the notion of the immortality of the soul is not necessarily to be found in the ancient accounts of metempsychosis. Furthermore, the justification of the doctrine of metempsychosis in terms of the persistence of the same reflexive consciousness presupposes that the unity of consciousness is already established and unproblematic, whereas the doctrine itself, I will now argue, was initially an expression of the fluidity of mentality. I want to show that the essential elements at work in metempsychosis are memory and forgetting, and metamorphosis; the ideas of disembodiment and immortality often implicated in the doctrine are late additions.

In the Greek accounts of metempsychosis, those of Pythagoras, Plato, and to a lesser extent Empedocles, the notions of forgetting and memory are essential. A supposed seat of consciousness aware of itself as the same throughout incarnations is on the whole absent. Other lives are only remembered during ecstatic or inspired states, or, ultimately, after death. Our notion of memory, as guarantor of the continuity of the seat of consciousness, is in fact what is at stake. Just as when drunk, people remember things they had said and thought the last time they were drunk but had forgotten in between, there arises in metempsychosis the possibility of *different* continuities obeying a hidden law. Moreover the early Greek awareness of the ubiquity of coming-to-be and passing away in the physical world meant that one could not explain the constancy involved in memory, such as it is, by means of the constancy of the body either. Rather the constancy is due to the *economy* that governs the movement of an essential soul through different bodies. This essential soul, or the possibility of it, however, is only intermittently experienced, and from many perspectives.

The Greek mystics attempted to master these perspectives. Empedocles recounts how Pythagoras 'had obtained the greatest wealth of mind… for when he stretched out with all his mind, he easily saw each and every thing in ten or twenty human generations' (B 129)[21]. He praises those who have 'far ranging thoughts', and the flight of the mind in general (B17, B11). We know that the later Pythagoreans powerfully cultivated the religious practice of memory.[22]

The links between early Pythagorism and the Orphic doctrines are well attested, although priority is often disputed. But if we look into Orphic eschatology we see the themes of memory and death coalescing in the idea of metempsychosis. In the myths of the afterlife found at strategic points in Plato we find transmissions of Orphic doctrine. The Myth of Er at the end of the *Republic* echoes the inscriptions on the tiny gold plates excavated in Southern Italy, which give instructions from sacred literature on what the dead soul should do when it arrives in Hades. The one kept in the British Museum reads as follows:

> You will find to the left of the House of Hades a spring
> And by the side of it, standing a white cypress
> To this spring do not approach near
> But you will find another, from the Lake of Memory
> Cold water flowing forth, and there are guardians before it.
> Say, "I am a child of Earth and starry Heaven;
> But my race is of Heaven. This you know yourselves.
> But I am parched with thirst and I perish. Give me quickly
> The cold water flowing forth from the Lake of Memory."
> And they will give you drink from the holy spring,
> And thereafter among the other heroes you shall have lordship.

In Plato's myth, Er looks on as the dead drink from the waters of memory and remember their place in the cycle of rebirths. They then must choose in what form they want to return to the earth. They themselves must choose their *daimon* – the *daimon* will not choose for them – before they drink from the spring in the plain of Lethe, of Forgetting, whence they will ascend back into the world. Klossowski points out the similarities between this myth and Nietzsche's first published account of the eternal return in section 341 of the *Gay Science*: in the *anamnesis* of the eternal return, the demon asks the subject if he will will *this* life again – innumerable times.[23] Here, the option of transmigration into a *different* soul seems precluded by Nietzsche's fatalism. But, as we have seen, if we take the economy of forgetting and remembering in the return seriously, the possibility of metamorphosis is granted with more power than before. We must forget this vision, and enter into a new life, and actualise a different affective potential of the great Circle of which we are a discontinuous part.

The *Phaedo* contains Plato's longest treatment of the notion that the soul must discipline itself in this life in order to remember its place in eternity. Philosophy is practice for death, Socrates famously says. The body must be ceaselessly attenuated, in order that divine memory may return to the mind, disoriented and addled by the sensible world. What Plato advocates here is a kind of death by degree; the more one whittles away the body, the more one becomes permeable to the divine objects of memory. In the Orphic doctrines too, the focus is on death, in the event of which the soul regains its full memory. What is interesting here is that the very nature of the cycle in which the soul wanders, despite being limited in duration, conceptually does not allow for an exit. The doctrine becomes confused here: escape from the cycle is promised to the few, but in the myths of the afterlife, it is the return to earth that is always emphasised. The cycle seems to sweep everything up into it, and precludes a place of rest. The words of another Orphic gold tablet read:

> I have flown out from the circle of heavy grief
> and stepped swift-footed upon the circle of joy[24]

Nevertheless, Empedocles seems to grant that no one, not even the gods, survives the transition to a new cosmic cycle. Moreover, the drink from the waters of memory does not reveal any sense of immortality as we know it; on the contrary, the soul at death must admit into itself a plurality of alien souls. Such an influx of entities into the soul is so opposed to the Christian idea of immortality as to appear demonic.

The idea becomes even more foreign as we examine the religious practices committed under the auspices of the idea of metempsychosis. For Pythagoras and Empedocles, the aim of *this* life was to cultivate memory, and knowledge of the past. Thus Empedocles, advocate of mind-stretching, tells us 'Already have I once been a boy and a girl and a bush and a bird and a silent fish in the sea' (B 117). In fact, in Plato, death is only the most extreme pole of the recovery of memory. The types of divine madness related in the *Phaedrus* – prophecy, divination, poetry and the experience of beauty – are all means of *anamnesis*. They are all relatively *ecstatic* experiences, and approximations in degree to death.

Thus while Plato is usually held to have been one of the first systematic reinforcers of the scission between sensible and intelligible realms, in fact if we attend to the notion of *anamnesis* and its attendant mystical pedagogy, we find rather a plurality of passages between 'realms', all involving the access to an order of time incommensurable with the everyday 'successive' temporality that was to be schematised only later by Aristotle in the *Physics*. The proper context for these ideas and practices lies in the mantic tradition. In his *Principium Sapientiae*, Francis Cornford traces the poet and the prophet back to a common root in archaic Greece.[25] Hesiod tells us that the Muses 'tell of things that are, that will be, and that were, with voices joined in harmony'[26], while in the *Iliad*, 'the past, present and future hold no secrets' to Calchas the seer.[27] Thus Cornford notes that the prophet scries the future by invoking the hidden past and present, while the poet's traditional role as recorder of the past extends into the zone of divine inspiration usually associated with the prophet. Now, if we recall Plato's own union of prophecy, divination, poetry and beauty in terms of the mantic capacities,[28] then we begin to glimpse a truly ecstatic theory of temporality at work in the Platonic theory of *anamnesis*.[29]

These mystical passages of the soul, their ubiquity and their high value in Greek culture, can be seen as the highest expressions of an amazing freedom in the articulation of ideas of the soul in early Greece. There seems to have been no single word or concept for the soul or mind and the various concepts that we can now identify as involving specifically nonphysical animal or human attributes seem to denote essentially mobile and multiple entities or potentialities, whose transformations are ever present. It is possible to find in early cultures many examples of the wandering soul; see for instance Frazer's chapter towards the end of *The Golden Bough*. In Homer the *psyche* as such enters the picture only at the moment of death, or in swooning; in a fragment of Pindar, we find the *psyche* active during dreams[30]: only later did *psyche* come to denote soul in general.[31] During waking life the attribution of action is distributed amongst *nous*, *thumos* (often now translated as 'spirit', a term whose opacity is the sign of a real loss of complex meaning), and many other designations, such as *menos*, *phrenes*, and *prapides*, the latter which we encounter in Empedocles' aforementioned account of the 'stretching of the mind.'[32] These terms still jostle for priority in the fourth book of the *Republic*. It is possible to find the disciplines of the mind referred to just now carried out systematically, with the blessing of official culture, in shamanic tribes; and a number of attempts have been made to find an indirect shamanic influence on mystical Greek cults. It is impossible to go into any of this here, but what we should keep in mind through a dim awareness of this context, is the idea that the domain of ideas of the soul essentially involves movement, an idea that survives right up through Aristotle.

In Greek mystical thinking arising from Orphic and Pythagorean influence, and centering around the idea of metempsychosis, this movement of the soul is anchored, as we have seen, in the mystery of death. Death promises complete *anamnesis*; memory, dreams, prophecy, and in Plato thought and beauty, are approximations to death, ecstases. Memory haunts each of these experiences, but it is a wider memory, in which I myself am ultimately lost as an individual. This is found first in the *experiences* of *ecstasis*, and most powerfully in the overarching doctrine of metempsychosis, where memory of my true self is equivalent to memory of a chain of *other* lives. The soul essentially wanders along the wider circle to which it belongs.

It is essential to emphasise two ideas here. Firstly, metamorphosis. Contrary to the idea that the faculty of memory brings me back to myself, that memory is an index of my continuity as consciousness, memory here signifies the capability of transformation. In the *Phaedrus*, wings begin to scratch and itch under the skin of the beholder of beauty. In the *Meno*, *Phaedo* and *Republic* learning itself involves transformation because it dissipates the veil of forgetting; one doesn't merely accumulate new knowledge, one remembers who one really is. This experience of metamorphosis is present even before it assumes its glorious form in metempsychosis. But once the theory is formulated, anomalous memories and imaginings may in principle finally find their reason as incursions of past lives into the present. One becomes at the mercy of *anamnesis* of one's other participations and incarnations. Sacred dreams are at liberty to become memories.

Secondly, the idea of disembodiment in these constructions is lacking. There are only other embodiments which are remembered. The constancy is provided not by a self-identical wandering soul, but by the memory of one's wider history, which is more or less accessible depending on one's mastery of various esoteric disciplines, or one's luck in finding beauty on this earth. It follows that the soul here is not conceived of as immortal in any Christian sense, but is rather conceived as distributed across a wider coherence, an essential elusive Ur-soul, that is no more an origin than a *telos*, as it is subject to a circular temporality. The idea of metempsychosis, however, does not restore a unity to memory – it scatters the individual through numerous lives. Metempsychosis does not allow the rest of the individual in a grand unicity of the intellect. The circle never stops. The soul's unity with itself is thus only possible through the influx of other souls into the present.

One final connection needs to be made before we can put together the pieces. The Orphic theogonies have a number of interesting details that set them apart from the traditional Hesiodic one. The important role of Chronos, Time, in the theogony, is one such detail, probably of Eastern derivation, that could be dealt with but I will concentrate on the essential, that is, the role of Dionysus, the most important god in the Orphic canon. The theogony tells how Dionysus is born to Persephone (not Semele as in Hesiod) and Zeus. In the traditional version Hera, Zeus's jealous wife, creates the circumstances that lead to Semele's incineration by a thunderbolt, but in the Orphic version she instructs the Titans to kill the child Dionysus. They dismember him and eat the flesh, in a ritual echo of the older Dionysiac rituals. Zeus then punishes them by striking them all with a thunderbolt, reducing them to ashes. Out of these ashes man is formed to bear the guilt of the slaying of Dionysus. Man bears an essential Dionysiac part in himself, but is mostly comprised of the old, sinful Titanic nature. The purpose of his life is to release the Dionysiac element of himself.

Now, it is interesting for our argument that in Nietzsche's account of Dionysiac religion in *The Birth of Tragedy*, when he recounts the myth of Dionysus's birth, he in fact recounts the version of the Orphic theogony (BT 10). Nietzsche would have been well aware of the difference between the Orphic Dionysus and the traditional Dionysus, and it is important to note the spiritualisation that Dionysus undergoes almost immediately in *The Birth of Tragedy* ('the horrible witches' brew of sensuality and cruelty becomes ineffective; only the curious blending and duality in the emotions of the Dionysiac revelers remind us – as medicines remind us of deadly poisons – of the phenomenon that pain begets joy' (BT 2)); Orphic doctrine spiritualised Dionysiac religion probably some time before the emergence of tragedy. Nietzsche's friend Erwin Rohde would in turn make the distinction between the Orphic and traditional Dionysus vital for his argument in his book *Psyche*. Now, with the aid of the metempsychotic reading of eternal return advanced here, we can begin to see that Nietzsche's final invocations of Dionysus, as god of recurrence, in his late works are also tinged with an Orphic taint. Is it possible that throughout his life Nietzsche had really been talking about the *Orphic Dionysus*?

In Orphic doctrine, our eternal soul is *Dionysiac*. The Dionysiac nature of the soul here should alert us that we are not concerned here with immortality as we know it, but rather with the *communion* invoked in Dionysiac ritual. It was Rohde in fact who became famous for defending the thesis that it was Dionysiac religion that first introduced the idea of immortality into Greece in the form of communion. In the tearing of the flesh of the god we identify or communicate with the essential indestructible life that lives in us and through us.[33] But in the Orphic version, what guaranteed communion before is now tainted, because of the Titanic guilt at the slaying of Dionysus. In the mystical tradition we are tracing now, sacrifice has become an abomination. A fragment of Empedocles says 'With the foul slaughter of bulls their altars were not washed, but this was the greatest defilement of life among men: to bereave of life and eat the noble limbs' (B 128.8–10). This is what really separates the mystery religions from state religion, as the latter remained essentially sacrificial; the *event* of sacrifice was essential to all communion.[34] It may appear that the theory of metempsychosis offers an immediate justification for the vegetarianism of the mystics, through the encouragement of the suspicion that one may be eating one's friends or relatives, an idea familiar from the Indian tradition. But it may be more complicated than that, due to the introduction of a peculiar temporality into what was before the raw presence of communion. Here the eternal soul, the Dionysiac part of the soul, is the image of a *memory* of communion, one that issued in dismemberment. The eternal present that is revealed in the communion of the purely Dionysiac cult, becomes shattered into the temporality of metempsychosis in the Orphic cult, in which the forever dismembered soul finds its eternity. It is guilt that keeps us in this single, decentred body, 'paying for an ancient doom,' as Pindar puts it in the second Olympian Ode, which is quoted by Plato before his treatment of *anamnesis* in the *Meno*. This guilt is felt as a lack in the *Phaedo*, where the singleness and crudity of one's earthly body makes one yearn for one's higher, more spiritually extensive body, with its greater memory. Thus one abuses this earthly body, one insults it for its paucity; one tears it until the light of the immemorial past starts to show through the seams. If the body is the anchor of the present, the 'function of reality', to disrupt it is to disrupt one's very unity; the focus of the present is lost, and the body becomes open to the virtual multiplicity it conceals.

I have left out until now the famous Greek mystical notion that 'the body is the tomb of the soul', which is often deemed so vital in Orphic-inspired mystery doctrines, but usually comes to us with attendant proleptic associations with the Christian idea of original sin.[35] Perhaps it is possible to see now that another interpretation of this phrase is possible. The Orphics may well have been the first classic ascetic priests in Nietzsche's sense – haters of both self and world. But the ambivalence in Nietzsche's account of the ascetic is well known – and indeed, what kind of inhuman will to power was necessary for the early shaman-priests to cultivate their esoteric practices to such dangerous levels? As well as being haters of the inadequacies of the body, they were unparalleled thirsters of eternity, thirsters after the Great Body that would dwarf and then shatter the individual, present-bound body. The earthly body is a tomb because it imprisons the lives of the past – and reduced to their minimal form as memory-images, wisps of smoke eluding the dominion of the present (Achilles' grasping hands), they become ghosts inhabiting the sepulchre. Spirits taunt the present-bound body; their fluttering is heard only through echoes, their forms glimpsed only out of the corner of the eye; and yet they set blood racing through the pumping heart, disturbing the temporal centre of this body.

Nietzsche, exemplar of the 'modern soul' coursing with a multiplicity of drives and phantasms, saw that the only way out of the tomb for the Prophet of nihilism was through the Redemption made possible by the invocation of the ancient idea of eternity. The tomb of the memory-haunted body is exploded and redistributed under the law of eternal return. But Dionysus must first be sacrificed – not crucified but dismembered and scattered across the circle of time – before communion with him is able to transcend the present. The circle of eternity channels the flows of history so that the body may participate in each, one at a time, at the cost of forgetting. The more that is remembered, the more the mind and body are besieged by disquiet and unrest; the more the mobility of the body is invoked and goaded. Communion is now experienced as an influx of memory that can so overwhelm the body that it must be forgotten again, so that the body may get up again and continue to stumble on the earth.

Nietzsche sometimes imagines the eternal return as a dance of gods. Nevertheless it is difficult to tell, from our station on the vicious circle of eternity, whether the flailing limbs of Dionysus are really dancing, or whether, like glimpses of shooting stars, they show the movements of an ongoing dismemberment.

III

According to Klossowski, an understanding of the necessity of eternal return helps us to see that the *dramatis personae* of *Thus Spoke Zarathustra* are conjurations of ancient and historical parts of humanity repressed but still at work in the present. 'Not only the reason of millennia – the madness of millenia breaks out in us. It is dangerous to be an heir,' says Zarathustra in 'Of the Bestowing Virtue'. Furthermore, it is not just *personae* that break out; all of those creative acts that we call *personifications* – in which life is attributed to the sun, to rock, vegetable and star – are in fact metamorphoses set free by the law of the return.[36] In the chapter entitled 'On the Islands of the Blest' (itself a Greek mystical term for the place where the good rest from the cycle of metempsychosis), Zarathustra says

> Truly, I have gone my way through a hundred souls and through a hundred cradles and birth-pangs. I have taken many departures, I know the heartbreaking last hours.
>
> But my creative will, my destiny, wants it so. Or, to speak more honestly: my will wants precisely such a destiny.
>
> All *feeling* suffers in me and is in prison: but my *willing* always comes to me as my liberator and bringer of joy.

This willing that wants the destiny of the incarnation of multiple souls can only be conceived under the law of the eternal return. The nightmare in 'The Prophet' describes the pressure of this *feeling*, these affective potentialities, suffering in the prison of one body. The multiplicity of this feeling can only be willed under the law of eternal return which *eternalises*, rather than *unifies* the multiplicity, on condition that forgetting is instituted for each individual soul. Otherwise the body, the site of the closest yet most ancient forces, would shatter. As Nietzsche says, contemplating the idea of eternal return: 'if we could *bear* our immortality – that would be the highest thing.'[37]

In the *Phaedo* Plato counterposes his metempsychotic theory of the soul to the rival theory of the soul as attunement, as the harmony of the elements of the body, which therefore dies with the body. Here, in the Nietzschean vision, we have a bizarre harmony of the two theories. The soul is in effect a detunement of the body into its chaotic impulses and configurations of impulses, that receives a wider, incomprehensible harmony in the circle of eternal return, echoes of which the soul hears at various stations of its circle. Perhaps here we find the reason why Nietzsche says that chaos and circularity are not incompatible.

What is forgotten and remembered in Nietzsche's doctrine of eternal return is no longer the ideal forms, as Plato avows; rather, as Klossowski says, 'forgetting conceals eternal becoming and the absorption of all identities in being.'[38] In the *ecstasis* that marks the vision of the soul into its own eternity, it is an original ecstacy that is recollected, the distribution of the soul across a circle that can never be experienced as a whole. The mortal *experience* of ecstacy is a revelation that seems to promise the dissolution of the soul across time – and all that remains through the fog of oblivion following ecstasis is the strange rhythm of another temporality, whether it be the non-linear temporality of dreams, or the shimmering vortex of beauty created in the sensible world. In all these forms, *anamnesis* marks a returning to eternity. The chaos that produced us is eternalised in a circle in the doctrine of metempsychosis, where everything that is not allowed into the everyday memory of the narrative of this life, returns in phantasms of another life. Metempsychosis is the return to eternity. Nietzsche's renewed version of metempsychosis in the eternal return, as interpreted by Klossowski as a vicious circle, is an eternal returning to eternity.

In *Ecce Homo* Nietzsche relates that the first thing he wrote after the experience of the vision of eternal return was a note dated 'Early August, 1881, in Sils-Maria, 6,000 feet above sea level and much higher above all human things.' It is a plan, largely conceived in terms of the theme of incorporation. He writes: 'What will we do with the *remnants* of our lives – we who have spent the greater part of them in the most essential uncertainty? We shall *teach the teaching* – that is the most potent means of *incorporating* it in ourselves. Our kind of beatitude, as teacher of the greatest teaching.'[39] Precisely in the immediate wake of such an experience, as forgetting begins to encroach, Nietzsche speaks of the difficulty of incorporating it in one life.[40] He must resign himself to *teaching* it – perhaps then he will be able to incorporate it, and begin to glimpse some order to the remnants of his life, each lived in the most essential uncertainty.

By teaching the teaching, he will *learn* it. The teaching fulfils Nietzsche's need to dis-incorporate the affects of the body, but at the price of a unified memory, hence personality. To the extent that Nietzsche continues to live and function as a human being, and to be a teacher of the eternal return, the eternal return itself recedes as a lived reality, and becomes an almost religious belief. 'It is the truth, and it will be experienced in my moments of madness, and I will finally experience it fully when I die. I shall continue to live knowing that it is the truth inscribed in light behind the pierced canopy of the heavens.' The eternal return becomes a mystery doctrine, the simulacrum of a ritual sheltering an impossible experience, like the reflection of light from the flash of steel in the blazing fires at Eleusis.

Recall the terribly moving moment in the Second Dance Song in *Zarathustra*: a personified female incarnation of Life says to him: 'you think, O Zarathustra, I know it, you think of leaving me soon!' She intimates that she has divined his suicidal thoughts. ''Yes', I answered hesitatingly, 'but you also know....' And I said something into her ear, in the midst of her tangled, yellow, foolish locks.' He whispers, in some form, his belief in the eternal return. She replies 'You *know* that, Zarathustra? No one knows that.' They gaze at each other and weep.

No one can know that, not simply because the idea is unprovable, like an ontological argument cut off from the crucial attribute of existence, but because it remains separated off from the knower as self-identical knower. Whatever one brings back from the *anamnesis* of return dissolves in forgetting of necessity, in order to make the next moment return.

In the song that follows, the 'Song of Yes and Amen', Zarathustra sings of his love for eternity. 'Joy *wants* eternity' he says. Recall the Orphic words cited earlier:

> I have flown out from the circle of heavy grief
> And stepped swift-footed upon the circle of joy

Joy, the fullest, least lacking form of existence, *wants* eternity – but it does not *have* it.

I would like to thank Ruth Blue, Graham Parkes and William Large for their comments on an earlier draft.

Bibliography of cited works by Nietzsche

'Assorted Opinions and Maxims' in *Human, All Too Human* (Cambridge: Cambridge University Press, 1996, trans. R. J Hollingdale).

Beyond Good and Evil (London: Penguin, 1973, trans. R. J. Hollingdale).

The Birth of Tragedy (New York: Vintage, 1967, trans. Walter Kaufmann).

Daybreak (Cambridge: Cambridge University Press, 1997, trans. R. J. Hollingdale).

Die Unschuld des Werdens, II (Stuttgart: Kroner, 1978).

On the Genealogy of Morality (Cambridge: Cambridge University Press, 1994, trans. Carol Diethe).

The Gay Science (New York: Vintage, 1974 trans. Walter Kaufmann).

Untimely Meditations (Cambridge: Cambridge University Press, 1983, trans. R. J. Hollingdale).

The Will to Power (New York: Vintage, 1968, trans. Walter Kaufmann & R. J. Hollingdale)

Thus Spoke Zarathustra (London: Penguin, 1969, trans. R. J. Hollingdale).

Notes

1 For a rare and illuminating account of Nietzsche's ideas on memory, see G. Parkes, *Composing the Soul* (Chicago: University of Chicago Press, 1994), p. 123f.

2 Although see *Republic* 515d–517a. People who remain in the cave look upon the anamnesiac initiate staggering around and accustoming himself to the dark, and declare that 'the visit to the upper world ha[s] ruined his sight' (517a).

3 *Iliad* 23.120f.

4 *Odyssey* 11.80f, 11.205.

5 P. Klossowski, *Nietzsche and the Vicious Circle* (London: Athlone, 1997, trans. D. Smith), p. 23.

6 Klossowski, 'Nietzsche, le polythéisme et la parodie', in *Un Si Funeste Désir* (Paris: Gallimard, 1963), p. 197.

7 Klossowski, *Nietzsche* p. 70.

8 Klossowski, *Nietzsche* p. 56f.

9 See Klossowski, *Un Si Funeste Désir*, p. 189f. He bases his analysis on GS 333.

10 Klossowski, *Nietzsche*, p. 192.

11 *Ibid*, p. 216.

12   Klossowski, 'Sur quelques thèmes fondamentaux de la Gaya Scienza de Nietzsche', in *Un Si Funeste Désir*, p. 21.

13   Klossowski, *Nietzsche*, p. 57.

14   *Ibid*, p. 70.

15   *Ibid*, pp. 57–8.

16   *Ibid*, p. 59.

17   Klossowski, *Un Si Funeste Désir*, p. 211.

18   This is how J. Barnes presents the idea in *The Presocratic Philosophers* (London: Routledge, 1982) pp. 103–120, 488–507.

19   J. Locke, *An Essay Concerning Human Understanding* (London: Penguin, 1997), II.27.14.

20   Cf. Locke, *Essay*, II.27.26 on 'Person, a forensic term'.

21   *Early Greek Philosophy* (London: Penguin, 1987, trans. and ed. J. Barnes), p.83. Subsequent references are to Diels-Kranz numbering, but in this edition.

22   Cf. J-P. Vernant, *Myth and Thought among the Greeks* (London: Routledge, 1983), chs. 3–4.

23   Klossowski, *Un Si Funeste Désir*, p. 23f.

24   M.L. West, *The Orphic Poems* (Oxford: Clarendon Press, 1983) p. 23.

25   F.M. Cornford, *Principium Sapientiae: The Origins of Greek Philosophical Thought* (Cambridge: Cambridge University Press, 1952), ch. 5.

26   *Theogony* 39–43.

27   *Iliad* 1.69.

28   Recall Plato's etymology of the words 'mantic' and 'manic' at *Phaedrus* 244.

29   In the *Meno*, where Plato introduces the notion of *anamnesis* with reference to Orphic doctrine, we seem nevertheless to find what seems to be the most rational account of *anamnesis*. Recollection seems to become simply the ability to draw implications from premises that one already knows. However, if we recall the analysis of the procedure of knowledge in the *Republic*, we see that the grounding of these definitions is a somewhat mystical process, while mathematical reasoning is only the second highest form of knowledge in the hierarchy. Only when the 'assumptions' involved in rational inference are converted into true 'starting points' do we find what can be called a true definition. In the light of this elusiveness of the Ideas, Deleuze comments that Platonic dialectic is limited to the method of *diaresis*, or division, on the basis of assumptions set up in terms of problems (cf. *Difference and Repetition* (London: Athlone, 1994) pp. 59–64). Platonic dialectic is problematisation, hence the ubiquity of irony in Plato concerning whether one has reached a true definition or not. Hence perhaps also the irreducibility of *anamnesis* even in the supposedly most rational parts of Plato.

30   Pindar, fragment 131b. Cf. also *Odyssey* 11.205, cited above, where the *psyche* at death 'flitters out like a dream'.

31   Jan Bremmer, *The Early Greek Concept of the Soul* (Princeton: Princeton University Press, 1983).

32   Cf. Bruno Snell, *The Discovery of the Mind* (New York: Harper & Row, 1960), ch. 1; E.R. Dodds, *The Greeks and the Irrational* (Berkeley: University of California Press, 1951) ch. 1.

33   Erwin Rohde, *Psyche* (New York: Harper & Row, 1966) ch. 8.

34   Walter Burkert, *Greek Religion* (Oxford: Blackwell, 1985) ch. 5; also his *Homo Necans* (Berkeley: University of California Press, 1983) ch.5.

35   For a summary, see W. K. C. Guthrie, *Orpheus and Greek Religion* (Princeton: Princeton University Press, 1993) pp. 156-164; also Dodds, *Greeks*, ch. 2 & 5.

36   Klossowski, *Un Si Funeste Désir*, p. 209.

37   *Die Unschuld des Werdens*, II (Stuttgart: Kroner, 1978) 1298.

38   Klossowski, *Nietzsche*, p. 56.

39   Nietzsche, *Grossoktavausgabe* (Leipzig, 1905ff.) XII, 425, quoted in Heidegger, see n. 40 below.

40   Heidegger overlooks that what is suggested here is the very difficulty of incorporating the eternal return, rather than the promise of eternal return as a grand incorporation of being and becoming. See *Nietzsche* Vol. II (New York: Harper & Row, 1984, trans. D. Krell) p. 76.

9

Nietzsche and the Bhagavad Gita: elective or ironic affinities?

Richard Brown

Introduction

Did Nietzsche know the text of the *Bhagavad Gita*? If he did, did he perhaps 'elect' to borrow from it as he did from Emerson, Lange, Boscovitch, and others?[1] In 'Nietzsche's Trans-European Eye' Sprung systematically debunks the persistent claim that Nietzsche was, in any important sense, influenced by Indian thought.[2] We know that Schopenhauer made several references to the *Gita* in *The World as Will and Representation*, which Nietzsche read.[3] But Nietzsche also read *The System of the Vedanta* written by his friend, the Indologist, Deussen, a text that makes numerous references to the *Gita*.[4] Did Nietzsche perhaps know the *Gita* through these two sources and, as a consequence, come to understand the text as they did?

According to Sprung, Nietzsche had no real knowledge of Indian thought in general or the *Gita* in particular and he had precious little sympathy with what he did know as evidenced by his published and unpublished writings, his personal library, his correspondence, and especially by his relationship with Deussen. Indeed, of the two texts on Indian thought written by Deussen that Nietzsche could have read, namely, the aforementioned *The System of the Vedanta* and *Das Sutras des Vedanta* (published in 1887), Sprung thinks there is little reason to suspect that Nietzsche ever read more than the first and that there is no evidence that the second, primary material on Vedanta, was even opened by Nietzsche. Nevertheless, according to Sprung, 'Vedanta served Nietzsche as the perfect model of a world-denying way of thought'.[5]

Remembering Nietzsche's penchant for learning about other philosophies (Eastern or Western) second or even third hand (via Lange, Überweg, Fisher, Schopenhauer), there is little doubt that Nietzsche (falsely) regarded both Buddhism and Hinduism (Brahmanism, Vedanta), like Schopenhauer, as singularly life-denying. And, like Schopenhauer, Nietzsche regarded Indian philosophy as essentially pessimistic not only because it accepted universal suffering but also because genuine happiness was only possible through the ascetic denial of the will to live or by self-hypnosis.[6] So Nietzsche's understanding of Hinduism (including the *Gita*) is decidedly Schopenhauerian and, as a consequence, his understanding of Hinduism is predominately, if not exclusively, of the non-dualist or Advaitic variety following Sankara's interpretation of the texts even as Deussen does.[7]

A single example of this particular non-dualist interpretation should suffice. Both Nietzsche and Schopenhauer share the Advaitic or non-dualist view of *maya* although neither understands it very well.[8] From the point of view of *The Birth of Tragedy* and well beyond it, Nietzsche regarded *maya,* just as Schopenhauer did*,* as the metaphorical equivalent of a dream, illusion, or delusion.[9] In a word, *maya* was thought to be synonymous with the unreal.[10]

However, there is no good reason to regard *maya*, the phenomenal world, to be any the less real than the noumenal realm of the One, either in the *Gita* or in the *Upanishads* for that matter. It is only because of the influence of Advaita Vedanta that *maya* has become synonymous with illusion, and not only in Nietzsche's mind. But *maya* in the *Gita* is simply the manifestation of the creative power of God and therefore *maya* and nature or the manifest world (*prakriti*) are equivalent terms.[11] In the *Gita, maya* is also uniquely described as the cosmic body of God, a body that has interdependent parts which, as we shall see, is ironically akin to Nietzsche's own understanding of the 'will to power'. Both *maya* and will to power transcend the distinction between organic and inorganic, between mental and physical, mind and matter. Both are incessantly creative and in constant flux. And while Nietzsche thinks the concept of 'will to power' monistically, that is, as a single explanatory principle, like the *Gita*'s monism or non-dualism in its use, it needs to be 'qualified' (that is, understood through Ramanuja rather than Sankara) in order for it to make any genuine sense.

By the same token, the *Gita* is not pessimistic nor does it advocate any form of life-denial, world-denial, or escapism in spite of what Nietzsche thought. It is not a means for 'sneaking' (*schleichen*, Z 'Of the Afterworldsmen') away from life, the general charge that Nietzsche makes against those philosophies and religions that he regards as otherworldly or after-worldly. Nietzsche certainly believed that Indian philosophy was essentially nothing more than pessimistic escapism. He therefore completely misunderstood it.

Morrison has demonstrated quite convincingly the extent to which Nietzsche misunderstood the rudiments of early Buddhism.[12] He has demonstrated that, following the appropriate corrections in Nietzsche's own thinking about Buddhism, there are actually many real affinities, ironically enough, between Nietzsche's thought and that of Buddhism. I argue the same kind of case can be made for Nietzsche and the *Gita* within the Hindu tradition. Whatever the depth of Nietzsche's knowledge and understanding of the *Gita* and whoever it was that might have influenced his thinking, it can be demonstrated that Nietzsche's own philosophical position on a number of key issues is ironically, if not uncannily, akin to the *Gita*. The affinities between Nietzsche and the *Gita* are therefore one and all ironic since, on the surface, Nietzsche and the *Gita* not only have nothing in common but, from Nietzsche's perspective at least, they are diametrically opposed to each other.[13] But as Sprung remarks, 'in some matters Nietzsche is in substantial agreement with thinkers from another, remote, tradition. *Ironically*, he denied this throughout, with vehemence'.[14] Nietzsche's relationship with the *Gita* is, as we shall see, ironic in precisely this sense.

Visions and riddles

There are several 'ironic', but nonetheless important, affinities that can be found between Nietzsche's thought and the *Gita*. Danto, for example, regards both Arjuna and Zarathustra as moral paradigms.[15] Indeed, Zarathustra starts as the teacher of the overman but, having failed to find or create the requisite disciples, himself embarks on becoming the overman. The entire process which Zarathustra undergoes typifies Eastern thought: rather than attempt, albeit in vain, to disclose the truth verbally to those who may not have ears to hear it, the more prudent method is simply to become the very embodiment of the truth which you wish to tell. Zarathustra eventually comes to embody the 'eternal return of the same' and thereby becomes the 'overman'. In the *Gita*, Arjuna eventually comes to embody the truth disclosed to him by Krishna and thereby becomes the perfect yogin. In this regard, Zarathustra as 'overman' is just the Western equivalent of what might be called the enlightened one, the Bodhisattva type according to which the wise man is or lives the truth.

On this deeper level, both the *Bhagavad Gita* and *Thus Spoke Zarathustra* unfold as personal dramas in which Arjuna and Zarathustra must undergo self-transformations towards the embodiment of their respective truths. In this regard, both Arjuna and Zarathustra are posed riddles that they have to solve in order for them to be able to attain the highest stage of their respective self-transformations. In Arjuna's case, he needs to come to understand the principle contained in the riddle: 'He who sees action in inaction and inaction in action – he is wise, a yogin,' (BG IV 18) because his coming to know the meaning of this principle, ['once you have understood my words'] means his deliverance or liberation (*moksa*) from rebirth;[16] 'for once you know this, you will win release' (BG IV 32). What Arjuna must come to know is that all actions are performed by the body alone and that the self (*atman, purusa,* consciousness) does nothing even though Arjuna is engaged in action.[17] In sum, Arjuna must come to know the distinction between *prakriti* (active) and *purusa* (passive). Hence Arjuna needs to gain the kind of self-control and self-discipline required for him to perfect himself, that is, for Arjuna to become a perfect yogin.

Zarathustra too must come to perfect himself.[18] In Zarathustra's case, he must solve the riddle encapsulated in the soothsayer's phrase; 'All is empty, all is the same, all has been' (Z 'The Prophet'). While the riddle itself is complex, the solution to the riddle is obvious namely, the 'eternal return'. But both Arjuna and Zarathustra are able to solve their respective riddles only subsequent to experiencing a terrific vision, a vision which, in both cases, is not only essential for their personal self-transformations but for their ultimate deliverance or redemption as well.[19] It should also be stressed that both visions are terrifying because they are visions of the nature of time. I shall not rehearse Zarathustra's vision of time here, namely, the 'eternal return of the same' and its special connection with Zarathustra's nightmare in the 'The Funeral Song' since it is well worn. Instead, I shall briefly outline what Arjuna learned about the nature of time from his vision since it is perhaps less familiar.

In Arjuna's vision, he sees the entire cosmos with all of its manifold diversity united in the body of God.[20] Arjuna realizes through his divine vision that since God is imperishable time, the ultimate being is both the annihilator and the creator of everything.[21] As time, God is 'world-destroying, grown mature, engaged here in subduing the world' (BG XI 32). Apparently, even without Arjuna's help or participation in the war and seemingly against Arjuna's will, the warriors on the opposing side of the battle will perish anyway having already been doomed by God/time.[22]

Three metamorphoses of the spirit

Following their respective visions, neither Arjuna nor Zarathustra is immediately able to accept the truth of their vision. Both require time to gain or to regain composure or to convalesce. Both Arjuna and Zarathustra undergo three metamorphoses of the spirit and all three are required of each of them since they must be undergone serially or pro-gressively.[23] There does not seem to be any textual evidence to suggest that anyone, including Zarathustra, can pass directly from camel to child without passing through the transformation of the lion. Similarly, although Arjuna might be the single exception to the *Gita*'s rule (given the special relationship he has with God and the unique vision he beheld with his divine eye), no one is able to reach the 'ultimate goal', namely, the child-like stage of the perfected yogin, without passing through all three yogas.[24] In other words, there is an important similarity between Nietzsche's three metamorphoses of the spirit and the transition that the three *gunas* of *prakriti* or qualities of nature demand in the *Gita* in order for an individual to transform (and thereby progress) through the three yogas or spiritual pathways.

Zarathustra defines 'spirit' as life that cuts into itself.[25] Given Niet-zsche's principle that life must always overcome itself again and again the transforming spirit is basically equivalent to life and ultimately to will to power because 'only where there is life is there also will: not will to life but ... will to power' (Z 'Of Self-Overcoming').[26] The three metamor-phoses of the spirit are the ways that the 'will to power' must overcome itself. The camel represents the beast that kneels under the weight of its own voluntarily imposed burden. It is a 'revering will' (Z 'Of the Famous Philosophers') that adopts the higher and noble values of the past even if it tries to surpass them as challenges to be met. Eventually, the camel speeds off into the desert of loneliness to become the ascetic ideal.[27] The camel tenaciously clings to ideals having a temperament that is essen-tially deluded.

The lion is the spirit who attempts to become master by mastering his master (the dragon of duty). The lion commands itself (I will) rather than obey another (thou shalt). The lion breaks the revering heart of the camel; it is hungry and war-like as it searches, seeks, and conquers.[28] The lion ushers in nihilism by destroying the old values without creating new ones to take their place. The lion's temperament is the cause of its action inspiring heroism, vigour, steadiness, resourcefulness, generosity, and leadership and persons who never pass up a good fight.

The child represents innocence, or the return to innocence insofar as the child is without guilt, and, like the perfected yogin in the *Gita*, has quite literally gone beyond both good and evil. To become an overman, one 'must yet become as a child and without shame' (Z 'The Stillest Hour').[29] The child's temperament is the cause of illumination and health that are both related to happiness and knowledge. Such temperaments are serene, self-controlled, austere, pure, and wise. And curiously enough, given Nietzsche's acceptance of Moleschott's/Feuerbach's principle that 'you are what you eat', lambs and rose apples must promote life, vitality, strength, health, and cheerfulness.[30] These qualities aptly describe the child and would tend to be dominant in any being who was able to win what the East generically refers to as enlightenment.

However, in spite of the need for personal self-transformation in both *Zarathustra* and the *Gita*, it is only with the final stage (the child/overman and the perfect yogin) that deliverance or redemption becomes possible. Michel Hulin is therefore not off the mark when he suggests that, 'viewed as an individual, the Brahmin [perfect yogin] bears a strange resemblance to the philosopher of the future, or even to the *Übermensch*, as Nietzsche imagines him.'[31] It should also be pointed out that deliverance or redemption for neither Zarathustra nor Arjuna really entails a belief in anything that might be characterized as out of this world, world-denying or life-denying. For Arjuna and Zarathustra, deliverance or redemption demand nothing less than a radical change of attitude, a wholesale acceptance of this world, without addition or subtraction. In sum, both Arjuna and Zarathustra need to learn how to 'deify' the world: Nietzsche through *amor fati* or the love of fate and Arjuna through *bhakti yoga* or the path of devotion or love.

Body

Ironically, one of the concepts which the *Gita* and Nietzsche have in common is the centrality of the body. However, to claim that the body is central to both Nietzsche and the *Gita* is not to claim that they have a strict correspondence in their thinking but rather that a genuine understanding of their respective philosophical positions is impossible without first taking the role of the body into account.

In *The Gay Science*, Nietzsche explicates the reason why certain individuals have different feelings and tastes. He says that it 'is usually to be found in some oddity of their life style, nutrition, or digestion perhaps a deficit or excess of inorganic salts in their blood and brain; in brief, their *physis*' (GS 39). Kaufmann claims that although Nietzsche used the word '*physis*' in this passage, what he undoubtedly meant by the term was 'physiological make-up'.[32] In 'On the Despisers of the Body' we find Zarathustra's most sustained account of the body which begins with his announcement that 'the awakened and knowing say: body am I entirely, and nothing else; and soul is only a word for something about the body' (Z 'On the Despisers of the Body').[33] Nietzsche regarded 'the body and physiology [as] the starting point' (WP III 492) and claimed that we ought 'to start from the *body* and employ it as guide' (WP III 532) because, in the body, we find the origin of all 'physiological valuations and racial conditions' (BGE 20). Coming to know or understand the body, as that astute physiologist and hygienist the Buddha did[34] would therefore be the best means for discovering the specific 'physiological demands for the preservation of a certain type of life' (BGE 3); indeed, the very 'physiological capacity for life' (GM III 11). This is why Alistair Moles can correctly speak of Nietzsche giving the body 'ontological primacy'.[35]

While Nietzsche divides bodies into two types: 'healthy' and 'sick', each having a corresponding value structure (so-called 'physiological values'), the same is also true for Nietzsche's understanding of life in general. Nietzsche divides life (a monistic principle like nature and will to power) into those who represent the ascending type of life (strong, healthy, active, noble, master, yes-saying) and those who represent the descending type of life (weak, sick, reactive, herd, slave, no-saying).[36] Life is also divided into lambs and birds of prey (GM I 13). Ultimately, Nietzsche even divides his most fundamental principle, namely, the will to power, as well.[37] Although it seems to be a monistic (that is, non-dualist) principle of explanation, Nietzsche is obliged to qualify it (by dividing it into two) in order for it to make any real sense. Even at the most basic level, namely, in terms of quanta of power, Nietzsche distinguishes between those, on the one hand, who have power and are able to use it to gain more power and those, on the other hand, who do not have power and therefore attempt to maintain the *status quo*. While Nietzsche thinks of them both as colours albeit on opposite ends of a single palette, he paints them as if they were black and white. They function as contraries. Take, for instance, Moles's apt description of the workings of the 'will to power',

The drives express themselves in action by overcoming outer resistance and obstacles. Without this resistance, there is no way for a drive to discharge itself... Nietzsche therefore interprets the gaining of power as dialectical; it proceeds by overcoming resistances to itself, obstacles which if unresisted would diminish power.[38]

If opposition and conflict entail otherness and difference, the 'will to power' as a functional, monistic concept that inherently demands opposition and difference, becomes a form of qualified non-dualism. George Feuerstein, in his commentary on the *Gita,* states that, the notion of *prakriti* as the root-principle of all cosmic manifestations corresponds perfectly with the concept of *physis* in pre-Socratic philosophy...it would be absolutely inaccurate to suggest that *prakriti*, or *physis*, is merely the common pool of 'dead' matter. On the contrary, it is a highly dynamic principle.[39]

The concept of *prakriti*, like Nietzsche's 'will to power', also conflates the distinction, and thereby collapses any distinct boundary, between the psychological and the physical. This is why Moles claims that Nietzsche 'is not a dualist, or one who believes that mind and body are equally real, although each irreducible to the other. He tends more towards the position of the neutralists, who regard mind and body as equally unreal, in the sense that mental and physical phenomena are both reducible to some different underlying reality.'[40] Even the 'material' aspect of *prakriti* as it evolves (*tanmatras*) are to be thought of as 'energy potentials' which is suggestive of Nietzsche's thinking of 'will to power' in terms of power quanta and dynamic force points.[41]

Fate and temperament

Johann Figl claims that Nietzsche was first introduced to Indian thought by his high school teachers when he was asked to compare the Indian epics, *Ramayana* and *Mahabharata*, to Greek and German epics.[42] Hence, Figl concludes, the influence of India on Nietzsche's own thought can already be found in the 'fate essays' of 1862, some three years prior to the reading of Schopenhauer. To support his claim, Figl quotes a passage from Nietzsche's essay, 'Freedom of the Will and Fate' which he believes has a distinctly Indian origin: 'the Hindu says: "Fate is nothing other than actions performed during an earlier phase of our existence"'.[43]

In spite of Nietzsche's reference to 'the Hindu' in this passage, he probably did not come to this understanding of fate, at least directly, through Hinduism. As George J. Stack has demonstrated at length, Nietzsche undoubtedly found this particular idea concerning fate in Emerson.[44] In his earlier essay on fate entitled 'Fate and History' (1862), Nietzsche wrote the following, acknowledging his indebtedness to Emerson,

> What determines our happiness in life? Do we have to thank the events from whose whirlpool we shall be swept? Or is it not rather our temperament as it were which colours all events? In the reflecting mirror of our own personality, do we not encounter everything? And do not the events give as it were only the key of our history while the strengths and weaknesses with which it confronts us depend merely on our temperament? Emerson says, ask astute physicians how much temperament does not decide; indeed, what is not decided by temperament?[45]

The Sanskrit term for 'fate' is *daivam*. It generally means the collective force of one's past actions or *karma*. However, the net result of that force is exactly what we are at the present time. So in a sense, *karma* simply means, as both the Nietzsche passage quoted by Figl and the last passage from 'Fate and History' indicate, we are our fate. In a phrase, beings follow their nature. Indeed, fate and temperament are, as Novalis is alleged to have said, simply two words for the very same thing. What is most important to note, however, is that the doctrine of *karma* only makes sense on the assumption that individual human beings are free, that is, are able to make choices and are therefore responsible for the choices they make and the actions they perform. This is the case even though *karma* is a strictly causal principle. Nevertheless, *karma* appears to be fatalistic, and never more so than in the *Gita*, because it advocates that what one is now has been determined by what one did in the past just as what one is now determines what one will be able to do in the future. However, what this means is that individuals are free to choose but only free to choose within the restrictions and limitations of their own creation. In other words, individuals are born with certain capacities, propensities, and dispositions (in a word, temperaments), which have been determined by their own past deeds and which will determine their own future deeds.

How does this difference in personal temperaments play itself out in the *Gita*? Initially, Arjuna wants to know the one thing by which he can attain the highest goal.[46] But Krishna says that all depends on one's temperament or psychological make-up (gunic mix: *sattva, rajas, tamas*) and distinguishes between Samkhyan theory or knowledge and Yogic practice as the unselfish performance of action.[47] The path of knowledge (*jnana yoga*) is only appropriate for contemplative persons with the corresponding *sattvic* temperament while *karma yoga* is reserved for men of action, like Arjuna, because of their *rajasic* or passionate temperaments.[48] But although theory and practice seem to differ, the wise do not see a difference and Krishna's initial distinction between theory and practice soon collapses into a yoga of praxis (*jnana-karma yoga*) since theory and practice are mutually entailed: one needs to know about action/inaction in order to be able to act unselfishly.[49]

But what is most extraordinary about the *Gita* is that liberation or becoming *Brahman* through knowledge is a necessary condition for loving God. Only those who know Brahman (the Absolute) by knowing both God's higher and lower nature (*jnana yoga*), who know the Self (*atman*) and its relation to action and have therefore become self-controlled (*karma yoga*) and who are also devoted to God (*bhakti yoga*) can win the highest goal. The *Gita* offers as a new and distinct goal the attaining of God's own particular mode of Being.[50] Liberation through knowledge precedes loving God and makes it possible. *Jnana-karma yoga* then, taken as a single path, and *bhakti-yoga* are distinct steps in a two-step process.[51]

Krishna describes the practitioner of *bhakti yoga* or devotion as someone with obvious 'overmanliness' (*Übermenschlichkeit*): he harbours no ill will towards any being; he is friendly and compassionate, and free from egoism.[52] But lest anyone think that the devotee has fatalistically given up acting in the world, Krishna says explicitly that he no more shrinks from the world than the world is able to shrink away from him. While this devoted yogin seems to have 'given up all initiative in action' (BG XII 16) having recognized that, in the great scheme of things, he is merely the occasion for God's will to be done, it simply means that the duties that he ought to perform are those actions that are determined by his own nature.[53] After all, beings follow their nature. This is the guiding principle of the *Gita.* Arjuna should therefore perform his prescribed duty according to his own nature and do 'the works that must be done' (BG III 19) not out of moral necessity (because we ought to do them) but out of physical or biological necessity because we have no choice but to follow our own natures.[54] If these actions have to be done anyway, then Krishna is really just calling on Arjuna to radically change his attitude toward these actions, 'it is material Nature's [three] constituents that do all works wherever [works are done]; [but] he whose self is by the ego fooled thinks, "It is I who do"' (BG III 27). All action is done by the modes (*gunas*) of nature (*prakrti*) and the ego deludes the self into thinking that it is the doer, 'for no one can remain even for a moment without doing work; everyone is made to act helplessly by the impulses born of nature [*gunas of prakrti*]' (BG III 5).[55]

In sum, *bhakti yoga* in the *Gita* demands the adoption of an attitude or stance towards existence which entails recognition of one's self as a necessary part of the whole, that is, as a piece of fate. But the kind of liberation which the *Gita* has in mind is not the annihilation of the individual in the nothingness of Nirvana, as Nietzsche understood it to be in Buddhism. Nor is it wishing for an after-world like the heaven of St. Paul. Liberation in the *Gita* is much more akin to what Nietzsche believed the kingdom of God to be for the historical Jesus, namely, a happiness (peace, bliss, *ananda*) that was attainable here and now.[56] In Sanskrit, the concept is referred to as *jivan mukti*: freedom while living. It means to exist as an individual human being, albeit with a radically new attitude towards existence, based squarely on realizing one's necessary relationship to the cosmic whole.

A case can readily be made that Nietzsche was a determinist of this same ilk. Richard Schacht says that Nietzsche was not a strict determinist.[57] But if Nietzsche is a determinist, strict or otherwise, he seems to have been a determinist by default since he took great pains to rid himself, and others, of the belief in a free will. Since there is no 'free' will and the concept of a 'free will' is the cornerstone of libertarianism, Nietzsche appeared to have no other place to turn except to the determinist camp. Nietzsche sometimes appears to work on the assumption that determinism and libertarianism are mutually exclusive and jointly exhaustive so that rejecting one automatically forced him to accept the other.[58] This did not prevent Nietzsche from ultimately rejecting both, however, insofar as the concept of an unfree will was just as problematic and philosophically empty as was the concept of a free will.[59]

However, I think a better case can be made that Nietzsche was really much more of a compatibilist than a determinist although he did not seem to understand the concept. Compatibilism also conveniently fits Nietzsche's concept of the 'will to power'. Compatibilism abandons the principle that causality and freedom are mutually incompatible states of affairs so that if something is caused, it cannot be free and if something is free (like the will), it cannot be caused. According to compatibilism, something is to be regarded as free simply if it falls within our power, our capacity or ability. In distinguishing between 'ascending' and 'descending' types of life, Nietzsche is drawing a distinction between those who have power (potential, ability, capacity) and those who do not. Those who do not have power cannot do otherwise. They are, if you will, fated. But those who have power can be called upon to use it, to actualize their potential. If it is within their power to do something, then they are free and ought to be held accountable. Schacht comes fairly close to this point when he says, 'freedom', [Nietzsche] suggests, should be understood as 'facility in self-direction' and such facility, which he regards as presupposing both 'fortunate organization' and the various forms of self-mastery …is a possibility which may be realized.'[60]

One thing for certain is that Nietzsche was not a fatalist even though he espoused the love of fate.[61] A fatalist believes that everyone is fated because fate itself acts as an external force, which is always working against them, constantly frustrating their actions. Hence nothing can be done so we should just resign ourselves to what is inevitable. Nietzsche rejects this view wholesale. He referred to it as 'Turkish fatalism' and claimed instead that 'in reality every man is himself a piece of fate; when he thinks to resist fate… it is precisely fate which is here expressing itself' (HH 61). Remembering that fate and temperament are the same thing, that beings follow their nature, it is not difficult to understand what this might mean. As Stambaugh says, 'if fate is not to be equated with Turkish fatalism [that is, simple resignation because one believes change is impossible] it is nothing above man against which man is powerless (and thus exempt from really doing anything). Fate is *in* man.'[62] Nietzsche's concept of *amor fati* therefore seems to function like the 'eternal return of the same' but without its cosmological baggage. The person who is able to answer the demon's question posed in the *The Gay Science*[63] in the most affirmative of ways has obviously adopted what Nietzsche calls a 'Dionysian relationship to existence' (WP IV 1041), that is, by definition, the highest possible affirmation of the world, 'without subtraction, exception or selection' (WP IV 1041).[64] *Amor fati*, like *bhakti yoga*, is the demand that we embrace existence in its entirety (though not necessarily for all eternity as eternal return would have us do). No element or aspect of existence can be denied or rejected; indeed, every aspect of existence must be regarded as necessary, as a piece of fate, and therefore it becomes imbued with desirability and with beauty. In other words, this life, this world, this existence has to become deified and made divine.[65] As Nietzsche states, 'my formula for greatness in a human being is *amor fati*: that one wants nothing to be different, nor forward, not backward, not in all eternity. Not merely bear what is necessary, still less conceal it…but *love* it' (EH 'Why I am so Clever'

10). This means essentially that, like the devotee in *bhakti yoga*, those who live according to the *amor fati* formula must actually come to love existence.[66]

Conclusion

One of Nietzsche's most pressing claims is that there is *only* a perspective knowing. However, the more eyes, even foreign eyes, that we permit to speak about one thing, even if that one thing happens to be about Nietzsche himself, the more complete and the more objective our understanding will become.[67] While the number of differences between Nietzsche and the *Gita* undoubtedly outnumber (but not outweigh) the number of similarities, in the essential thrust of their thinking, their *raison d'etre* as it were, Nietzsche and the *Gita*, indeed, Nietsche and Eastern thought as a whole, have a great deal in common. I believe that Heinrich Zimmer best sums up this 'thrust' when he writes,

> the primary concern – in striking contrast to the interests of the modern philosophers of the West – has always been, not information, but transformation: a radical changing of man's nature and, therewith, a renovation of his understanding both of the outer world and of his own existence; a transformation as complete as possible, such as will amount when successful to a total conversion or rebirth.[68]

It never fails to be a fruitful exercise to reflect Nietzsche, the philosopher of perspectives, in as many mirrors as possible, and particularly so in mirrors which are cross-culturally framed and therefore usually not found within anyone's immediate focus.

Bibliography of cited works by Nietzsche

Nietzsche Contra Wagner in *The Portable Nietzsche* (Toronto: Penguin, 1976, trans. W. Kaufmann)

On the Genealogy of Morals and *Ecce Homo* (Toronto: Random House, 1967, trans. W. Kaufmann)

The Gay Science (Toronto: Random House, 1974, trans. W. Kaufmann)

The Will to Power (New York: Random House, 1967, trans. W. Kaufmann and R.J. Hollingdale)

Thus Spoke Zarathustra (New York: Viking Press, 1972, trans. W. Kaufmann)

Twilight of the Idols and *The Anti-Christ* (Toronto: Penguin Books, 1990, trans. R.J. Hollingdale)

Notes

1 Stack uses 'elect' in this fashion. See George J. Stack, *Nietzsche and Emerson: An Elective Affinity* (Athens: Ohio University Press, 1992) as well as *Lange and Nietzsche* (Berlin: Walter de Gruyter, 1983).

2 Mervyn Sprung, 'Nietzsche's Trans-European Ee' in Graham Parkes (ed.): *Nietzsche and Asian Thought* (Chicago: University of Chicago Press, 1991) pp. 76–90.

3 Arthur Schopenhauer, *The World as Will and Representation* (New York: Dover, 1958, trans. by E.F.J. Payne) Vol. I pp. 284, 388; Vol. II pp. 326, 473. Sprung has shown that in his copy of Schopenhauer's text Nietzsche underlined only three passages which dealt specifically with Eastern thought and only one of them made reference to the *Gita*: 'Death is *Schein*'. See Sprung, 'Nietzsche's Trans-European Eye', p. 82.

4 Paul Deussen, *The System of the Vedanta* (New York: Dover, 1972, trans. C. Johnston). Originally published in 1883.

5 Sprung, 'Nietzsche's Trans-European Eye', see pp. 79, 82, 86.

6 See GM III 17.

7 There are several references in Schopenhauer to F.H.H. Windischmann, *Sancara, siva de theologumenis Vedanticorum*. See, for example, Schopenhauer, *The World as Will* II, pp. 508, n.32 and II, 607. There are three distinct schools of Vedanta, that is, three different interpretations of the so-called Vedic (Upanishadic) texts. They differ primarily in how they understand the relationship between the essence of the external world (*Brahman*) and the essence of the internal world or person (*atman*). Sankara's non-dualism (*Advaita*) regards them as absolutely identical; Ramanuja's qualified non-dualism (*Visisitadvaita*) regards them as identical but only in a qualified sense; Madhva's dualism (*Dvaita*) regards them as absolutely different. Nietzsche, sympathetic to Deussen's non-dualistic reading, tended to view all Hindu thought the same way. However, for the *Gita* at least, the qualified non-dualistic reading of Ramanuja is much less hostile to the text.

8 Nietzsche describes Apollo metaphorically as art, beauty, a veil, dream, and *maya* but he also uses more traditional concepts such as appearance, phenomenon, and empirical reality. Although Nietzsche describes Apollo as the 'sole and highest reality' (BT 18), he nevertheless regards it as the 'truly non-existent' (BT 4). At best, Apollo is only an inadequate appearance of the reality which lies beneath it. Since empirical reality is characterized by the phenomenality of space, time, and causality (BT 4, 18), everything temporal, spatial, and causally related must be illusory or *maya*. See D.W. Hamlyn, *Schopenhauer* (London: Routledge and Kegan Paul, 1985) pp. 65, 77.

9 See Richard S. G. Brown, 'Nietzsche and Kant on Permanence', *Man and World*, vol.13 (1980), pp. 39–52.

10 *Maya*, strictly speaking, is neither real nor unreal. Nevertheless, Nietzsche equated *maya* with illusion and therefore as unreal.

11 Throughout I refer to R.C. Zaehner's translation of *The Bhagavad-Gita* (London: Oxford University Press, 1973) hereafter BG. Reference is to chapter and verse.

12 Robert G. Morrison, *Nietzsche and Buddhism: A Study in Nihilism and Ironic Affinities* (Oxford: Oxford University Press, 1997).

13 This is the position taken by Morrison *vis-à-vis* Nietzsche and early Buddhism.

14 Sprung, 'Nietzsche's Trans-European Eye', p. 89, emphasis added.

15 Arthur C. Danto, 'The Discipline of Action in The Bhagavad Gita', in *Mysticism and Morality: Oriental Thought and Moral Philosophy* (New York: Basic Books, 1972) p. 86. My thanks to George J. Stack for bringing this book to my attention.

16 See BG IV 16.

17 See BG IV 20–21

18 See Z 'Of the Afterworldsman', 'Of Involuntary Bliss'.

19 See BG IX and Z III 'Of the Vision and the Riddle' respectively.

20 See BG XI 13. All contingent beings, both human and divine (see BG IX 15), are in God's body which has no discernible beginning, middle, or end (see BG XI 16). Arjuna trembles before the sight of God's open mouths (see BG XI 24). The scene is graphically described: God's mouths are 'like Time's devouring flames' (BG XI 25) and the host of heroes arrayed on the battlefield rush headlong to their destruction having their heads crushed to a pulp as they are caught between God's teeth (see BG XI 27, 28). Knowing this, indeed, having seen it with his own eye (so to speak), Arjuna should stop being afraid, get up, and fight, the *Gita*'s moral paradigm for doing one's duty in general (BG XI 33). By God alone, his enemies have been slain already. Arjuna should therefore come to consider himself as merely the occasion for God's will to be done since whatever is done is just the action of God's body (see BG XI 33).

21 See BG X 30, 33, 34.

22 See BG XI 32 XI 34.

23 I am not interested here whether or not Zarathustra himself, or Nietzsche for that matter, transformed from camel to lion to child, or when he might be said to have so transformed in the text, if he does at all, or whether or not he ultimately becomes the child ('overman'), or what the relationship might be between accepting the 'eternal return of the same' and becoming an 'overman'. While these are undoubtedly important questions that do need to be addressed, what I wish to stake out is that there is no reason to suspect that the three metamorphoses of the spirit are not progressive or serial, that being a camel must precede becoming a lion just as being a lion is a necessary condition for becoming a child.

24   The progression would be through a series of karmic rebirths (alien to Niet-
     zsche regardless of the truth of 'eternal return') which assumes the transi-
     tion through three temperaments each reflecting a dominant quality of
     nature (*gunas* of *prakriti: tamas, rajas, sattvas*).
25   See Z 'Of the Famous Philosophers'.
26   See also Z 'Of the Tarantulas'
27   The characteristic, if not actual requirement of strength or degree of power,
     is what makes the camel a positive element or spirit. According to Lampert,
     Zarathustra does not criticise the camel because the camel represents a cer-
     tain capacity for deeds. The camel is a positive moment in the evolution of
     the spirit because it answers the call to actualise in itself what is only poten-
     tial. As Lampert states, 'the sole motive for heroic behaviour as described
     here is the delight of the spirit in its own strength'. See L. Lampert, *Niet-
     zsche's Teaching: An Interpretation of 'Thus Spoke Zarathustra'* (New Haven:
     Yale University Press, 1986) p. 34. Is Zarathustra a camel? According to
     Lampert, Zarathustra is a camel insofar as he reveres the 'overman'. But
     even into Part III of *Zarathustra*, we find that Zarathustra has not yet, by his
     own admission, even become the lion, let alone the child, '"as yet I have not
     been strong enough for the finaloverbearing, prankish bearing of the lion.
     Your gravity was always terrible enough for me; but one day I shall yet find
     the strength and the lion's voice to summon you."' (Z 'Of Involuntary
     Bliss').
28   See Z II 'Of the Famous Philosophers'.
29   But like the ass in the ass festival in Z IV, we can also say of the child:
     'Beyond good and evil is your kingdom. Innocence is not even to know
     what innocence itself is.' (Z 'The Ass Festival'). This is why the child is char-
     acterized as a forgetting. It represents the very 'innocence of becoming' (Z
     'Of Immaculate Perception'); it is a new beginning, a game (of creation), a
     self-propelled wheel, a sacred yes. It is not self-evident, however, whether
     the child's sacred yes is the same 'Yes and Amen' which is tantamount to
     accepting the 'eternal return of the same' (see Z 'Before Sunrise'). If it is
     the same yes, it seems that it might be necessary for someone to accept
     the 'eternal return of the same' in order for them to become the child,
     assuming that the child is, in fact, the 'overman'. The child is not necessar-
     ily the 'overman', for Lampert, but only represents that time when the spirit
     is fully at home in this world (*Heimlichkeit*) because there will no longer be
     any other-worldly values.
30   See Z 'The Convalescent'.
31   Michel Hulin, 'Nietzsche and the Suffering of the Indian Ascetic' in G.
     Parkes (ed.): *Nietzsche and Asian Thought* p. 70. Morrison says that 'the
     qualities required to become a Buddha seem to be similar to those required
     to become a Nietzschean *Übermensch* (overman)', *Nietzsche and Buddhism*
     p. 36, and that what the Buddha's teaching offered his followers 'was the

prospect of a more meaningful ideal of what a human being can become' (ibid) p. 39. I would argue that this is the transformative message of all Eastern philosophy, especically the *Gita*.

32   See Kaufmann's comment, GS 39, n. 34. In a subsequent note Kaufmann adds, 'It would surely be much more plausible if Nietzsche had spoken of psychology instead of physics. Even 'physiology' would have been more plausible, and 'physics' seems far-fetched unless we assume that what is meant is the study of nature (*physis* in Greek)' (GS 335, n. 67). See also Walter Kaufmann, *Nietzsche: Philosopher, Psychologist, Anti-Christ* (Princeton: Princeton University Press, 1974) p. 295. Stanley Rosen echoes Kaufmann's claim when he states 'more explicitly than Descartes, Nietzsche adocates that we tear down the dwellings which constrict and distort man's spirit; but whereas for Descartes the instrument of liberation is physics, for Nietzsche it is poetry or creativity', *Nihilism: A Philosophical Essay* (New Haven: Yale University Press, 1969) p.106. Jon Franklin argues that human thought, emotion, and behaviour as mental processes can, and should be quantifiable in chemical terms. As he states, 'beneath the molecular level, biology drops away and there is only physics, *Molecules of the Mind: The Brave New Science of Molecular Psychology* (New York: Atheneum, 1987) p. 44. See also Richard S. G. Brown, 'Nihilism: "Thus Speaks Physiology"' in Tom Darby, Bela Egyed, Ben Jones (eds.): *Nietzsche and the Rhetoric of Nihilism: Essays on Interpretation, Language and Politics*, (Ottawa: Carleton University Press, 1989) pp. 133–144.

33   Zarathustra says, 'the body is a great reason, a plurality with one sense, a war and a peace, a herd and a shepherd. An instrument of your body is also your little reason, my brother, which you call 'spirit' – a little instrument and toy of your great reason…Behind your thoughts and feelings, my brother, there stands a mighty ruler, an unknown sage – whose name is Self. In your body he dwells; he is your body…I am the leading strings of the Ego and the prompter of its concepts' (Z 'On the Despisers of the Body'). Zarathustra also states that, 'thought is one thing, deed is another. The wheel of causality does not roll between them (Z 'Of the Pale Criminal'). Nietzsche reiterates this thus, 'there is no 'being' behind doing, effecting, becoming; 'the doer' is merely a fiction added to the deed – the deed is everything' (GM I 13) and 'it thinks; but that this 'it' is precisely the famous old 'ego' is, to put it mildly, only a supposition, an assertion, and assuredly not an 'immediate certainty'' (BGE 16). Nietzsche was not the first to think this way. Compare, for example, Berkeley's claim, 'Substance of a Spirit is that it acts, causes, wills, operates, or if you please (to avoid the quibble that may be made on the word it) to act, cause, will, operate', D.M. Armstrong (ed.): *Berkeley's Philosophical Writings,* (New York: Collier Books, 1965) p. 370.

34   See AC 20.

35 Alistair Moles, *Nietzsche's Philosophy of Nature and Cosmology* (New York: Peter Lang, 1990) p. 97.

36 See TI 'Expeditions of an Untimely Man' 33.

37 Wilcox understands Nietzsche's concept of 'will to power' to have developed over time having started as a principle which was limited to explaining the psychology of human motives. It then expanded to become a biological principle used by Nietzsche to explain all life and nature. Finally, 'will to power' became an ontological principle which was universal. See John T. Wilcox, 'Comment on Paper by Maudemarie Clark "Nietzsche's Doctrines of the Will to Power"', *Nietzsche-Studien*, vol. XII (1983) pp. 469–472.

38 Moles, *Nietzsche's Philosophy of Nature and Cosmology* p. 107.

39 Feuerstein, *Introduction to the Bhagavad Gita: Its Philosophy and Cultural Setting* (London: The Theological Publishing House, 1983) p. 101.

40 Moles, *Nietzsche's Philosophy of Nature and Cosmology* p. 97.

41 See Feuerstein, *Introduction* p. 108. Visistadvaita Vedanta of Ramanuja, which finds its fullest flower in his interpretation of the *Gita*, is a qualified form of non-dualism since it insists that *purusa* (the spiritual element) and *prakriti* (the material or natural element) are both modes or attributes of something else, namely, God. In many ways then, both Nietzsche and the *Gita* advocate a neutral monism which makes sense only when it is qualified.

42 Johann Figl, 'Nietzsche's Early Encounters with Asian Thought' in G. Parkes (ed.): *Nietzsche and Asian Thought* pp. 51–63.

43 *Ibid* p. 52.

44 As Stack states, 'in this terse essay there is a reference to the role of temperament in relation to personality and behaviour that specifically refers to Emerson's thoughts on this question in "Fate"', *Nietzsche and Emerson* p. 179. See also pp. 20–22. This is not to forget that Emerson's poem, 'Brahma' quotes the *Gita*. As Gay Wilson Allen states, 'a man's morals, his thoughts, his experiences, depends on his "structure and temperament"', *Waldo Emerson* (New York: Penguin, 1982) p. 436.

45 Hans Joachim Mette (ed.), *Friedrich Nietzsche: Werke und Briefe, Historisch-Kritische Gesamtausgabe, Werke/2.Band. Jugendschriften 1861–1864* (Muenchen: C.H.Beck'sche Verlagsbuchhandlung, 1934) pp. 57–58.

46 See BG III 2

47 See BG II 39.

48 See BG III 3.

49 See BG V 4.

50 That God's mode of being is not the same as liberation or becoming *Brahman*, see BG IV 10, VIII 5, XIII 18, XIV 19.

51 Zaehner refers to the 'progressive stages on the way to liberation' in BG p. 173. See also pp. 195, 384. Compare the hierarchy of *yoga*s at BG XII 12 which excludes mention of *bhakti* as well as BG XIII 24–25. *Bhakti-yoga* is

obviously possible at all stages (compare Zaehner, BG p. 398) but they
differ in kind not by degree. Sacrifice (*yajna*) to other gods which Krishna
guarantees would be the lowest kind of *bhakti*. *In nuce*, one kind of knowledge wins liberation which allows for one kind of devotion to God. Being
devoted to God then wins the devotee a different kind of knowledge,
namely, knowledge of God as he truly is, which then affords the devotee a
new and higher kind of devotion which is the ultimate and highest goal in
the *Gita*.

52 See BG XII 13.

53 See BG XVIII 57.

54 See BG III 8.

55 See also BG IX 8, VIII 19, XVIII 59–61.

56 See AC 21.

57 See Richard Schacht, *Nietzsche* (London: Routledge and Kegan Paul, 1983)
    pp. 26, 311. The best evidence that Nietzsche was probably a strict deter-
    minist is 'The Waterfall' (HH 106).

58 See BGE I 21.

59 See BGE I 21, WP III 671.

60 Schacht, *Nietzsche* p. 309.

61 Schacht equates strict with hard or necessitating determinism, see *ibid* p.
    311.

62 Joan Stambaugh, *Nietzsche's Thought of Eternal Return* (Baltimore: John
    Hopkins University Press, 1972) p. 58. Stambaugh adds, 'Nietzsche's con-
    cern lies not in the subjection of man to fate but in man's relationship to
    the fate. It makes no sense for man to prostate himself on the ground
    before fate, because he himself belongs to, *is*, that fate' *ibid*, p. 56. Com-
    pare also Pfeffer's claim, 'man's fate is inextricably interwoven with the
    totality of the cosmic fate. The significance and meaningfulness of the
    human will and its history is found within the nonhuman world, within the
    necessity of the cosmic whole' in Rose Pfeffer, *Nietzsche: Disciple of Diony-
    sus* (Lewisburg: Bucknell University Press, 1972) p. 185.

63 See GS IV 341 (see above).

64 Given the fact that *amor fati* is a Dionysian affirmation of existence, and
    insofar as this parallels the *Gita's* understanding of *bhakti yoga*, Feuerstein
    seems to be misguided to think that the '*Gita's* message calls on man's
    Apollonian nature', *Introduction* pp. 126. For further instances of *amor fati*
    see EH 'Why I am so Clever' 10, 'The Birth of Tragedy' 2; TI '"Reason" in
    Philosophy' 8, 'Morality as Anti-nature' 6.

65 See GS IV 276; WP IV 1041, 1051.

66 See F. Nietzsche: *Nietzsche Contra Wagner* Epilogue 1.

67 See GM III 12.

68 Heinrich Zimmer, *Philosophies of India* (Princeton: Princeton University
    Press, 1967, ed. J. Campbell) p. 4.

10
Nature and the human 'redivinised':
Mahāyāna Buddhist themes in
Thus Spoke Zarathustra

Graham Parkes

> At least we are today far from the laughable immodesty of decreeing from
> our own little corner that perspectives are *permissible* only from this corner.
> The world has rather become 'infinite' for us once more, insofar as we
> cannot dismiss the possibility that it *contains within it infinite interpretations.*
> Once more the great shudder grips us – but who then would want straight
> away to divinize *this* monster of an unknown world again in the old way?
> (GS 374)

Nietzsche's infamous proclamation in 1882 of the death of God would
seem to be reinforced by the publication the following year of *Thus
Spoke Zarathustra*, in which the protagonist reaffirms at the start the
deity's demise, and soon universalizes the obituary by announcing the
death of '*all Gods*'.[1] The trenchant and eventually harsh criticisms of
Christianity delivered up to the end of his writing career with *The Anti-
Christ* have tended to confirm Nietzsche's reputation as a godless
immoralist. But if we reflect on that magnificently timed stroke of fate
which brought the realization, two weeks before he was first struck by
the thought of eternal recurrence, that he had a genuine precursor in
Spinoza, we may well see that his understanding of the world is closer
than generally assumed to the *deus sive natura* of that 'God-intoxicated
man'.[2]

In a previous essay advocating our taking Nietzsche seriously as an
ecological thinker and philosopher of nature, I referred to the passage
that serves as the epigraph to the present chapter and suggested that he
wouldn't want 'straight away to divinize *this* monster of an unknown
world again in the old way', but that 'he gives every indication that this
monster of an unknown world *presents itself* as divine, in the new way of
a Dionysian pantheism, to those who are able to emerge from their own
little corner with sufficient reverence for what lies beyond their human

horizons.'[3] I should like here to amplify that suggestion with reference to *Thus Spoke Zarathustra*.

It was over fifty years ago that the Japanese philosopher Keiji Nishitani drew attention to the importance in Nietzsche's thought of what he called 'a new religion with a Dionysian new god', remarking its similarity to 'the standpoint of Meister Eckhart, who speaks of "living without why, within the Godless desert of divinity"'.[4] Aware of the limitations of Nietzsche's understanding of Buddhism, Nishitani makes the further comment: 'Ironically, it was not in his nihilistic view of Buddhism but in such ideas as *amor fati* and the Dionysian as the overcoming of nihilism that Nietzsche came closest to Buddhism, and especially to Mahāyāna'.[5] While there has been some discussion of Nietzsche as a religious thinker, not much has been said about the nature of this new, Dionysian religion – or about its remarkable similarities to Mahāyāna (a later form of Buddhism with which Nietzsche was not acquainted).[6]

A comprehensive comparison would enhance our understanding of both sides, but would best be carried out with respect to a particular school or thinker in the multifarious Mahāyāna tradition.[7] Having found that reading *Zarathustra* from a Mahāyāna perspective highlights some hitherto ignored aspects of the text, I here adopt this kind of perspective in order simply to limn the outlines of Nietzsche's 'new Dionysian pantheism' (as Nishitani calls it), which turns out to involve some remarkable revaluations of the divinity of nature and the human.

Nietzsche will have read in Hermann Oldenberg's book *Buddha* that 'the noblest task of [the Buddha's] life was the preaching of the teaching of liberation and the attracting of all kinds of people to follow him in the monk's habit'.[8] Nietzsche's Zarathustra also has a teaching of liberation to impart, and after gathering a number of disciples he delivers numerous speeches whose style and content parallel Oldenberg's accounts of the Buddha's sermons and relations with his audience. (The parallels with Jesus and his sermons are, of course, more numerous and extended.) Both the Buddha and Zarathustra realize that if their teachings of liberation are to be imparted successfully, their speeches must be carefully adjusted to the level of their audiences. Since Zarathustra begins by haranguing the people in the marketplace, continues with a series of speeches to disciples, and ends up addressing himself (as well as his animals, his soul, and a female figure called Life), and since his understanding of himself and the world progressively deepens, we can best gauge his (and by extension Nietzsche's) attitude to the divine by following the development of his discourse as the story unfolds.[9]

'Dead are all Gods!'

At the beginning of the book, Zarathustra seems well on the way to becoming what the Mahāyāna Buddhists call a *bodhisattva*, a being who attains enlightenment but refuses to enter nirvana until all beings have become enlightened. The *bodhi* in the term means 'enlightenment' while the *sattva* means 'being' – but also has the connotation of 'warrior'.[10] The bodhisattva's two main qualities are consummate wisdom and boundless compassion, wisdom being associated with ascent out of the world of ignorance, and compassion with descent back into the world for the salvation of all beings.[11] On *Zarathustra's* first page we hear the protagonist, after ten years of accumulating wisdom in his mountain-top cave, address the sun as follows:

> Behold! I am overfull of my wisdom, like the bee that has gathered too much honey, and I need hands outstretched to receive it....Bless the cup that wants to overflow, that the waters may flow from it golden and carry everywhere the reflection of your delight! Behold! This cup wants to become empty again, and Zarathustra wants to become human again. (Z 'Prologue' 1)

It is the same with the bodhisattva: the attainment of wisdom, which involves the realization of the emptiness of the self through its interrelatedness with all things, naturally leads to an abundant generosity and a re-engagement with the world. Zarathustra could well be describing a bodhisattva when he says:

> I love him whose soul squanders itself, who wants no thanks and does not give back: for he always bestows and does not want to preserve himself. ...I love him whose soul is overfull, so that he forgets himself and all things are in him: thus all things become his going under. (Z 'Prologue' 4)

Next to a sketch for this passage in one of Nietzsche's notebooks from the period is another note saying: 'We are to be a mirror of Being: we are God on a small scale'.[12]

On the way down from his mountain-top to the world of his fellow human beings, Zarathustra encounters an old holy man who immediately recognizes him as *ein Erwachter*, 'an awakened one' (Z 'Prologue' 2) – an appellation customarily applied to Buddhas and bodhisattvas.[13] Applied to Zarathustra it suggests not only an awakening to the true nature of his self but also to the realization that such an awakening must be enacted through re-engaging the human world. The old man counters Zarathustra's profession of love for humanity by professing his own

love for God, just as the Arhant (the early Hinayāna Buddhist counterpart to the bodhisattva) strives to attain nirvana primarily for himself.
Zarathustra restrains himself from depriving the holy man of the object
of his love by telling him: *'God is dead'* (Z 'Prologue' 2).

We learn something about the implications of this death from
Zarathustra's first speech to the people in the market-place, with its
opening proclamation of the *Übermensch* and its admonition that 'The
human being is something that is to be overcome' (Z 'Prologue' 3).
Theism is not simply to be replaced by humanism, nor is Zarathustra, in
admonishing the crowd to *'stay faithful to the earth* and not believe those
who speak of over-earthly hopes' (Z 'Prologue' 3), merely advocating a
renunciation of transcendent perspectives in favor of a focus on the
human. To urge that the human must be overcome is on one level to call
for a transcendence of the anthropocentric perspective to a view that
sees the inanimate world – 'the earth' – as itself divine.

> Once sacrilege against God was the greatest sacrilege, but God died, and
> with Him these sacrilegious ones too. Sacrilege against the earth is now the
> most terrible thing, and to revere the entrails of the unfathomable more
> than the sense of the earth! (Z 'Prologue' 3).

Hopes directed to what is beyond the earth are to be renounced, and
with the demise of a transcendent divinity the earth and nature become
the proper locus of the sacred. A late Buddhist sutra claims that the
Buddha's enlightenment brought about the enlightenment of the whole
world: 'I and the great earth are simultaneously enlightened. Mountains,
rivers, grass, and trees have all realized their intrinsic Buddha-nature'.[14]
This exemplifies an idea that was elaborated in later Indian Buddhism
under the name *tathāgata-garbha,* which signifies that all beings intrinsically possess 'buddha-nature' and have the capacity to be enlightened.
This idea became central to the forms of Mahāyāna Buddhism that
developed in China, Tibet, and Japan.

By the time of Zarathustra's seventh speech, however, his apparent
atheism is moderated to an agnosticism: in response to those who maintain that life is a heavy burden, he says: 'I would only believe in a God
who could dance' (Z 'On Reading and Writing'). The ground for this
potential belief is revealed in the ecstatic ending to the speech: 'Now I
am light, now I am flying, now I see myself beneath myself, now a God
dances through me' (Z 'On Reading and Writing'). This is an epiphany
– the first of several in the book – of Dionysus, God of wine and the
dance. As the climax of Zarathustra's most lyrical flight so far, it may be

taken as an involuntary revelation of his belief in divine forces to an audience from whom he is currently withholding his deeper feelings as he tries to disabuse them of their belief in God.

By the end of the first part of the book Zarathustra has gathered an audience of disciples, but he realizes they are immature in being more inclined to follow him rather than his teaching. He therefore resolves to leave them and return to his solitude, but not before delivering a speech that ends by reiterating his emphasis on staying loyal to the earth, at the high pitch of a sentence entirely in italics: '"*Dead are all gods: now we want the Übermensch to live*"' – may this be at the great noontide our ultimate will!' (Z 'On the Bestowing Virtue' 3). On one level this admonition is a reflection of the idea (derived from Feuerbach) that Gods are the result of a projection of unconscious human qualities. Nietzsche had outlined the consequences of the withdrawal of such projections in a passage written shortly before *Zarathustra*:

> There is a lake that one day refused to let itself flow off and threw up a dam where it had formerly flowed off: since then this lake has been rising ever higher. Perhaps this very refusal will also grant us the strength with which the refusal itself can be borne; perhaps the human being will from then on rise ever higher, when it no longer *flows out* into a God. (GS 285)

The refusal to allow one's energies to drain off through projections of divinity is a necessary step – but not the last – on the way to understanding one's place in the cosmos. Even after human beings have risen higher thanks to this refusal, they still may find themselves inferior to other forces in the cosmos.

Taken in context, Zarathustra's apparent declaration of a radical atheism may be understood as what the Buddhists call *upāya*, 'skill in means', a strategy aimed at directing an audience unprepared for the full revelation of the truth some way along the appropriate path. When the Buddha sends his disciples out into the world he says to them, 'I am released from all bonds, both divine and human. You, too, are released from all bonds, you disciples, both divine and human'; but he then tells them to go out and spread the teachings 'to the joy of gods and humans'.[15] In order to throw the practitioner back on his or her own resources, Mahāyāna Buddhism keeps its respect for the Buddhas and Patriarchs in perspective through the use of injunctions such as, 'If you meet the Buddha on the road, kill him!'[16] Correspondingly, Zarathustra would rather that his disciples at first rid themselves of all belief in forces transcending the human, than move too soon to a more salutary polytheism – from which they might then relapse into some other form of 'monotonotheism'.[17]

As a last lesson Zarathustra encourages his disciples to cultivate in themselves what he proclaims as the highest, *bestowing* virtue – 'You shall compel all things toward you and into you, so that they may flow back out of your wells as gifts of your love' – and retreats to his mountain-top cave (Z 'On the Bestowing Virtue' 1).

'Divine shall all beings be for me.'

The first chapter of the book's second part, 'The Child with the Mirror', opens with Zarathustra's awakening from a dream in which a child approaches him with a mirror and invites him to look at his reflection – an allusion to the myth of Dionysus-Zagreus in which the Titans abduct the infant Dionysus as he stares at his reflection in a mirror.[18] He interprets the dream as a sign that he must go back down to human beings and to being human again, after a further period of accumulating wisdom in his mountain-top solitude. Again, as with the bodhisattva, it is love that prompts him to go back down and pour out his self into the world:

> My impatient love overflows in torrents, downwards, toward rising and setting. Out of silent mountains and thunderstorms of pain my soul rushes into the valleys.... Mouth have I become through and through, and the roaring of a stream out of high cliffs: downward would I hurl my speech into the valleys. ...There is a lake in me, solitary and self-sufficient; but the river of my love carries it away – down to the ocean! (Z 'The Child with the Mirror')

The Dionysian imagery of his speech, which rushes through him as a force of nature, then veers from features of landscape to the trappings of war, as Zarathustra braces himself for the struggle against hostile forces with images of riding wild steeds and hurling spears at his enemies.

His first speech to his disciples after coming down from the mountain, 'In the Isles of the Blessed', explains why the Gods must die before the *Übermensch* can come to life. The death of God as the collapse of the plausibility of any permanent absolutes brings the individual face to face with the radical impermanence of all existence, and especially the impermanence of the human self. To suffer a Dionysian dissolution of one's own person is suffering indeed, but subsequent participation in the broader processes of destruction and regeneration brings a realization of the possibilities of new creation.

Creating – that is the great redemption from suffering, and life's becoming lighter. But that the creator may be, that itself requires suffering and much transformation. Yes, much bitter dying must there be in your lives, you creators! Thus are you advocates and justifiers of all that is transitory. (Z 'In the Isles of the Blessed')

The impermanence of all existence, the suffering associated with that, and the fabrication of a self-construct in response – all are central teachings of Buddhism. Nishitani quotes an unpublished note of Nietzsche's that echoes Zen ideas: 'Becoming as inventing, willing, negating the self, as self-overcoming: no subject, but a doing, positive, creative.'[19] And indeed Nietzsche himself associates this kind of Dionysian process with impermanence: 'Dionysos: sensuality and cruelty. Impermanence could be interpreted as enjoyment of the procreative and destructive energies, as constant creation' (KSA 12 2 106). For Zarathustra, as long as human beings feel themselves subordinated to transcendent forces in the form of divinities they will lack confidence in their own will to create. But if they are able to face up to the impermanence of 'becoming' and fully engage the cycles of death and rebirth and destruction and creation that characterize the world of a deity like Dionysus, such self-overcoming will allow the forces of the creative will to work and play – perhaps even dance – through them. Captivated by a vision of what the human being could become, Zarathustra claims to have no need for divine epiphanies: 'The beauty of the *Übermensch* came to me as a shadow. Ah, my brothers! What are the Gods to me now!' (Z 'In the Isles of the Blessed').

But in his speech 'On the Famous Wise Men', where Zarathustra shows how much previous philosophers have been lackeys in the service of religious leaders or political rulers, it becomes clear that atheism is merely a provisional stage in the transformations of the human spirit. In questioning his predecessors' pretensions toward the truth, he alludes to the 'three transformations' (camel to lion to child) described in his very first speech.

> Truthful – thus did I call the one who goes into godless deserts and has broken his reverential heart. In yellow sand and burned by the sun, he squints thirstily at islands rich in springs, where living things repose beneath dark trees. But his thirst does not persuade him to become like these comfortable ones: for where there are oases, there are always images of idols. Ravenous, violent, solitary, godless: thus would the lion-will have itself be.

Free from the happiness of vassals, redeemed from gods and worship, fearless and fearsome, great and solitary: thus is the will of the truthful one. (Z 'On the Famous Wise Men')

At the stage of the camel one has to 'break one's reverential heart' in order to be able to endure the godless desert with the strength of the lion and not be seduced by mirages harboring idols. But we recall that the lion's 'holy No' is incapable of genuine creativity: the best it can manage is 'the creation of freedom for new creation' (Z 'On the Three Transformations'). For 'the play of creation' the 'holy Yes-saying' of the child is required; after the Gods who impede human creativity have been denied, they return in the form of the child. For it turns out that among the living things reposing under dark trees will be a little God.

In the next chapters Zarathustra's speeches modulate into songs, as he approaches the central topic – and figure – of Life. Before breaking into 'The Dance Song' he addresses, in the presence of his disciples, a group of young maidens dancing in a meadow:

God's advocate am I before the devil: but he is the spirit of gravity. How could I, you light-footed ones, be an enemy of divine dances? Or of girls' feet with well-turned ankles? Indeed I am a forest and a night of dark trees: but whoever does not fear my darkness will also find rose-bowers under my cypresses. And the little God will one find as well, who is to girls the dearest one: beside the spring he lies, still, with his eyes closed. (Z 'The Dance Song')

The God whose advocate Zarathustra is before the devil is Dionysus, since it was thanks to this divinity's dancing through him that he was going to be able to overcome the spirit of gravity (Z 'On Reading and Writing'). In the context of the dance song the child Dionysus appears as *Erôs* (or Cupido, as he is referred to here), though Nietzsche closely associates these two Gods of the life-force.

In 'The Tomb Song' the divine recurs in the form of 'divine moments' made for 'tender eternities' from Zarathustra's youth. (The conjunction of 'moments' *[Augenblicke]* and 'eternities' *[Ewigkeiten]* anticipates the thought of eternal recurrence, in which the moment plays a key role.) Zarathustra now mourns the loss of those divine moments, while accusing his 'enemies' of strangling 'the songbirds of his hopes', because of the even greater loss they cost him.[20]

For you cut short what was eternal for me, as a tone breaks off in coldest night! Scarcely as a glinting of divine eyes did it come to me – as a moment! Thus did my purity once speak to me in a fair hour: 'Divine shall all beings be to me.'[21] ...'All days shall be holy to me' – thus did the wisdom of my youth once speak: verily, the speech of a joyous wisdom! (Z 'The Tomb Song')

Prevented by resentment toward his enemies from regaining his former attitude of 'holy Yes-saying' to the world, Zarathustra now places his hope in the redemptive power of his creative will, trusting that the deaths and tombs by which he is surrounded will turn out to be harbingers of resurrections and new life.

In his next speech, 'On Self-Overcoming', Zarathustra announces the outcome of his inquiries into the living: life is best understood as 'will to power'. Just as Plato (in the *Symposium*) had Diotima intimate life's deepest mysteries to Socrates, so Nietzsche has Life herself tell Zarathustra that she is continual 'self-overcoming' and 'will to power' (Z 'On Self-Overcoming'). When Nietzsche later elaborates this insight as a challenge to understand the whole world (not just the animate part of it) as 'will to power, and nothing besides', he signifies that while this would mean that the transcendent God of morality is refuted, a pantheistic cosmos full of immanent Gods is not.[22] But to experience the world this way, as a play of will to power engaged in perpetual self-overcoming, one has to understand from experience the thought of eternal recurrence.

Circulus vitiosus deus?

The second chapter of part three, 'On the Vision and the Riddle', presents the first full intimation of this thought – the 'basic conception' of *Zarathustra* and 'the highest formula of affirmation that can possibly be attained' (EH 'Thus Spoke Zarathustra' 1). The thought of eternal recurrence had first been presented at the end of *The Gay Science*, where we are asked what our response would be if a demon (or *daimôn*?) were to say to us: 'This life, as you now live and have lived it, you will have to live once more and innumerable times more' (GS 341). Would you curse the demon? 'Or have you ever experienced a tremendous moment where you would answer him: "You are a God and never have I heard anything more divine!"' (GS 341). Corresponding to the nihilistic and affirmative responses to the prospect of eternal recurrence, then, are the demonic and the divine aspects to the thought.

In 'On the Vision and the Riddle' Zarathustra is voyaging across the sea when he has a vision in which he is climbing a mountain-path in defi-

ance of the spirit of gravity, his 'devil and arch-enemy', who in the form
of a dwarf sits on his shoulders (Z 'On the Vision and the Riddle' 1). The
dwarf asserts his superiority over Zarathustra by reminding him that, no
matter how high he may climb, however high he throws himself up,
he will always come down again and will ultimately suffer the fate of
all mortal beings and go under altogether. The spirit of gravity, modeled after Mephistopheles in Goethe's *Faust* ('the spirit that always
negates'), represents the force whereby 'all things fall' and always wants
'the earth and life' to be *heavy*.[23] But Zarathustra then experiences a
sudden access of courage, a courage powerful enough to strike even
death dead that ultimate manifestation of impermanence insofar as it
says: 'Was *that* life? Well then! One more time!' (Z 'On the Vision and
the Riddle' 1).[24]

When the thought of eternal recurrence is reiterated in similar words
in *Beyond Good and Evil*, there is another allusion to the divinity of the
cosmos. Here Nietzsche claims that in his confrontation with nihilism
he has at least overcome the Eurocentric perspective, if not the anthropocentric perspective too, insofar as he has looked 'with an Asiatic and
supra-Asiatic eye into the most world-denying of all possible ways of
thinking …beyond good and evil' (BGE 56) – and has thereby had his
eyes opened to 'the opposite ideal …of the most exuberant, vital, and
world-affirming human being' (BGE 56). Such a human being, who
could joyously affirm the world *'just as it has been and is'* (BGE 56),
would understand the enigmatic end of the aphorism, *circulus vitiosus
deus* (BGE 56), in this way: what had looked like a vicious circle (the
thought of recurrence in its nihilistic aspect) turns out to be divine – *deus
ex natura*, one might say.

To return to Zarathustra: to the extent that he can summon the
courage to say (and live) Yes! to the question – in his every action, at
every moment – 'Do you want this once again and innumerable times
more?', he will overcome the spirit of gravity with levity and laughter. To
say and live Yes! to this question requires courage because it requires an
affirmation of the whole of existence, insofar as every action of each self
is inextricably linked with all other actions and selves. As Zarathustra
asks the dwarf: 'And are not all things knotted together so tightly that
this moment draws after it *all* things that are to come?' (Z 'On the Vision
and the Riddle' 2). The question also receives an affirmative answer in
the central Buddhist teaching of 'dependent arising' (*prātītya-
samutpāda*), which similarly emphasizes the interconnectedness of all
things and the consequent 'emptiness' of any 'self-nature' to them. This

idea receives its ultimate Dionysian expression at the culmination of *Zarathustra*'s fourth part, when Zarathustra sings:

> Did you ever say Yes to a single pleasure? Oh, my friends, then you said Yes to *all* pain. All things are interlinked, intertwined, enamoured – (Z 'The Night-Wanderer Song' 10)

This passage exemplifies what Nishitani has called 'Dionysian pantheism' with reference to Nietzsche's explication of the term 'Dionysian' as involving 'rapturous affirmation of the total character of life [and] the great pantheistic sharing of joy and suffering' (WP IV 1050). As Nishitani states:

> Nietzsche's use of the term 'pantheistic' is not unimportant, for what is overcome by eternal recurrence is only 'the God of morality', and belief in recurrence opens one to a pantheistic affirmative attitude toward everything. He asks himself, and then answers, the question of whether it is possible to think of a God not in moral terms but 'beyond good and evil'.[25]

Nietzsche even sees this possibility as one that was latent in German philosophy (Hegel) but went undeveloped: 'to think through a *pantheism* in which evil, error, and pain are *not* felt as arguments against divinity' (KSA 12 2 106).

In the second phase of his vision Zarathustra sees himself as a shepherd writhing on the ground because a huge black snake has crawled into his mouth and bitten fast to his throat.[26] The shepherd eventually bites the snake's head off, spits it out and leaps to his feet, 'No longer a shepherd, no longer human – one transformed, enlightened, who *laughed!*' (Z 'On the Vision and the Riddle 2) A laughter that is 'no human being's laugh' (Z 'On the Vision and the Riddle 2): *übermenschlich* then, with accents, at least, of the divine.

The effects of this experience on Zarathustra's understanding of himself and the world come to light in the chapter 'Before Sunrise'. Still on board ship on the open sea, he rises before dawn and delivers a speech to the open sky in response to the divine feelings the prospect engenders in him: 'O heaven above me, you pure one! profound one! You abyss of light! Beholding you I shudder with divine desires' (Z 'Before Sunrise'). His reaction echoes the response of the Epicurean thinker (as described by Lucretius) to the revelation in which 'Nature is revealed as rid of haughty overlords, as the free autonomous agent of everything, without the participation of the gods.'[27] Such a revelation affords a peculiar pleasure: 'At these things some godlike delight seizes me and a shuddering of awe, to think that nature is thus made so clear and manifest, laid open and unveiled in every part.'[28]

To Zarathustra's eyes the heavens before dawn, in which the stars have been extinguished and the sun has not yet risen, are an expanse of pure openness that illuminates everything evenly, without bias or slant – by contrast with the sun's illumination which always comes from a particular direction, casting shade and shadows. 'Before Sunrise' is of crucial importance since it seems to go beyond Nietzsche's customary perspectivism and allow for an experience of the world that is not merely 'from our own little corner' but from a horizon that transcends anthropocentric views. There are remarkable parallels here with Nishitani's explication of 'the standpoint of śūnyatā [emptiness]' in Mahāyāna Buddhism, from which things are experienced not as representations of a subject but rather in their own 'suchness' or 'as-they-are-ness' (*tathātā*).[29]

Somewhat enlightened by the vision he has just seen, and addressing the most open audience imaginable, Zarathustra can afford to be totally open himself and claim without reservation that he now has something in common with the pre-dawn heavens: 'the enormous, unbounded saying of Yes and Amen'. As a participant in this unbounded affirmation he is moved to bless all things in the 'innocence of their becoming' (to borrow a phrase Nietzsche uses elsewhere):

> But this is my blessing: to stand over each particular thing as its own heaven, as its round roof, its azure bell and eternal security: and blessed is he who blesses thus! For all things are baptized in the well of eternity and are beyond good and evil; for good and evil are themselves mere intervening shadows and damp depressions and drifting clouds. Verily, it is a blessing and no blasphemy when I teach: 'Over all things stands the heaven Chance, the heaven Innocence, the heaven Contingency, the heaven Exuberance.'
> 'Lord Contingency'[30] – that is the oldest nobility in the world, which I restored to all things when I redeemed them from their bondage under purpose. (Z 'Before Sunrise')

When a particular thing is what it is only thanks to the role assigned it under some overarching divine Providence, or the position occupied in some scientific projection of the world, it is not free to be itself. Just as the Daoist sage (a precursor of the Zen master) is able to broaden his perspective to the point where he is able to 'illumine all things in the light of heaven,' and by acting in a way harmonious with heaven and earth can 'help the ten-thousand things be themselves',[31] so Zarathustra's blessing lets each particular thing generate its own horizons and be (or, rather, *become:* arise and perish) just as it is. And ultimately he understands that all things would far rather, more than anything, '*dance on the feet of chance*' just as the bodhisattva works for the en'lighten'-ment of all things.

One should note that these stances are by no means biocentric in being restricted to a celebration of all life: they concern rather a celebration of *all things*. In a preface written in 1886 to a book in which he first emphasized the importance of 'small things' and the 'inconspicuous truths' of life, Nietzsche writes of himself as one who re-engages the world after a period of alienation from it:

> It is almost as if his eyes are only now opened to *what is near*. He is amazed, and sits still: where *was* he then? This near and nearest things: how they seem to him transformed! what bloom and enchantment they have acquired in the interim! He looks back with gratitude... (HH 'Preface' 5)

It is from this kind of perspective that one might experience all things as having been 'baptized in the well of eternity'.

Returning to *Zarathustra*, we learn that Zarathustra's purity, which we heard announce the divinity of all beings to him, is a reflection of the vaster purity of the heavens:

> O heaven above me, you pure one! on high! That is what your purity means to me, that there is no eternal reason-spider and spider's web: that for me you are a dance-floor for divine accidents, that for me you are a gods' table for divine dice and dice-throwers! (Z 'Before Sunrise').

The heavens are a dance-floor not because the Gods are above but because Zarathustra's boundless affirmation has overturned all traditional hierarchies of the 'heavens above, earth below' variety. Earth's materiality is to be seen through, deliteralized, so that it can be rebaptized 'the light one' (Z 'On the Spirit of Gravity 2), and Zarathustra can begin his apostrophe to the open sky with the appellation, 'you abyss of light' (Z 'Before Sunrise').

We learn more about Zarathustra's theism when he tells the hilarious tale of how the ancient gods died:

> Theirs was no mere 'twilight' death – that is a lie![32] Rather did they *laugh* themselves to death! That happened when the most godless word issued from a god himself – the word: 'There is only one God! Thou shalt have no other god before me!'[33] – an old wrath-beard of a god, a jealous one, forgot

himself thus: And thereupon all the gods laughed and rocked on their chairs and shouted: 'Is that not precisely godlike [*göttlich*, divine], that there are gods but no god?' He that hath ears, let him hear. – (Z 'On Apostates' 2).

These are Zarathustra's last words in the last speech that he makes before returning to his mountain-top solitude for the last time, and the quotation from *Matthew* suggests that there is more to come, deeper implications to what has been said than the audience has grasped. If the old gods laughed themselves to death, and the divine consists in there being Gods but no God, then presumably the old gods may be laughed back to life again – by transformed shepherds who understand the world as 'will to power'.

How the world appears on such an understanding is conveyed by Zarathustra's speech 'On Old and New Tablets', where he tells of how his flying into a far future granted him an experience of the world as a force-field of divine play:

> Where all becoming seemed to me a Gods'-dance and Gods'- willfulness, and the world released and exuberant and fleeing back to itself: – as an eternal fleeing-and reseeking-themselves of many Gods, as the blissful self-contradicting, self-rehearing, self-rebelonging of many Gods. (Z 'On Old and New Law Tablets' 2)

Such was the power of this experience that he retroactively transforms his previous interrogative into an affirmative by claiming to have said earlier 'That precisely is godlike, that there are gods, but no god' (Z 'On Old and New Law Tablets' 11).

The book as Nietzsche originally conceived it culminates in three lyrical chapters celebrating the mystic marriage of Zarathustra with Life, on the model of the nuptials of Dionysus and Ariadne.[34] At the end, in the 'Yes- and Amen-Song', Zarathustra reaffirms the way the ring of recurrence sets a seal on the world as a playing field for divinities:

> If ever I laughed with the laughter of creative lightning, grumblingly but obediently followed by the rumbling of the long thunder of the deed: If ever I played with Gods'-dice at the Gods'-table of the earth, so that the earth quaked and broke and snorted forth rivers of fire: – for a Gods'-table is the earth, trembling with creative new words and Gods'-throws – Oh how could I not be lusting after eternity and the nuptial ring of rings – the ring of recurrence? (Z 'The Seven Seals' 3)

The world as divine play, then, the ultimate game of chance, with the enlightened human being as a full participant.

'What can we best give *in return*?'

Nietzsche was attracted at an early age to the religiosity of the ancient Greeks through his reading of Homer and the Hellenophilic writings of Goethe and Schiller. His admiration only increased with time, and after several decades later he writes: 'What astounds us in the religion of the ancient Greeks is the unrestrained abundance of gratitude that it exudes: it is a very noble kind of human being that stands *thus* before nature and life!' (BGE 49). Zarathustra is naturally an exemplar in this respect:

> Thus does the nature of noble souls wish it: they want to have nothing for free, and least of all life. Whoever is of the rabble wants to live for free: we others, however, to whom life has given itself – we are always wondering *what* we can best give *in return!* (Z 'On the Old and New Law Tablets' 5)

This kind of gratitude is again reminiscent of Epicurus, for whom meditation cultivates a keen appreciation of the 'once-only' character of existence in a radically contingent universe. When the world is experienced as arising anew at every moment, yet with no necessary connection between this moment and the next, one comes to celebrate each moment as a unique miracle. As Epicurus writes: 'One cultivates profound gratitude to nature for granting us the gift of life'.[35] Zarathustra cultivates such gratitude by striving to live each moment (which for him, too, is unique and 'once only') *as if* it and the rest of the past were going to recur eternally. A similar gratitude informs Mahāyāna Buddhist practice, which is also based on an understanding of the unique and radically contingent character of each and every moment.

And yet for Nietzsche there seems to be something that persists throughout the constant flux, which he characterizes in a late note as the Dionysian: 'rapturous affirmation of the total character of life, as what is the same in all change, similarly powerful, similarly blissful' (KSA 13 14 14). Nishitani's gloss of this 'total character' is apt, coming as it does from the Mahāyāna perspective:

> For Nietzsche, what remains the same throughout the process, never departing from ever-changing arising and perishing, is the will that affirms eternal recurrence. This is the perspective of the new 'pantheism' – qualitatively different from previous and subsequent pantheistic ideas – and Dionysus is the god who embodies it.[36]

A Dionysian pantheism by no means excludes – indeed by its nature it includes – other forms of the divine, and indeed one of Nietzsche's last words on the topic keeps such possibilities open. In a note written several months before his mental collapse, under the title 'History of the Concept of God', he bemoans the impoverishment consequent upon a move away from God as a being (like nature) that one can thank and yet that can be harmful as well as helpful, to 'a God of *the Good*' alone. He contrasts a God (like Dionysus) who 'knows the dangerous *ardeurs* of destruction' with 'the pitiful God of European monotono-theism', who he trusts is finally giving way to something new:

> – And how many new Gods are still possible!..To myself, in whom the religious, that is to say God-*forming* instinct wants every now and then to become active again: how differently, how variously the Divine has revealed itself to me every time!..So much that is strange has already passed before me, in those timeless moments that fall into one's life as if from the moon, where one no longer has any idea how old one is already and how young one will yet become …I should not doubt that there are many kinds of Gods. (KSA 13 17 4).

And insofar as humans are natural beings, one should not doubt that there are many kinds of participation in the divine play open to them too.

I trust that this essay reinforces the conclusion of an earlier one, which argued that Nietzsche's ideas about nature deserve to be taken seriously in current debates about 'the environment', especially in the light of their consonance with ideas from such a different tradition as that of Mahāyāna Buddhism.[37] Both views go beyond a naive romanticism that would see nature as simply beneficent, regarding its perpetual creativity and destructiveness rather as deserving our awe and respect. Indeed Nietzsche associates 'the naturalizing of the human' precisely with the cultivation of awareness of the tremendous *contingency* of our existence: 'We can protect ourselves only a little in the great matters: a comet could smash the sun at any moment…To the naturalizing of the human belongs readiness for the absolutely sudden and thwarting' (KSA 9 11 228). The Mahāyāna Buddhists too understand that, to the extent that we can give up our death-anxiety-engendered desire to subjugate the natural world, and cultivate instead a readiness for the absolutely sudden and thwarting (of which the ultimate paradigm is my death), there will open up a way of being that verges on the divine through its fullness of sorrows and joys.

Bibliography of cited works of Nietzsche

Sämtliche Werke: Kritische Studienausgabe. (Munich: Walter de Gruyter, 1980, eds. G. Colli, M. Montinari).

Notes

1 See GS 108, 125; Z 'Prologue' 2, 1 'On the Bestowing Virtue' 3. I refer to passages from *Zarathustra* using my own translation (forthcoming from Stanford University Press, 2001).

2 Nietzsche, letter to Franz Overbeck, 30 July 1881 in *Briefe* (Munich: Walter de Gruyter, 1986) 6 111.

3 Graham Parkes, 'Staying Loyal to the Earth: Nietzsche as an Ecological Thinker' in John Lippitt (ed.), *Nietzsche's Futures* (Basingstoke: Macmillan, 1999) pp.167–188. See p. 182.

4 Keiji Nishitani, *The Self-Overcoming of Nihilism* (Albany: State University of New York Press, 1990, trans. Graham Parkes with Setsuko Aihara) p. 48.

5 Nishitani, *The Self-Overcoming of Nihilism* p. 180.

6 Laurence Lampert in his forthcoming book, *Nietzsche's Task: An Interpretation of 'Beyond Good and Evil'* (New Haven: Yale University Press), emphasizes Nietzsche's conviction that a new philosophy such as his needs to be complemented by a new religion, such as his religion of Dionysus. On Nietzsche and Buddhism, see the essays by the Japanese contributors to Graham Parkes (ed.), *Nietzsche and Asian Thought* (Chicago: University of Chicago Press, 1991) as well as my review article, 'Nietzsche and Early Buddhism', and 'Reply to Robert Morrison', *Philosophy East and West* 50:2 (2000) pp. 254–267 and pp. 279–284.

7 See, for example G. Parkes, 'Nietzsche and Zen Master Hakuin on the Roles of Emotion and Passion', in Joel Marks and Roger T. Ames (eds.) *Emotions in Asian Thought: A Dialogue in Comparative Philosophy* (Albany: State University of New York Press, 1994) pp. 213–233.

8 Hermann Oldenberg, *Buddha. Sein Leben, seine Lehre, seine Gemeinde* (Berlin: Wilhelm Hertz Verlag, 1881) p. 121. See also Nietzsche's notes on this book in the context of *Zarathustra*, in KSA 11 26 220–221.

9 For the sake of (relative) brevity, I confine myself to the first three parts of *Zarathustra* which constitute the book as Nietzsche originally conceived it.

10 Har Dayal, *The Bodhisattva Doctrine in Buddhist Sanskrit Literature* (London: Kegan Paul, 1932) p. 9. It has also been suggested that *sattva* may mean 'strength, energy, vigour, power, courage' (*ibid* p. 7).

11 Gadjin Nagao, *Mādhyamika and Yogācāra: A study of Māhāyana Philosophies* (Albany: State University of New York Press, 1991, trans. Leslie Kawamura) pp. 32–33.

12 Nietzsche, KSA 105 1 240. See also the claim: 'I am too full: thus I forget

myself, and all things are in me, and beyond all things there is nothing more: where have *I* gone?' (KSA 5 1 238)

13   The Buddha is often referred to as *ein Erwachter* in Oldenberg's *Buddha.*

14   Cited in Kōgaku Arifuku, *Deutsche Philosophie und Zen-Buddhismus* (Berlin: Akademie Verlag, 1999) p. 115.

15   Oldenberg, *Buddha* p. 133.

16   See, for instance, the first of the collection of Zen stories entitled *Mumonkan* (The Gateless Gate).

17   The advantages of polytheism are eloquently exposited in GS 143.

18   See the account by Nonnos: 'The Titans cunningly smeared their round faces with disguising chalk, and while [Zagreus] contemplated his changeling countenance reflected in a mirror, they destroyed him with an infernal knife' in *Dionysiaca* (Cambridge, Mass.: Harvard University Press, 1940) vol. 7 p. 169. Also *Diodorus of Sicily* (Cambridge, Mass.: Harvard University Press, 1932) vol 5 75 4.

19   Nietzsche, KSA 12 7 54, WP III 617, cited by Nishitani in *The Self-Over-coming of Nihilism* pp. 47–48.

20   The context and the biographical background suggest that these 'enemies' were the Wagners and also Lou Salomé and Paul Rée.

21   This saying, as well as 'All days shall be holy to me,' is adapted from a passage from Emerson's *Essays* of which Nietzsche was especially fond, and which he used for the epigraph to *The Gay Science* (1882). The original reads: 'To the poet, to the philosopher, to the saint, all things are friendly and sacred, all events profitable, all days holy, all men divine' (*Essays*, 'History'). In a letter to Overbeck written on the Christmas after the fateful summer when his relationship with Lou Salomé foundered so painfully, Nietzsche writes: 'I have here the most beautiful opportunity to demonstrate that "all experiences are useful, all days holy, and al human beings are divine" to me !!!!' (25 December 1882), *Briefe* 6 312.

22   See BGE 36, 37. As Laurence Lampert says of the import of these two aphorisms for the idea of the world as will to power: 'That wasteful, indifferent, throbbing abundance, the world as it is, must be seen as the not refuted, vindicated divine'. See L. Lampert, 'Nietzsche's Best Jokes' in Lippitt (ed.), *Nietzsche's Futures* p. 79. Nietzsche wrote to Jacob Burckhardt that *Beyond Good and Evil* 'says the same things as my *Zarathustra*, but differently, very differently' (22 September 1886), *Briefe* 7 254.

23   See Z 2 'On the Tarantulas', 3 'On the Spirit of Gravity' 2.

24   For a comparison of Zen Buddhist and 'existentialist' (including Nietzsche's) understandings of death with respect to a momentary conception of time, see G. Parkes, 'Death and Detachment: Montaigne, Zen, Heidegger, and the Rest', in Jeff Malpas and Robert C. Solomon (eds.) *Death and Philosophy* (London: Routledge, 1998) pp. 164–180.

25   Nishitani, *The Self-Overcoming of Nihilism* p. 65.

26   See Z 3 'On the Vision and the Riddle' 2, 3 'The Convalescent' 2.

27   Lucretius, *The Way Things Are: The ' De rerum natura' of Titus Lucretius* (Indianapolis: Indiana University Press, 1968, trans. Rolfe Humphries) 2 1100.

28   *Ibid* 3 16–17, 28–30.

29   Nishitani Keiji, *Religion and Nothingness* (Berkeley: University of California Press, 1982, trans. Jan Van Bragt) chapter four. See also my elaboration of some of the parallels in G. Parkes, 'Nietzsche and Nishitani on the Self through Time', *The Eastern Buddhist* vol. 17:2 (1984) pp. 55–74.

30   *Von Ohngefähr.* The phrase means 'by chance,' but Nietzsche is playing on the use of the prefix *von* to indicate a noble family (as in the name Alexander von Humboldt).

31   *Zhuangzi,* chapter 2, Laozi, *Daodejing,* chapter 64.

32   An allusion to the last part of Wagner's *Ring* cycle, *Twilight of the Gods.*

33   Compare *Exodus* 20 3–5, where the Lord introduces the ten commandments by saying: 'Thou shalt have no other gods before me. ... for I the Lord thy God am a jealous God, visiting the iniquity of the fathers upon the children unto the third and fourth genration of them that hate me.'

34   See Laurence Lampert's commentary on these chapters in *Nietzsche's Teaching* (New Haven: Yale University Press, 1986) pp. 223–44.

35   Epicurus, *Vatican Sayings* 19, 69, 75. For the parallels between Epicurus and Zen see G. Parkes, 'Practicing Philosophy as a Matter of Life and Death', *Zen Buddhism Today* 15 (1998) pp. 58–67.

36   Nishitani, *The Self-Overcoming of Nihilism* p. 65.

37   See G. Parkes, 'Staying Loyal to the Earth'.

11

Ecstatic philosophy

Tyler T. Roberts

The political madness, about which I smile just as my contemporaries smile at the religious madness of earlier times, is above all secularization, faith in the world and a putting the 'beyond'…out of one's mind (KGW 2, 403).[1]

Nietzsche and the divine

Perhaps above all, Nietzsche prided himself on his untimeliness, on the fact that he was a posthumous man, on unflinching questions directed at questioning the concepts, categories, and values by which his contemporaries mapped their world. 'The philosopher,' Nietzsche writes, 'being of necessity a man of tomorrow and the day after tomorrow, has always found himself, and had to find himself, in contradiction to his today' (BGE 212). But after a century in which Nietzsche's influence has been perhaps unmatched by any other philosopher, can he still be untimely for us? For instance, can he really help us to think in an untimely fashion about religion when it has become all but automatic to assimilate him to modern secularism, which, at least in the academy and more generally in western intellectual culture, must be regarded as a reigning cultural and political ideology? If Nietzsche is still untimely with respect to religion, doesn't his untimeliness consist not in the unmasking of religious consolation or ascetic ideals, but in the subversion of a powerful dichotomy constitutive of modern western culture: the dichotomy between the secular and the religious.

Certainly, Nietzsche offers much to make the assimilation to secularism seem uncontroversial. His is a writing characterized by the cold chemistry of genealogical unmaskings, a deep animosity toward Christianity and, not infrequently, the explicit rejection of what he calls 'religion'. But then why, as he claims in the passage with which I began, does he smile at the political madness that insists on putting the beyond out of one's mind I think we find a certain beyond inscribed in the exuberance of his writing, a writing at times carried away by intoxicated, grateful affirmations and, as I note below, even 'deifications'. As William Connolly suggests, Nietzsche's is writing that confounds 'the dour division between the enchanted world of medieval Christianity and the disenchanted world of secular modernism... [so that we] might cultivate those fugitive spaces of enchantment lodged between theistic faith and secular abstinence.'[2]

In what follows I want to attempt to identify just one of these fugitive spaces of enchantment and discuss the role I think it plays in Nietzsche's philosophy. To do so, I will explore what I describe as a 'mystical thematics' in Nietzsche's thought.[3] I will not argue that Nietzsche 'is' a mystic, for recent historical studies of this term persuade me that its constructed and contested status make such definitions all but useless. Instead, I seek to identify a constellation of themes, ideas, and practices that in one sense or another have been acknowledged as mystical – a mystical thematics – in order to show that reading Nietzsche through the lens of this thematics radically complicates the manner in which we should interpret his thinking and writing when it comes to the question of religion. In turn, this allows Nietzsche to question us with respect to the way we deploy categories such as 'religion' and 'secular.' In short, it allows Nietzsche, once again, to be untimely.

Nietzsche and mysticism

> Concept of the mystic: one who has enough and even too much of his own happiness and seeks a language for the happiness with which to give it away (KSA 11 25 258).

This passage is an exception, for one only rarely finds the word mystic in Nietzsche's writing. Accordingly, the issue of mysticism in Nietzsche has not played a significant role in the secondary literature. There are some exceptions to this rule, such as Georges Bataille and, more recently, Joan Stambaugh's description of the Nietzsche of *Zarathustra* as a 'mystical poet'.[4] Neither Bataille nor Stambaugh, however, has explored the mystical themes in Nietzsche's thought in any sustained way or connected these themes to his larger philosophical project. I attempt to do both here.

Mysticism was a problem central to Nietzsche's engagement with Schopenhauer, primarily because mysticism was at the centre of

Schopenhauer's major philosophical work, *The World as Will and Representation*. There Schopenhauer argued, from his deep philosophical pessimism, that the inevitable suffering of individual beings could be ended only in the dissolution of individuation. This, in turn, was possible only when the will – Schopenhauer's ultimate metaphysical principle – ended its insatiable striving by turning against or denying itself. Schopenhauer saw this denial of the will accomplished in the *unio mystica* of the saint.[5] Further, he contended that his view of the mystical dissolution of the individual was the truth underlying all religion and philosophy, leading him to claim that 'Buddha, Eckhart, and I all teach essentially the same.'[6]

It was precisely Schopenhauer's pessimistic denial of life that Nietzsche would come to reject as he attempted to think through to the affirmation of life. But early in his philosophical career, Nietzsche was deeply impressed by Schopenhauer's ideas. Not surprisingly, then, certain mystical themes are easy to find in Nietzsche's early work. In his first book, *The Birth of Tragedy,* Nietzsche located the roots of Greek tragedy in the Greek mystery religions. At the heart of Greek tragedy, in fact, was a 'mystery doctrine,' namely, 'the fundamental knowledge of the oneness of everything existent, the conception of individuation as the primal cause of evil, and of art as the joyous hope that the spell of individuation may be broken in the augury of a restored oneness' (BT 7, 10).[7] The book describes how tragedy was born in this hope, but also tells of tragedy's death, at the hands of Socrates, whom Nietzsche describes as a 'typical non-mystic'(BT 13). Socrates was something new for the Greeks, revolutionizing their art and their philosophy. In an unpublished work of the same period, *Philosophy in the Tragic Age of the Greeks*, Nietzsche argues that in pre-Socratic philosophy the intuition and rapture rejected by Socrates played a major role: for example, he argues that Heraclitus grasped truth in intuition rather than logic and 'in Syballine rapture gazes but does not peer, knows but does not calculate.'[8] With Socrates, then, Greek voices of rapture are silenced: the mystical consciousness of tragedy and philosophy died with the advent of Socratic rationalism.

Now, even if one accepts the presence of certain mystical themes in his first book, it will be noted immediately that in the years following its publication, Nietzsche became disenchanted with Schopenhauer's philosophy. It is not surprising, then, that the kinds of mystical themes one can locate in the early work seem to all but disappear, along with metaphysical thinking more generally, from Nietzsche's writing. This would seem to be confirmed in a preface Nietzsche prepared for the second edition of *The Birth of Tragedy* in 1886, entitled 'Attempt at Self-Criticism' and written while he was at the peak of his powers. There, Nietzsche levels severe criticism at his first book and explicitly rejects its call for 'metaphysical comfort,' suggesting that the therapy for pessimism is not a return to primordial unity but rather the 'this-worldly comfort' exemplified in the golden laughter of Zarathustra. It would seem to follow that by rejecting so categorically 'metaphysical comfort,' Nietzsche would leave little room for a positive role for mysticism in his work.

This may be, in fact, what Nietzsche himself thought, though I will note evidence to the contrary. Nonetheless, I think arguments that would limit the significance of mysticism for Nietzsche to the period of the early 1870s, and tying it directly to his adherence to Schopenhauer, must fail. It is, no doubt, essential to take seriously Nietzsche's embrace of 'this-worldly comfort' and his rejection of metaphysical otherworldliness, exemplified, as he asserts, in *Zarathustra*. But it also is the case that in this text the idea of 'this-worldly' becomes complicated in ways unacknowledged by Nietzsche's 'Attempt at Self-Criticism'. As I have indicated, Joan Stambaugh views the Nietzsche of *Zarathustra* as a 'mystical poet' and identifies in the book classic mystical motifs such as *coincidentia oppositorum* and cosmic union. I think Stambaugh is right on this score and have elsewhere pushed her argument further by showing that certain mystical themes not only can be found in, but are at the heart of *Zarathustra*.[9] I can only gesture toward this argument here by looking at the end of Book Three and the penultimate section of Book Four of *Zarathustra*.

Book Three describes Zarathustra's struggles with his abysmal thought. Near the end of the book, Zarathustra finally allows himself to be overtaken by the thought. This marks a turning point, for in the remaining sections of the book, Zarathustra overcomes the abysmal thought and finds himself in love with Life and Eternity. This love is manifested in the final two songs of the book, 'The Other Dancing Song' and 'The Seven Seals (Or, The Yes and Amen Song)'. In the course of the first, when Zarathustra and Life finally pledge their mutual love for one another, something strange happens. The dialogue ends and the figures of both Zarathustra and Life recede. The reader is left with only a short, untitled poem/song, describing the tolling of a midnight bell with words that, significantly, have no apparent source (Z 'Other Dancing' 3). In each of the sections of *Zarathustra*, the speaker/singer is identified clearly in the text. However, this song and the song that follows ('Seven Seals'), are conspicuous for the absence of an identifiable voice.[10] Zarathustra undergoes an ecstatic experience, born of the painful experience of the abyss, in which the boundaries of his self dissolve in a song of love and participation with the cosmos.

The final song of Book Three – 'The Seven Seals (Or: the Yes and Amen Song)' – is a love song to eternity. It is also a song of affirmation, for it sings of clouds 'pregnant with lightning bolts that say Yes and laugh Yes.' And it is a song of participation: the singer 'hangs on the mountains,' sails on the sea, soars in the sky and dances 'star-dances'. In each of these respects – love, affirmation, and participation – the song attests to Zarathustra's ecstasy. He is lost to himself, less the singer than the one who is sung, less the dancer, than the one who is danced, as he had already suggested earlier in the book when he proclaimed: 'Now I am light, now I fly, now I see myself beneath myself, now a god dances through me' (Z 'Reading'). Despite what the late Nietzsche says about his first book, Zarathustra's ecstasy refigures the Dionysian as delineated in *The Birth of Tragedy*: 'In song and dance man expresses himself as a member of a higher community; he has forgotten how to walk and speak and is on the way toward flying into the air, dancing' (BT 1).

In the penultimate section of Book Four, after his 'Last Supper' with the higher men, Zarathustra undergoes a visionary experience that reprises the ecstasy of Book Three. As it opens, Zarathustra's spirit flies ahead and comes to rest on the 'high ridge' that was the scene for the opening lines of 'The Seven Seals' (Z 'Drunken' 2). Again, the midnight bell tolls, drawing Zarathustra to exclaim: 'Did not my world become perfect just now?' And, as the bell tolls, Zarathustra whispers to the higher men, not in his own words, but in the 'words' of the bell, which tell of a complex intertwining of pain and joy in which joy desires the return of all pain. In the moment of perfection, it seems, opposites such as pain-joy, day-night, time-eternity collapse. Nietzsche offers here another version of the idea of eternal recurrence, which he claimed was the basic idea of *Thus Spoke Zarathustra*.

> Just now my world became perfect; midnight too is noon; pain too is a joy; curses too are a blessing; night too is a sun – go away or you will learn; a sage too is a fool.
>
> Have you ever said Yes to a single joy? O my friends, then you said Yes to *all* woe. All things are bound together, entangled, enamored; if ever you wanted one thing twice, if ever you said, 'You please me, happiness! Abide, moment!' then you wanted *all* back. All anew, all eternally, all bound up, entangled, enamored — oh, then you *loved* the world (Z 'Drunken' 10).

Zarathustra does not end with this 'perfect moment,' for, in the final section of the book, Zarathustra shakes off his pity for the higher men and returns to his work. Nonetheless, the presence of ecstatic moments of perfection and joyful eternity both invoke certain themes from *The Birth of Tragedy* and complicate the sense of Nietzsche's 'this-worldly comfort'. From beyond his perfect moment, Zarathustra signals that joy's love for eternity includes the desire for suffering. Unlike other-worldly answers to the problem of suffering that promise some kind of final escape from suffering, Nietzsche here writes of suffering as integrally bound up with joy, eternity with the world. Love for eternity *is* love for the becoming of the world; the desire for joy is the desire for suffering. Such love does not distort the reality of self and world, for 'woe,' 'hatred,' and 'the cripple' remain: the love for eternity is love for the real. Clement Rosset, characterizes this love for the real as 'beatitude' and argues that it is the central theme of Nietzschean philosophy.[11] In the perfect moment, the joy of eternity floods the present of the world, so that the present is affirmed by all that leads to it and from it. Nietzsche here describes a movement of transcendence toward eternity that is completed only in a return to the world and the finite self. 'The world' is not left behind as false or incomplete, as it would be in certain monistic religious systems, or, it seems, as in *The Birth of Tragedy*, as read by Nietzsche in 1886; nor is the experience of eternity seen as a hint of better things to come, as it might be in certain understandings of Christianity. This is transcendence not as escape, but as an expansion and reorientation of awareness in which one's life in the earthly and finite finds a new center 'beyond' itself or 'deeper' than itself. Although Nietzsche rejects the comfort of metaphysical dualism, he continues to value an ecstatic abandon that has as its goal a certain reoccupying of the self, a resettling of or rebinding of the self to itself and world.

A mystical thematics

The primary mystical theme I have identified as playing a role in both Nietzsche's early work and in *Zarathustra* – an ecstatic union with the cosmos or ultimate reality – is relatively easy to recognize as mystical because for many in modern western culture, and this includes both Schopenhauer and Nietzsche, such experience is, in fact, definitive of 'mysticism'. But my discussion of Nietzsche and mysticism also identifies elements of Nietzsche's thought that seem clearly out of place in a discussion of mysticism, for example Nietzsche's this-worldliness and, with it, his affirmation of suffering and temporality. In turning now to a brief examination of some contemporary efforts at thinking through and beyond modern constructions of mysticism, I want to suggest that these aspects of Nietzsche's thought are not necessarily alien to mystical thinkers.[12]

Recent work in the study of mysticism has shown that the emphasis on private, individual dramatic experiences of selflessness and divine union as definitive of mysticism is a historically specific construction of modern western culture. This construction emerged from a complicated set of circumstances including the efforts by modern philosophers to marginalize religious truth claims, the colonial encounter with so-called mystical eastern religions, and the modern theological turn to religious experience as the basis for theological truth.[13] This construction has served certain apologetic efforts, as noted recently by John Bagger: 'Since the 19th century [the] hope for an experiential defense of religion has governed discussion of the historical mystics.'[14] This construction also has distorted our understanding of certain mystical thinkers, for whom the preoccupation with extraordinary experience is tangential, if not alien.[15] This is not to say that extraordinary experiences are not often found in historical mystics, but to emphasize that this is not always the case and that to make such experience definitive is to refuse to see the plurality of mystical phenomena. Again, Bagger: 'The farrago we label mysticism proves upon reflection far less homogenous that we often imagine.'[16]

Denys Turner's account of the apophatic strand of Christian theology is particularly instructive on this score. *Apophasis*, which literally means 'unsaying,' describes a way of doing theology in which movement towards God takes place by negating all propositions, images or metaphors – unsaying them – by which God is defined or described. Apophatic theology is often called negative theology and is rooted in the recognition of the absolute transcendence of the God of Biblical monotheism. Turner's study of apophatic thinkers such as Meister Eckhart and John of the Cross argues that the contemporary focus on mysticism as a kind of experience does not capture the radical negativity of apophatic traditions in which the self is emptied not only of all conceptions of God, but of all experience of God, even the experience of God's absence. It is better, he argues, to see as characteristic of the apophatic, 'that God is what is on the other side of anything at all we can be conscious of, whether of its presence or of its absence.'[17] He goes on to argue that historically, apophatic theology is a critique of the 'baroque, over-florid, technology of spiritual experientalism.'[18] Negative theologians were concerned not with experience but with cultivating a space of emptiness in all religious thought and experience, a 'moment of reserve, of denial and unknowing within worship, prayer and sacrament.'[19] This claim is significant. As a critical claim, it views the apophatic critique of experientialism as an attack on a Christian 'positivism' which seeks in mystical experience a ground for theological truth claims. More positively, though, it brings negative theology, as it were, down to earth, to ordinary Christian worship. The point of the apophatic path, on this reading, is not to cultivate an extraordinary, esoteric experience of God's absence or negativity, but rather to indicate the 'hiddeness' of the divine transcendent within the public, accessible, common cult, a 'moment' of negativity within the affirmative,' in other words, to bring to bear on ordinary Christian experience the *mystery* of God.[20]

What Turner's study suggests, and what other scholars of mysticism, such as Bernard McGinn and Robert Gimello, also argue is that for certain theological and spiritual traditions commonly referred to as mystical, extraordinary experiences of the divine are not the point.[21] They may in fact be a by-product of certain mystical practices, but what is at stake is first of all an overall pattern of life distinguished by disciplined practices oriented to the divine or ultimate. One consequence of the deemphasis on experience and the focus on practice has been increased attention to mystical writing as itself a form of religious practice. Instead of approaching mystical texts – which can take a wide variety of forms, such as aphorism, biography, visions, instruction, prayer, and poetry – with the intention of getting at the 'experience' behind the text, such research focuses on the text and writing itself as practice and performance.

Michel de Certeau, for example, uses the term 'mystics' to refer to a particular form of discourse, not to a particular kind of person. This is a discourse, he argues, that emerged in 'proximity to a loss,' specifically in the wake of the destruction of the Thirty Years War, a time in which Christianity was humiliated by the disintegration of its sacred world, a time when both Church and Scripture were being questioned as theological authorities.[22] As a discourse, 'mystics' is a practice of writing that is not simply 'about' the divine other, but is itself the very site and enactment of that otherness: 'The Other that organizes the text is not an outside the text. It is not the (imaginary) object that one might distinguish from the movement by which it is sketched.'[23] Like Turner, Certeau upsets the reigning assumption that Christian mysticism appeals, in a quasi-positivistic fashion, to a personal experience of the Christian God.[24] For the otherness organizing the mystic discourse is performed not in a conceptual or experiential determination of God, but in a series of departures that mirror the historically specific absence of God to which mystics responds. Mystics, Certeau writes, 'is a "manner of speaking," figured as a kind of "walking" or "gait," especially as a "wandering": he or she is a mystic who cannot stop walking and, with the certainty of what is lacking, knows of every place and object that it is not that; one cannot stay there nor be content with that.' It is here, I think, that we can make a first, extremely tentative, link with Nietzsche's writing insofar as it is marked by a departure or exile demanded by the death of God.

I approach this argument, however, only by means of a detour through the work of another contemporary theorist of writing and loss, Stanley Cavell. I turn to Cavell for three reasons. The first is philosophical: in Cavell I find the elucidation of a philosophical practice of writing that I think helps make an interesting link between the kind of writing of loss described by Certeau and by Nietzsche's own philosophical writing. The second reason for turning to Cavell is historical: Cavell articulates his view of philosophy in and through his readings of Emerson, Thoreau and Heidegger. He thereby invokes a constellation of thinkers whose historical relationship is mediated to a significant extent by Nietzsche's reception of Emerson. Much of what Cavell says about these figures applies in specific ways to Nietzsche's own writing and thought. Finally, although Cavell himself would likely resist giving his works a mystical inflection, he is not unaware that Emerson, Thoreau and Heidegger – along with Wittgenstein, another crucial figure for Cavell – are often viewed as having the aura of the mystical about them.

Following Wittgenstein, Cavell views philosophy as therapy. Specifically, it is a therapy of language, responding to our tendency to be 'bewitched' by language into trying to force an epistemological relationship with the world that, as finite creatures, is not available to us. This forcing comes about through the challenge of skepticism, which Cavell defines as the conversion of 'metaphysical finitude into intellectual lack.'[25] Traditionally, philosophy has responded to skepticism by seeking to create extraordinary, transparent philosophical languages that offer the certainty about our relation to the world skepticism finds lacking in ordinary language. But Cavell thinks that the philosophical response should be fundamentally different, for philosophy has usually only distorted the relationship to the world language does make possible.

Instead, philosophy should bring us back to the ordinary, for it is our ordinary words that connect us most solidly to the world and to others, not in an epistemological relationship of knowledge, but through what Cavell names 'acknowledgement', an openness or responsiveness to the world as a whole, and as something other than the knower.[26]

Philosophy, for Cavell, is writing 'in quest of the ordinary' but this quest must take a path through the extraordinary. Cavell does not reject outright the challenge of skepticism to our relationship with the world, for a certain alienation from language and the world is necessary in order to find an ordinary intimacy with it. Thus Cavell's embrace of a certain romantic response to skepticism. He defines romanticism as 'the discovery that the everyday is an exceptional achievement. Call it the achievement of the human.'[27] Cavell appeals to Emerson's view of poetry as a 'grand empiricism' to argue that true intimacy with the world takes place through the poetic imagination and its reception of language. Poetry gives voice to humanity in its passionate effort to push and expand its language. 'The simplest words, we do not know what they mean except when we love and aspire.'[28]

Cavell seeks to bring this poetic sensitivity to the life of words to philosophy as therapy or what I might call, following Pierre Hadot, a spiritual exercise.[29] For Cavell, we are always already embedded in the world through language and specifically through the conditions or agreements that make possible the intimacy between word and world.[30] Through writing, though, and particularly through figurative language, we can test and contest our words, pushing against, without rejecting the conditions of language, working with a tension between the ordinary and extraordinary, through which we try to bring life to our intuitions. Such writing is a process of giving inflection to the language we receive: 'in the realm of the figurative, our words are not felt as confining but as releasing, or not as binding but as bonding.'[31] A philosophical writing that embraces this perspective becomes a means by which one struggles with words by living them beyond habit and necessity, hearing them from all sides, listening for their resonance, resisting the temptations, as Nietzsche recognized, to which they tempt us: either blind conformity or transcendence.[32]

With his classic ascetic gesture of going to the woods to live 'deliberately', Thoreau becomes for Cavell a particular embodiment of this discipline. In his writing Thoreau endeavors to find the way that each word he reads or writes links him, here and now, to world and life. Such engagement with language becomes for Thoreau the model for engagement with nature and people: all his experiences are shaped by the incessant demand to make life come alive in each moment. In other words, Thoreau's writing performs a meditation on the present – 'the present was my next experiment of this kind' – a meditation that mediates Thoreau's experience of the divine: 'God himself culminates in the present moment.' Of this latter claim, Cavell offers his own inflection: 'To discover what is being said to us, as to discover what we are saying, is to discover the precise location from which it is said; to understand why it is said from just there, and at that time.'[33]

As Cavell reads it, Thoreau's 'experiment' requires a constant turning, a constant departure from or dying to the past, as a precondition to the birth of language in the present. Writing relinquishes words, but this loss or departure is always also a finding and arrival. 'Not till we are lost, in other words, not till we have lost the world do we begin to find ourselves, and realize where we are and the infinite extent of our relations.'[34] It is only in this loss that one finds life, because it is only in this loss that one opens oneself for new words, a new place of inhabitation, finding oneself, as Thoreau puts it, next to, or neighboring the world.[35] Cavell glosses this condition of intimacy with the following: 'You may call this mysticism, but it is a very particular view of the subject; it is not what the inexperienced may imagine as a claim to union, or absorption in nature.'[36] One does find accounts of such absorption in Thoreau's work, but Cavell indicates that if one is going to describe Thoreau as a mystic, what is significant is not self-dissolving union but a practice of intimacy in which one is always both bonded with and other than self, others, the world.

But why use the term 'mystical' to describe this writing? If one is convinced that the mystical is all about extraordinary experiences beyond words and beyond the human or about a selfless immediacy, then Cavell's orientation to the problem of ordinary language and human finitude will seem precisely to preclude the mystical. Despite the affirmation of the extraordinary in Cavell, he always turns us back to the ordinary, in what he describes as a reinhabiting of the world.[37] And if we read the mystic as a relative of the Cavellian skeptic – which I think the modern construction of mysticism does implicitly – that is, as one who desires and seeks to accomplish a relationship to the world and/or God that is closer, more immediate than our words, isn't Cavell an antimystic? Maybe; but I am trying, through Turner, Certeau and Cavell, to offer a different inflection of the mystical. I do this, however, without trying to redefine mysticism, but to instead articulate a 'mystical thematics'. What this means is that I seek to identify aspects of historical mystical traditions by which one might resist collapsing all mysticism into its modern, experiential construction and to thereby consider anew connections between the past and the present. Cavell and Thoreau, on the one hand, and apophatic mysticism as analyzed by Turner and Certeau, on the other hand, present us with a practice of writing in which the point is not any final transcendence of world and language, but rather the cultivation of a certain emptiness, a loss or departure, within ordinary, worldly experience and, indeed, within the self. This emptiness is the site of a certain intensification and deification. It makes possible, that is, a mode of thinking and writing that resists the deadening habits of language and constitutes a vivifying relation to the world before us, both connected intimately to us and radically other from us.

Ecstatic philosophy

> A philosopher is a human being who constantly experiences, sees, hears, suspects, hopes, and dreams extraordinary things; who is struck by his own thoughts as from outside, as from above and below, as by his type of experiences and lightning bolts. (BGE 292).

I turn now to an elucidation of a practice of writing that informs Nietzsche's post-*Zarathustra* texts, in order to show how this mystical thematics can offer insights into Nietzsche's mature view of philosophy. My interpretation begins with an uncontroversial observation. Nietzsche sought to rethink the task of philosophy. In doing so, he produced a body of writing that stands out from the canon of western philosophy – especially as that canon existed in his lifetime – for its stylistic diversity and resistance to straight-forward argumentation, studied objectivity, and system. Nietzsche's is writing highly controlled in image and in the concentrated insight of the aphorism, but it also is writing freed from many of the restraints that determined good taste, scholarship, and philosophy in nineteenth-century Europe. Nietzsche claimed to possess, 'the most multifarious art of style.' (EH 4) The reader is vividly reminded of this not only by the presence of *Zarathustra* at the centre of his corpus, but also by the poems and songs at the margins of his 'philosophical' texts and by the irony, hyperbole, and metaphor that figure throughout them. Nietzsche's writing draws attention to itself as liminal writing: writing situated at the boundary between philosophy and poetry, body and consciousness, emotion and reason. This liminality is crucial, I argue, to understanding Nietzsche's late view of philosophy, for in a significant and precise sense his writing creates an opening whereby the philosopher brings self and culture beyond themselves. What I offer here is an interpretation of Zarathustra's declaration, in a speech entitled 'Reading and Writing': 'Now a god dances through me' (Z 'Reading'). I describe this writing as 'ecstatic philosophy'.

Consider *Ecce Homo*, Nietzsche's literary autobiography and final book. There, Nietzsche describes the period of his life during which he wrote the first book of *Zarathustra* (about six years previous to *Ecce Homo*). *Zarathustra*, he writes, 'overtook me' and the main idea of the book, eternal recurrence, struck him like 'lightning' (EH 'Zarathustra' 2, 3). Nietzsche goes on to describe 'my experience of inspiration', which I quote here, at length.

> If one had the slightest residue of superstition left in one's system, one could hardly reject altogether the idea that one is merely incarnation, merely mouthpiece, merely a medium of overpowering forces. The concept of revelation – in the sense that suddenly, with indescribable certainty and subtlety, something becomes visible, audible, something that shakes one to the last depths and throws one down – that merely describes the facts. One hears, one does not seek; one accepts, one does not ask who gives; like lightning, a thought flashes up, with necessity, without hesitation regarding its form – I never had any choice. A rapture whose tremendous tension occasionally discharges itself in a flood of tears – now the pace quickens involuntarily, now it becomes slow; one is altogether beside oneself… .Everything happens involuntarily in the highest degree but as in a gale of a feeling of freedom, of absoluteness, of power, of divinity [*Gott-lichkeit*].The involuntariness of image and figure [*des Bildes, des Gleich-nesses*] is strangest of all; one no longer has any notion of what is an image or a figure: everything offers itself as the nearest, most obvious, simplest expression. It actually seems, to allude to something Zarathustra says, as if the things themselves approached and offered themselves as figures. ('Here all things come caressingly to your discourse and flatter you; for they want to ride on your back. On every figure you ride to every truth… .Here the words and word-shrines of all being open up before you; here all being wishes to become word, all becoming wishes to learn from you how to speak') (EH 'Zarathustra' 3).

There is much to say about this strange passage, particularly with respect to the way it both traces and effaces a series of boundaries: for example, the boundary between Nietzsche, the writer, and what he describes as 'overpowering forces'; or, the boundary between Nietzsche, the writer, and Zarathustra, his character, whose experiences are used to describe Nietzsche's own (Nietzsche borrows images – lightning, the flood of tears – central to the joyful songs of Zarathustra); or, more generally, the boundary between experience and writing (Nietzsche's experience of inspiration comes in and through his writing); and, finally, the boundary between self and world (where 'all being' and the 'things themselves' speak through the writer). In short, as he writes about writing *Zarathustra*, the book, and about the character Zarathustra's experience of eternity, Nietzsche writes his own ecstasy.

But one also should note the suspicion. With his use of the subjunctive in this passage, Nietzsche puts into question its status as a simple testimony to extraordinary experience: 'If one had the slightest residue of superstition left in one's system, one could hardly reject altogether the idea that one is merely incarnation.' With this ambiguous, tortured sentence Nietzsche reminds us -as if we could ever forget – of his deep suspicion of intoxication and ecstasy. Hence, the possibility that although in places Nietzsche may describe his experiences in terms which gesture towards the mystical and the divine, this does not entail that, as a philosopher, he would argue that such experiences are, in fact, what they 'seem' to be.

Nietzsche's suspicion marks the ambivalence with which he views all intoxications, his own included, for he recognizes that although such states can be the mark of high, strong spirits, they can also be traced to pathological states of weakness or fear. But there are two issues to keep in mind in this context. First, Nietzsche does value and celebrate certain kinds of intoxication – those deriving from overflowing strength – and, especially in his notebooks, writes about such intoxication with figures of the divine. Second, any glance at literature from Christian mystical traditions reveals that mystics often have been exceptionally acute psychological observers who have examined their own experiences with great care and realism, and who often have displayed chronic suspicion of their own ecstatic and visionary states. Nietzsche himself appears to recognize this when he writes, in his notebooks from the period just before beginning *Zarathustra*, 'In the union of skepticism and yearning, the mystic is born' (KSA 1 274). We might, then, view Nietzsche's suspicion in this case not simply as an effort to reduce ecstatic experiences of inspiration to physiological or psychological causes, but instead as a practice that purifies the experience by placing a question mark next to it, indicating that the experience itself is ultimately unfathomable and that what is most important about it is the life it generates, not what it, in the end, is. As such, this passage exemplifies something crucial about Nietzsche's view and practice of philosophy, namely an attitude that is at once both suspicious of and open to that which exceeds philosophy. The passage acknowledges something extraordinary, something one cannot grasp or comprehend, something that strikes the philosopher 'as from outside.'

Dionysus and becoming

Nietzsche acknowledges the excess of philosophy in numerous ways, but most importantly with the figure Dionysus. In his first book, Nietzsche charged Socrates with antipathy to mysticism, yet also expressed the hope that one day an 'artistic Socrates' would be possible (BT 14). He wondered, in other words, about a philosophy that does not deny the positive and productive role of the Dionysian in the apprehension of reality and the living of life. Does Nietzsche's late philosophy embody this hope for an artistic, or Dionysian, Socrates? Though Dionysus played a major role in Nietzsche's first book, the figure was absent from Nietzsche's writing for the following fourteen years, making a reappearance only at the end of *Beyond Good and Evil*. There, Nietzsche describes Dionysus as a 'philosopher god' from whom 'everyone walks away richer...in himself, newer to himself than before, broken open, blown at and sounded out by a thawing wind...more broken but full of hopes that as yet have no name' (BGE 295).

This philosophical Dionysus appears different from the god that played the central role in *The Birth of Tragedy*. For instance, in his late work, Nietzsche refers to Dionysus as a philosopher. Yet, this late Dionysus is still a god and Nietzsche makes an explicit connection between them, introducing this late incarnation as 'the great ambiguous one...to whom I once offered, as you know, in all secrecy and reverence, my first-born – as the last, it seems to me, who offered him a sacrifice' (BGE 295). John Sallis offers an interpretation of the early Dionysus that I think can elucidate the link to the late Dionysus. He argues that in *The Birth of Tragedy*, Nietzsche already was engaged in a critique of Schopenhauer and a 'twisting away' from metaphysics.[39] On this reading, Nietzsche's early Dionysus is a figure of excess, determining the course of tragedy through a 'logic of ecstasy'. This logic is characterized by a simultaneous transgressing and delimiting of limits – limits, for example, of individuality, reason, and metaphysics – in an ecstatic, excessive movement. Since limits themselves are a function of the Apol-

Ionian principle of individuation or determination, the Dionysian, as its opposite, blurs the boundaries that constitute individuation. But this means, then, that the opposition that separates the Dionysian from the Apollonian is itself disrupted: the Dionysian not only disrupts the Apollonian but, in that very movement, disrupts 'itself' as well, meaning that there is no 'itself', no being, as such, to the Dionysian: the Dionysian 'is' only as excess, in ecstasy. It therefore cannot be experienced as such, but only in a flash on the margins of its Apollonian manifestation. The identity of the Dionysian, writes Sallis, is 'abysmal': realized only in 'the movement, the figure' not 'in some originary being over against the individual, who in Dionysian ecstasy, would then return. For there is no origin.'[40] It is as a figure of divine excess – an invocation marking and transgressing the limits of self, knowledge, and philosophy – that Dionysus returns in Nietzsche's late work.

Looking back on his philosophical efforts in 1888, Nietzsche claimed that he was the first to transpose 'the Dionysian into a philosophical pathos' (EH 'Birth' 3). Sallis' view of Dionysian excess is a key for understanding this transposition and particularly for interpreting Nietzsche's late efforts to subvert metaphysical views of philosophy and subjectivity. The attack on metaphysics concentrates on the traditional philosophical privilege granted to the concept of Being. In *Beyond Good and Evil*, Nietzsche criticizes what he calls 'the faith in opposite values', which relegates all transitoriness to the false and the worldly and all truth to the eternal stability of Being; in the *Genealogy*, he unmasks modernity's otherworldly ascetic ideal, which finds in the perfection of Being a ground from which to denigrate this-worldly life. And, in *Twilight of the Idols*, Nietzsche describes metaphysical philosophy as a kind of necrophilia, a 'vampirism', sucking the life blood from thought and an 'Egyptianism', mummifying thought in concepts. Philosophy, in other words, worships the dead stasis of Being rather than the life of becoming.[41]

In these works, Nietzsche also develops an opposing, life-affirming view of philosophy. In *Twilight of the Idols*. Nietzsche contrasts the Socratic philosopher with the Dionysian artist. Led astray by *ressentiment* and the metaphysics of language, the Socratic philosopher grounds all philosophy in a metaphysical distinction between the 'True world' and the 'Apparent world', between an eternal realm of Truth and Being, accessible only to the philosopher or the saint, and the illusoriness of the everyday world.[42] By contrast, the Dionysian artist – who, in this text, is Nietzsche's paradigm of strength and affirmation – immerses himself in becoming, happy to abolish the metaphysics of the 'True world'. Nietzsche's distinction between the Socratic philosopher and the Dionysian artist is, however, more subtle than may appear at first glance, for the artist's affirmation of becoming is not a simple affirmation of this-worldly reality understood as empirical appearance. Indeed, Nietzsche points out that the artist, like the philosopher, also relies on a distinction between appearance and reality – but with an important difference. For the Dionysian artist, Nietzsche asserts, 'appearance …signifies reality once more, only selected, strengthened, corrected' (TI 'Reason' 6). In other words, the artist affirms both appearance and reality, makes appearance real in the process of artistic play. A different way of putting this is that where the philosophical tradition grounds itself in a *metaphysical opposition* between the true and apparent worlds, Nietzsche's Dionysian artist works with a *relative difference* between 'reality' and appearance. Appearance, in this case, is not opposed to reality, but is, as Nietzsche puts it, 'reality once more.'

With this, Nietzsche distinguishes between two attitudes toward becoming. Dionysian art undercuts the philosophical distinction between truth and appearance by rejecting the idea that there is any intelligible ground or transcendent reality – Truth or Being – 'beneath' the surface of the flux of appearance. As Nietzsche puts it in *The Gay Science*, truth does not remain truth 'when the veils are withdrawn' (GS 'Preface' 4). Beneath the veil there is only 'becoming', a never-ending movement of concealing and revealing, that is never known 'in itself', for, as Nietzsche writes in his notebooks from the period of *Twilight of the Idols*: 'knowledge and becoming exclude one another' (WP 517). In one sense, Nietzsche is making a metaphysical claim here, but it is a claim that follows a logic of ecstasy. That is, Nietzsche subverts metaphysical dualism by claiming that becoming cannot be known apart from appearance: becoming is not in itself, it 'is' only as excess. Like lightning, a mark of the Dionysian, we can only glimpse becoming in the reiteration of the 'once more'. Or, as he puts it at the end of *Twilight of the Idols*, it is only through a Dionysian 'faith' that one can realize 'in oneself the eternal joy of becoming' (TI 'Ancients' 5).

Becoming marks the point where the philosopher must let go of concept and philosophy. Nietzsche is well-aware that such letting go is anathema to modern philosophy, for not only does it undermine the privileged status of the concept of Being, it also undermines a principle, which, for Nietzsche, grounds the philosophical attachment to Being. In the same chapter of *Twilight of the Idols* that introduces Dionysus, Nietzsche asserts that the philosophical aversion to becoming is a consequence of the belief in the ego: 'Being is everywhere thought in, foisted on, as cause; it is only from the conception 'ego' that there follows, derivatively, the concept 'being'' (TI 'Reason' 5). Underlying the metaphysical concept of Being, in other words, is the attachment to a unified, self-grounded ego or subject, which, in turn, Nietzsche links to *ressentiment*. In the *Genealogy*, for instance, Nietzsche argues that the idea of the ego, the idea of a self-conscious source for all that is and happens – whether God or moral agent – is itself a consequence of the priestly attempt to make the strong take responsibility for their strength and therefore to curtail it (GM I 13). Kant is a good example of the metaphysics of selfhood that Nietzsche attributes to a resentful morality. For Kant, morality finds its source in a freely reasoning and willing 'I' that can divorce itself from and subjugate body, instincts, desire, relationships – the whole of its material and historical matrix – in order to will solely on rational/moral grounds. Such willing is definitive of Kantian holiness. Nietzsche despised this domesticated holiness that opposes the ego, as consciousness or rational will, to the wildness of body and becoming. Such holiness no longer breathes in the element of mysterious attractions, births, transformations, deaths, which disclose the permeability of the self, its constitution through unbiddable forces. The Dionysian strand of Nietzsche's late philosophy informs a concept of self radically at odds with the modern view of the unified subject, marking a certain vulnerability of self, a radical openness in which one is exposed to flux and chaos. This is a self, as Nietzsche writes when he reintroduces us to Dionysus, 'more broken but full of hopes.' It is a self more akin to that inscribed by Certeau's mystical writers than Kantian philosophers: 'I is an other' Certeau writes, '- that is the secret told by the mystic long before the poetic experience of Rimbaud, Rilke, or Nietzsche.'[43] Finally, it is a self Nietzsche enacts in his writing.

Departure and return

For Nietzsche, participating in the eternal joy of becoming means renewing oneself only in losing oneself, cultivating openness or responsiveness to the forces of life in a practice of writing to and on the boundaries of consciousness and body, being and becoming. As Pierre Hadot has made clear, for Nietzsche, like many of the Greek philosophers he knew so well, philosophy was a practice, 'a way of life', and not simply an intellectual discourse.[44] And his practice of philosophy is akin to mystical apophasis in that both move in a paradoxical cycle of exhaustion and revivification. Nietzsche's writing mortifies the philosophical temptation – one might argue that it is the philosophical imperative for the Socratic tradition – to stabilize and hold language in the permanence of conceptualization. Of course, philosophy has always involved certain kinds of mortification. But in the Socratic case, as viewed by Nietzsche, philosophy is grounded in a necrophilic, life-denying renunciation of art, poetry, and figure as it seeks to achieve the stasis of Being. By contrast, Nietzsche engages in a life-giving mortification of philosophy that finds in the eternal joy of becoming the inspiration and liberation of language and life.

Nietzsche's renunciation is figured as departure. As in the mystics of Certeau and the philosophy of Cavell, Nietzsche writes 'in proximity to a loss.' At the end of the fifth book of *The Gay Science*, Nietzsche writes of being 'homeless' and departing from the shores of the present and familiar into uncharted waters of 'new seas'. He casts himself and his hoped-for companions as the 'argonauts of the new ideal' who, by means of a 'great health', distance themselves from their 'time' in undertaking this search (GS 377, 382). This great health, however, is not something that one simply attains, as a means to an end, or as the end itself, for it is something that 'one does not merely have but also acquires continually, and must acquire because one gives it up again and again, and must give it up' (GS 382). The ideal for which Nietzsche and his companions search, is a 'strange' ideal, always running ahead, luring them to announce but also to renounce the great health. The constant departures and reversals of Nietzsche's writing indicate, in fact, that the ideal is 'discovered' only as it is also, always, relinquished; the ideal, then, is never simply possessed, for it is only present to the extent that one is ready to leave it for the ever-arriving future.

This motif of departure figures not just in what Nietzsche writes about, but in his very idea of writing itself. Nietzsche describes his writing as having 'a knack for seeking out fellow-rhapsodizers and for luring them on to new secret paths and dancing places'(ASC 3). He seeks to communicate the joy of becoming by transfiguring the dancing of the Dionysian ecstatic into the dancing of the pen (TI 'Germans' 7). Yet this effort is doomed to a certain frustration, which requires Nietzsche always simultaneously to affirm and deny his writing. 'Our true experiences are not garrulous,' he writes, 'They could not communicate themselves if they wanted to, they lack words. We have already grown beyond what we have words for' (TI 'Expeditions' 26). Profundity of thought, he also claims, manifests itself in a certain 'evasion of communication'

(BGE 40). The problem of communication reverberates through all Nietzsche's writing: he despairs over his failure to make himself heard by his contemporaries, yet he insists on silence, masks, secrets, and the inability of language to communicate elevated states. His writing, then, inscribes only to always erase, it is both a revealing and a concealing. Conceptually and graphically, with suspicion, shifting perspective, and aphorism, Nietzsche surrounds his writing with silence and space. In the crossing of his affirmations and his demystifying unmaskings, in the movement from one aphorism to the next, he points us to something other than what is said.

There are some obvious modes of unsaying in Nietzsche's texts. In the final section of both *The Gay Science* and *Beyond Good and Evil*, Nietzsche looks back on what he has written – in one case with humor, in the other sorrow – to take leave of the ideas he has expressed in the text. For Nietzsche, having been 'said' – written or 'immortalized' – they are on the verge of losing their life. So he takes his departure from them, continues his wandering. In each case, Nietzsche leaves his philosophical writing and moves to poetry and song, repeating, in a different register, the movement at the end of Book Three of *Zarathustra* from 'abysmal thought' to joyous song. Nietzsche abandons philosophy for affirming song, but it is only through his philosophy that he gets to that point.

Through these departures from the philosophical text, Nietzsche marks that text itself as fundamentally tropological, as much image as concept.

> Alas, what are you after all, my written and painted thoughts! It was not long ago that you were still so colorful, young and malicious, full of thorns and secret spices... .what things do we copy, writing and painting, we mandarins with Chinese brushes, we immortalizers of things that can be written – what are the only things we are able to paint? Alas, always only what is on the verge of withering and losing its fragrance! Alas, always only storms that are passing...(BGE 296).

The apophatic character of Nietzsche's writing is registered to a significant extent in his use of figure or trope. Tropes bring together and hold in tension the ordinary and the extraordinary. Tropes allow one to say, at the same time, that something both 'is' and 'is not'. Certeau argues that the trope, where a single word or phrase marks the collision of different meanings, introducing strain and strangeness, is the fundamental unit of mystical discourse. Tropes, he writes, are 'deviant', they are 'exit, semantic exile, already ecstasy' and 'machines for voyages and ecstasies out-side of received meanings.'[45] Nietzsche inscribes tropes at the bound-aries of philosophy and thus indicates and performs becoming without arresting it conceptually in any final way, figuring not so much the straight line of argument than a dance of thought and language.[46]

The play of figure and concept in Nietzsche marks the boundaries of philosophy as well as the path of departure and return he traces over and over again with the figure of the dance. On the one hand, the recourse to figure is an occasion for mourning, as we see above at the end of *Beyond Good and Evil*. 'Alas!' Yet, by insisting on the figurative charac-ter of his philosophy, Nietzsche subverts the life-denial of the concep-tual, working through his mourning in a departure from the word. Departing, Nietzsche at once acknowledges the death of the figure at the same time that he is able to affirm the life, the joy, in which it was born – and to affirm that there will be another birth, another dawn. Fig-uring and transfiguring self and world, each trope offers a new perspec-tive on something familiar, and in doing so it also acknowledges the 'once more' beyond all things. In Nietzsche's writing, the moments of the ordinary and extraordinary, departure and return resist one another, performing a kind of 'unsaying' that continually brings the reader back to the movement of life – its cycle of joy and suffering, its becoming.

Such writing generates what Cavell describes as a neighboring or nextness among words and world and what Connolly describes as 'fugi-tive spaces of enchantment.'[47] This takes place not through the concep-tual mirroring or grasping of the world, but in following the movement or dance of becoming. Recall how Nietzsche borrows from *Zarathustra* to describe his inspiration: 'The involuntariness of image and figure is strangest of all; one no longer has any notion of what is an image or a figure: everything offers itself as the nearest, most obvious, simplest expression.' Everything is simple, everything is near – inspiration not as escape from the world, but as return.

> The free spirit again draws near to life – slowly to be sure, almost reluc-tantly, almost mistrustfully...It seems to him as if his eyes are only now open to what is *close at hand*. He is astonished and sits silent: where *had* he been? These close and closest things; how changed they seem! What bloom and magic they have acquired! He looks back gratefully – grateful to his wanderings, to his hardness and self-alienation, to his viewing of far dis-tances and bird-like flights in cold heights. What a good thing he had not always stayed 'at home', stayed 'under his own roof' like a delicate apa-thetic loafer! He had been *beside* himself; no doubt of that (HH 8).

'He feels himself a god'

In departure and return the world becomes enchanted again, an enchantment which, not infrequently, Nietzsche figures as divine. As we have seen, Nietzsche describes his inspiration as a feeling of *Gottlichkeit*. There are three things to keep in mind about this description, and about Nietzsche's appeals to 'divinity' in general. First, insofar as Nietzsche discusses a *feeling* of divinity and makes no ontological claim about the ultimate source of the feeling, he invokes the divine as a figure. Second, to say that Nietzsche's use of 'divinity' is figurative should not be taken to mean that it is *merely* figurative, as if Nietzsche imagined some other, non-divine reality under the appearance of the figure. Following Nietzsche's subversion of the distinction between appearance and reality, one should say, instead, that to the extent that this feeling of divinity is an expression of Dionysian appearance, it is 'reality once more.' Third, on frequent occasions in his late work, Nietzsche does invoke the divine from the perspective of Dionysian art. In fact, there Nietzsche suggests that deification is the highest expression of Dionysian art. In this sense, I think Nietzsche's striking comments about Jesus in *The Antichrist* have to be taken seriously as indicative of Nietzsche's own, positive, view of divinity. There, he writes that Jesus 'knows that it is through the *practice* of one's life that one feels "divine", "blessed", "evangelic", at all times a "child of God." It is *not* "penance", *not* "prayer for forgiveness", which leads to God: *evangelic practice alone* leads to God, it *is* God!' (AC 33).

Divinity for Nietzsche is not found in some entity that exists beyond and above humanity, nor is it simply a human-all-too-human projection. Rather, divinity is realized, made real, in and through human creativity as both the state of Dionysian creativity and that which is created from this state. Nietzsche describes 'Dionysian art' as the 'transfiguring power of intoxication' rooted in the noble soul's overabundant 'gratitude and love' (GS 328) and he identifies gratitude as that quality of noble (Greek) religion that distinguishes it from Christianity (CW 'Epilogue'; BGE 49). And, at the end of *Twilight of the Idols*, Nietzsche identifies Dionysus as the 'religious' symbol for the eternal joy of creation. In his notebooks, particularly from the period between 1887–8, Nietzsche invokes the divinity of creation and affirmation numerous times. 'Existence,' he writes, is an 'eternal deifying and undeifying' (WP 712). He characterizes Dionysian art as 'perfection of existence, [the] production of perfection and plenitude,' 'essentially affirmation, blessing, deification of existence' (WP 821). And the artist, as a lover, he writes, 'becomes a squanderer...he believes in God again, he believes in virtue, because he believes in love' (KSA 13 14 120). Finally, in an oft-cited passage, Nietzsche describes his own deifications:

> And how many new gods are still possible! As for myself, in whom the reli-gious, that is to say god-forming instinct occasionally becomes active at impossible times – how differently, how variously the divine has revealed itself to me each time! So many strange things have passed before me in those timeless moments that fall into one's life as if from the moon, when one no longer has any idea how old one is or how young one will yet be – I should not doubt that there are many kinds of gods (WP 1038).

As a philosopher, Nietzsche's Dionysus makes possible a kind of self-knowledge. This is 'knowledge' of the self as strange to itself, divided from itself in ecstatic awareness and the abandonment of love, value, ideal. Knowing oneself as becoming, one knows oneself as already having become 'something else'. This space of emptiness in which self is divided from self is, for Nietzsche, as it is for mystics like Eckhart and Thoreau, life-giving and divinizing. Nietzsche finds life in the act of giving meaning and striving for goals, but he finds a certain death in being imprisoned by that which he gives and creates. The effort to grasp meaning too tightly or to rest in stability, is for Nietzsche to lose the life-giving power of becoming. But – to invoke a different loss, another departure – to sacrifice that which one loves and values, including one's own 'great health', is to begin again the process of bestowing meaning. Self-knowledge, therefore, requires an apophatic subversion of self and language. The philosopher, in other words, must be a 'tragic artist' who manifests 'the will to life rejoicing in its own inexhaustibility through the sacrifice of its highest types' (TI 120). In this rejoicing, the divine comes to existence. Or, as Nietzsche writes, in a poem entitled 'Ecce Homo', 'I consume myself, and glow' (GS 'Joke' 62).

Bibliography of cited works by Nietzsche

The Antichrist. Translated by R.J. Hollingdale. London: Penguin Books, 1990.
Beyond Good and Evil. Translated by Walter Kaufmann. New York: Vintage Books, 1989.
The Birth of Tragedy. Translated by Walter Kaufmann. New York: Vintage Books, 1967.
Dawn. Translated by R.J. Hollingdale. Cambridge: Cambridge University Press, 1982.

Ecce Homo. Translated by Walter Kaufmann. New York: Vintage Books, 1969.

On the Genealogy of Morals. Translated by Walter Kaufmann and R.J. Hollingdale. New York: Vintage Books, 1969.

The Gay Science. Translated by Walter Kaufmann. New York: Vintage Books, 1974.

Human, All Too Human. Translated by R.J. Hollingdale. Cambridge: Cambridge University Press, 1986.

Philosophy in the Tragic Age of the Greeks. Translated by Marianne Cowan. Washington, D.C.: Regnery Publishing, 1962.

Sämtliche Werke. Kritische Studienausgabe in 15 Bänden, edited by G. Colli and M. Montinari. Berlin: de Gruyter, 1980.

Twilight of the Idols. Translated by R.J. Hollingdale. London: Penguin Books, 1990.

Untimely Meditations. Translated by R.J. Hollingdale. Cambridge: Cambridge University Press, 1983.

The Will to Power. Translated by Walter Kaufmann and R.J. Hollingdale. New York: Vintage Books, 1968.

Thus Spoke Zarathustra. Translated by Walter Kaufmann. London: Penguin Books, 1978.

Notes

1   I would like to thank Jim Urpeth and John Lippitt for their helpful comments on a previous draft of this paper, as well as the Friedrich Nietzsche Society of Great Britain and Ireland for the opportunity to present and discuss the paper. I also would like to thank Princeton University Press for permission to use previously published material in this paper.

2   W. Connolly, *Why I am Not a Secularist* (Minneapolis: University of Minnesota Press, 1999), p. 15.

3   For the more complete argument see T. Roberts, *Contesting Spirit: Nietzsche, Affirmation, Religion* (Princeton: Princeton University Press, 1998). For a useful discussion of the historical construction of the concepts 'religion' and 'mysticism,' see R. King, *Orientalism and Religion* (London: Routledge, 1999).

4   G. Bataille, *On Nietzsche* (New York: Paragon House, 1992, trans. B. Boone); J. Stambaugh, *The Other Nietzsche* (Albany: State University of New York Press, 1994).

5   Schopenhauer also claimed that the artist, to some degree, was able to accomplish this reversal of the will. For further discussion see T. Roberts, *Contesting Spirit* pp. 25–9.

6   Quoted in R. King, *Orientalism and Religion* p. 125.

7   In his notebooks of that period Nietzsche claims that 'art and religion in the Greek sense are identical' (KSA 7 9[102]).

8   'Philosophy in the Tragic Age of the Greeks', 9.
9   J. Stambaugh, *The Other Nietzsche* pp. 137–9.
10 T. Roberts, *Contesting Spirit* pp. 128–37.
11 In *Zarathustra* each chapter ends in one of three ways: the vast majority are speeches or songs spoken/sung by Zarathustra, all of which conclude with either 'Thus spoke Zarathustra' or 'Thus sang Zarathustra'; alternatively, some end with the voice of the narrator, describing, for instance, Zarathustra's journey; finally, a few sections end in conversation, either Zarathustra's internal dialogue or a conversation between Zarathustra and another character. In all these cases, the voice is identified clearly.
12 C. Rosset, *Joyful Cruelty* (New York: Oxford University Press, 1993), p. 25.
13 Though I will not argue the point here, one could make the case that Nietzsche's own adherence to a modern conception of mysticism did much to color not only his view of mysticism but of religion and Christianity more generally. Consequently, the question of mystical themes in Nietzsche's thought should not be determined solely by Nietzsche's own view of mysticism or by commonly accepted contemporary views of the subject.
14 For one discussion of this history, see R. King *Orientalism and Religion*.
15 J. Bagger, 'The Uses of Mysticism', *Religious Studies Review*, vol. 25: (1999) p. 369.
16 This is not to say that some mystics do not describe or undergo extraordinary experiences.
17 J. Bagger, 'The Uses of Mysticism', p. 370.
18 D. Turner, *The Darkness of God* (Cambridge: Cambridge University Press, 1996), p. 264.
19 *Ibid.*, p. 210.
20 *Ibid.*, p. 259.
21 *Ibid.*, pp. 257–8.
22 See B. McGinn *The Foundations of Mysticism* (New York: Crossroad, 1994) and R. Gimello, 'Mysticism in its Contexts,' in *Mysticism and Religious Traditions*, ed. S. Katz (Oxford: Oxford University Press, 1983).
23 M. de Certeau, 'Mystic Speech' in *Heterologies* (Minneapolis: University of Minnesota Press, 1986), p. 80.
24 M. de Certeau, *The Mystic Fable* (Chicago: University of Chicago Press, 1992 trans. M. Smith), p. 15.
25 D. Turner, *The Darkness of God*, p. 259.
26 S. Cavell, *The Claim of Reason* (Oxford: Oxford University Press, 1979), p. 493.
27 S. Cavell, *Senses of Walden: An Expanded Edition* (Chicago: University of Chicago Press, 1981), p. 107 and *Conditions Handsome and Unhandsome* (Chicago: University of Chicago Press, 1990), p. 39.
28 S. Cavell, *The Claim of Reason*, p. 463.

29 S. Cavell, *In Quest of the Ordinary* (Chicago: University of Chicago Press, 1988), p. 24.

30 P. Hadot, *Philosophy as a Way of Life* (Oxford: Blackwell, ed. A. Davidson, 1995).

31 S. Cavell, *In Quest of the Ordinary*, p. 38.

32 *Ibid.*, p. 148.

33 *Ibid.*, p. 14.

34 S. Cavell, *Senses of Walden*, p. 64.

35 *Ibid.*, p. 50.

36 *Ibid.*, pp. 105–6.

37 *Ibid.*, p. 106.

38 S. Cavell, *This New Yet Unapproachable America* (Albuquerque, N.M.: Living Batch Press, 1989), p. 106.

39 J. Sallis, *Crossings: Nietzsche and the Space of Tragedy* (Chicago: University of Chicago Press, 1991).

40 *Ibid.*, p. 71.

41 This is a theme present in Nietzsche's work from early on, for instance in his unpublished but influential essay 'Truth and Lie in an Extramoral Sense.'

42 Hence, the third chapter of *Twilight of the Idols*, which Nietzsche entitles, 'How the 'True World' Finally Became a Fable: The History of an Error.' For a useful interpretation of this chapter, which helps to support my argument here, see M. Heidegger, 'Nietzsche's Overturning of Platonism,' in *Nietzsche*, vol. 1 (New York: HarperCollins, trans. D. F. Krell, 1979), pp. 200–10.

43 Certeau, 'Mystic Speech', p. 96.

44 P. Hadot, *Philosophy as a Way of Life*.

45 Certeau, *The Mystic Fable*, pp. 142–8.

46 Eric Blondel writes of Nietzschean metaphor that it 'is like a world made dynamic by a play of attraction and repulsion that continually creates interaction and intersection among different movements ... without this play ever coming to rest in an absolute knowledge that would reabsorb all the tensions.' E. Blondel, *Nietzsche: The Body and Culture* (Stanford: Stanford University Press, 1991 trans. S. Hand), p. 245).

47 W. Connolly, *Why I am Not a Secularist*, p.15

12

'Health' and 'Sickness' in religious affectivity: Nietzsche, Otto, Bataille

Jim Urpeth

In different ways Nietzsche, Otto and Bataille are profoundly religious thinkers whose critical engagement with, for instance, Christianity, springs from a passionate avowal of the 'divine' or 'sacred'. In their respective accounts of the nature of religion these thinkers insist on the primacy of affectivity: the feelings that characterise 'religious experience'. Indeed, Nietzsche, Otto and Bataille each accord affectivity in general an ontologically constitutive status and stress the primordiality of a 'religious' form of it.[1] They reject reductionist conceptions, in either socio-political or psychoanalytical terms, of religion and contest the supposed radicality of the secular, anthropocentric orientation of modern thought. Nietzsche's, Otto's and Bataille's respective conceptions of religious affectivity will be clarified in order to show that, in each case, a contrast is drawn between a 'healthy' and 'sick' form of religious feeling. This diagnostic perspective forms the basis of these thinkers' different evaluations of Christianity, responses to it that will be comparatively assessed throughout.

I

For Nietzsche the categorical and doctrinal content of a religion is the product of a more primordial process of evaluation, itself the expression of an affective-libidinal economy or type of 'will'. It is this constitutive domain of value and desire that has to be addressed in any radical evaluation of a religion.[2] The criterion Nietzsche employs in assessing the values underpinning a religion (and hence its value as such) is the extent to which they are an expression of an 'affirmation' rather than a 'denial' of 'life'. The most distinctive feature of Nietzsche's genealogical critique of Christianity is his assessment of its contribution to the 'health' of the human species, the index of which is its propensity for 'affirmation'. In pursuing this Nietzsche often initially adopts a merely 'psychological' perspective. However, he explicitly seeks a 'physiological' source of the values in question and thereby broaches the question of the role of Christianity in the 'biological' uniqueness he associates with the 'human' namely, the triumph of the 'weak' over the 'strong'.[3]

It is possible to locate in Nietzsche's texts the main features of this contrast between 'health' and 'sickness'. A key symptom of 'health' for Nietzsche is the capacity for a positive evaluation of 'life' or 'this world' – 'becoming', the 'body', the sensuous and so on. In contrast 'sickness' is manifest in a predisposition for hostility toward, and denial of, the basic constituents of embodied life. In Nietzsche's view this inability to valorise 'this world' is the source of the 'illusion' of an 'other world' or 'ideal' order of being characterised as distinct in kind from material, embodied life. Such an evaluative sensibility is prone to conceive desire in terms of 'lack' and constructs the 'metaphysical' arsenal of categories and values, premised upon the alleged primacy of negation, out of its need for them.

This fundamental condition of dissatisfaction with the insubordination of 'life' in relation to metaphysical ideals is, Nietzsche claims, the source of the conception of 'spirituality' in suprasensuous terms. The 'sick' align transcendence with the transcendent and sustain an exclusively 'moral' interpretation of 'this world'. Nietzsche identifies the constitutive affectivity that generates this régime of value as 'pessimism'. This arises in those defined by it upon recognition of the extent to which human beings are inextricably embroiled in and determined by instinctual primary processes. The philosophical optimism that imagines that, theoretically and morally, life might be comprehensible and determinable is, for Nietzsche, an even greater pathology insofar as its commitment to the value of the allegedly non-naturalistic domains of reason and morality and its fantasies concerning the teleological alignment of life and theologico-humanist ideals presuppose pessimism's negative evaluation of 'this world' but fail to attain to even its insights.[4]

For Nietzsche this *a priori* tendency toward either the 'affirmation' or 'denial' of life is physiologically determined. 'Health' is the manifestation of determination by the primary process of the 'will to power', its demand for 'self-overcoming' beyond all utilitarian and teleological definition. Nietzsche accords this instinctual necessity for self-expenditure priority over the derivative impulse of 'self-preservation' that determines the 'sick'.[5] He thereby contests the alleged primacy of 'hunger' and 'need' over 'excess' and 'superabundance'.[6] In summary, Nietzsche identifies 'health' with 'life-ascending' and 'sickness' with 'life-descending' phenomena.[7] 'Health' consists in the degree to which a valorisation is possible of the fundamental conditions of material existence and the derivative and inconsequential status of the individual within an impersonal 'sea of forces' (WP IV 1067) is embraced.[8] Rejecting the derivative ontology of individuation and negation, a *'healthy* morality' (TI 'Morality' 4) is developed in which ethical self-problematisation is not premised upon a pre-given constitutional hostility to the 'body', the senses and so on from which 'redemption' is needed.[9]

Nietzsche's negative assessment of Christianity within this critical context is manifest in a weight of blisteringly ferocious textual material.[10] The Christian God is 'not merely an error but a *crime against life…*' (AC 47) and, due to its intrinsic 'hostility to life' (ASC 5), Christianity is a 'nihilistic religion'(WP II 156), one of the two main *'décadence* religions' (AC 20). Nietzsche's 'physiological' assessment of Christianity is clear: 'without any exaggeration we are entitled to call it the *real catastrophe* in the history of the health of European man' (GM III 21). It is, he claims, only rivaled in its deleterious effect by 'alcohol-poisoning' with both placed far ahead of syphilis![11] A number of causes, digestive and gynaecological, are suggested as the causes for the sickness of Christianity.[12] Nietzsche sketches a *'physiology of the nihilistic religions'* describing them as 'a systematized case history of sickness employing religious-moralistic nomenclature' (WP II 152).[13] A 'conscience for the collective evolution of mankind' (BGE 61) is evoked that, in the case of the triumph of Christian values, argues that the 'law of *selection* has been crossed' (EH 'Destiny' 8), a situation that requires a certain 'moral code for physicians' (TI 'Expeditions' 36).[14] Nietzsche writes of 'the physiological depravity of the typical Christian' (AC 47) and describes the Christian God as 'the God of the physiologically retarded, the weak' (AC 17). Such an enfeebled constitution is, in Nietzsche's view, incapable of any affirmative contact with the 'sacred', with the form of ecstatic surrender he identifies with the 'Dionysian' in which the derivative nature of individuation is acknowledged.

The 'pessimism' that defines the 'sick' affectivity of Christianity is evident in its inability to celebrate the a-symmetry between the primary instinctual drives of life which, for Nietzsche, are irretrievably dysteleological in trajectory and the theologico-humanist ideals of a rational-moral teleology. This affectivity produces the notion of a transcendent 'other world', 'the concept 'God' invented as the antithetical concept to life' (EH 'Destiny' 8). Nietzsche's contestation of the implicit *sensus communis* of 'pessimism' is the key to his rejection of all religions which valorise the transcendent or 'pessimistic religions' (HH 141).[15] As he states, 'according to the same logic of feeling, all pessimistic religions call nothingness *God*' (GM III 18). The main symptom of the 'sick' affectivity of pessimism that characterises Christianity in Nietzsche's view is its 'moral' evaluation of existence, its 'antithetical values' (BGE 2). This constitutional dissatisfaction with 'this world' generates a 'need for redemption' (HH 132). Nietzsche seeks the '...*physiological realities*...out of which the doctrine of redemption has grown' (AC 30). In identifying Christianity with this 'moral' perspective Nietzsche underlines his basic conception of its shortcomings as a religion, its failure to appreciate that, 'in itself, religion has nothing to do with morality' (WP II 146) and that 'religions are destroyed by their belief in morality' (WP II 151).

Nietzsche identifies the *ressentiment* felt by the 'slave' in response to the well-being and 'health' of the 'noble' as a crucial source of Christian morality.[16] He offers a 'physiological' account of such features of Christian affectivity as 'guilt' and 'bad conscience' conceiving them as complex transformations in the economy of instincts necessitated by the advent of 'society', an 'internalization' of drives that can no longer be discharged externally.[17] Nietzsche argues that the febrile affectivity of Christianity produces its own specific 'physician' – the 'ascetic priest'. Crucially, this type is as riddled with the physiological deficiencies as those they tend. However, the 'ascetic priest' has, Nietzsche claims, an opportunistic investment in, and talent for, controlling and manipulating the 'sickness' in question, in merely containing and directing the symptoms rather than removing the underlying cause of the pathological states of those treated.[18]

Nietzsche identifies a number of characteristics of the affective-libidinal economy of Christianity. Two important examples concern its interpretation of 'suffering' and investment in 'pity'. Nietzsche contrasts 'healthy' and 'sick' conceptions and evaluations of suffering, particularly in relation to the theme of the overcoming of individuation. The 'sickness' of Christianity is contrasted with the 'healthier' interpretation of 'suffering' characteristic, in Nietzsche's view, of the 'tragic' religious sensibility of the pre-Socratics.[19] The following passage clarifies this contrast of sensibilities in relation to suffering:

> One will see that the problem is that of the meaning of suffering: whether a Christian meaning or a tragic meaning. In the former case it is supposed

to be the path to a holy existence; in the latter case, being is counted as *holy enough* to justify even a monstrous amount of suffering. The tragic man affirms even the harshest suffering: he is sufficiently strong, rich, and capable of deifying to do so (WP IV 1052).

The 'sickness' of Christian affectivity is also manifest in its investment in the feeling of pity or compassion (*Mitleid*). In raising 'the problem of the *value* of pity and the morality of pity' (GM 'Preface', 6) Nietzsche wished to establish the '*worthlessness* of pity' (GM 'Preface' 5) and expose its negative effects on 'health':

> Christianity is called the religion of *pity*. – Pity stands in antithesis to the tonic emotions which enhance the energy of the feeling of life: it has a depressive effect. One loses force when one pities… it can bring about a collective loss of life and life-energy…it gives life itself a gloomy and questionable aspect…this depressive and contagious instinct thwarts those instincts bent on preserving and enhancing the value of life: both as a *multiplier* of misery and as a *conservator* of everything miserable it is one the chief instruments for the advancement of *décadence*…(AC 7).

Nietzsche does not conduct his critique of Christianity from a humanist perspective. Rather he is deeply suspicious of the fundamental continuity and complicity in terms of values that he uncovers behind the traditional Christian/secular opposition. Instead Nietzsche seeks to contrast the 'sick' religious sensibility of Christianity with the 'healthy' religiosity of, among others, the pre-Socratic Greeks that he unequivocally valorises.[20] It is, after all, a question of '*Dionysus against the Crucified*' (EH 'Destiny' 9). The religious orientation of Nietzsche's critique of Christianity is evident in his criticism of its conception of God as 'a *reduction* of the divine' (AC 17) and description of it as 'the low-water mark in the descending development of the God type. God degenerated to the *contradiction of life*, instead of being its transfiguration and eternal *Yes*!' (AC 18). Nietzsche frequently positively deploys religious terminology both for the articulation of key themes in his thinking and in his condemnation of Christianity. For Nietzsche, the Christian evaluation of existence is a sacriligious insult to the intrinsic sanctity of 'this world'. As he states, 'we deny God…only by doing *that* do we redeem the world' (TI 'Errors' 8).[21]

The most radical trajectory of Nietzsche's thought is its post-suspicious affirmation of a transvalued religiosity, a rethinking of the 'divine' in response to the 'death of God'. As he states, 'it seems to me that the religious instinct is indeed in vigorous growth – but that it rejects the theistic answer with profound mistrust' (BGE 53). The basic features of Nietzsche's religiosity spring from his most general project – the overcoming of anthropomorphism. Hence an 'affirmative' religion is characterised by the rejection of the notion of a personal deity and by dissociation of religion from morality. Such a 'religious affirmation of life' (WP IV 1052) celebrates the immanent sublimity of 'this world', its intrinsic irreducibility and incomprehensibility, its unmasterable nature and complete anonymity, its profound disinterest in individuated existence. This is a religious perspective in which a transvalued sense of dysteleology is the criterion of the 'sacred'.

However, although it exceeds the 'will to truth', the immanent sublimity of 'this world' is accessible to affectivity – it is felt not known. The transvaluation of the 'divine' discernible in Nietzsche's thought concerns the rethinking of both transcendence and the affectivity that discloses it. Transcendence, conceived in immanent rather than transcendent terms as a dimension of 'otherness' inherent to 'this world' without remainder (i.e. beyond 'incarnation'), and the religious feeling through which it accesses itself are both envisioned by Nietzsche in terms of 'affirmation'. At work throughout Nietzsche's texts, as their most radical promise, is what can be termed *religious materialism*. Alongside the much discussed 'physiology of art' Nietzsche develops a physiology of religion that he deploys both critically and affirmatively in outlining a non-reductive renaturalisation of both 'sick' and 'healthy' religious phenomena.[22]

Nietzsche's religious conception of this immanent transcendence is signaled in his texts in themes such as the 'deification of existence' (WP III 821) and the 'spiritualisation of passion' (TI 'Morality' 1).[23] Nietzsche develops a radically impersonal vision of the 'sacredness' of material becoming, conceiving the 'eternal return' of its intrinsic power of self-differentiation as an auto-consecration in which '…existence celebrates its own transfiguration…'(WP IV 1051). He undertakes a re-naturalisation of, to borrow a term from Eliade, 'hierophany' – the disclosure of the 'sacred'.[24] As Nietzsche states, 'this world: a monster of energy, without beginning, without end…a play of forces and waves of forces, at the same time one and many…blessing itself as that which must return eternally…my *Dionysian* world of the eternally self-creating, the eternally self-destroying…'(WP IV 1067).

However, this sketch of Nietzsche's conception of the inherently religious nature of impersonal and 'extra-moral' materiality is too focused on 'content'. Given the all-determining place he accords to the question of the 'type of will' animating and constituting any phenomenon, the key issue concerns the clarification and evaluation of the difference between the affectivities that generate these contrasting religious perspectives – on the one hand, the 'healthy' affectivity that affirms the immanent sublimity of 'this world' (desire as excess), and on the other hand, the 'sick' sensibility that yearns for the transcendent and seeks passionately to extirpate the passions (desire as lack).

It is, of course, to the theme of the 'Dionysian' in Nietzsche's texts that we must turn for his conception of 'healthy' religious affectivity. The valorisation of the 'Dionysian' is synonymous in Nietzsche's texts with the attempt to recover the essentially religious origins of tragedy.[25] The key feature of this affirmative religiosity is 'tragic joy'. Having described the 'mysteries of sexuality' that characterise the Dionysian as the 'sacred road', Nietzsche describes this affectivity thus:

> an overflowing feeling of life and energy within which even pain acts as a stimulus provided me with the key to the concept of the *tragic* feeling…Affirmation of life even in its strangest and sternest problems, the will to life rejoicing in its own inexhaustibility through the *sacrifice* of its highest types….*to realize in oneself* the eternal joy of becoming – that joy which also encompasses *joy in destruction*…(TI 'Ancients' 5)

Here the distinctive features of a 'healthy' religious sensibility are enunciated and its underlying physiological determinants suggested. Nietzsche describes a complex affective condition of pre-oppositional duality. This arises with the individuated entity's acknowledgment of the ontological priority of non-anthropomorphic life or the 'innocence of becoming'(TI 'Errors' 8).[26] The affectivity of the 'sacred' concerns the feelings arising with the dissolution of self-identity in the inter-play of the anonymous force of affirmative destruction. As Nietzsche states, 'a spirit thus *emancipated* stands in the midst of the universe with a joyful and trusting fatalism, in the *faith* that only what is separate and individual may be rejected, that in the totality everything is redeemed and affirmed – *he no longer denies*' (TI 'Expeditions' 49)

Nietzsche's conception of 'healthy' and 'sick' religious affectivities seems clear: 'pessimistic' and 'affirmative' religions are contrasted, the principal examples being Christianity and the pre-Socratic Greeks respectively. Numerous texts underwrite Nietzsche's refusal to identify the 'sacred' with Christianity toward which he seems to maintain a stubbornly oppositional stance.[27] Of course, Nietzsche's critique of Christianity is not without qualification and nuance. In *The Anti-Christ* he famously valorises the existential exemplarity of Christ and identifies Paul and organised Christianity as the principal target of his critique.

Most importantly in this respect Nietzsche's analysis of Christianity also stresses its intense and complex affective-libidinal constitution, particularly its relation to asceticism. As Nietzsche states, 'man takes a truly voluptuous pleasure in violating himself...' (HH 137).[28] The main instinctual pleasure of Christianity is, in Nietzsche's view, 'cruelty' (*Grausamkeit*).[29] Nietzsche's concern with the difference between the artist's, philosopher's and priest's appropriation of the 'ascetic ideal' and insistence on returning all phenomena to the non-dualist terrain of the 'total economy of life' (BGE 23) considerably complicate his contrast between 'health' and 'sickness', ruling out any account of it in terms of, for instance, a distinction between 'nature' and 'civilisation'.[30] It is, for Nietzsche, always a question of degree and it is never possible to identify 'health' and 'sickness' exclusively with any particular form of life – there can be 'healthy' ascetics and 'sick' sensualists and so on. His project of a renaturalisation of culture is not only not synonymous with a 'return to nature' but undermines it – it is not possible to return to what it's impossible to leave.

Nonetheless although Nietzsche acknowledges the intensity of feeling that characterises the lives of many of the Christian mystics, his evaluation of them is predominantly negative. He states that, 'all the visions, horrors, exhaustions and raptures of the saint are familiar states of illness' (HH 126). Nietzsche's account of the varieties of Christian 'passion for God' (BGE 50) is often uncharacteristically reductive in orientation. Rather than positively evaluating the intoxication of the Christian mystics Nietzsche analyses its 'excess of feeling' (GM III 19) as a side effect of the procedures of the 'ascetic priest'. Hence St.Theresa of Avila's 'voluptuous inundations and ecstasies of sensuality' (GM III 17) are dismissed as 'spiritual disturbances' (*ibid*) induced by one such method. This illustrates that Nietzsche did not indiscriminately valorise 'excess' and condemn 'measure' but distinguished between 'healthy' and 'sick' forms of both.[31] Yet Nietzsche's overwhelming rejection of Christian intoxication exposes, when compared to the different assessments of it made by Otto and Bataille, a limitation in his thought.[32]

However, in the crucial case of Christian saints and mystics Nietzsche hints at a more nuanced approach when he states 'other portraits might result in a more favourable impression. Isolated exceptions to this type stand out...by the magic of their unusual energy' (HH 144). Indeed

Nietzsche sometimes seems to be aware that the phenomenon of Christian mysticism cuts across his general criteria of 'health' and 'sickness'. This is implicitly acknowledged in the description of saintliness as, 'basically a rare form of voluptuousness...perhaps that voluptuousness in which all others are wound together in one knot' (HH 142).[33]

Nietzsche not only emphasises the constitutive nature of the affective-libidinal dimensions of religion but also distinguishes between 'healthy' and 'sick' religious sensibilities identifying a 'physiological' basis for them. Furthermore, Nietzsche conducts his critique of specific religions as an advocate of a 'healthy' religiosity. However, it seems that Nietzsche's critique of Christianity remained predominantly oppositional and even, occasionally, reductive in nature.[34] This indicates that, at least in the case of Christianity, Nietzsche fell short of his insights into the plasticity of the impersonal appropriating 'forces' he identifies and underestimated their intrinsic neutrality in respect of the phenomenon they, by possessing, constitute.[35] To this extent Nietzsche remained largely unable fully to endorse the possibility of a 'healthy' form or dimension of Christianity. Nietzsche's critique of Christianity needs to be radicalised from its predominantly merely oppositional stance to a more immanent gesture in which 'life-ascending' tendencies are identified within it. In short, an affirmative critique of Christianity is required.[36]

II

A seminal study of the nature of religious affectivity is provided by Rudolph Otto in *The Idea of the Holy* and its sequel, *Religious Essays: A Supplement to 'The Idea of the Holy'*.[37] Otto's main task is to describe the 'non-rational elements' of the 'holy', the non-conceptual field of feelings and emotions that, he claims, constitute the essence of religion.[38] For Otto the affective dimension of religion needs to be emphasised to correct an ingrained tendency in philosophy and theology that privileges the rational and moral, or conceptual, aspects of religion.

For Otto 'religious experience' is conceived as a feeling for what he terms the 'numinous' or *mysterium tremendum*, the divine or 'wholly other' that surpasses all comprehension. A key characteristic of religious affectivity that Otto identifies is 'religious awe', a feeling of the 'uncanny', 'eerie' and 'weird' that is stimulated by the 'absolute unapproachability' (IH p. 19) of the numinous object.[39] Closely related to this is what Otto describes as a 'feeling of one's own submergence' in response to the 'absolute overpoweringness' of the 'numen' that is the source of 'religious humility' (IH pp. 19-20). Otto notes the importance for mysticism of this 'self-depreciation' or 'self-annihilation' that acknowledges 'the absolute superiority or supremacy of a power other than myself' (IH p. 21). In relation to this Otto identifies an element of 'energy' or 'urgency', a sense of the numinous as 'a force that knows not stint nor stay, which is urgent, active, compelling, and alive' (IH p. 24). In describing the affectivity induced by a sense of the 'wholly other' Otto stresses how the encounter with the unintelligible and unfamiliar nature of the divine induces a feeling of 'blank wonder and astonishment' (IH pp. 26) and from which we 'recoil in a wonder that strikes us chill and numb' (IH pp. 28).

The aspect of religious affectivity Otto identifies that most immediately resonates with Nietzsche's thought is his account of the 'element of fascination'. As he states, 'the daemonic-divine object…allures with a potent charm…The 'mystery' is…something that entrances…something that captivates and transports…with a strange ravishment, rising often enough to the pitch of dizzy intoxication; it is the Dionysiac-element in the numen' (IH p. 31). For Otto this is the source of what he describes as 'the feelings of positive self-surrender to the numen' (IH p. 32). In the following overview of religious affectivity as a whole Otto stresses its essentially 'ambiguous' character:

> these two qualities, the daunting and the fascinating…combine in a strange harmony of contrasts, and the resultant dual character of the numinous consciousness…is at once the strangest and most noteworthy phenomenon in the whole of the history of religion…this dual character, as at once an object of boundless awe and boundless wonder, quelling and yet entrancing the soul…constitutes the proper *positive* content of the *mysterium* as it manifests itself in conscious feeling (IH pp. 31, 41).[40]

Otto undertakes thoroughly to expose the anthropomorphic nature of religious language in order, as with Nietzsche and Bataille, to reinforce rather than undermine the 'divine'.[41] For Otto, uncritical anthropomorphisation reduces the 'wholly other' nature of the 'holy'. Inadvertently echoing Nietzsche's conception of a 'healthy' religious sensibility, Otto writes:

> religion…has developed not from the homely and the familiar but from the uncanny, rising to the 'wholly other', which is remote from everything human. This 'wholly other' is the mysterious underlying framework to which all that is rational is but the superstructure; it permeates all that is

'anthropomorphic' and the anthropomorphic element is not primary but an accretion...the divine in God ...cannot be reduced to idea, world-order, moral order, principle of being or purposive will (RE pp. 78–79; IH p. 96).

The most rigorous aspect of Otto's critique of anthropomorphism is his avowal of a 'supra-personal' conception of the divine given that the notion of a 'personal God' is an objectification of the 'wholly other'.[42] Otto insists on an extraordinarily impersonal conception of religious affectivity and its 'object', which he asserts to combat the forgetful literalisation of anthropomorphic analogies and concepts. As he states of the 'wholly other':

> in drawing more near to earth and to humanity, it comes...to acquire human traits, and, that this tendency may not be carried too far, it is necessary now and then to melt down...the human lineaments of God in the more elemental entirety of the original experience...all gods are more than mere (personal) gods, and that all the greater representations of deity show from time to time features which reveal their ancient character as *'numina'* and burst the bounds of the personal and theistic...this personal character is that side of his nature which is turned manward (IH pp. 198, 199, 203).

This anti-reductionism also characterises Otto's account of the 'subjective' side of the relationship to the divine, 'all that we call person and personal, indeed all that we can know or name in ourselves at all...beneath it lies, even in us that 'wholly other', whose profundities, impenetrable to any concept, can yet be grasped in the numinous self-feeling' (IH p. 203).

On the basis of this recovery of the 'non-rational' elements of the 'holy' Otto addresses its role in Christianity. He uncovers an impersonal, errant religious affectivity within the Judaeo-Christian tradition that resists the process of moralization to which it has been subjected.[43] Otto persuasively uncouples the religious and the moral and, prioritising the former, argues that many key Christian themes such as sin, atonement, 'lostness', 'original guilt', and the 'battle between flesh and spirit', are *not* first and foremost 'moral' in orientation. Otto's conception of a distinctly religious rather than moral realm of value is evident in the following claims:

> Sin is a religious, not a moral concept...if sin, expiation, lostness, salvation from the state of being lost, the fall, and original guilt, are drawn into the moralistic, not to say the juridical sphere, they must lose their original meaning which lies entirely within the ancient numinous sphere of the Old and New Testament...sin remains primarily that which lies *purely* within

the realm of *religious* relationships: it is primarily the failure, inhibition, or atrophy of the purely religious spiritual functions themselves, of reverence and awe…it is made up not of moral badness, but of godlessness…it is entirely *sui generis*, and not reducible to the merely moral order…flesh is primarily not an antagonism against moral laws but a deficiency in the divine…the religious conscience..transcends all morality and makes profanity, that is to say our estrangement from God itself into guilt…redemption…is not a moral education or improvement, it is a rebirth, stirring the profundities of our metaphysical being itself…in the realm of pure contact with the supernal divine itself (RE pp. v, 7, 14, 27, 28–29).[44]

For Otto, religious value concerns primarily the extent to which the human affirms or resists the 'wholly other', an issue quite distinct from, even at variance with, adherence to moral codes. In a phrase which could be echoed by Nietzsche and Bataille, the task for Otto is, 'to overcome the natural aversion, indeed the horror, against that 'wholly other'' (IH p. 15). Otto is drawn towards mysticism as an aspect of Christianity in which the feeling for the 'numinous' is best preserved. As he states:

mysticism is the stressing to a very high degree…of the non-rational or supra-rational elements in religion…mysticism…retains the *positive quality* of the 'wholly other' as a very living factor in its overbrimming religious emotion…above and beyond our rational being lies hidden the ultimate and highest part of our nature, which can find no satisfaction in the mere allaying of…needs…and cravings…The mystics called it the ground of the soul…the non-rational energy…fundamentally independent of *moral* elevation or righteousness…Western mysticism has…an element inimical to the church and menacing to the community and to organized religious use…the religious feelings associated with the mystical love of God…readily assume an erotic tinge (IH pp. 22, 29, 36, 107; RE p. 105).[45]

Clearly Otto's conception of the 'holy' as 'wholly other' is conceived in terms of the transcendent, albeit critically delimited in the Kantian sense. Otto bases his conception of the 'autonomy' of religious affectivity on Kant's notion of 'reflective judgment' and *a priori* conception of feeling in the 'Critique of Aesthetic Judgment', in particular the 'Analytic of the Sublime'.[46] Hence, unlike Nietzsche and Bataille, Otto does not develop an immanent conception of the radical 'otherness' of the divine.

However, the force of Otto's vivid description of religious feeling is not compromised by his commitments to the transcendent. In fact, the religious feelings of human 'impotence' and 'insignificance' that Otto identifies are strikingly akin to Nietzsche's conception of 'healthy' religious affectivity. The three thinkers considered here define the religious in terms of the collapse of egoic willing; a radical disabling of what Nietzsche dismissively termed the 'will as cause' (TI 'Errors' 3). Human willing, or what Bataille terms 'project', is brought to its knees by an impersonal, dysteleological process (e.g. 'will to power') for which it is inconsequential.[47] Unquestionably Nietzsche's and Bataille's ontology of religious sublimity is considerably more radical than Otto's. However, all three thinkers share a positive valorisation of the religious feeling of being submerged, overwhelmed and engulfed.

Otto's account of religious affectivity demands a reconsideration of Nietzsche's negative assessment of the 'health' of Christianity. Unlike Nietzsche, Otto pursues a universalist agenda that claims to uncover a religious *sensus communis*.[48] From Otto's perspective, Christianity, if rebalanced in favour of its 'non-rational' elements, is not as 'sickly' as Nietzsche claims. Otto's work raises the possibility of considering religious affectivity as a nomadic cluster of 'extra-moral' affects that can appropriate *any* doctrinal-conceptual religious system. This is, of course, the standard Nietzschean point that phenomena are constituted by the 'forces' that, for a time, appropriate them. Hence, Christianity is not intrinsically 'healthy' or 'sick' as this is dependent upon the type of 'will' that inhabits it. Otto's texts manifest aspects of Christianity that can be considered 'healthy' in Nietzsche's sense, a 'noble' form of Christianity. The mystic, possessed by an wave of impersonal affectivity to the point of total self-expenditure, could be considered as a rare moment of the becoming-sacred of Christianity.

That, for Otto, Christianity is the pre-eminent religion in both the conceptual and affective domains, including in the latter a 'Dionysiac-element', challenges Nietzsche's assessment of it. Otto's work should induce a hesitation in those impressed by Nietzsche's critique of Christianity on two counts. Firstly, the question arises as to whether Nietzsche conflates the religious and moral spheres of value in his critique of Christianity and thereby merely condemns its moralized self-image, its irreligious drift from its non-anthropomorphic affective essence.[49] Secondly, Otto offers an immanent critique of Christianity that locates *within* Christianity the very elements of intense religiosity that are to be deployed in a critique of it. This is an affirmative or non-oppositional critical approach that unleashes a suppressed religiosity immanent to Christianity that reanimates a conflict of forces within it, confronting it with its inherently non-Christian essence. Unlike the less radical gesture of opposition, immanent critique seeks to put a phenomenon at odds with itself, to instill sedition thereby stimulating a re-prioritisation of elements within it. The critical stance Otto adopts toward Christianity surpasses Nietzsche's, which remains predominantly oppositional in nature, bent on locating a 'healthy' religious affectivity outside of Christianity.

In response to the first issue, the question arises as to what extent Otto offers a radically non-moral account of Christianity. Whilst he effectively demonstrates the 'autonomy' of religious affectivity in relation to the moral it is not obvious that he has distinguished Christianity from the 'moral' in the more significant sense Nietzsche identifies, that is the pre-given negative evaluation of the fundamental material and instinctual characteristics of 'this world'. This raises the issue of Otto's and Nietzsche's respective conceptions of the relationship between the religious and moral spheres. Otto insists that, especially in the case of Christianity, religious affectivity and morality are autonomous but mutually reinforcing.[50] It is through his elaboration of this point that Otto makes a rare reference to the issue of 'health' in the religious sphere. As he states, 'the degree to which both the rational and non-rational elements are jointly present, united in healthy …harmony, affords a criterion to measure the relative rank of religions – and one, too, that is specifically religious…Christianity, in the healthily proportioned union of its elements, assumes an absolutely classical form' (IH pp. 141–142). For Otto, the autonomous elements of the 'holy', in the exemplary case of Christianity, compliment each other 'like the interweaving of warp and woof in a fabric' (IH p. 46). In contrast, Nietzsche claims that anything other than an opposition to morality fatally compromises the religious instinct. A related charge that could be made against Otto from a 'Nietzschean' perspective is that the intoxication of Christian affectivity he valorises is merely the religious feeling of the 'slave', it is a 'sick' rather than a 'healthy' excess.[51]

It could also be said that, even granted the 'universality' of the type of religious affectivity Otto describes, his claims for Christianity's pre-eminence are too uncritical. For Otto, not only are the 'rational' and 'non-rational' elements of the 'holy' of *a priori* origin and status, but so also is their 'schematization'. Otto details the translation of the non-rational feelings of the *tremendum, fascinans* and *mysteriosum* into the 'rational ideas' of 'justice, moral will and the exclusion of what is opposed to morality' (*tremendum*), 'goodness, mercy, love' (*fascinans*) and *'absoluteness'* (*mysteriosum*) (IH pp. 140–141) and accords this relation between affect and concept *a priori* status.[52] Nietzsche would no doubt condemn this Christian appropriation of religious affectivity masquerading behind claims to the universality and necessity of the translation process in question. He would, insofar as he accepted Otto's account of 'healthy' religious affectivity, suggest other, more religious, expressions of such feelings.

The comparison of Nietzsche's and Otto's accounts of religious affectivity raises a number of significant issues. These include the description and evaluation of the affectivity of Christianity, the relation between the rational-moral and emotional elements of religion, and the degree to which religious affectivity is autonomous, radically separable from the categorical and doctrinal. It is in relation to these questions that the comparison between their different critical stances toward Christianity arises. I shall now turn to Bataille and suggest that his thought can be described as a synthesis of the radical elements of both Nietzsche's and Otto's conception of religious affectivity and evaluation of Christianity.

III

No thinker has developed more powerfully the religious dimension of Nietzsche's thought than Bataille. Like both Nietzsche and Otto, Bataille pursues a religious critique of religion as he states, 'I regard…religion from a religious point of view'.[53] Although Bataille's critical stance towards Christianity is formally more akin to Otto's than Nietzsche's his overall evaluation of it is clear: 'the Christian religion is possibly the least religious of them all' (E p. 32). Bataille also prioritises 'religious experience', synonymous in his texts with the notion of 'inner experience'. As he states:

> my theme is the subjective experience of religion…religion in the sense I mean it is not just *a* religion, like Christianity. It is religion in general…My concern is not with any given rites, dogmas or communities, but only with the problem that every religion sets itself to answer…I am describing an experience without reference to any special body of belief, being concerned essentially to communicate an inner experience – religious experience…outside the pale of specific religions (E pp. 32, 34)

Bataille undertakes a radical transvaluation of the 'divine' in response to the 'death of God' which he interprets as a positive religious, sacrificial event – 'what the love of God finally rises to is really the death of God' (E p. 141) and, 'the *absence of God* is no longer a closure: it is the opening up to the infinite. The absence of God is greater, and more divine, than God' (AM p. 48).[54] This transvaluative trajectory aligns 'God' with an impersonal movement of self-transcendence without transcendent determination: 'God is nothing if not a transcendence of God in every direction' (E p. 269). In agreement with Nietzsche, Bataille rethinks transcendence in immanent terms as the 'apotheosis of that which is perishable...the passion of giving the world an intoxicating meaning'.[55]

Underpinning Bataille's thought is a conception of the accumulation and expenditure of energy that overturns the primacy traditionally accorded to the notions of utility, scarcity and lack. Bataille proposes an 'economics' which prioritises 'consumption' over 'production' on the basis of a 'Nietzschean' insight into the originary surfeit of energetic resources, a prodigality that surpasses the requirements of mere self-preservation and which is irreducible to teleological appropriation whether critically or dialectically conceived.[56] This 'accursed share' of excess energy has, ultimately, to be expended gratuitously without reference to productive ends. There is, Bataille paradoxically claims, a 'need for limitless loss' (VE p. 123) that characterises material life within which he locates, non-reductively, human activity without remainder.

On the basis of this 'economics' Bataille develops a series of contrasts of which the most relevant here are those between the 'continuity' and 'discontinuity' of being and 'intimacy' and the 'order of things'.[57] In relation to these distinctions Bataille develops his principal contrast between the 'sacred' and 'profane'. For Bataille 'continuity' and 'intimacy' are terms for the most fundamental plane of being, a material field of self-differentiation prior to negation, a domain in which the oppositions which make possible the field of 'discontinuity' and the 'order of things' have not yet been instituted and into which they are dissolved in a sacrificial process. It is this domain of 'continuity' and 'intimacy', akin to Nietzsche's conception of the non-unified 'mystical oneness' of the 'Dionysian', that, for Bataille, characterises the 'sacred'. Given that this realm is a dimension of 'this world', the only one Bataille acknowledges, it can be conceived as a terrain of immanent self-transcendence. Bataille writes of an 'immanent immensity, where there are neither separations nor limits' (TR p. 42). In contrast, the realm of 'discontinuity' and the 'order of things' is the mode of being of distinct, self-identical, spatio-temporal, causally related entities as conceived by representational and calculative thought. Bataille aligns the realm of 'discontinuity' and the 'order of things' with the 'profane' world of work and rational calculation, founded upon taboo, especially in relation to sexuality and death. The containment of the expenditure of the realm of 'continuity' and 'intimacy' can only be temporary. Inevitably excess has to be affirmed and its primacy acknowledged. In the following passages Bataille's conception of religious affectivity in this context can be discerned:

> there are transitions from continuous to discontinuous or from discontinuous to continuous. We are discontinuous beings…but we yearn for our lost continuity. We find the state of affairs that binds us to our random and ephemeral individuality hard to bear. Along with our tormenting desire that this evanescent thing last, there stands our obsession with a primal continuity linking us with everything that is…This nostalgia is responsible for the three forms of eroticism in man…physical, emotional and religious…with all three…the concern is to substitute for individual isolated discontinuity a feeling of profound continuity (E p. 15).[58]

The pre-individuated, impersonal nature of the 'sacred' in Bataille's sense is clearly stated here. Also apparent is his radically a-subjective conception of the ecstasies of the most intense religious feelings conceived in terms of affirmative self-annihilation. As with both Nietzsche and Otto, Bataille privileges affectivity, 'I will say…this of continuity of being: it is not in my opinion knowable, but it can be experienced' (E pp. 22–23).

Bataille identifies 'health' with an affective-libidinal economy in which self-expenditure predominates over self-preservation. This produces a sensibility open to the auto-consecrative processes of material life. Like Otto and Nietzsche, Bataille conceives the affectivity of the 'sacred', which occurs on the cusp of the contrasts described above, as intrinsically 'dual' in character. For Bataille, the 'anxiety' and 'horror' felt by the 'discontinuous' entity upon encountering the 'limit' vies with the 'ecstasy' and 'joy' of affirmative self-loss. Religious affectivity is necessarily ambiguous as it concerns the transvaluative surrender of individuation at the limits of the 'human' or the 'extreme limit of the possible' (IE p. xxxiii). Bataille writes in this respect that the 'mind moves in a strange world where anguish and ecstasy coexist' (IE p. xxxii).[59]

Bataille valorises this affirmation of self-overcoming and identifies it with 'sovereignty', or the attainment of the 'summit' in contrast to 'decline', terms that repeat Nietzsche's contrast of 'health' and 'sickness' in terms of 'ascending' and 'descending' life.[60] A crucial characteristic of this condition is an affirmative embrace of the 'death' of the discontinuous entity in its numerous senses. Bataille vividly described this state as one of 'joy before death'. Its affinity with the affirmative religious sensibility Nietzsche terms 'tragic joy' is clear:

a joy that has no object other than immediate life. 'Joy before death' belongs only to the person for whom there is no *beyond*; it is the only intellectually honest route in the search for ecstasy...to a sufficiently happy *loss of self*...the religious forms it rediscovers are the naïve forms that antedate the intrusion of a servile morality: it renews the kind of tragic jubilation that man 'is' as soon as he stops behaving like a cripple, glorifying necessary work and letting himself be emasculated by the fear of tomorrow (VE pp. 236–237).

A key notion in this area of Bataille's thought is 'religious eroticism'. This illustrates the non-reductive nature of Bataille's materialism which is best conceived as a libidinal monism. This is stated thus:

> The cohesion of the human spirit whose potentialities range from the ascetic to the voluptuous may...be sought. The point of view I adopt...reveals the co-ordination of these potentialities. I do not seek to identify them with each other but I endeavour to find the point where they may converge beyond their mutual exclusiveness...flights of religious experience and bursts of erotic impulses are seen to be part and parcel of the same movement (E pp. 7, 9).

All three forms of 'eroticism' or self-transcendence that Bataille identifies, the 'physical', 'emotional' and 'religious', are equiprimordial. As a form of affirmative self-oblivion, 'religious eroticism' is not viewed by Bataille as a 'sublimation' to be decoded in sexual terms. It is, no less than the other types of eroticism, a first-order process of material expenditure, an auto-transfiguration of impersonal energy.

Like Nietzsche, Bataille was personally familiar with mystical states, a mysticism 'missing a God' (IE p. 9). For Bataille mysticism concerns 'contagions of energy', 'streaming of electricity' and is a 'celestial bacchanalia' (IE pp. 94–95).[61] It is a mysticism that accesses an immanent otherness, a state of enraptured fusion with a self-transfiguring world, a 'wave of life losing itself' (IE p. 95). Bataille describes his own mystical experience as an 'ecstasy before the void' (IE pp. 112–113).[62]

Nonetheless Bataille maintains an equivocal relationship toward mysticism. He acknowledges the intensity of ecstatic self-loss that characterises Christian mysticism but also distances himself from its theistic commitments: 'I hold the apprehension of God...to be an obstacle in the movement which carries us to the more obscure apprehension of the *unknown*: of a presence which is no longer in any way distinct from absence' (IE p. 5). Bataille seeks to affirm 'the mystical mode of feeling in the sense of experience, not mystical philosophy' (ON p. 175). In terms of the ontological contrasts discussed above Bataille thematises mysticism thus:

> mystical experience...brings to a world dominated by thought connected with our experience of physical objects (and by the knowledge developed from this experience) an element which finds no place in our intellectual architecture except negatively as a limiting factor...mystical experience reveals an absence of any object. Objects are identified with discontinuity, whereas mystical experience, as far as our strength allows us to break off our own discontinuity, confers on us a sense of continuity (E p. 63).

Bataille's reluctance to adopt unequivocally the term mysticism can be read as, following Nietzsche, his commitment to the radicalisation of Kant's critique of metaphysics. Bataille is gesturing toward a post-critical conception of mysticism that subjects the notion of the transcendent (or 'noumenon') to an even stronger critique than Kant who, in any case, was unable to valorise religious feeling. Bataille's attempt to dissociate the mystical from the transcendent rather than merely developing a negative as opposed to a positive account of possible access to it is stated thus:

> the states described by the mystics had ceased to be closed to me. This experience was independent, it is true, from the presuppositions to which the mystics imagine it to be linked...Can one not free from its religious antecedents the possibility for mystical experience – this possibility having remained open to the non-believer, in whatever way it appears? Free it from the *ascesis* of dogma and from the atmosphere of religions? Free it, in a word, from mysticism...? (IE pp. 93, 169).

Bataille describes mystical experience as 'that ultimate in human poten-tialities' (E p. 221). He develops Nietzsche's insights into the libidinal investment and intensity of Christian mysticism but, unlike Nietzsche, he evaluates these affective states positively as the highest form of 'health' insofar as the mystic, burning with 'divine love', seeks total self-immolation. Bataille addresses the 'burning question of the relationship between mysticism and continence' – the suspicion that Christian mys-ticism is based on a 'fear of sex' (E p. 221). Given his insistence on the equiprimordiality of the different forms of eroticism, Christian mysti-cism is not for Bataille, in its highest forms, analysable as a 'neurotic' reaction to an originary, essentially non-religious, material process. Rather it is the manifestation of a *becoming-religious of matter* – 'spiritu-ality' as a primary material process of sacred self-expenditure.

Bataille finds this religious propensity of matter operative in the 'evangelical law' that 'man must die in order to attain the divine life' (E

p. 228). He hears in this edict not the life-negating yearning for 'other-worldly' redemption but the 'death' and 'violence', affirmatively heard, that characterise the transition from individuation to self-annihilation. From this perspective 'mystical passion', the process of 'dying to one-self', contests the 'dragging weight of attachment to the self' (E p. 230). It is one of a number of affirmative senses of death or 'self-overcoming' that Bataille identifies. In the religious context he describes it thus:

> The religious…will die to the divine life he desires…Dying can take on the active meaning of behaviour…that sets at nought the cautiousness incul-cated by the fear of death…to live for the moment, no longer to heed these instincts for survival: this is dying to oneself…Beyond pride and mediocrity we keep glimpsing a terrifying truth.The immensity of everything that is, unintelligible…no place is left for the limited being who judges the world through calculations …Immensity…spells death to the one it attracts (E pp. 233–234).

This passage resonates with many 'Nietzschean' themes, the displace-ment of the supposed primacy of the 'instinct for self-preservation', the immanent sublimity of impersonal life and so on. Yet, beyond Nietzsche, Bataille locates these features of a 'healthy' religious sensibility *within* Christianity. In energetico-economic terms, Christian mysticism is con-ceived as a process of intensificatory self-expenditure concerning a 'desire to live to the limits of the possible and the impossible with ever-increasing intensity…to die without ceasing to live' (E p. 239). Bataille seeks, having established the autonomy of religious eroticism, to iden-tify its shared element with sensuality. This proximity is stated thus:

> the desire to fall, to fail, to faint and to squander all one's reserves… a start-ing point to investigate the way that sexual and mystical experience are linked… harmonise in the nostalgia for a moment of disequilibrium… toward transcendence in which concern for the preservation of life is scorned… non-attachment to ordinary life, indifference to its needs, anguish felt in the midst of this until the being reels, and the way left open to a spontaneous surge of life that is usually under control but which bursts forth in freedom and infinite bliss. The difference between this experience and that of sensuality is only a matter of confining these impulses to the domain of inner awareness… communication is always possible between sensuality and mysticism, obedient as they are to the same motive force (E pp. 229–230, 246–247).

IV

Bataille combines Otto's evaluation of Christian mysticism with Nietzsche's non-reductive materialism such that he can state that, 'in the sphere of mysticism we reach complete sovereignty' (E p. 249). This religious-materialist valorisation is reiterated thus, 'little by little, desire lifts the mystic to such utter ruin and expenditure that the life of the person becomes more or less a solar brightness' (ON pp. 31–32). However, apart from its mystical strain Bataille can find no other significant trace of the 'sacred' within Christianity. Like Nietzsche, Bataille condemns Christianity as a highly deficient and domesticated religion that bears no comparison with a range of archaic religions which, Bataille argues, are far more in tune with the economic and religious material imperatives he identifies. From the perspective of the religious criteria he proposes, Bataille finds Christianity to be resolutely 'profane' and 'utilitarian' in orientation.

Hence, Nietzsche and Bataille would both vehemently contest Otto's claim concerning the superiority of Christianity. For Bataille, Christianity is religiously impoverished insofar as it mistakenly prioritises and hypostatises the derivative ontology of 'discontinuity' (a personal God, 'immortality of the soul' and so on) and inhabits the relation between taboo and transgression that constitutes the human, in oppositional or 'moral' terms rather than the pre-oppositional valorisation of their reciprocity that he recommends.[63]

In his valorisation and non-reductive materialist interpretation of Christian mysticism Bataille surpasses both Nietzsche's and Otto's relation to Christianity. He develops, through his conception of mysticism, an immanent critique of Christianity. In this respect a similarity can be discerned between Bataille's and Otto's thought. However, in that Bataille offers a radical materialist-libidinal thematisation of Christianity he is more akin to Nietzsche than Otto. Bataille also follows Nietzsche in developing an immanent conception of the 'wholly other' which forms the basis of their respective critiques of the ontology and values of Christianity. In this respect the limitations of Otto's critique of Christianity are revealed.

All three thinkers share a commitment to the radicality of a 'religious' orientation in contemporary critique and to the primacy of affectivity within religion itself. They each also tend toward an interpretation of religious feeling as an impersonal phenomenon. Furthermore, they each distinguish between 'healthy' and 'sick' forms of religious affectivity only disagreeing on the balance of them within a religion and the identification of a specific religion as pre-eminently affirmative – in broad terms, the pre-Socratic Greeks (Nietzsche), the Aztecs and Christian mystics (Bataille) and post-Reformation Christianity (Otto). Bataille emerges as the most radical of the three thinkers in that he combines the 'content' of Nietzsche's critique of the ontology and values of Christianity with the 'form' of Otto's stance toward it. Bataille, uniquely, pursues an immanent trajectory in both the rethinking of transcendence demanded by the 'death of god' and in his affirmative critique of Christianity.

Bibliography of cited works by Nietzsche

'Attempt at a Self-Criticism' in *The Birth of Tragedy* (see below).

Beyond Good and Evil (Harmondsworth: Penguin Books, 1973, trans. R.J. Hollingdale).

Ecce Homo (Harmondsworth: Penguin Books, 1979, trans. R.J. Hollingdale).

Human, All Too Human (London: Penguin Books, 1984, trans. M. Faber and S. Lehmann).

On the Genealogy of Morality (Cambridge: Cambridge University Press, 1994, trans. C. Diethe).

On the Genealogy of Morality (Indianapolis: Hackett Publishing Co., 1998, trans. M. Clark and A.J. Swenson).

The Birth of Tragedy (London: Penguin Books, 1993, trans. S. Whiteside).

The Gay Science (New York: Random House, 1974, trans. W. Kaufmann).

The Will to Power (New York: Random House, 1968, trans. W. Kaufmann and R.J. Hollingdale).

Thus Spoke Zarathustra (Harmondsworth: Penguin Books, 1969, trans. R.J. Hollingdale).

Twilight of the Idols and *The Anti-Christ* (Harmondsworth: Penguin Books, 1968, trans. R. Hollingdale).

Notes

1 In according affectivity such status each thinker seeks to surpass the merely anthropological perspective of the 'psychology of religion'.

2 See WP II 251.

3 For statements of this broad set of claims about the nature of Nietzsche's critical stance see AC 47, ASC 5 and GM 'Preface' 6, I 17, III 14.

4 I discussed Nietzsche's surpassing of the optimism/pessimism distinction in 'A "Pessimism of Strength": Nietzsche and the Tragic Sublime' in J. Lippitt (ed.), *Nietzsche's Futures* (London: Macmillan, 1999) pp. 129–148.

5   See, BGE 13, TI 'Expeditions' 14, WP II 254, 372, III 650.
6   See WP III 846.
7   See TI 'Expeditions' 36–37.
8   That the contrast between 'health' and 'sickness' is always a matter of degree for Nietzsche is clearly stated at WP I 47, III 812. These terms are part of a network of themes in Nietzsche's thought that include the 'aesthetic'/'moral' and 'noble'/'slave' contrasts.
9   I explored Nietzsche's non-moral conception of ethics in 'Noble *Ascesis*: Between Nietzsche and Foucault', *New Nietzsche Studies*, vol. 2:3/4 (1998) pp. 65–91.
10 Examples include AC 2, 5, 20, 22, 39, 51, 59, 62, ASC 5, BGE 61, 62, EH 'Destiny' 7–9.
11 See GM III 21.
12 See GM III 15. In assessing the 'seriousness' of such diagnostic claims the qualifying comment made in GM III 16 is important.
13 See also WP II 154.
14 See also AC 2, 14, BGE 62, WP II 246.
15 See also BGE 56, 59, WP II 195.
16 See AC 24, 51, GM I 4–16.
17 See GM II 16.
18 See GM III 15–21.
19 See BT 10, BGE 46, 62, GM II 7, III 14, 17, 28, GS 370.
20 See BT 3, 10, GM II 23.
21 For further examples see BT 2, 7, 10, GM II 24, Z 'Of Redemption'.
22 Even T. Roberts stumbles in the face of Nietzsche's tranvaluative fusion of materialism and religion. See his otherwise impressive text *Contesting Spirit: Nietzsche, Affirmation, Religion* (Princeton: Princeton University Press, 1998) pp. 151–152, 161–162.
23 See also WP III 820.
24 See M. Eliade, *Myths, Dreams and Mysteries* (Glasgow: Collins, 1968, trans. P. Mairet) pp. 124–126.
25 See BT 7.
26 See also GM II 19, 20.
27 For example see AC 16, ASC 5, GM II 23, WP II 147–50, 196.
28 The 'unmasking' of the affective-libidinal investments of Christian asceticism as harnessed by the 'ascetic priest' is the fundamental task of GM III 11–22. I discussed Nietzsche's insights into the pleasures of denial in 'Noble *Ascesis*: Between Nietzsche and Foucault'. For an excellent discussion of related issues see T. Roberts, *Contesting Spirit* pp. 77–102.
29 See BGE 55, 229, GM II 18, III 12, Z 'Convalescent' 2. This claim is generalised to all religions at GM II 3.
30 For the important notion of the 'economy of life' see also GM III 27, TI 'Morality' 6, WP II 432.

31 I discussed this issue in 'Noble *Ascesis*: Between Nietzsche and Foucault'. Nietzsche also criticises the 'sick excess of feeling' of Christianity in HH 114.

32 Nietzsche's criticism of Socrates as 'the very embodiment of the non-mystic' (BT 13) seems to suggest an implicit valorisation of mysticism, albeit of a non-Christian variety. Socrates is, of course, a 'mystagogue of science' (BT 15). For Nietzsche's negative assessment of the *unio mystica* see GM I 6. T. Roberts is insightful on this topic: see *Contesting Spirit* pp. 103–137.

33 See also BGE 51.

34 The tentative suggestion that 'fear' might be the 'origin of the gods' (GM II 19) is an example of this 'reductive' tendency. Another might be the inverse relation proposed between frequency of sexual intercourse and the fecundity of the 'sensual imagination' used to explain the phenomenon that 'many Christian saints' imaginations were exceedingly dirty' (HH 141).

35 See GM II 12–13.

36 That Nietzsche's critique of Christianity is 'immanent' in another sense, as characterised by and reliant upon certain specifically 'Christian' attitudes and values (eg. 'probity', 'truthfulness' and so on) such that it could be regarded as the 'self-overcoming' of Christianity itself (a possibility Nietzsche explicitly acknowledged), is the basic stance adopted by K. Jaspers in *Nietzsche and Christianity* (Washington D.C.: Henry Regnery Co., 1961, trans. E.B. Ashton) pp. viii, 9–11, 51, 64–66, 69, 80–83, 88–89. However, I am suggesting an immanence in respect of Christianity itself rather than aspects of Nietzsche's critical perspective toward it.

37 R. Otto, *The Idea of the Holy* (London: Oxford University Press, 1958, trans. J.W. Harvey), originally published in 1917 (hereafter IH) and *Religious Essays: A Supplement to 'The Idea of the Holy'* (London: Oxford University Press, 1931, trans. B. Lunn), hereafter RE. For a positive, if somewhat begrudging, comment on Otto's thought see G. Bataille: *The Absence of Myth: Writings on Surrealism* (London: Verso, 1994, trans. M. Richardson) p. 117, hereafter AM.

38 See IH p. 6.

39 See also IH pp.125–129.

40 See also IH pp. 52–53, 193.

41 It is important to note that highlighting the anthropomorphic elements of religion is not necessarily hostile to the divine. Whilst for some (e.g. Marx and Freud) this is the case, for others, including Kant and those considered in this paper, the critique of anthropomorphism is made in order to defend the 'divine'. In other cases (e.g. Hume and Feuerbach) it is more ambiguous.

42 See IH pp.197–203.

43 See IH pp. 72–93, RE pp. 30–52. These texts can be usefully compared with Nietzsche's evaluation of the relative merits of the Old and New Testaments. See BGE 52, GM III 22.

44 For an occasion when Nietzsche seems to make a similar point see GM III 17.

45 See also IH pp. 46, 141, 197.

46 See IH pp. 41, 46, 62–63, 132–135. For an interesting account of the relation between sublime aesthetic feeling and religious affectivity in Kant's thought that draws upon Otto's work see A. Lazaroff, 'The Kantian Sublime: Aesthetic Judgment and Religious Feeling' in C. Cazeaux and R.F. Chadwick (eds.): *Immanuel Kant: Critical Assessments, Volume 4* (London: Routledge, 1992) pp. 355–377.

47 For Otto's formulation of this point see RE pp. 18–24. All three thinkers align the religious with a non-pacifistic passivism or non-egoic willing.

48 See RE pp. 95–120.

49 Nietzsche, as texts such as ASC 5 demonstrate, didn't acknowledge the possibility Otto proposes – that the religious and the moral can be dissociated in Christianity.

50 See IH p.111, RE p. 15.

51 For occasions on which Otto invites this response see IH pp. 51, 82.

52 See also IH pp. 45–49.

53 G. Bataille, *Eroticism* (London: Marion Boyars, 1962, trans. M. Dalwood) p. 123, hereafter E. See also G. Bataille, *Inner Experience* (Albany: State University of New York Press, 1988, trans. L.A. Boldt) p. 134, hereafter IE.

54 See also G. Bataille IE pp. 130–134, 152–157.

55 G. Bataille, 'The Practice of Joy Before Death' in *Visions of Excess: Selected Writings 1927–1939* (Minneapolis: University of Minnesota Press, 1985, trans. A.Stoekl, C. Lovitt, D.M. Leslie, Jr.) pp. 237, 245, hereafter VE.

56 The *locus classicus* here is G. Bataille, 'The Notion of Expenditure' (VE pp. 116–129). See also G. Bataille, *The Accursed Share: Volume One* (New York: Zone Books, 1988, trans. R. Hurley) pp. 21, 27, 106, 182, hereafter AS.

57 For the 'continuity/discontinuity' contrast see E pp. 11–15, 21–24; for the 'intimacy/order of things' contrast see G. Bataille, *Theory of Religion* (New York: Zone Books, 1989, trans. R. Hurley) pp. 45–48, 50–52, 92–104, hereafter TR.

58 In a similar vein Bataille claims that 'man is *in search of a lost intimacy* from the first' (TR p. 57).

59 See also IE pp. 142–147, E pp. 38–39.

60 For examples of the role of these themes in Bataille's thought see G. Bataille, *The Accursed Share: Volumes II and III* (New York: Zone Books, 1993, trans. R. Hurley) pp. 103–105, 198–200, 217–222, *On Nietzsche* (New York: Paragon House, 1992, trans. B. Boone) p. 17, hereafter ON.

61 See also IE pp. 58–60
62 See also IE pp. 126–127.
63 For this severely critical dimension of Bataille's response to Christianity
    see, E pp. 89–90, 117–128, ON pp. 17–19, TR pp. 69–90, AS pp. 115–142,
    VE pp. 119, 242–245.

13
Lunar rapture: Nietzsche's religion of the night sun

Jill Marsden

As the evening sun gently bleeds into the horizon and healthy human beings slide into the snore of oblivion, an alien species stirs into life, enraptured by a universe that rivets it to its gaze. Only the insomniac knows the *profundity of night*. To remain awake when others sleep is to observe a vigil quite foreign to the waking hours of the day. Night is the unlived world, indifferent to the working hours of calm, productive thought and for Nietzsche these restless hours are strangely exalted times. In the *Nachlass* one encounters the following fragment:

> There is one part of the night about which I say, 'Here time ceases!' After all these moments of nocturnal wakefulness, especially on journeys or walks, one has a marvellous feeling with regard to this stretch of time: it was always much too brief or far too long, our sense of time suffers some anomaly. It may be that in our waking hours we pay recompense for the fact that we usually spend this time lost in the chaotic tides of dreamlife! Enough of that! At night between 1 and 3, we no longer have the clock in our heads. It seems to me that this is what the ancients expressed in the words *intepestiva nocte...* 'in the night, where there is no time'... (KSA 9 11 260).[1]

Never the woeful insomniac, wretchedly nailed to eternity, Nietzsche enthuses about the tremendous feeling to which only the night-wanderer is privy. In nocturnal wakefulness time loses its steady ordinal flow and dissolves into the anomalies of excess beyond measure – always too much or not enough. For the wakefulness of the night is not of the same order as the lethargic flickerings of consciousness, nor simply inverse to the wild flights of dreamlife. More than mere attentiveness, its light survives within you: 'one does not see in the dark with impunity'.[2] An alien voyager from an uninhabited realm, the nightwanderer infiltrates the sun-lit world, entrancing it with its mystic spell and rendering the familiar strange at every turn. As Nietzsche writes in *The Gay Science*:

> Oh, these men of former times knew how to *dream* and did not find it necessary to go to sleep first. And we men of today still master this art all too well, despite all of our good will toward the day and staying awake. It is quite enough to love, to hate, to desire, simply to feel – and *right away* the spirit and power of the dream overcome us, and with our eyes open, coolly dismissive of all danger, we climb up on the most hazardous paths to scale the roofs and spires of fantasy – without any sense of dizziness, as if we had been born to climb, we nightwanderers of the day! We artists! We concealers of what is most natural! We are moonstruck and God-struck! (GS 59).[3]

I want to ask what it would mean to be moon-struck and God-struck (*Mond- und Gottsüchtig*) – to be literally addicted to the lunar and the divine – and why it is the wakeful dreamer who has access to this experience. It seems that it is enough to throb with love, hate, desire, simply *passion* in order to become enraptured by the spirit and power of that which leaves the natural order behind. Liberated from the torpid values of a senescent humanism, the nightwanderer attains a different quality of sentience – a vibrant second nature. As every insomniac knows, in sleeplessness it is the *body* that is disturbed and encountered anew, as if in default of dogmatic slumber the inner forces beat to a fundamentally different rhythm. But why should exile from the natural and temporal order have any bearing on divinity? A fragment from Nietzsche's *Nachlass* provides a first tantalising clue.

> – And how many new gods are still possible! As for myself, in whom the religious, that is to say, god-*forming* instinct, wants, from time to time, to come back to life, how differently, how variously the divine has revealed itself to me each time! So many strange things have passed before me in those timeless moments that fall into one's life as if from the moon, when one no longer has any idea how old one is or how young one will yet be – I should not doubt that there are many kinds of gods – (WP IV 1038)

Divinity appears to be revealed in those timeless moments that fall into one's life as if from the moon, moments in which the religious, god-*forming* instinct is reanimated, and more precisely, awakened ever again anew. In many ways this is a surprising thought in the wake of the death of God, an event which Nietzsche characterises as solar eclipse and collapse of being into night: 'Is not night continually closing in on us? Do we not need to light lanterns in the morning?' (GS 125). Yet if the religious instinct is to be located in timeless moments, *lunar* moments which ruin the seriality of a life and rob thinking of its co-ordination by the sun, might it be that night admits a clarity which is also divine?

As is well known, Nietzsche's thought of eternal return – a thought which radically reconfigures our understanding of time – is always revealed in moonlight, where demons become gods and 'many a thing can be heard which may not speak by day' (Z 'The Nightwanderer's Song' 3). As the famous *The Gay Science* passage intimates, to *affirm* eternal return as *sacred* hinges upon the experience of a 'tremendous moment' which would prompt one to sanctify the diabolical prophet of recurrence: 'You are a god and never have I heard anything more divine' (GS 341). Elsewhere in the same text Nietzsche declares that religion is the means by which the human animal 'learns to hunger and thirst for *himself*' (GS 300) and we are told that it is the happiest who, in the 'most profound enjoyment of the moment' are prepared to risk all festively, 'impelled by the longing for undiscovered worlds and seas, people and gods' (GS 302). Affirming the moment appears to be the wellspring for a religious ecstasy of an extraordinary kind but what would *affirming the moment as divine* actually mean? Intriguingly, it is in 'The Nightwanderer's Song' in *Thus Spoke Zarathustra* that an avowal of eternal return is made and it is the murderer of God who utters its pronouncement. Might this be a key to understanding the divinity of lunar moments or will our nocturnal journey carry us elsewhere through the 'spiriting night'? In the words of Zarathustra, *'the hour has come: let us walk into the night!'* (Z 'The Nightwanderer's Song' 2)

The Nightwanderer

Night 'is sacred to those astray',[4] a mythic world of dream and derangement, peopled by dark and vagrant souls. But strange are the night-time pathways travelled by Zarathustra who from the outset identifies himself with the gratuitous self-expenditure of the sun. It is at 'noontide' that he basks in his most perfect happiness and it is night that plunges his spirit into darkest despair. In *Ecce Homo* Nietzsche quotes the entirety of 'The Night Song', a Dionysian dithyramb of deepest melancholy, which tells of one who through his nature as a 'sun' is condemned not to love: 'Oh wretchedness of all givers! Oh eclipse of my sun! Oh craving for desire! Oh ravenous hunger in satiety!' (EH 'Thus Spoke Zarathustra'). Elsewhere in *Thus Spoke Zarathustra* the sun is associated with innocence and creative desire, eliciting the sea to rise with a thousand breasts, 'to be kissed and sucked' by its hot thirst whereas the moon is a symbol of stealth and deception: 'When the moon rose yesterday I thought it was about to give birth to a sun, it lay on the horizon so broad and pregnant. But it was a liar with its pregnancy…Behold, the moon comes along catlike and without honesty' (Z 'Of Immaculate Perception'). This is the first of many riddles that constellate around the sacred moment and its perpetual lunar unfolding.

Indeed, Nietzsche's extraordinary text 'The Nightwanderer's Song' is set against the backdrop of an immense full moon and explicitly recalls the earlier epiphanies of moonlight from 'The Greatest Weight' (GS 341) and 'Of the Vision and the Riddle' (Z). At this point in the narrative, the band of Higher Men go out to 'greet the night' after having finished celebrating their bizarre acts of idolatry at the 'Ass festival' in Zarathustra's cave. Unlike the prisoners in Plato's cave, they do not emerge from darkness into light but enter what Zarathustra calls his 'nocturnal world' – the deep mystic night of unknowing. As the 'mystery of the night' draws nearer and nearer to their hearts, an astonishing event takes place. The ugliest man and 'murderer of God' finally attains the point of speech and turns to address the gathered throng:

> 'My assembled friends,' said the ugliest man, 'what do you think? For the sake of this day – *I* am content for the first time to have lived my whole life. And it is not enough that I testify only this much. It is worthwhile to live on earth: one day, one festival with Zarathustra has taught me to love the earth. 'Was *that* – life?' I will say to death. 'Very well! Once more!' My friends, what do you think? Will you not, like me, say to death: 'Was *that* – life? For Zarathustra's sake, very well! Once more!' Thus spoke the ugliest man; and it was not long before midnight (Z 'The Nightwanderer's Song' 1).

It is tempting to interpret this proclamation as a sign that Zarathustra has successfully communicated his teaching; indeed, after the ugliest man has finished speaking the Higher Men fling themselves upon Zarathustra, thanking, adoring and caressing him as if *he* were a god and his teaching divine. But their messiah is oddly unmindful of their adulation. Standing there like one intoxicated, Zarathustra's eyes grow dim, his tongue stammers and his feet totter as if the organs of the body suddenly forget their proper functions: 'And who could divine what thoughts then passed over Zarathustra's soul? But it seemed that his soul fell back and fled before him and was in remote distances and as if "upon a high ridge", as it is written, "wandering like a heavy cloud between past and future" '(Z 'The Nightwanderer's Song' 2). No words are uttered to the ugliest man, no response is given to his surprising disclosure. Instead, in a state of bodily entrancement, Zarathustra is overcome with thoughts so potent that they sever him from the ensuing commotion. More precisely it is his soul, which seems to travel vast distances fore and aft, as if a chasm opens in the night into which all connection to the present is swallowed. Nietzsche's reference to the wandering soul strongly echoes the opening of 'The Seven Seals' in which Zarathustra declares that if he were a prophetic spirit, wandering between past and future, pregnant with lightening flashes which affirm 'Yes!', how ardently he would *lust* for eternity and the ring of recurrence. Zarathustra's rapture – both his mystic transport into the vastness of becoming and his deeply sensual longing – disrupts the narrative with the force of trauma.

Or perhaps we might say that it is the power of *Traum*, of the waking dream, that takes possession of this nightwanderer. In a startling passage in *The Gay Science* Nietzsche writes:

> How wonderful and new and at the same time how dreadful and ironic I feel my position to be with respect to all of existence in light of my realisation! I have *discovered* for myself that primeval human and animal kind, indeed, the whole primal age and past of all sensate being continues in me to poetise, to love, to hate and to conclude: I suddenly woke up in the middle of this dream but only to the consciousness that I am still dreaming and that I *must* continue dreaming so as not to perish just as a sleepwalker (*Nachtwandler*) must go on dreaming in order not to fall. (GS 54)

Nietzsche suggests that the continuation of all affective force within the compass of a single life is experienced within a waking dream – as if liberated from the sanity of the day, the self becomes a vessel for alien inhabitation. A vast virtual phylum flows through the self like a main line artery, linking a life to possibilities no longer *owned*. Ironically, whilst the ugliest man is able to avow his existence in his own name – '*I* am content…to have lived my whole life' – it is Zarathustra adrift in the seas of cosmic ruin who appears to have been touched by the moon. For in his lunar intoxication, Zarathustra is borne away by a soul that streams out in as if in 'slow rivers through the inky sky'.[5] When he finally begins his 'Nightwanderer's Song', the moon-crazed ravings which ring out in the night air displace the temporal location of the narrative once again, but this time enigmatically recasting and *condensing* the moment into that of 'Of the Vision and the Riddle': 'Woe is me! Where has time fled? Did I not sink into deep wells? The world is asleep – Ah! Ah! The dog howls, the moon is shining. I will rather die, die, than tell you what my midnight-heart is now thinking. Now I am dead. It is finished. Spider, why do you spin your web around me?' (Z 'The Nightwanderer's Song' 4).

From the heart of 'ancient, deep, deep midnight', the gateway of moment returns: "'And this slow spider that creeps along in the moonlight, *and this moonlight itself*, and I and you at this gateway whispering together, whispering of eternal things – must we not have been here before?"' (Z 'Of the Vision and the Riddle' 2, emphasis added). Liberated from the moment of self-presence, Zarathustra returns anew to the revelation of recurrence. Perhaps moonlight is not simply the background within which events unfold but is *lunar unfolding* itself, the regeneration of the moment *within itself*. Past and future emerge together in the timeless moment but this moment is not 'in' time: it 'is' time. One recalls that Zarathustra's dialogue with the dwarf is interrupted by a dog howling at the moon, a howling from the past – Zarathustra's most distant childhood. Yet this is also a howling from the future, as events no longer *succeed* one another but, as if in a dream, collapse in a vertiginously spiralling depth, drawing in and out of focus like shapes in the night sky. Night has no points, no sequence, no arching sun by which to map the passing of a life. In lunar rapture one has no idea how old one is or how young one will yet be. And Zarathustra, in his moon-struck madness proclaims his own crushing demise as a subject, as an 'I'. The lunacy of eternal return is such that it excludes the thinker at the very moment it is thought.[6]

According to Maurice Blanchot: 'Wakefulness is without beginning and end. To wake is neutral. 'I' do not wake: someone does, the night does, always and incessantly, hollowing the night out into the other night where there can be no question of sleeping'.[7] If night is sacred to those astray might this be because it marks the awakening of the *inhuman*? In the 'wavering moment'[8] of sacred sleeplessness the self becomes irrevocably estranged from the familiar species co-ordinates that anchor a life in its passage. For we inhabit the day but night inhabits us: the chaos of the starry skies *within* twinkle in the dark tangled capillaries of a sentience no longer *ours*. Across the dark canvas of the sky, a sinister destiny is realised. It is at the level of affective yet *anonymous* force that lunar rapture impacts. Perhaps to affirm a tremendous moment as divine is to consecrate oneself to the night to submit to the ecstasy of overwhelming passions and to be entranced like the nightwanderer of the day. Could it be that affirmation of eternal return is nothing attitudinal, rather, something libidinal? We recall that Zarathustra in his

mystic flight from self-presence voraciously lusts for the ring of recurrence and in his rapture it is the body that is undone. Yet this is not a
flight from the body, rather a re-encountering of corporeality at a physiological frequency different to that of the day and its regular pulse of the
'clock in the head'. Earlier in the text, he proclaims that the body does
not say 'I' but performs 'I', that the bodily self thirsts to create beyond
itself (Z 'Of the Despisers of the Body'). Is this the key to the creation
of new gods, the source of the religious instinct?

The sleepless and the sacred

In the *Nachlass* Nietzsche characterises the human body as that in which
'the most distant and most recent past of all organic development again
becomes living and corporeal, through which and over and beyond
which a tremendous inaudible stream seems to flow' (WP III 659). In
this exquisite formulation, Nietzsche implies that the body is a conduit
for forces that it neither wholly controls, nor discretely contains. It is as
if all sentient being continues in us to invent, love, hate and infer. In
another remarkable passage he speculates that if we imagined our body
on analogy with the stellar system we would abandon belief in a consciousness that determines purposes (WP III 676). Yet the mute intensity of the tremendous pulsions that flow through, over and beyond the
body is only rendered intelligible at the price of commuting its power to
the rational order of signs and exposing its dark complexity to the glare
of sun. What might be termed the '*levelling* power of gregarious
thought'(NVC p.7) functions by stabilising primary affectivity within its
pre-established codes where it must surrender its intensity to the colum-
barium of concepts. But perhaps things are different for the nightwanderer. In the night of consciousness, the afflux and reflux of corporeal
excitations attain a clarity no longer assimilable within the representational matrix. Cloaked by the gentle veil of darkness, the senses no
longer subordinate themselves to the speculative gaze of the eye and the
silent libidinal forces impose themselves more insidiously on thinking.
Such a reattunement of the body has been described by E. M. Cioran as
insomniac sensibility:

> The pure passing of time, naked time, reduced to an essence of flux, with-
> out the discontinuity of the moments, is realised in our sleepless nights.
> Everything vanishes. Silence invades – everywhere. We listen; we hear
> nothing. The senses no longer turn toward the world outside. What out-

side? Engulfment survived by that pure passage through us that *is* ourselves, and that will come to an end only with sleep or daylight…'[9]

To think the self as pure passage, as sheer intensity, holds in abeyance
the prejudice that consciousness should coincide with 'a' subject and
give the measure to 'inner sense'. However much the imperious ego
might be invoked to contest such a thesis, its material coexistence with
the forces it seeks to suppress enables the latter to intimate their power
at the level of thought. Hence, perhaps, the *lunacy* of the one who no
longer succeeds in mapping his life in terms of the serial order of personal self-identity.

In a letter to Karl Fuchs dated 14th December 1888 Nietzsche makes
explicit reference to the fluctuating currents of his tortured, inner
depths:

> *The vehemence of my inner oscillations* has been terrifying, all through these
> past years; now that I must make the transition to a new and more intense
> form, I need above all a new estrangement, a still more intense deperson-
> alisation. So it is of greatest importance what and who still remain to me.
>
> What age am I? I do not know – as little as I know how young I shall
> become…[10]

Nietzsche speaks of inner oscillations so frightful that they command an
intense depersonalisation, forces so violent that they struggle to register
themselves within a consciousness constantly under siege. Yet in many
respects, consciousness is a fragile dictator for it is only insofar as it com-
mensurates with the unity of an organism that it is able to maintain its
tyranny. The identity of the self seems to depend on the creation of an
irreversible history of the body, a temporal horizon or 'linkage of causes
and effects' (NVC p. 29). As Pierre Klossowski has so convincingly
argued in his reading of Nietzsche, the body is only the *same* body
insofar as the self in its singularity is able to coincide with it, the
body being nothing other than a locus where individuated impulses
confront each other 'so as to produce this interval that constitutes a
human life' (NVC p. 26). Intriguingly, Klossowski expresses these ideas
as follows:

> What is born from this chance association of impulses is not only the indi-
> vidual they constitute at the whims of circumstance, but also the eminently
> deceptive principle of a cerebral activity that progressively disengages itself
> from sleep. Consciousness seems to oscillate continually between somno-
> lence and insomnia, and what we call the *waking state* is merely the com-

parison of the two, their reciprocal reflection, like a play of mirrors (NVC p. 26).

If consciousness is a mere fluttering between dormancy and attentiveness, it lacks the inherent unity that would enable it to bind and temporarily reconcile the contradictory impulses that comprise the body, yet as a reactive force it has the power to stifle those impulses which seem to proceed from corporeal states hostile to its own sense of cohesion. On this basis, Klossowski conjectures that by 'passing through the *limit* that is constantly redrawn by the *waking state*' the self establishes a strategic unity:

> the waking state *never lasts more than a few seconds*. At every instant, the brain is flooded by excitations of greater or lesser intensity, excitations whose *overwhelming reception* must constantly be filtered. The new excitations are filtered through the traces of prior excitations, which have already been absorbed. But the new excitations can be co-ordinated with prior ones only through assimilation, namely by comparing what is 'habitual' with what is foreign (NVC p. 31).

This means that intensive energy is bound by consciousness via the reduction of difference to sameness, a process that inhibits the generation of new connective pathways which might bypass its channelling mechanism. In other words, the bodily self is reiterated as the same through oscillations that reinscribe identity *in the present*. One is reminded in this context of Nietzsche's claim that the greater the impulse towards unity, the more firmly one can conclude that weakness is present, the greater the force towards variety and differentiation – even at the cost of inner decay – the more force is present (WP III 655). This said, perhaps the bodily self which 'thirsts to create beyond itself' must risk this inner collapse if it is to attain the intense depersonalisation which Nietzsche desires. Everything hinges, it would seem, on attenuating the waking state.

In Nietzsche's *Nachlass* from Winter 1888 one encounters the following astounding passage:

> Five, six seconds and no more – then you suddenly feel the presence of eternal harmony. Man in his mortal frame cannot endure it; he must either physically transform himself or die. It is a lucid and ineffable feeling. You seem to be in contact with the whole of nature and you say: 'Yes, this is true!' God, when He created the world, said at the end of each day: 'Yes, it is true, it is good.' It is not emotion, it is joy. You forgive nothing because there is nothing to forgive. Nor do you really love anything – oh, this feel-

ing is higher than love! The most terrible thing is the horrific *certainty* with which it expresses itself and the joy with which it fills one. If it lasted longer the soul could not endure it, it would have to disappear – In these five seconds I live the whole of human existence, I would give my life for it, the price would not be too high. In order to bear this any longer one would have to transform oneself physically. (KSA 13 11 337)

If the fragile waking state constitutes consciousness through the assimilation of difference to the same, what happens when multiplicity in all its fullness floods the system, facilitating connections with all of nature? Such a high point of intensity compels a new estrangement from man in his mortal frame. One would sacrifice one's life for this feeling. One would literally expend oneself. For some time I interpreted this passage as an expression of the sublime feeling that Nietzsche attributes to the 'experience' of eternal return until I came upon a near identical extract in Dostoyevsky's novel *The Devils*. It would seem that these remarks made such an impact on Nietzsche that he copied them down in his notebook, perhaps perceiving in these awe inspiring lines something akin to his own encounter. The words are spoken by the insomniac Kirilov, who urged by his interlocutor that he really must get some sleep at night 'came out of his dream and – strange to say – spoke more coherently than he usually did'.[11] It is as if in sleepless clarity, the self cohesion constantly redrawn by the waking state, short-circuits at the insomniac state *and begins to oscillate there*, forging connections with all of nature at the price of its own self reassimilation. For in his wakefulness *beyond waking*, this nightwanderer speaks of a marvellous yet *unendurable* joy – a feeling which mortal being cannot *sustain* without physically transforming or perishing. Kirilov wakes from his dream but perhaps to the consciousness that he is still dreaming and must go on dreaming lest he fall. The demon's chilling words ring out: 'If this thought gained possession of you, it would change you as you are or perhaps crush you' (GS 341). At this high point of intensity the self-present subject literally cannot endure.

To bear such a thought one would have to transform oneself physically. Might it be that libidinal forces here succeed in deindividuating themselves from cranial identity, tending towards the variety and differentiation that consciousness functions to hold in check? As active forces these pulsions go to the limit of their power, even if this means to make a sacrificial offering of the self for the sake of its desire to *create beyond itself*. Perhaps it is in this register that the nightwanderer experiences

incarnation otherwise: as if struck by the moon, he must physically transform or perish. Nietzsche tells us that the 'feeling of rapture' is an
'exalted feeling of power' – sensations of space and time are altered,
tremendous distances are surveyed and organs are refined to apprehend
that which is extremely small and fleeting (WP IV 800). Overcharged by
exorbitant and impossible passions which again become 'living and corporeal', insomniac physiology is refractory to the discontinuous
moments of personal self-presence. If the waking state lasts merely a few
seconds, perhaps the insomniac state – wakefulness beyond waking –
frustrates duration precisely because it cannot be endured or can only
be endured through repeating itself as *other*: 'I live the whole of human
existence, I would give my life for it'. In a kindred passage, Dostoyevsky
says that in these moments the vital forces are strained to the utmost all
at once and 'the extraordinary saying that *there shall be time no longer*'
becomes 'somehow comprehensible'.[12]

Nietzsche's religion of the night sun

In our nocturnal wanderings might we have encountered finally the
source of the religious instinct, the god-*forming* force that in timeless
moments wills to come back to life? This force emerges in a life, in a
body, independent of human agency: 'As for myself, in whom the religious, that is to say god-*forming* instinct wills, from time to time, to come
back to life, how differently, how variously the divine has revealed itself
to me each time!' (WP IV 1038). It is life itself which returns to life,
repeats itself as other to itself in its depersonalised intensity. Lacking any
constitutive identity, this life is sensitive to the panoply of its variegated
possibilities and the necessary impossibility of sustaining a self-identical
state. It is in precisely this sense that Nietzsche conceives of divinity as
instinctive – an immanent economy of sacred self-expenditure. In his
heightened sleep-deprived fervour, Kirilov enthuses about a marvellous,
unbearable, God-like feeling of immense connection with all of nature.
In a passing yet prescient remark, Klossowski comments that if everything in us is conscious there would be a simultaneous activation of all
available bodily intensities, a state he calls *generalised insomnia* (NVC p.
39). Formulated thus, such a notion calls to mind the idea of God as a
total sensorium, a view which Nietzsche elsewhere in the *Nachlass*
descries as symptomatic of the elevation of consciousness to the
supreme standard and condition of life, the erroneous perspective of *a
parte ad totum* (WP III 707); however, might it be possible to retain the

notion of a generalised insomnia as an account of the flux of libidinal, transhuman energies liberated from the *unifying power* of the ego? Beyond the conscious waking state, such forces perpetually generate and disperse a life in their striving to differentiate themselves from the stabilising oscillations of consciousness and from one another, indeed, from bodily integrity itself. This tension is so extreme because in default of psychic equilibrium, in the wake of the death of God, the highest feeling can only be attained in violent conflict. A force differentiates itself in its perpetual overcoming of its rivals whilst remaining materially continuous with them, much as we might distinguish a shooting star from the night sky. Affirmation of self can only be won at the price of affirming *everything*.

In this respect we might think of generalised insomnia as the night-pool from which the divining of identity emerges. In the heart of darkness it is the affective potential of the vast differentiated richness of a single existence which is incarnated as the most exalted feeling. Nietzsche writes that anyone who manages to experience the history of humanity as a whole as *his own history* will feel in 'an enormously generalised way' all the grief of an invalid who thinks of health, of an old man who thinks of youth, of a lover deprived of his beloved, of the hero vanquished in battle, an immense sum of grief of all kinds. Yet if one could endure this feeling, welcoming the glimmering dawn like a person whose horizon encompasses 'thousands of years' past and future, a religious pathos of unprecedented magnitude will be the reward: 'if one could finally contain all this in one soul and crowd it in one feeling – this would surely result in a happiness that humanity has not known so far: the happiness of a god full of power and love, full of tears and laughter, a happiness that like the sun in the evening, continually bestows its riches, pouring them into the sea' (GS 337).

This evening sun offers a glorious vision of extravagant expenditure but if Nietzsche's philosophy has a religion it is a religion of the *night sun*. Just as the insomniac experiences a clarity quite alien to the day and to the mediating structures of representation, there is a mystic sensibility which illuminates the lunarscape without delivering it over to the levelling power of signs: 'It is a lucid and ineffable feeling'. This sensuality is resistant to all idealising gestures and can only be endured as a perpetual deviation from itself. Most importantly, it is a delight which can never be conceived 'redemptively' in terms of the absence of pain for it is only felt in terms of its affirmation of everything, its self differentiation from, and determination by, the vast libidinal maelstrom of becoming. Such is a god-like feeling, the *affirmation of eternal return as divine*. 'The Night-wanderer's Song' does not end with Zarathustra's cries of woe but with mounting tension oscillates between outbursts of despair and jubilation reaching a final crescendo of bliss born from pain: 'it ruminates upon its woe in dreams, the ancient, deep midnight hour, and still more upon its joy. For joy, though woe be deep: *Joy is deeper than heart's agony*' (Z 'The Nightwanderer's Song' 8).

> Do you not hear it? Do you not smell it? My world has just become perfect, midnight is also noonday, pain is also a joy, a curse also a blessing, the night is also a sun – be gone, or you will learn: a wise man is also a fool. Did you ever say Yes to one joy? O my friends, then you said Yes to *all* woe as well. All things are chained and entwined together, all things are in love; if you ever wanted one moment twice, if you ever said: 'You please me, happiness, instant, moment!' then you wanted *everything* to return! You wanted every-thing anew, everything eternal, everything chained, entwined together, everything in love, O that is how you *loved* the world…and you say even to woe: 'Go, but return!' *For all joy wants – eternity!* (Z 'The Nightwanderer's Song' 10)

The collapse of midnight into noonday signals the annihilation of any notion of temporal order that maintains the axes of a human world and divides sleepers from the inhumanly awake. Perhaps it could be said that in 'The Nightwanderer's Song' the moon, characterised as clandestine much earlier in the text, finally does give birth to a sun. For it comes to light up the dark Dionysian underworld of inhuman passion and hence to overcome the wisdom of the day, much like the Apollinian power of dream comes to radiate and intensify Dionysian night. The nightwan-derer wakes to the realisation that he is dreaming and whispers: 'It is a dream. I shall dream on!' – affirming the moment, however gruesome and melancholy his insights might be (BT 1). The crushing torment of sexual longing, epitomised in the 'The Night Song', is transfigured into the perfect moment of noonday, in an affirmation of every joy and every pain.

As Zarathustra's nocturnal incantations exemplify, joy wants the eter-nity of all things: '*what* does joy not want! It is thirstier, warmer, hun-grier, more fearful, more secret than all woe, it wants *itself*; it bites into *itself*, the will of the ring wrestles within it, it wants love, it wants hatred, it is superabundant, it gives, throws away, begs for someone to take it, it would like to be hated' (Z 'The Nightwanderer's Song' 11). This is not the contentment of which the ugliest man speaks but manic, insatiable desire. Return is not willed for the sake of one day, one festival, for Zarathustra's sake, but for its own sake – an affirmation so excessive it is illegible within the balance sheets of satisfaction and recompense. Might it be that eternal return is so terrible to endure because of the raw intensity of its rapture – a 'mad tension that puts every moment of your life on the plane of eternity'?[13] Joy is not acceptance of the moment, it *is* the moment, a moment without duration, unendurable, excruciating bliss. Affirmation – monstrous, tremendous, terrifying, exorbitant – can never endure for it is only produced through its rhythmic tension with, and overcoming of, an immensity of pain. In passing the moment must return, eternally open to past and future. Indeed, the moment's returning returns in every moment, lunar moments in which divine happiness is resuscitated ever again anew. This is the lunacy of a love that is so voracious it bites into itself, recoils on itself, eternally, insatiably needing itself again and again: 'And would this not be – *circulus vitiosus deus*?' (BGE 56).

Nietzsche's religion of the night sun is a sacred energetics of desire, a divine eroticism which demands self-annihilation. As Nietzsche's texts subtly indicate, one only 'exists' as the eternal joy of becoming, the profound delight 'in which existence celebrates its own transfiguration' (WP IV 1051). Zarathustra's ardent lust for eternity is deeply sexual yet ruthlessly impersonal, for it is the upsurge of a wholly inhuman eroticism which, in lunar rapture, thirsts for its own overcoming. This sacrificial force defines the religious instinct which Nietzsche determines as a longing for the most intense feeling and in the name of which the human animal learns to hunger and thirst for itself (GS 300). We recall Nietzsche's claim that it is the happiest who long for new gods, who in the 'deepest joy of the moment' are overcome 'by tears and the whole crimson melancholy of the happy' (GS 302). This is the deep, deep eternity of which Zarathustra sings and it is in this state that the Greeks are said to have 'invented' their gods. Yet with such happiness in one's soul 'one is also more capable of suffering than any creature under the sun' (GS 302). If suffering is identified as 'evil' then one can never proceed beyond the religion of pity, comfort and otherworldly redemption for the latter only knows how to share affliction, not to share joy. Nietzsche maintains that the 'path to one's own heaven always leads through the voluptuousness of one's own hell' (GS 338). To affirm eternal return is to affirm this darkness.

The revelation of the highest feeling in those timeless moments is an affirmation of 'God' as the high point of power, not as a sensorium of

being but as an expression of a sacred will to overcome being as such –
to eternally recome, *'the universe being nothing but a perpetual flight from
itself, and a perpetual re-finding of itself in multiple gods'* (NVC p. 65). The
religious impulse is a libidinal charge which in wanting to be more,
thirsts to overcome itself and to do so ever again anew. It is a carnal pul-
sation, the rapturous tension of differential forces, which inexhaustibly
renew themselves in the moment wherein all things are enchained and
entwined together or as Zarathustra, puts it, 'all things are in love'. For
love, even the love of God, remains the same in its roots (WP IV 808).

> A people which still believes in itself still also has its own God. In him it
> venerates the conditions through which it has prospered, its virtues, – it
> projects its joy in itself, its feeling of power on to a being whom one can
> thank for them. He who is rich wants to bestow; a proud people needs a
> God in order to *sacrifice*... Within the bounds of such presuppositions reli-
> gion is a form of gratitude. One is grateful for oneself: for that one needs a
> God. (AC 16)

Moon struck and god struck the nightwanderer soars through the star-
splashed night, intoxicated by demons and madmen, seared by eternity:
wanting it, hating it, loving it, crazed for it, wracked by torments that
glisten through the pores, galvanising every nerve ending and burning
with a slow, cruel passion, as the soul combusts in lunatic worship to the
blank, incurious moon. If lunar rapture fades with the dawn like an
evanescing dream, its afterglow colours the day with its indelible night-
mares and its poetry, a deftly spreading contagion, communicates
beyond the pulse of reason its delicately proliferating disaster. A convalescent from time, the nightwanderer inhabits the waking life of a myth-
ically inspired people which 'more closely resembles a dream than it
does the waking world of a scientifically disenchanted thinker' and 'as in
a dream, anything is possible at each moment, and all of nature swarms
around man as if it were nothing but a masquerade of the gods, who
were merely amusing themselves by deceiving men in all these shapes.'[14]

To conclude, a discarded draft from Robert Musil's *The Man Without
Qualities*, entitled 'Lunar Rapture'.

> Every inner and outer occurrence of lunar nights possesses the nature of
> the unrepeatable. Every occurrence possesses an enhanced nature. It has
> the nature of an unselfish liberality and dispensation. Every communica-
> tion is a sharing without envy. Every giving a receiving. Every reception
> inextricably interwoven in the excitements of the night. To *be* this way is our
> only way to *know* what is happening. For the 'I' does not retain for itself any

elixir of its past possession, scarcely a memory; the enhanced self radiates outward into a boundless selflessness, and these nights are full of the senseless feeling that something will have to come to pass that has never come to pass before, something that the impoverished reasonableness of the day cannot even visualise. And it is not the mouth that gushes forth but all the body from head to foot, and the body above the darkness of the earth and beneath the light of the sky, the body that is yoked to an excitement that oscillates between two stars. And the whispers we share with our companion are pervaded by an utterly unfamiliar sensuality, which is not some person's sensuality, but the sensuality of the earth, of all that compels our sensibility, the suddenly unveiled tenderness of the world that touches all our senses and that all our senses touch.[15]

Bibliography of cited works by Nietzsche

Beyond Good and Evil (London: Penguin 1973, trans. R. J. Hollingdale)

Ecce Homo (London: Penguin 1979, trans. R. J. Hollingdale)

Philosophy and Truth: Selections from Nietzsche's Notebooks of the Early 1870's (New Jersey: Humanities Press International, 1979, trans. D. Breazeale)

Sämtliche Werke: Kritische Studienausgabe (Berlin: Walter de Gruyter, 1980, eds. G. Colli and M. Montinari)

The Antichrist (London: Penguin 1986, trans. R. J. Hollingdale.

The Birth of Tragedy (New York: Vintage, 1967, trans.W. Kaufmann)

The Gay Science (New York: Vintage, 1974, trans. W. Kaufmann)

The Will to Power (New York: Vintage 1968, trans.W. Kaufmann and R. J. Hollingdale)

Thus Spoke Zarathustra (London, Penguin 1961, trans. R. J. Hollingdale).

Notes

1 I am indebted to D. F. Krell for his translation of this fragment in *Lunar Voices: Of Tragedy, Poetry, Fiction and Thought* (Chicago: University of Chicago Press, 1995) p. 146.

2 E. M. Cioran, *A Short History of Decay* (London: Quartet, 1990, trans. R. Howard) p. 170.

3 Whilst indebted to Walter Kaufmann's translations of *Die Fröhliche Wissenschaft* and *Der Wille zur Macht* I have occasionally suggested alternative translations to highlight the theme of 'lunar rapture'.

4 Hölderlin, 'Bread and Wine' (second stanza) in Hölderlin, *Selected Verse* (Middlesex: Penguin, 1961, trans. M. Hamburger) p. 106.

5 See G. Bataille's eloquent depiction of lunar ecstasy in *Guilty* (U.S.A.: The Lapis Press, 1988, trans. B. Boone) p. 18.

6   See P. Klossowski's subtle elaboration of this thought in *Nietzsche and the Vicious Circle* (London: The Athlone Press, 1997, trans. D. W. Smith) p. 64. Hereafter NVC.

7   M. Blanchot, *The Writing of the Disaster* (Lincoln: University of Nebraska Press, 1986 trans. A. Smock) p. 48.

8   Hölderlin, *Selected Verse* p. 106

9   E.M. Cioran, *Anathemas and Admirations* (London: Quartet, 1992, trans. R. Howard) p. 120.

10 F. Nietzsche, *Sämtliche Briefe: Kritische Studienausgabe* (Berlin: Walter de Gruyter, 1986, eds. G. Colli and M. Montinari) 8 521.

11 F. Dostoyevsky, *The Devils* (London: Penguin, 1953, trans. D. Magarshack) p. 586.

12 F. Dostoyevsky, *The Idiot* (London: Penguin, 1955, trans. D. Magarshack) p. 244.

13 E. M. Cioran, *On the Heights of Despair* (Chicago: University of Chicago Press, trans. by I. Zarifopol-Johnson) p. 22.

14 F. Nietzsche, 'On Truth and Lies in a Non-Moral Sense' in *Philosophy and Truth: Selections from Nietzsche's Notebooks of the Early 1870's* (New Jersey: Humanities Press International, 1979, trans. D. Breazeale) p. 89.

15 Once again I am indebted to D. F. Krell's *Lunar Voices* (p. xix–xx) for bringing this fragment to my attention.

14
Nietzsche's Götterdämmerung

Ullrich Haase

> Religion perishes as a consequence of the belief in morality: the Christian
> God of Morality is no longer possible: "Atheism" follows – as if no other
> breeds of Gods were possible. (KSA 12 114)

> We only want to be the inheritors of Christian meditation and sensibility ...
> to overcome all Christianity by means of a *hyperchristianity*, rather than
> being content by freeing ourselves from it. (KSA 11 626, 682)
> Friedrich Nietzsche

The return of religion

The last ten years of the second millennium have seen what some have
called a *return of God*, a new actuality of religion[1]. Following the victory
of positivism, cheered on by the apparently infinite ability of the natural
sciences and their technological deployment to manipulate the world,
the catastrophic experiences characterising the 20th Century have led
the human being to realize that some-*thing* went missing. As Nietzsche
puts it, we human beings are members of a race that cannot live without
a certain notion of truth, and this idea of truth is intimately linked to religious faith. And as if such a realization could have an effect on reality, it
has led, not only to a *theological turn of French phenomenology*, but to a
return of God. That is to say, that the need disclosed by this experience
has led to the return of a God who had already left us and who has now
returned on account of our despair. Just as we Europeans thought our
souls lost to an awesome infinity, we are called to find them again in his
returned presence. For a long time philosophy had joined the natural sciences in their conviction that the question of God was passé. Now,
according to Vattimo, God has returned, not only as a topic for philosophical reflection, but in reality, which can be seen in the fact that Vat-

timo does not merely turn to discuss the divine being, but seeks a way to return to his faith.

And yet, to have said that some-*thing* went missing with the Death of God is quite misleading. What 'true' knowing and 'true' religion have in common, and, indeed, where we might find their common origin, is that they are not dealing with the world by way of objectification, that is, that they do not deliver some-*thing*. Rather they have always been directing themselves toward the concrete life, which cannot find its mediation within the realm of distinct objects. The 'objective world' might be understood as the consequence of the secularization of Christian faith, but as such it does not remain within the bounds of faith. While the scientist does indeed believe in his subject matter, this belief is quite hollow and it fails to bestow the permanence on to life bestowed by religious faith.

And yet, if there is, in the form of the objectivist modern sciences, a continuity of the Christian revelation; if it is possible to understand them as shadows of a dead God[2], then we should ask ourselves what it is that returns to our attention under the title of 'religion'. Thinking about the historical position that I have already indicated, it is not too far a step to Derrida's answer: 'the question of religion is first of all the question of the question'[3]. While such an affirmation remains rather vague, ranging from an endorsement of Plato's argument that the human being cannot sustain its life without the belief in Gods, right up to an imposition on Heidegger's account of questioning as the piety of thinking, it still expresses the insight into the universality of religion, which has shaped much of the thinking of the 19th and 20th centuries. We are then dealing with a contradiction between two questions: on the one hand, we philosophers have never been able to understand how the human being could exist without a God, while, on the other, it seems impossible to allow that a God might return on account of our insight into the inability to exist without him.

Derrida, Vattimo and others speak on the occasion of a conference about the question of religion. This is only one example of a plethora of publications concerning a return to God. Suddenly philosophy turns back to one of its most haunted questions. Two questions arise: what is the motivation of such a turn back to religion? What is it that returns with this topic of religion? The suspicion is that we are not returning to faith, but at best to the problem of the loss of faith. While any philosophical reflection about a God falls far short of religion, the realization of the need involved in such reflection represents an advance on the naïve atheism of our contemporary world-picture.

In the following essay I am going to consider the unfolding of this return of the problem of religion. This problem is twofold, in that it not only concerns the question of what is thought when philosophy thinks religion, but also reflects on the essence of philosophy itself, as soon as thought thinks about religion. I will follow through Vattimo's claim of a rejuvenation of the Christian God by way of the weakening of religion, not only in terms of Nietzsche's text, which is one of Vattimo's most decisive sources, but also on account of the necessity that binds the human being to the existence of its Gods. This problem will carry me towards the question of the *Eternal Return* as a new religion and the question of the mystic experience as a counterweight to the progressive secularization of Christianity on which Vattimo pitches his hopes. In the course of this consideration it will become clearer that what has returned here is but a problem and not a God, a problem that might be better described as the helplessness of modernity in the face of the invisible.

This helplessness shows itself first of all in the inability to understand the question of God's existence in any other way than that given by proofs concerning the demonstration of the visible. What has returned to philosophy is not a God, but a problem; and, indeed, a problem that has become *the* aporia of humanity. To say it in simple words: 'God is dead! And God remains dead!' (GS 125), while the end of the positivist dream has made the conclusion inescapable that without God the human being cannot *be* either. In this sense the death of God forces the human being to face up to its most existential crisis. Nietzsche describes this crisis as arising from the essence of modern man as *everything that does not know where to turn*. The human being has become everything, insofar as with the death of God the human world has been deserted by the last being distinct from the anthropomorphic constitution of the objective world. But what has become everything has lost all direction and has then lost all becoming. In this respect what has become everything has become nothing: a paradox which characterises the ambiguous self-understanding of humanity in the modern age. While modernity is the age of humanism, bestowing an absolute value on human life, at the same time its sciences have reclaimed the human being as part of their subject matter, dealing with it as with any material mass.

After the death of God the human being can no longer remain what and where it is. In this respect the death of God leads to a crisis, that is to the decision that Nietzsche lodges within the thinking of the *Eternal Return*. This decision refers to either the return of the human to animal life or its disappearance in that existence that Nietzsche enigmatically calls the *Overman*. The main point that Derrida makes in his essay, regarding the word 'religion' is quite succinct and indeed touches on the *word* that is at the beginning. If the question of religion is the question of the question, then we return the question of religion to the paradox that Kierkegaard has already pointed out in terms of faith. 'True religion' withdraws from the plane of philosophical investigation, since it is that which itself cannot be thought. '"Thinking religion?" you say. As if such a project would not in advance dissolve the question itself'[4].

But it is not only a question of the ability to 'think religion', rather, as Heidegger points out, for the philosopher it is somewhat indecent even to try. The philosopher of the 20th Century has realized the historical 'unity' of philosophy as onto-theo-teleology, a unity of a very strange kind, considering that since the enlightenment we Europeans have got used to representing philosophy and religion as antithetical on the ground that reason leads to the refutation of all authority. Furthermore we have got used to representing the origin of philosophy as the displacement of *mythos* by *logos*. Thus Deleuze, in his *Nietzsche and Philosophy*[5], still attempts to explain the religious image of the philosopher as a mask hiding the essentially anti-religious essence of philosophy. The unity between philosophy and religion appears in the progressive Christianization of any theme of philosophy, if it is ethics or politics, epistemology or cosmology, ontology or metaphysics. To say that it is indecent for the philosopher to speak about religion leaves her in limbo as to the question 'what is thinking?', unless she gives up on the notion of freedom as it falls within the domain of metaphysics. The modern philosopher lives indeed in a deeply confusing state, the more so when confronting the return of God. He is not quite sure if it would not have been better to follow Heidegger: 'whoever has experienced Theology, that of Christian belief as well as that of philosophy, from out of its genealogical origin, prefers today, in the realm of thought, not to speak about God.'[6]

'God is dead! And God remains dead!' How shall it then be possible to speak of a return of religion? It seems as if we have not yet stopped confusing religion with Christianity and hence with the Christian God. But this is what Vattimo appeals to, namely that if the God who died is only one particular God – *and, indeed, why not just the metaphysical God, that is, the God of the philosophers?* – then we might be allowed to draw the consequence from Nietzsche's and Heidegger's work by concluding that 'the end of the metaphysical God prepares the rediscovery of the

Christian God.'[7] Somebody might object that *dead* means *dead* and that, furthermore, the experience of the progressive secularisation of the Christian church, while conserving Christian values, has put an end to religion, but that still leaves us with the following problems.

How can the death of God affect Christianity in any *negative* way, considering that Christianity *is* that religion building upon the experience of the death of God? The death of God is certainly not just a modern event, nor is it a mystery that Nietzsche had suddenly discovered. Already Hegel describes 'this pain, that God himself is dead' as 'the birthplace of sanctification and of the ascendance to God,'[8] and with these words he describes the specific nature of Christianity as that religion in which God himself and the world become what they are by way of the death of God. From the death of its God springs the life of the Christian world.

If we consider the Christian experience of this death – first in the negation through which the Father becomes the Son, who is still the God becoming mortal; then in the form of the sacrifice of the Son of God himself – that is, if we consider that the Christian faith believes in a God who makes himself mortal so as to allow his people to put him on the cross, then one might begin to see how Vattimo can claim that the historical development of 'secularisation … is a positive effect of the teaching of Jesus Christ and precisely not a way to distance oneself from it'[9]. The special mission of Christianity can hence be seen in the liberation of religion from all naturalist, absolute, threatening and bizarre images of divinity,[10] while the last service in the ongoing process of the Christian revelation has consequently been performed by psychoanalysis, 'insofar as it has dissolved the illusion of the sacred substantiality of consciousness.'[11] And yet, one might be tempted to look at this Hegelian account of the sublation of religion and ask whether all these reasons do not rather point towards the impossibility of a rebirth or of a return of the Christian God, because His unique historical mission was to fulfil *his* death, so that what remains is but a vague idea of universal love. In this sense, then, one could really talk about a universal destiny of Christianity, to that degree that it brings about the death of all religion.

And yet, Vattimo can draw on the authority of Nietzsche's text itself: 'the refutation of God: – properly speaking it is only the moral God who *is* refuted' (KSA 11 264). Adding to this the clear distinction that Nietzsche makes in *The Anti-Christ* between the psychology of Jesus Christ, on the one hand, and St. Paul, on the other, then you will find again a similar motive. But it does not follow that the true Christianity of Christ could, would or should re-emerge once the Moral God has died. Rather one wonders if that is not precisely Nietzsche's point, namely that the Christian God *is* the Moral God of the religion of love. 'Religion perishes as a consequence of the belief in morality: the Christian God of Morality is no longer possible,' (WP 151) Nietzsche says, thereby sealing the fate of Christianity. And, against Heinrich Heine, who hears the death bells toll for the Christian God on the eve of the 21st of January 1781, that is, on account of the publication of the *Critique of Pure Reason,*[12] Kant might be better understood as one of the most important steps on the path of the secularization of Christianity that Vattimo has in mind. As Derrida makes clear,

> the unconditional universality of the categorical imperative is Evangelical. The moral law inscribes itself at the bottom of our hearts as a memory of the Passion of Christ. Whenever this law address us, it speaks a Christian idiom – or it keeps quiet.[13]

And we should keep in mind, that it was Nietzsche who showed us that our morality and our customs, the very fabric of our thought, our notions of freedom, equality and fraternity are deeply Christian.

Nietzsche describes the highest type of man, who has left the moral God behind, as 'the Roman Caesar with the soul of Christ' (KSA 11 289). And, so as to make clear in what sense a return of religion finds its first expression in Nietzsche's work, and seems to legitimate Vattimo's claim, I will again quote the former. 'It seems to me that the religious instinct is growing rapidly – but that it rejects precisely the theistic gratification with deep suspicion'[14], Nietzsche says and promises God's return: 'You call it the self-dissolution of God: yet it is only his sloughing [*Häutung*]: – he only takes his moral skin off! And you shall soon see him again, beyond good and evil' (KSA 10 105).

There are, then, at least two quite distinct ways of understanding the 'return of religion' as the first step towards the realization of the death of God. Both these possibilities are to be found in form of the *atheist* discourse that animates many of Nietzsche's writings. Insofar as Nietzsche has proclaimed the realization of the death of God as the task of a future time, we still find ourselves at the beginning of this process. And yet, because 'we' are those animals that cannot exist without this God, we can only see this return as that of *our* God not returning to *us*. When Nietzsche speaks of the *Eternal Return* as a new religion *and* as the crisis of the human being between animal and Overman, one should bear in mind that the concept *Overman* contains the word 'man' only negatively.

That is to say, it is called Overman only on account of rising out of mankind, not on account of an identity binding one to the other: 'we' humans are never to be 'overmen'. But how should such a realization of the death of God be able to call itself *the return of God* or *a new actuality of religion*? Should it not rather be its final end – as Nietzsche has said that it might be just a question of His final decomposition? Are we not speaking of another dawn of Gods, of another dawn of another *Dasein* separating itself clearly from us? And is not that *being-there* to take its position within this 'universe, which is a machine for the making of Gods'?[15]

The death of God leads humanity – and 'we' know how difficult it is, in what Derrida calls the mondialatinisation[16], to restrict our claims to 'European Humanity' or to the history of the Occident, or even to Christianity in opposition to the other world religions – before its most fundamental crisis, and this crisis has hence to be brought about in terms of the *Death of God*. To speak of a *mondialatinisation*, rather than of a Europeanisation of the world at large, is to say that Europe has been so effective and infective because it has always 'signified the death of God'[17].

It seems to me that rather than being privy to the return of God or even a new actuality of religion, what we do see today is an increasing receptivity to this imperative of a spiritual renewal that has attempted to make itself heard since Nietzsche's time. Such a 'spiritual renewal' derives its problematic nature from the impossibility of conceiving of a community without religion. Nietzsche's great politics derives its impetus from this problem of conceiving community after the death of God.

Consequently Nietzsche determines his 'great destination' as 'bringing about a kind of crisis and the highest decision in the problem of atheism'[18]. This decision shall be brought about through the *Eternal Return*, which decides about those that can and those that cannot sustain themselves in a world whose being is no longer guaranteed by the Christian God. Here I will restrict myself to approaching this issue by way of a minor decision, namely that between two strands of interpretation and their middle. There are, on the one hand, interpreters like Weischedel, who proclaim that Nietzsche is not radical enough, because he allows for another possibility of God. On the other hand, there is Vattimo, who sees in Nietzsche a thought grasping the problem at its root thereby preparing another, purer possibility of a God who has never yet appeared, insofar as he has withdrawn behind the history of Christianity. The crisis of philosophy which Nietzsche brings about might be yet better represented by Heidegger's interpretation of Nietzsche as that philosopher who begins to think a non-metaphysical relation between the mortals and the immortals, between heaven and earth. And, it is high time for such a crisis, considering the scandal of Christianity which Nietzsche characterises in his famous words: 'two millennia, nearly, and not a single new God'[19]. It is high time for such a crisis once the suspicion arises that religion – or maybe the source of religion; the sacred, the holy – is the *conditio sine qua non* of human life. 'We find in the past, we could find to-day,' as Bergson puts it, 'human societies with neither science nor art nor philosophy. But there has never been a society without religion.'[20]

Interlude: the necessary nature of religion

The nineteenth century is marked by the discovery of the universal fact of religion wherever there is human life. But is it really possible to speak of such a universality? When discussing the idea of such a universality we go back to the meaning of the word 'religion' itself. Yet this is a Latin word, essentially linked to the history of the Christian Church and it thus seems to be limited to the Occident and the two millennia of the history of Christianity. Already the Greeks, as Heidegger assures us, were not religious. In fact, the Christian religion first gains its universality with its signification as the death of religion.

In other words, the problem concerning a claim about the necessary existence of religion begins with the assertion that, indeed, we are speaking about a universality of the 'sacred' or the 'holy', of 'belief' or 'awe' as the *sine qua non* of human existence, while all the reasons we might give for such a necessity will depend on what Greek philosophy has taught us since its Latinisation. Furthermore, we will claim that there cannot be any human being without religion, while that is just what we are, human beings without religion, lacking a relation to the holy, suffering from the absence of God.

But on what grounds should we presume that the human being could not be without religion? The human being, as Greek philosophy understands it, is ζῷον λογον ἔχον (*zoon logon echon*), the animal that 'has' the λόγος (*logos*). In the λόγος we find the appearance of language as that in which reason grounds. To the extent that language becomes reasonable, language harbours concepts, especially those without which thinking seems to be impossible, like those of unity, identity, universality. These concepts are necessary preconditions for all experience: they are *a priori*. And yet, how should concepts be possible as concepts, rather than remaining mere words? How should they grasp anything, if it was not that they are identified with what they think? The λογος presupposes – already in the fragments of Heraclitus – unity. This unity is in-itself the essence of the divine being. This identity is not the empty logical equivalence of two concepts but the identity of thinking and being thought and it hence concerns the possibility of thinking generally. For the *merely* logical to be possible, there first has to be a metaphysical foundation of all thinking generally. That is why one of the more formal names of God is simply A = A. As is well known, St. Anselm's ontological argument is and is supposed to be a tautology.

One of the stems of the word *religion* is hence *relegere* (to pick up, to take into account), closely related to the Greek λόγος. And yet, it needs the second root, given as *religare* (to connect, to fasten) too.[21] That there is language speaking its unity with the world is due to the possibility of communication. Not to the actuality of communication by means of the use of words, but by its being made possible in the communion of faith. It is in this sense that the religious community precedes language while not existing outside of language. The question of religion then accounts for the impossibility of a pure origin of language as it is expressed in the opposition of *langue* and *parole* in Saussure's linguistics. It is indeed impossible to think an origin of language, precisely because language reduced to its formal constitution cannot give rise to communication. For the same reason there is neither a private language, as language cannot exist without communication, nor can we understand language as a means of communication. When Nietzsche says that he fears we will not get rid of God as long as we still believe in grammar, then he has this essential dependency of language on religion in mind. For the same reason the atheist is locked into a desperate contradiction: while he wishes to speak without God, all he can speak about is the loss of God.

Insofar as 'religion' signifies the origin of the identity of thinking and being as well as the possibility of communication, it follows that it is the origin of difference. Religion harbours the *principium individuationis* of and between human beings and their necessary union. That is why Bataille can show, in the *Theory of Religion*,[22] that the ground of communication lies within the communion arising from the sin of putting God onto the cross. The 'success' of Christianity hence lies in this image of the *Death of God*.

Consequently, if there is to be a return of a God, a new actuality of religion, then we will have to find the signs of such a God outside of

Christianity. And indeed, reading Vattimo, it often appears as if he was not so much looking for a new actuality of religion at all, because in this sense the survival of the Christian God depends on the secularisation of Christianity and hence on its universality of the experience of the death of God. But that only leads to a slow decomposition of Christianity, following Nietzsche's claim that the Christian God has died on account of his insidious claim to be the only and hence universal God.

How shall we then approach the question of a return of religion? Given that we do not dispose of any absolute or 'real' outside of history, our finite mode of access takes the route of a return to an historical possibility, that is to say, it depends on a move backwards on the lineage of descent towards *The Two Sources of Morality and Religion*.

The proof and the existence of God

> The religious is never destroyed by logic, but only through the withdrawal of the God.
>
> Martin Heidegger[23]

The aim of posing the question of a return of religion in the vicinity of the thought of Friedrich Nietzsche cannot consist in yet another attempt to prove the existence of God. And yet, to understand what is at stake in the question of religion, one might learn from the *degeneration* of the very question evidenced in attempts to prove the existence of God. Not only as regards the import of these proofs, but also insofar as we might become aware of the fact that to the question 'do you believe in God?' it does not make much sense to answer either 'yes' or 'no'. To answer negatively remains naïve; to follow St. Anselm's argument concerning the intimate relation between faith and knowledge, it would require me to suspend belief in the world as 'I know it'. To answer in the affirmative would remain inconsequential, insofar as faith expresses itself in action rather than in mere judgement. What Nietzsche has in common with Heidegger – at least as far as the above quotation is concerned – is that he does not doubt that Gods do indeed exist.

What does it mean to ask about the belief in the existence of something, especially if this something is to be a God? Posing the question of the truth of such existence, are we really thrown back on to the logical form of thought? Let us presume that somebody would be willing to prove the existence of God by means of that infamous syllogism which we call the ontological argument. In a manner to which we are by now accustomed, the argument is rejected on the grounds that a thought can never penetrate into the realm of really existent things. We wonder about this misunderstanding and compare the attempt at a proof for the existence of God with the desire to argue a hundred imagined Talers into existence, or maybe the most perfect island that we have conceived in our minds. Such a rebuttal of the ontological argument says more about ourselves than about this particular proof for the existence of God.

First of all, our refusal to take the ontological argument seriously makes clear what we understand by being, which is to say, which entities we take for real and what status we extend to *mere* inventions or possibilities. It tells us as well about our understanding of time, given that we tend only to think of facts – that is of 'having beens' – as sufficient evidence for existence. But, most importantly, such a critique expresses our frustration about thinking itself, because we lean to the conviction that thought is an abstract and vague non-entity, which could never produce enough evidence. And this is precisely the point at which we depart from St. Anselm. Where he tried to prove that we can trust thought on condition of our faith in God, we have long turned with a nihilistic suspicion against all thinking.

In other words, as long as we claim that this syllogism does not leave the realm of the merely logical, we have already given a reply to the question whether we believe that God does exist. This follows clearly from the point that claiming the existence of the *merely logical*, that is, of an ideal realm independent of the world itself, we despair of the fact that it does not *really* exist, given that it is unable to transcend towards the 'actual' world of facts. Yet this is tantamount to saying that one believes that the Christian God was once alive and yet that, now, he is dead.

We then move from the logical to the psychological, which here is a short slide, especially because we would still want to say that – while believing in the historical existence of the Christian God, given through a society that believed in Him and that, through this belief, gave birth to our modernity – God did not *really* exist, but did so only as a part of the culture of European humanity. On account of this psychological explanation we might claim that human beings had to believe in divinities, because, originally, their intellect was not yet fully developed and accustomed to living in the world. We might explain this belief by recourse to (1) the weakness of the human being generally, in that it needs to believe in order to survive; (2) the victory of reactive beings over active beings; (3) the historical necessity to hide from the understanding its own forces, at least until it assumes their mastery. Such an argument is fairly reminiscent of the 19th Century arguments concerning the rise of Christianity from 'primitive religion' as the sign of the maturation of spirit paralleled in the progressive revelation of the Christian God.

And yet, all these arguments fail to show how the invention of a God should have been possible. They are as absurd as saying that Kant attempted to prove one hundred Talers into existence, so as to pay his bills. We have proclaimed that human beings have invented an omnipotent and omniscient being, and yet we have no idea from where they should have received this power of invention. The invention of something new is, according to Nietzsche, a prerogative of the Gods. In this sense any real origin depends on the presence of the divine being. We moderns, on the other hand, have not even found out why – presumably having gained the mastery that would allow us to let these imaginations die – we still cannot find peace with ourselves. This is the case especially in respect of the intellect itself which defines itself the more radically in terms of the divine abstraction the more dead God becomes. In other words, that we are progressively more convinced of the vacuous nature of thought, is a result of the nihilism that Nietzsche has analysed as the history of the progressive secularization of Christianity.

It is in this context that we can understand Nietzsche's dictum that 'religion belongs in its totality to the psychology of error.'[24] Without preparation one might have concluded that such a sentence refers us to the 'fact' that God has never existed and is revealed as an illusion. On further reflection we realize that Nietzsche speaks about religion and we might conclude from this that he separates the question of faith from the existence of a specific religion. But such a conclusion relies on a modern and liberalist conception of personal faith. Yet the idea of a private God is as absurd as that of a private language, and the questions of the divine, of the sacred, of God are inseparable from the question of community as it is raised in the idea of religion. Our problem with the 'psychology of error' lies again in that we presume that the 'psyche' is something that does not really exist. Nietzsche, on the other hand, neither sides with a realism denying the reality of psychical life, nor with an idealism which would hypostasise spirit, while maintaining its separation from the world. And yet, these two abstract ideologies have served as the ground on which the question for the existence of God has mostly been based over the last two hundred years.

What we try to understand is the relation between the mortals and the immortals. We have seen that any human society finds its origin in religion, that is, that the human being finds its possibility in the existence of Gods, so that it becomes practically impossible for it to deny their existence. On the other hand, it appears as if the immortals depend for their existence on the human being. Insofar as it seems incomprehensible that human beings should give rise to a God, one concluded that whatever the human being 'creates' in such a way cannot but be an illusion. To speak of the whole of religion as belonging to the psychology of error seems to say that the idea of human community based on religion is itself an illusion. Such an argument forcefully contradicts the modern myth that mankind has re-appropriated its powers that it had before alienated into the illusion of a God. It seems as if we have not progressed an inch in our quest to illuminate the question of religion in Nietzsche's text and that we are still prone to be thrown back and forth by contradicting sentences, wondering whether he was an atheist or a theist.

Maybe we could understand that sentence about the psychology of error better by listening to it with Heidegger's ears and on account of his interpretation of error. By this reading, in modernity, understood as a particular era in the dominion of error, it is precisely *psychology* that can reveal to us the truth about the being of God. This is what Nietzsche does in the famous § 125 of *The Gay Science*, called 'the Madman'. The German title *Der tolle Mensch* is maybe more revealing. First of all, because it describes an essential characteristic of mankind rather than referring to a particular individual. Secondly, because the German word *'toll'* is much more specific than the English 'mad'. A human being that is 'toll' is the one who is *'außer Rand und Band geraten'*, that is to say, who has lost the boundary and the bond of the community. The *'tolle Mensch'* is then the one who has been *'verlassen'*, i.e. deserted. But to be deserted is a passion. The one by whom one is deserted is the one who lets one go. This is an *'auslassen'*, i.e. a letting go. That is why the madman's *'Ausgelassenheit'*, his wildness, becomes the ground of his error, making possible his *being in error*, that is, his madness or *'Irrsinn'*. To speak of the madman hence illuminates our misunderstanding of psychology as regarding 'character', i.e. a substantial form which we call by the name of subject.

In short, and this is nothing new, the death of God does not issue in a liberation of the human being from superstition and does not set an end to the alienation of its powers on to non-existent entities. Rather the outcome of this death is nihilism itself and hence the historical question of whether the human being – whose ἀρχή (*arche*) is called religion – will meet in this death its own end and revert to animal life, or whether it can, as Nietzsche says, understand the Overman as the meaning of this earth. Yet the Overman has always had slight mystical undertones and in this respect the death of God throws open the question for the source of religion. The whole question of what the human being is and what the human being ought to be, reverberates around this question of religion. To the measure that from the history of Christian religion issues the necessity of nihilism for world history, we find in it our destiny. Nietzsche's *amor fati*: this nearly constitutes a confession in itself.

The genealogy of religion

We have arrived at that strange point where it becomes clear that any attempt to reduce the phenomenon of religion to an historical development of human need makes sense only on account of separating the Christian God from a more fundamental essence of the sacred itself. Both Bergson and Nietzsche describe Christianity as if it was merely an invention on the part of the human being. Yet both are able to do so only on the basis of positing a more original faith, binding the human being into a community which in turn takes such an invention out of the circumspection of an acting subject. How are they able to escape the problem that the question of religion seems to dissolve itself? How can religion serve as an answer to the question of the origin as long as it is the question of the question? In terms of Bergson's *The Two Sources of Morality and Religion* the answer is relatively straight forward. Religion is thought as a process that takes place on the basis of nature, yet in a way that *nothing really happens*, which is to say that nothing new originates at the beginning of religion. In other words, because Bergson claims that nature itself is characterized by self-identity and that it always remains accessible, the human being continues in its innermost being always identical with its origin. Consequently, it is always possible to leave aside the question for the ἀρχή (*arche*) of the human being, insofar as religion becomes the answer to the question of a beginning which is not an origin at all. This interpretation of the origin of religion necessitates a reduction of history in a rather Hegelian manner.

Bergson understands history as the passing of the creative impetus through matter. Religion appears here as a safety device against problems appearing with the lack of self-mastery on the part of the intellect.

Religion is hence the name of the process of the emancipation of the intellect and, at the same time, of the production of culture hiding nature. The history of a religion is then a process of decline, even if it develops on the original intention. That is to say, a religion appears for everybody out of the mystic experience of a few individuals. Consequently the religion itself is not creative, it merely uses up its original impulse. The death of a God hence always requires the rejuvenation on the part of the individual that works back to its origin.

Religion thus appears as a fact of nature, finding its beginning in a cause according to which it can be analysed and understood. Understood as an effect, religion is itself condemned to a constant weakening, in which Vattimo sees its promise. But this promise is only made possible by ignoring Bergson's main point. The genealogy of religion seems to make of religion more completely an imagining on the part of the human being, the weaker its relation to its origin becomes. It is only on account of its origin that religion can exist, and it is thus in its origin, namely in the mystic experience, that the true unity and union of God and soul appears. On account of the history of the decline of religion this split between religion and the mystic experience appears in a progressively clearer way, affecting our relation to the world until, 'in truth' there are only facts and an inexplicable mystery. This mystery can find its fulfilment only in the mystic experience, which is not primarily that of the unity of man and God, but of God itself as the unity of man and world. From this point follows Bergson's desire to derive the existence of God from experience.

The real question, then, appears as that of the nature of faith. In other words, to understand the mystic experience and its relation to the problem of religion, we have to understand the relation between faith itself and that which it has faith in. On account of such understanding we might be able to intimate the reason for the mutual dependence of mortals and immortals. That the Christian God existed in faith, there can be no doubt for Nietzsche. 'Christianity should have erected the innocence of mankind as an article of faith – human beings would have become Gods: as in those days one could still believe (WP 149).

The religion of the Eternal Return

That the question of the origin of religion cannot be dissolved by a superior logic of the intellect, representing to itself its liberation from belief, is that insight which Nietzsche expresses in the already cited § 125 of

The Gay Science. Its content is not so much the question of religion following the death of God, as it is the question of the alienation of the intellect from the world. The people encountered by the madman in the *agora* are characterized as overtly atheistic, but, more to the point, as alienated from the world they are living in.

The madman arrives on the *agora*, he lights a lantern and he meets here '*Viele von Denen … welche nicht an Gott glaubten*', that is, 'Many of Those who did not believe in God'. It should not surprise anybody that 'Many' and 'Those' are capitalised;- they are the Platonic characterisations of the Many who live by beliefs or disbeliefs. While it might at first appear strange that Nietzsche uses Platonic metaphors, describing the atheists with the same words that Plato used in the allegory of the Cave, it makes much more sense bearing in mind that the death of God brings a circle to its end, so that the allegory of the Cave poses itself anew. In other words, if Christianity is Platonism for the people, then the end of Christianity throws us back upon Plato. And indeed, it is exactly those who believe themselves to be free of any belief (in God), who are living in a strange sort of cloud-cuckoo-land, in which they are everything to their sense of self-importance and yet nothing in the face of their sense of responsibility to themselves, which is to say, where they *are* everything so that they have to *become* nothing. This is the lot of modern man as Nietzsche takes it up again at the beginning of *The Anti-Christ*: '"I am everything that knows not which way to turn" – sighs modern man …' (AC 1).

This atheism is hence what Nietzsche calls passive nihilism. I have repeated this well known analysis here, in order to make clear that the question of nihilism is not one of not believing in anything, but rather derives from the form of thinking that has lost its inner unity and hence has always already decided from within its own essence, that God does not and cannot exist. When Nietzsche talks about our modern inability to believe, he is, first and foremost, thinking about the way in which the world appears to us, that is, he reflects on our relation to beings as a whole. This relation we designate nowadays by the term *Metaphysics of Presence*. This metaphysical relation to the world determines us to ask for the existence of God in a similar way as one might ask for one hundred Talers, or for a whole island, only in order then to decide that He rather joins the category of the unicorns and tooth fairies and, finally, of the ideas of Justice and Freedom.

All these ways of asking for God's existence have then not so much to do with God as with our way of thinking. And still, as this way of thinking derives from 2000 years of Christianity, there is no way that we can correct our 'vision' in order to re-invite the Christian God. Vattimo was right when he stated that our thinking derives from the secularization of Christian thought. Hence the very distinction between accidental and necessary existence that St. Anselm uses for his argument, will today – against the background of an absolutised difference between the true and the appearing world – be used for its refutation. If we see God as existing in and through history, in other words, if a God can die, then he is not a true God, but only a chimera. Yet, as soon as we speak about the God of philosophical theology, then we regard him as something that does not concern us. Consequently, God does not exist. And even if he existed, he would not concern us. And even if he concerned us, he could not help us.

The answer that we give to the question of God's existence hence shows us our own relation to truth and our mode of thinking. This mode of thinking is a consequence of the secularization of the Christian God. When I said above that the 'objective world' is itself a product of Christianity – which is the reason why our modern sciences are not only thoroughly metaphysical, but can even be seen as modes of worshipping the Christian God – then this point first of all aims at the relation of thinking to what is thought within it. What we can hold for true and what we cannot depends on this history of metaphysics, on the notion of eternal truth as the last remnant of Christian theology in philosophy[25]. That we have difficulties with the question of the existence of Gods – and with Nietzsche's philosophy generally – lies in this inability to unify thinking and thing thought. Yet that brings us equally to the root of religion as to the difficulty of Nietzsche's text, for the experience of the unity of thinking and thing thought is what we call the mystic experience.

> We are still unprepared and clumsy and small in relation to the thinking of the possible, that is, of a thinking that is always a creative thinking, because we are ... much too habituated to think from out of the real, that is, to interpret according to reality (presence, *ousia*).[26]

Bibliography of cited works by Nietzsche

The Anti-Christ (in *Twilight of the Idols and The Anti-Christ*) (London: Penguin, 1968, trans. R.J. Hollingdale)

The Gay Science (New York: Vintage, 1974, trans. W. Kaufmann)

Nachlaß
The Will to Power (New York: Vintage, 1967, trans. W. Kaufman and R.J Hollingdale)

Notes

1   C.f. Gianni Vattimo, '*Credere di credere*', (Garzanti) Milano 1996; references will be to the German translation: '*Glauben – Philosophieren*', (Reclam) Stuttgart 1997.

2   Nietzsche comes back to this interpretation in every part of his work. One might easily claim that his interest in sciences in relation to the idea of the *Eternal Return* lies in nothing but this link that binds both of them to the question of religion.

3   Jacques Derrida, *Foi et Savoir*, in: Thierry Marchaisse, éd. '*La Religion*' (Seuil/Laterza) Janvier 1996, p. 54.

4   Derrida, *Foi et Savoir*, p. 55.

5   Gilles Deleuze, *Nietzsche and Philosophy*, (Athlone) London 1983.

6   Martin Heidegger, *Die Onto-Theo-Logische Verfassung der Metaphysik*, in: '*Identität und Differenz*', (Neske) Pfullingen (1957) 91990, p. 45.

7   Vattimo, *ibid*, p. 33.

8   G.W.F. Hegel, '*Vorlesungen über die Geschichte der Philosophie*', Werke 18, 19, 20, (Suhrkamp) Frankfurt a. M. 1970, vol. 19, p. 526. 'Dieser Schmerz, daß Gott selbst tot ist, ist die Geburtsstätte der Heiligung und des Erhebens zu Gott'.

9   Vattimo, *ibid*, p. 37.

10 Cf. *ibid*, p. 46.

11 *Ibid*, p. 38.

12 Heinrich Heine, '*Zur Geschichte der Religion und Philosophie in Deutschland*', vol. 5 of *Werke und Briefe in zehn Bänden*, (Aufbau) Berlin und Weimar 21972, p. 256; 'Hört ihr das Glöckchen klingeln? Kniet nieder – Man bringt die Sakramente einem sterbenden Gotte'.

13 Derrida, *Foi et savoir*, p. 19.

14 Nietzsche, *Großoctavausgabe*, VII 78, quoted from Weischedel, *op. cit.*, p. 456.

15 Henri Bergson, '*The Two Sources of Morality and Religion*', (University of Notre Dame Press) Indiana 1977, p. 317.

16 Derrida, *Foi et savoir*, p. 21.

17 *Ibid*, p. 21.

18 Friedrich Nietzsche, *Großoctavausgabe*, XV 70, quoted from Weischedel, *ibid*, p. 434.

19 Nietzsche, '*Der Antichrist*'. KSA 6; Engl. trans.: *The Anti-Christ*, in '*Twilight of the Idols and the Anti-Christ*', (Penguin) London 1968, book 1.

20 Henri Bergson, *The Two Sources*, p. 102.

21 I am not trying to resolve the dispute about the true derivation of the word *religion*. I am just presuming that both make sense, Cicero's *relegere* as well as Lactanius' *religare*.

22 Georges Bataille, *Theory of Religion*, (Zone Books) New York, 1992.

23 Martin Heidegger, *Was heißt Denken*, (Niemeyer: Tubigen, 1954) p7.

24 Die 'Religion gehört ganz und gar unter die Psychologie des Irrtums' (Großoktav Ausgabe, VIII 99, quoted from Weischedel, p.435).

25 Heidegger, *Being and Time*, (Basil Blackwell) Oxford 1962, p. 272.

26 Martin Heidegger, '*Nietzsche*', (Neske) Pfullingen 1961 51989, vol. I, p. 393; 'Weil wir … allzusehr gewöhnt sind, nur aus dem Wirklichen zu denken, d.h. aus dem Wirklichen her (Anwesenheit, *ousia*) auszulegen, sind wir noch unvorbereitet und täppisch und klein in bezug auf das Denken der Möglichkeit, welches Denken immer ein schaffendes Denken ist'.

15
Nietzsche's deus ex machina

Michael Bowles

We should be wary of drawing any over hasty inference from the fact that Zarathustra's first significant remark is the declaration that 'God is dead' (Z 'Prologue' 2). Of course if *Thus Spoke Zarathustra* was a typical philosophical text which purported to offer propositions about the world, there indeed the matter would rest. All that would remain for the reader to decide is whether the proposition is true or false. But *Thus Spoke Zarathustra* is very far from a typical philosophical text. Rather it bears a close resemblance to a tragic drama. In a tragedy, whilst the protagonist might well begin his journey with the certainty that God is dead it is by no means the case that this is how the drama will conclude. Indeed one of the most puzzling claims which seems to lie within the tragic drama is that to bring the gods to life we must proclaim them dead. In the following I wish to suggest that this claim is also contained in Nietzsche's *Thus Spoke Zarathustra*. Thus while Zarathustra begins an atheist we must not forget that the section which closes the original version of the book presents an image of gods who are very much alive:

> if ever I have played dice with the gods at their table, the earth, so that the earth trembled and broke open and streams of fire snorted forth – for the earth is a table of the gods, and trembling with creative new words and the dice throws of the gods (Z 'The Seven Seals' 3)[1]

Before considering how Zarathustra comes to roll divine dice it is worth looking more closely at this picture of the activity of living gods. The image, of course, owes much to Heraclitus, but it is important to notice that Nietzsche has changed the game played from draughts to dice.[2] The game of the gods is not the solitary occupation of a lone child but a competition between jealous rivals. Further, by changing the game to dice, Nietzsche emphasises the point that it is a matter of chance who wins.

These divine gamblers do not have a system; in the *agon* of the gods it doesn't really matter what number is thrown as long as it is good enough to beat the opponent. What is celebrated in this image of divine play is the activity of throwing against an opponent, of risking a challenge precisely when there is no guarantee of success. But the gods who are tragically resurrected in *Thus Spoke Zarathustra* seem at the farthest remove from what is traditionally named with the term divinity. These jealous beings, whose one aim seems to be to overcome their rivals, who are devoid of any worthier purpose and who are so lacking in omniscience that they have to take chances. Surely such an image is too much like real life to be called divine? If this is where *Thus Spoke Zarathustra* takes us, back to life, then surely we will be justified in asking, why it requires the hand of a god, a dice thrower, to take us back to this most mundane of settings? In order to consider further the question why the return to life must be a divine act, let us begin with an account of what Nietzsche tells us about life.

Styles of eating

Nietzschean biology reduces life to one activity: eating. But before dismissing this oversimplification we should consider what is involved in digestion. Life takes other life into itself. That is to say, it takes and burns its energy; it breaks down the form and code which styles another life and uses the material to carry its own code. For example, the matter that carried one genetic code now carries another. Of course eating is not only a question of the incorporation of one form by another; we also eat to gain energy. Some of what is eaten is always used to repeat and carry the code of the eater, but some is always burnt and turned into raw energy. The energy that enables life to go and find more things to eat; but also the energy that can be enjoyed and squandered in dancing and singing, in the non-utilitarian acts which give life its spice. But whether life is only a question of survival or whether it indulges in more reckless activities, it always has to prevail over other life which it can then break down and take into itself.

   In the process of digestion the code, or style of eating, is the essential thing. It is the code which is nourished and given the opportunity to reproduce itself and expand. For example, DNA provides the template in terms of which the eaten matter is reconstituted; thus through successful eating this particular code is able to expand: more life now carries this pattern than did before. But the code is nothing other than a specific way of eating; a pattern for structuring matter. Hence nourishment is precisely the event where more and more life is encoded with a particular pattern and this pattern is itself a style of eating. Consequently it is essential to note that eating is not a univocal process. There are different ways and styles of eating. Moreover, some styles are superior to others. Hence Zarathustra warns us that 'to eat and drink well, O my brothers, is truly no vain art' (Z 'Of Old and New Law-Tablets' 13). To be a good eater one must gain a *superior* style. A superior style is defined simply as that which eats rather than is eaten.

For Nietzsche codes of digestion are not simply the concern of the body. The mind too is involved in the process of eating. Or rather the mind is itself a style or code of eating. Accordingly Zarathustra instructs us that 'the mind [*Geist*] *is* a stomach' (Z 'Of Old and New Law Tablets' 16). Nietzschean biology does not by any means dismiss the mind and its fixtures as a mere epiphenomenon, which, at best, can watch the more fundamental processes of life take place. The mind has an effective role; it too executes the procedure of breaking down other life and reconstituting it in its own image. The mind and its fixtures are very far from being an idealism that any rigorous approach to life must dismiss. For the mind is one of the ways, or styles, which directs digestion. And we should not let the fact that consciousness does not regard itself as an eating machine detract from this point:

> what we experience and absorb enters our consciousness as little while we are digesting it (one might call the process 'inpsychation' [*Einverseelung*]) as does the thousandfold process, involved in physical nourishment – so called 'incorporation' [*Einverleibung*] (GM II 1)

Now of course the mind offers a different way of eating, it has a different style from how the body digests its food. But for both it is always a case of taking in other life, of breaking it down and reconstituting it such that it now carries the style which has digested it. Thus whilst the stomach of the body employs enzymes and acids to digest its food, the mind uses a different style: its principal resource is morality. For Nietzschean biology the distinction between good and evil is a device for capturing food. Now we should not think that there is only one way, one morality, whereby the mind imposes its code on other life, as though good and evil had only one instantiation. Indeed the term mind is nothing other than the generic name for a whole variety of ways of eating. And we should not make the blunder of assuming that the mind's style of eating is weaker than the body's. Through much travelling Zarathustra 'discovered the good and evil of many peoples. Zarathustra has found no greater power on earth than good and evil' (Z 'Of the Thousand and One Goals'). Thus Nietzschean biology, far from dismissing the mind and its morality as mere superstructure, sees the mind as the most effective way whereby life is obliged to become the bearer of a code that has eaten it.

Undoubtedly the effectivity of mental incorporation owes its success to the, perhaps surprising, fact that the life which is eaten often *wants* to be eaten. A superior style of eating is immensely attractive. By incorporating it one gains its power; that is to say, one gains the capacity to digest other life forms; and thereby gain nourishment, and thereby experience the thrill of burning energy. Thus we can say that life *agrees* to be eaten – that is, to become organised in terms of a code – precisely because this empowers it. We should not always see the code which eats us as repressive, as obliterating our true identity; rather, in eating us, it gives us a style whereby we can, in turn, eat; the only price is that we now digest according to the code that has incorporated us. By being eaten life has been transformed into a productive force: it has been given a code which will enable it to face and overcome other life. Thus Zarathustra has no problem in solving the old Kantian riddle of heteronomy – of why life agrees to serve a law not of its own making – 'The will of the weaker persuades it to serve the stronger; its will wants to be master over those weaker still: this delight [*Lust*] alone it is unwilling to forgo' (Z 'Of Self-Overcoming').

Nietzschean biology is adamant that obedience is not something foreign to life and it is not something which represses life. Indeed it lays it down as a ground rule that, 'All living creatures are obeying creatures' (Z 'Of Self-Overcoming'). But the obedience spoken of here is very far from signifying that some inner purity has been repressed. Rather it is the claim that life survives precisely because it follows a law of eating, a style. It is the code which gives life the ability to eat rather than be eaten. And indeed the law is the primary thing. The particular individuals that instantiate the law are mere carriers of code, merely vehicles which the code employs to replicate itself. Zarathustra would not disagree with Richard Dawkins' claim that human beings are the vehicles of a specific pattern of the DNA code: that it dictates to them rather than they controlling it.[3] But what must be emphasised is that it is through such obedience to a law that life gains power.

Power is what life feels when it eats. That is, when it successfully meets and overcomes another form of life. It needs to feel a block which it then flows over; it needs to meet resistance which is then broken. If the feeling of power is to surge it is essential that eating be part of an *agon*: a contest between two life forms. Life wants to win, and that means that the other is subdued and takes in the code that has now mastered it. This can be exampled by physical digestion, when zebra meat is turned into lion DNA *and* the roars that echo over the Savannah; or mental digestion, when the teacher successfully converts the unenlightened *and* cannot help feeling a little pride and joy at another soul saved. Nietzschean biology is convinced that it is this feeling of power which all life seeks. That is why life is obedient to a law, for a law is nothing other than a style which gives life the ability to eat – and thereby experience the feeling of power. After victory at the *agon* life celebrates, it celebrates by burning the energy that constituted the life of its prey before the kill. This is the way in which a code not merely survives but comes alive. Indeed a young code, which takes all before it, so invigorates that the bearers of the code can easily be mistaken for gods: 'all becoming seemed to me the dancing of gods and the wantonness of god, and the world unrestrained and abandoned' (Z 'Of Old and New Law-Tablets' 2).

The festival of man

It will have been noticed that the above review of Nietzschean biology has so far failed to provide any detailed account of how a specific style of digestion carries out its function. Nietzsche is prepared to leave the analysis of how the body digests its food to others; his specialism is the digestion of the mind. In particular he devotes much of his work to a specific mental style of eating which he calls the human. We must not, however, assume that this category exactly coincides with how the term is used in other biologies. Nietzsche's use of this term picks out one of the many styles of the mind, one of the many ways in which food might be digested. A style is rarely the possession of a lone individual but marks out a people: there are as many different peoples as there are styles of eating; and Zarathustra tells us 'there have been a thousand peoples' (Z 'Of the Thousand and One Goals'). Nietzsche's use of the term 'human' names one of these peoples. Its origins are not precise; it owes something to the rise of reason in post-classical Greece; something to the birth of Christianity in the attempt by the Jewish people to resist the Roman empire; it developed, however, into the complex of moral and technological values that, for Nietzsche's eyes, dominated nineteenth century Europe. It is the style of eating that nearly all of modern life lives by.

We should never for a moment doubt Nietzsche's respect for the human code. We are told, in no uncertain terms, that of all the mental styles of digestion the human is by far the superior: 'man is the finest beast of prey' (Z 'Of Old and New Law-Tablets' 22). We should also note that the human eats so well because it can face down pain better than any other style of life: 'Man, however, is the most courageous animal: with his courage man has overcome every animal. With a triumphant shout he has even overcome every pain' (Z 'Of the Vision and the Riddle' 1) The courage described here, with some approbation, is the way the human code consumes its prey. The prey cannot withstand the pain, but the human code can. It is this ability to take the pain that is the secret of the human success.

The pain we are speaking of is the quite specific horror that occurs when a code collapses. We must remember that Nietzschean biology dismisses the fantasy of unorganised life. Every life form is always encoded; it always digests in terms of the law it obeys. Hence when consumption takes place it is a case of one code replacing another. The human achieves this by *first* destroying the other code, by removing its self-confidence. Thus the hungry Zarathustra, even though he is resisting the human way of eating, knows that he must start by breaking the self-certainty of his prey: 'Shatter, O my brothers, shatter these ancient law-tables' (Z 'Of Old and New Law-Tablets' 15). Should the code that one bears collapse, the experience is intensely painful. Codes, after all, are always solipsistic; they only know themselves. When they eat they digest and thus find that whatever it was they encountered is now wearing their clothes. The world that they live in is the product of their style of digestion. But should this way of processing collapse then we suddenly become naked and vulnerable. Indeed Zarathustra, who never tires of telling us that he is partly human, feels the pain of such vulnerability at precisely those moments when the human code loses its grip; he cries out, 'I should not know how to live' (Z 'Of Redemption'). Thus too Antigone, when she cannot ingest both the demand to obey the law of the *polis* and the requirement to honour her family, loses her bearings: 'I have no home on earth and none below.'[4] Her pain is that the code which she bore has collapsed: what is now encountered, is not the smooth surfaces of successful comprehension, not patterns of rationality that have always worked up until this moment, but, as Zarathustra declares when he faces a similar moment to Antigone's: 'fragments and limbs and dreadful chance' (Z, 'Of Redemption'). It is with the collapse of solipsism that life for the first time meets chance: it meets that which is not simply eaten as a matter of course. The pain of this moment derives from the fact that now life is without code: it has no style which tells it how to eat. At this point we should try and resist the temptation to assume that Antigone's encounter with 'dreadful chance' is not a biological event but rather, what might be called, an ontological event. As if here the veil of the human world is lifted and there is glimpsed being in all its contingency, alterity and questionableness. For the biologist, however, 'Dreadful chance' is that fleeting moment of paralysis that overcomes life just before it is eaten by the predator; when it ceases to consume in its own style and is about to be consumed by a superior style. A collapse of a code comes about because another eating style gets too near. The extraordinary capacity of the human code is, as we shall see, that it can suffer such moments and return back to itself. In other words, that, whatever it was that threatened it, is digested.

The secret of human success, that is, its prodigious capacity to incorporate fresh life into its code, lies in its willingness to replay the tragic moment. It shows its intended victim Antigone in all her pain and powerlessness, and declares that she arrived at this moment precisely *because* she did not carry the human code. It announces that the experience of dreadful chance befalls all those who do not follow the human way. Thus the paralysis and pain which always accompanies the meeting with dreadful chance is classified as a *punishment*. Indeed Zarathustra tells us that 'mankind's chief concern ... [is to declare] that where there was suffering, there was always supposed to be punishment' (Z 'Of Redemption'). It is by labeling the encounter with dreadful chance a sin, and thus Antigone as evil, that the human code is able to eat. For by means of such a classification it offers its prey a way to escape the paralysis of dreadful chance. As long as life resolves to become human it will avoid Antigone's pain. By becoming human, and only by becoming human, will life be able to purge itself of the awful pain that for an instance it felt and shared with Antigone.

What is so remarkable about this style of eating is that it manifests such a profound understanding of biology. Zarathustra knows well the subtlety of the Priests of humanity; when regarding one of the first human temples he tells us that: 'he who once towered up his thoughts in stone here knew as well as the wisest about the secret of all life!' (Z 'Of the Tarantulas'). The human code knows well the finitude of all that opposes it. In particular it knows that a tragic reading is always possible.

For all the bluster and confidence of the non-human it can always be taken out of itself and shown its limits – the moments where dreadful chance opens up and life loses its footing. The human consequently has a great need for profound art and thinking; that is, precisely those works which take understanding and morality to their limits – 'It would like to range heroes and honourable men about it, this new idol' (Z 'Of the New Idol'). By means of such devices the human is able, as it were, to stun its prey. For with the collapse of its code, life suffers the paralysis and pain of 'I should not know how to live.' And then, as we have seen, it is told that such an event took place precisely because of its non-humanness; that the non-human is a sin; and hence one can escape the pain by now living in the human style.

Of course, the question arises that if all codes can be pushed to their limits and shown the 'dreadful chance' that paralyses their bearers, then why is the human style immune from such a collapse? Zarathustra calls man 'the most courageous animal' precisely because this code accepts its finitude. It knows, just as Zarathustra and the Dionysians know, that dreadful chance is part of life. A code must not deny the encounter with chance, but codify it. Hence the human code does not merely declare that the experience of dreadful chance is a punishment meted out to the non-human; it also maintains that sin is inevitable for humans too. In this way once life is taken over by the human, it stays human. For it now knows that even the collapse of the human code is part of what it is to be human.

But flexible codes of comprehension, for all their cleverness, would never succeed in holding life if they were not also able to offer it food. How then does the human style enable its bearer to digest other life and thereby gain the thrill of power? The human would not survive without its festivals. Zarathustra tells us that 'More than anything on earth he [man] enjoys tragedies, bullfights and crucifixions' (Z 'The Convalescent' 2). And if Zarathustra had lived in the twentieth century he would almost certainly have added to this list those spectacles which are staged at the cinema and sports stadium. For on such occasions the code carriers of the human are taken once again to 'dreadful chance'. When the human audience views the plight of an Antigone their empathy does not have to be manufactured. They immediately recognise and remember such events and horrors from their own experience. But the drama, if it is to be a spectacle suitable for human festivals, must show that the only resolution for such pain is to become human once more (even Sophocles can be staged in this way). At the festival the audience eats: they are guided through the steps that must be undertaken for purging the non-human; for slaying their own sin. In this way the non-human, that incapacitating event suffered when the code collapses, has been successfully digested, or as is often said, purged. The function of the human festival is catharsis. And as with all overcomings, some of that which was consumed is burnt; the warm afterglow this occasions produces the feeling which is usually called pity, although Zarathustra suggests other names: 'Do you love tragedies and all that is heartbreaking? Your eyes are too cruel for me; you look upon sufferers lustfully. Has your lasciviousness not merely disguised itself and called itself pity?' (Z 'Of Chastity'). When we are able to pity Antigone it is because the horror has passed and we have returned, once more, to the human. But such a return is precisely the event of consuming the non-human, of incorporating it into the human code and thereby gaining the feeling of power. This is why humans enjoy festivals so much.

Nietzsche often compares the human style of eating to the way a spider deploys its web. Life is captured and consumed through the staging of festivals. However, it is important to note that the human, unlike the spider, is a parasite. For the human does not produce its own net; for that it is dependent on what Zarathustra classifies as a higher type. Without, for the moment, asking why the term 'higher' is used, let us simply note that the human *needs* that which does not simply obey man's law but rather pushes, explores and acts beyond the parameters of the human code: 'he who is of the highest type nourishes the most parasites' (Z, 'Of Old and New Law-Tables', 19). In his attempt to go beyond the human, to question and challenge its code, the higher man is the unintentional web spinner whose product is then used otherwise. In that such explorers do not simply give themselves to the human code Zarathustra suggests that we call them selfish. But we must emphasise that for the human code it is not a case of annihilating such selfishness, but of using it for its own development and growth. Indeed, speaking of human morality, Zarathustra tells us that: 'to ill-use selfishness – precisely that has been virtue and called virtue' (Z 'Of the Three Evil Things' 2). It is this capacity to use the works and acts of the higher man, to not simply deny or repress these yearnings for something else, that endows the human eating machine with such strength. It is the ability to display the non-human at the festival and then incorporate it that makes this code of digestion almost invincible. It can take on, defeat and consume all other codes. Indeed Zarathustra maintains that this is what has happened: 'Man has already robbed all beasts of their virtues' (Z 'Of

Old and New Law-Tables' 22). And it is this invincibility that leads Zarathustra to declare, of all those philosophers who would dismiss and reject the human, that: 'only a buffoon thinks: "Man can also be *jumped over*"' (Z 'Of Old and New Law-Tables' 4).

God is dead

Nietzsche's biology of life is not only concerned to analyse the human style of digestion. He also makes enquiry as to whether this style of eating might not itself, in turn, be the subject of predation. Clearly not all life is human. We can infer this from the fact that the human survives and flourishes: for this it needs the food of the non-human. What we can also know about the non-human is that it too needs to eat. But such knowledge can only be obtained by way of inference: we can never directly meet and comprehend the non-human. Or to be more accurate: the carriers of human code can never directly apprehend the non-human. For a code does not meet other codes, it digests them. A meeting with another style of life only occurs if the processes of digestion should fail; then the code collapses, then life is paralysed in this encounter with what for it can only be 'dreadful chance'. Certainly we have seen that such moments of paralysis do occur within human life, but these interruptions are the very lifeblood of the human code; for it is through such breaking down that the human eating machine functions. A mere flicker of life at the margin, a flash of *Id* – such occurrences are simply fuel for catharsis. There is no evidence here of style which could meet and threaten the human code. Rather than explore such marginal phenomena Nietzsche turns his attention to something that he finds much more interesting *within* the walls of the city founded by the Priests of humanity: 'it was on the soil of this essentially dangerous form of human existence, the priestly form, that man first became *an interesting animal*' (GM I 6). The form of life within the human world that Nietzsche finds so interesting he calls the higher man.

These creatures, at least in their youth, very much want to take a bite out of man. Observing this Zarathustra tries not to weep, for he shares their hunger but also knows the strength of their would-be prey; it is like watching lambs to the slaughter: 'Our flesh is tender, our skin is only a lamb-skin: – how should we not excite old idol priests! He still lives on *in us ourselves*, the old idol-priest, who roasts our best for his feast' (Z 'Of Old and New Law-Tables' 6). However, in the case of the higher man, the hunger remains. They want to eat the human but it is too strong for them. When they come round from this brief tussle they find that their very attempt is now used to fuel the human; it becomes the centre-piece for one of the festivals. Undeterred they make a fresh attempt and try to devise an even stronger joust, only to suffer the same fate. Thus when Zarathustra asks, 'What compulsion compels the high to bend to the low? And what bids even the highest – to grow higher still?' (Z 'Of the Three Evil Things' 1) – we can answer that it is nothing but the human code in its *agon* with the higher man.

Such repeated failure, however, is not without consequence. The higher man wants to eat but cannot digest the food that he hungers for and consequently suffers indigestion. And when such a creature goes to eat again, as it must, its indigestion will guide it. It has now learnt to avoid the foods that are too strong and directs its attention on the less well formed. In other words, it too starts to eat in the human way. It now seeks out the more youthful higher men who are still naively in battle with the human code and resolves to do its utmost to make them human. Zarathustra famously names this apostasy induced by indigestion, 'revenge'. Thus the higher man is that creature 'who takes revenge upon him who does not, like it, feel wrath and ill temper' (Z 'Of Redemption'). And yet whilst he now eats in the human way, and indeed contributes to the growth and prosperity of the human code, the higher man is not entirely human. For what spoils the human world for him is precisely his bitterness and rancour. He is not naively human, he is only human because he has failed to eat in any other way. This indigestion stays with the higher man; the food that he eats is insipid, he feels none of the delight and dance of those who have only ever wished to be human. Zarathustra is speaking of the higher man when he tells us that: 'all wells are poisoned for him from whom an aching stomach, the father of affliction, speaks' (Z 'Of Old and New Law-Tablets',16). It is thus the higher man, who whilst living in the human way, doesn't really believe in it. He still eats but 'life seems to him a desert' (Z 'Of the Spirit of Gravity', 2). It is the higher man who lives within nihilism and it is, of course, from the higher man's lips that we first hear the claim, that whilst life goes on, God is dead.

It is important to realize that whether God lives or dies is an issue decided by the stomach. It is certainly not a matter for proof. And yet there is much that Zarathustra says which makes it sound exactly as if God was simply a false proposition. After all he entreats us to: '*remain true to the earth*, and do not believe those who speak to you of celestial [*überirdischen*] hopes' (Z 'Prologue' 3). We must not, however, assume that such demands are a request to take life without prejudice. As if the distinction between earth and world, which is used throughout *Thus Spoke Zarathustra*, was but a repetition of the division between infrastructure and superstructure. As though all that is required for the material forces to stream forth, is to break and destabilize the overdetermining superstructure. As though by removing ideology we gain access to life in all its purity; with God out of the way we can at last commune with the body as it really is. If Zarathustra does on occasion demand that we join him in breaking and disproving the ideology of the world, it is not because such an activity is sufficient to take us to the earth. As we have seen, life without code collapses and is quickly taken back into the human world. Hence it is not a question of uncovering the earth, of demonstrating that an ideology is either true or false. The human style will only be overcome when it meets a stronger style of digestion: but for this to happen the process of digestion must be given a new, non-human, code; or as Zarathustra puts it, the issue is 'to give the earth its meaning' (Z 'Of the Bestowing Virtue' 2).[5]

God has died for the higher man, not because he has now discovered the truth and is at last able to view the earth as it really is, but because the food he consumes does not invigorate him in the way it should. He eats with no delight; he gains no feeling of power and jubilation precisely because he is not eating the food that he longs for; with a feeling that he dare not affirm, he still hankers for human blood. This is why he cannot whole-heartedly join and believe in the human dance. But far from this torn being representing a threat to the human world, he is in fact its chief resource. In one of the most famous scenes in Nietzsche's writings we are shown how the higher man comes to serve the beast he hates. After setting out on the path to try and overcome the human code, the higher man arrives at a crossroads, besides which squats a dwarf. Here he sees, just for a moment, a prospect open before him in which that part of himself which Zarathustra once described as 'Unutterable and nameless is that which torments and delights my soul and is also the hunger of my belly,' (Z 'Of Joys and Passions') is given a future: a future in which it differs from the past, the past of the human world. It is that moment of an *agon*, where two beasts, two different styles of eating, confront each other. But in spite of his hunger the moment vanishes. Now he only sees man: there is no longer a difference between the past and the future; the human world stretches out into infinity. Indeed it is this vision of eternity, where the human world endlessly repeats itself, where the future is not part of a moment, but is in fact nothing but the same, that is the

cause of his failure. All that he reads, all that he knows, all the festivals
he has attended, have demonstrated again and again that anything in the
future must *follow* from the past. The higher man's culture and education, his respect for science, all amply demonstrate that the future comes
out of the past: that the future is *determined* by the past. It is knowledge
and reason that prove to the higher man that the moment he once saw
was an illusion. Thus the higher man now bows to the dwarf. For the
dwarf does not see the moment; he denies that there is a difference
between past and future and maintains that 'time itself is a circle' (Z 'Of
the Vision and the Riddle' 2); that there must be an eternal return of the
same; that the human way of life, goes on for ever. For to think otherwise is as ludicrous as suggesting that stories must not have plots, that
life proceeds otherwise than by a rational development, in which the end
of a tale comes from what has gone before. Thus it is knowledge – the
insistence that each step be rational and probable – which breaks the
higher man; which makes him bow and become incorporated into the
human way of life. But the higher man, even after he has learnt the ways
of the world, remains torn: for what he knows and what he wants do not
coincide: 'It is all one, nothing is worth while, knowledge chokes' (Z
'The Convalescent' 2). But we must bow to knowledge, therefore this
discrepancy between will and representation can only be resolved by
silencing our hunger. This has the effect of making life insipid and
empty, it certainly no longer feels like the dancing of a god, but this is
what reality shows. And should the higher man now set his thoughts
down on paper, his writings will almost immediately take their place in
the canon of world literature; that is the canon of the human way of
eating.

But why should this broken, bitter, higher man be of *interest* for Nietzschean biology in its search for a human predator? It is and will remain
a paradox, but the path taken by these no-hopers is the source of
Zarthustra's greatest hope. For it is by no means necessary that the only
consequence of taking such a path is the death of God. In one of his
notebooks Nietzsche scribbles down his great discovery: 'nihilism …
might be *a divine way of thinking*' (WP I 15).

Deus ex machina

If it happens it always looks something like this. After the denouement,
a trap door bangs open, high up at the back of the stage. We hear a
creaking mechanism start up and see a figure, wearing a garish mask,

slowly begin to descend. The rope slips, the mask tilts – 'why that's only Quixada from the local village dressed up as a knight errant!' The figure crashes to the ground and in a very unconvincing voice announces he is a god come to fight dragons. His lance wobbles, his visor is made of papier mâché. This makes no sense, its idiotic and unbelievable – complains the audience. And yet from now on this figure has an effect on how the future unfolds. In the reviews and discussions that follow, it is universally declared that the drama was really very authentic, full of deep psychological insights, but only up to the point when that fool entered and ruined everything. The plot simply didn't justify it, it was gratuitous and spoiled that feeling of satisfaction that is demanded of all great drama.

Indeed the *deus ex machina* is always difficult to swallow. The young Nietzsche, for one, disdained Euripides' employment of the device. It threatened the true meaning of tragedy: that it should produce a 'metaphysical comfort' (BT 17) and reveal to the audience: 'that the existence of the world is *justified* only as an aesthetic phenomenon' (ASC 5). But after *Thus Spoke Zarathustra* Nietzsche comes to his senses and resolves to 'dispatch all metaphysical comforts to the devil' (ASC 7). Consequently we are not surprised when Zarathustra himself has a vision, a vision which bears all the hallmarks of a *deus ex machina*.

It comes after Zarathustra's own encounter with the dwarf at the crossroads. Now, whilst the higher man accepts the dwarf's view of the future, even though it poisons his life, Zarathustra sees a precedent here, that the higher man, for all his culture, missed. When the mighty Oedipus, hell bent on discovering the truth at all cost, encountered dreadful chance, when he at last confronted his own non-human acts, he collapses and flies back to the human city; there he determines to cripple himself by tearing out his own eyes. Zarathustra refuses to go the way of Oedipus and the higher man. He rejects the dwarf, who he sees as a modern version of the clubfooted King of Thebes: 'I shall leave you squatting where you are, Lamefoot [*Lahmfuß*]' (Z 'Of the Vision and the Riddle' 2). Zarathustra may recognise the situation but he cannot save himself from the horror of defeat. Like the higher man, Zarathustra cannot find any pleasure in the human style of digestion; he too feels the hunger for human flesh: 'man is something that must be overcome' (Z 'Of Old and New Law-Tables' 3); and he too is consequently choked by the thought that the human is in fact invincible: that there is an eternal recurrence of the same. At this denouement Zarathustra collapses, just as Oedipus and the higher man did. Because of the non-human in him

Zarathustra cannot bear the thought of the eternal recurrence of the human world. It is to admit that the human way is too strong even for him; that he too will be digested. Zarathustra also chokes on this disgusting thought. We are given a graphic image of his defeat: 'a young shepherd writhing, choking, convulsed, his face distorted; and a heavy, black snake was hanging out of his mouth' (Z 'Of the Vision and the Riddle' 2). And then it happens: the shepherd bites the head off this thought which has prostrated him – 'He spat far away the snake's head – and sprang up' (Z 'Of the Vision and the Riddle' 2).

Most hunters, going for the kill, know that it is dangerous to corner the prey. For when there is *absolutely no way out* the victim can suddenly hit on reserves of energy that it didn't know it had. Sometimes it will throw a lucky punch, the dice will land for it; and the hunter himself is suddenly destroyed in what should have been, what nearly always is, an everyday, run-of-the-mill, killing. When Zarathustra looks back on the event he tells us that 'disgust itself creates wings and water-divining powers' (Z 'Of Old and New Law-Tables' 14). He needed to be cornered, he needed to meet the blackest hour. For it is only when everything has failed, when he has all but lost the *agon*, that from nowhere, the strength comes which enables him to eat that which would otherwise have eaten him. It is *as if* one needs to go to this extreme situation, where nothing works and all is lost, for all the ideology to be thrown out and at last the body, unimpeded by the false doctrines of the mind, can act, and does act. On reflection, Zarathustra now sees, that his greatest nightmare – that the future necessarily follows out of the human past, that the same eternally returns – was in fact necessary. For it is by being overwhelmed by the thought of an eternal recurrence of the same that Zarathustra is made to act *blindly*. At last he ceases to try and understand and reason it out with the human; instead he *acts* in independence of the human code. Consequently, he is now in a position to thank his old enemy for providing this necessary spur. Speaking of the eternal 'It was' of the human world Zarathustra tells us that it will always be such until 'the creative will says to it: "But I will it thus! Thus shall I will it"' (Z 'Of Redemption'). Zarathustra can now say yes to the thought that the human world is eternal, because he now sees that such prostration *caused* him to at last come to himself, and thus to begin to eat and speak in his own name.

Now of course it's easy to be carried away with the joy that Zarathustra gives off after having found himself. But we cannot help but notice that what is said is somewhat contrived. Its all a blur of bright colours, painted on hollow papier mâché. It's far from clear that what Zarathustra says after the event really amounts to an explanation of what happened. He *seems* to assert a causal mechanism between being prostrated by the thought of the eternal recurrence of the same and his then being able to stand up and no longer live in the human way. But if there is such a mechanism, then why did the higher man, who was similarly overwhelmed with the thought, fail? Here is where philosophy must obtrude. It tells us that we must become serious and go beyond such romanticism. We must discover, if there is one, the clear and precise explanation of how Zarathustra was able to bite the thought's head off. Philosophy insists that we cannot make any progress until we have explained the conditions of possibility of such an event. Without this, the image of the shepherd biting and killing the snake, will remain an implausible contrivance, a mere *deus ex machina*. So whilst Nietzsche leaves it as an image, it seems we must go further and explain what exactly happens when Zarathustra thinks the eternal recurrence of the same.

Ontology

Thus Spoke Zarathustra is of course full of explanations of the eternal recurrence of the same; however, we would be wise to notice that none of them come from the mouth of Zarathustra. He is followed by a shadow which manifests in various forms: sometimes as Zarathustra's best disciple, sometimes as his ape, and, perhaps most significantly, as his animals. For it is the animals who take it upon themselves to explain what made Zarathustra's experience possible. They justify this presumption on the basis that Zarathustra himself has already done enough. He has slain the monster, he has completed it, now he must rest and recover and leave it to others to explain what happened. The animals command Zarathustra: 'Speak no further, ... convalescent' (Z 'The Convalescent' 2); and add, 'we know what you teach' (Z 'The Convalescent' 2). Thereupon they expound Zarathustra's doctrine. On reflection Zarathustra's victory was perhaps not so awe inspiring; it only seemed that way because, at the time, we did not really understand what was going on. Once we understand the doctrine we can see that it was, after all, destined to happen. For the animals know that the key to understanding tragedy is *hubris*. No matter what this term might signify in the original Greek, for them it indicates an overweening pride, an arrogance that maintains itself to be all that is the case. What tragedy shows us is that eventually this bubble will burst; and not because it has been defeated, but because it has become exhausted. It is precisely because it has raged unchecked that it, of itself, comes to its own limits. This is now what has happened with the human eating machine that Plato gave birth to so long ago. With Zarathustra we are merely seeing the final stage of an immanent unfolding whereby the human style collapses because it is too successful. And with this internal collapse we are at last free from a too limited identity that has been stamped on being. Thus Zarathustra is not really an alternative to man, he is that which lies within the human. His name marks the point where the human completes itself and begins to see that its system of comprehension is perhaps, after all, not coincident with being. And indeed, whatever might come after man and his metaphysics, it too will grow and then pop: it will reach saturation and then, as a matter of necessity, will collapse. Hence, for the animals, Zarathustra's adventure illustrates the necessity of becoming: that all things rise and fall, 'like an hour-glass, turn itself over again and again, so that it may run down and run out anew' (Z 'The Convalescent' 2). Zarathustra, when seen aright, did not actually *do* anything himself. His name merely marks the completion and collapse of an exhausted style of life. Zarathustra, in spite of his many remarks to the contrary, is not really his own self; he is but the creature and vehicle, whereby, that which is more fundamental than both Zarathustra and the human, flexes its muscles and ploughs its inevitable course. Thus if we should ask who Zarathustra is we can see that he is merely the manifestation of what was once called *Nemesis*. However, we should note that this way of reading tragedy comes in all shapes and sizes and different vocabularies. For example, here is how a famous twentieth century animal names Zarathustra and his apparent failure to explain himself:

> At all events, prior thinking is metaphysics, and Nietzsche's thinking presumably brings it to fulfillment. Thus something in Nietzsche's thinking comes to the fore which this thinking itself was no longer able to think. Such remaining behind what it has thought designates the creativity of a thinking. And where a thinking brings metaphysics to completion it points in an exceptional way to things unthought, cogently and confusedly at once[6]

If we approach tragedy as ontology we will always go wrong. For this is to make a mockery of the thought of the eternal recurrence of the same. It suggests that there is nothing essential about this thought. That instead of meeting the prospect of man, nothing but man, stretching into the infinite future, Zarathustra could, if only he had opened his eyes a little wider, have seen through man. Or, if Zarathustra, because of his historical situation and lack of the proper tools, could not avoid the horror of an infinity of man, we who come after can now dig deeper and so avoid the unnecessary histrionics. However, for the thought of eternal recurrence, all such unfoldings do not find the end of man but are a continuation of man. Zarathustra's horror is engendered precisely because no matter how far one looks into the human world, one only ever finds a repetition of the same. For Zarathustra, the tools of comprehension are human and will remain so no matter how refined. He comes to the point where he accepts and knows that his own advance is impossible, and yet still he goes on: 'Your foot itself has extinguished the path behind you, and over your foot stands written: Impossibility' (Z 'The Wanderer').[7] How can an immanent unfolding of the human ever capture such a moment? Such a method, even though its path is sometimes extremely difficult, always makes progress; it never meets with the moment of dreadful chance, of failure, that always opens, just for an instance, when two radically different life forms face each other.

It is the removal of the pain from the thought of eternal recurrence, that Zarathustra finds most disturbing. For if we disclose Zarathustra's experience as an unfolding of destiny, then we have ceased to deal with that which was not simply a thought but a thought that leads the thinker to become convulsed with disgust. Instead of pain we are now dealing with a problem worthy of serious thinking. It is this movement from pain to thought which provokes Zarathustra to speak out *against* his animals. What he sees in this attempt to *think* his experience, is a repetition of the movement of catharsis; that is, to take the encounter with dreadful chance back to the human world of comprehension. His complaint to the animals is that by removing the pain they have performed all that is necessary to enact the human festival. It is simply by not suffering the pain of the eternal recurrence of the same and instead taking it as something to be thought, that the basic step of catharsis has been performed. Hence Zarathustra's only question to his animals is: 'Did you desire to be spectators of my great pain, as men do?' (Z 'The Convalescent' 2).

However, it should not be suggested that the pages of *Thus Spoke Zarathustra* contain a proof which demonstrates, once and for all, the failure of all ontological readings of tragedy. Any such demonstration would require a ground from which to make its moves; but, as has already been noted, Zarathustra does not announce the correct interpretation which would provide such a basis. Instead of proofs, what we find is in fact the opposite. Zarathustra celebrates and makes every effort to defend the foolishness of what has happened to him. He speaks of 'the wisest soul, to which foolishness [*Narrheit*] speaks sweetest' (Z 'Of Old and New Law Tables' 19); and, each time he hears an animal, or disciple offer an explanation, he dismisses it. He in fact takes every step to preserve the incomprehensibility of the moment when he took the thought of the eternal recurrence otherwise than the higher man. His stage directions then are quite clear. The event must not be given a realistic presentation and neither must it be represented as the product of a slowly unwinding plot; rather it must be played such that it breaks any possibility of the audience empathising or comprehending what has happened. It must then be preserved as a *deus ex machina*. Or in other words, Zarathustra, through his numerous negative definitions, makes it quite clear that the event is not something immanent coming to the surface, but is, and must be maintained as, an absolute transcendence.

However, this transcendence is effective. Whilst foolish and implausible, it nevertheless has an impact on the outcome of the drama. Zarathustra's ability to bite the head off of the snake of eternal man, is not something buried deep within the snake's world. More specifically it is not the pure earth breaking out from under the repressive ideology. Zarathustra's capacity to make a difference, comes from the fact that he has given the earth a new style: that his name signifies a radically different process of digestion. To overcome man it is not a question of immanent critique, but of creating a new code of eating: 'he will baptize the earth anew' (Z 'Of the Spirit of Gravity' 2). Zarathustra has not, let the earth be, but has commanded it. He has given it a different style and by such a gift he has taken it: 'giving in such a way that in giving it *takes*' (Z 'Of Involuntary Bliss'). For Zarathustra it is not a question of renouncing eating, this was how the higher man reacted to his encounter with the thought of the eternal recurrence, but of creating a new, non-human, style of digestion; indeed Zarathustra speculates, 'My stomach – it is perhaps an eagle's stomach?' (Z 'Of the Spirit of Gravity' 1). Whilst this stomach remains an absolute transcendence, a *wholly different* style of eating from the human code, we can nevertheless infer its basic characteristic. It gives the bearer a new way to digest dreadful chance, to meet that which is radically other to it, and digest it. Accordingly Zarathustra declares: 'I cook every chance in *my* pot. And only when it is quite cooked do I welcome it as *my* food' (Z 'Of the Virtue that

Makes Small' 3). And we should be under no illusion as to what the prey of this stomach might be: it is man. To break the human code and thereby incorporate fresh material, that is its joy. Zarathustra is now the human predator.

Finally, we must ask why the coming of this new style has to be represented as divine? Zarathustra declares himself to be godless,[8] is that because as a law-giver and not an obeyer he has himself now become a god? Kant, after all, insists that divinity is an irreducible aspect of autonomy. But if we followed Kant and maintained that Zarathustra must be taken as a god because the event of autonomy, the making of code, is necessarily beyond all ready-made codes, we would not have grasped the Nietzschean notion of the divine. For the divine is not achieved simply by creating a new law. Such a creator might well be a god, but that is not sufficient to make him divine. Indeed Zarathustra accuses the god, who created the human style of digestion, of lacking divinity:

> 'There is one God! You shall have no other gods before me!' – an old wrath-beard of a god, a jealous god, thus forgot himself: And all the gods laughed then and rocked in their chairs and cried: 'Is not precisely this godliness, that there are gods but no God?' (Z 'Of the Apostates' 2).

If we ask why the God, who refuses to recognise any other code but his own, forgets himself, the answer is because he has forgotten the *agon*. He has forgotten that originally he only threw this code to beat the other dice players. Whilst the game was played it did not really matter what he threw, so long as it was good enough to win the round. A god who celebrates divinity does not want to obliterate the other players, for that would be to destroy the game itself. The Nietzschean notion of divinity is the celebration of the contest between codes: it is the act of throwing against a god which is divine. It is not a specific set of clothes or a certain type of mask which endows the *deus ex machina* with divinity, but the fact that he or she ventured out onto the stage, in spite of the derision and incomprehension of the human audience. But if divinity is the act of playing *against* another god, then it is necessary that there are other gods. This is why the label 'Anti-humanism' is much too blunt to capture Zarathustra. It misses altogether the fact that Zarathustra does not dismiss his enemy as a mere epiphenomenon, as simply how things seem prior to a rigorous immanent critique. Rather Zarathustra respects the strength and bravery of his enemy; he makes thanks to the human code – 'My enemies too are part of my happiness' (Z 'The Child with the Mirror'). This is not because the human code was a stage on the way to himself, but because it provides him with a worthy opponent; indeed an opponent which, given the nature of an *agon*, might yet overcome Zarathustra.

Bibliography of cited works by Nietzsche

On the Genealogy of Morals (New York: Vintage Books, 1989, trans. W. Kaufmann)

The Birth of Tragedy (New York: Vintage Books, 1967, trans. W. Kaufmann)

The Will to Power (New York: Vintage Books, 1968, trans. R. J. Hollingdale and W. Kaufmann)

Thus Spoke Zarathustra, (Harmondsworth: Penguin, 1969, trans. R. J. Hollingdale).

Notes

1   This is the last section of Part III. Nietzsche's original intention was that this would close *Thus Spoke Zarathustra*. However, he came back to *Zarathustra* a year later resolving to compose a further four parts; of these he only produced one and this now comprises Part IV.

2   'Time is a child playing draughts', in J. Burnet, *Early Greek Philosophy* (London: Adam and Charles Black, 1908) Fragment 79, pp. 146–156. Elsewhere Nietzsche makes his debt to Heraclitus apparent: 'lucky throws in the dice game of Heraclitus' 'great child', be he called Zeus or chance' (GM II 16).

3   'The true 'purpose' of DNA is to survive, no more and no less. The simplest way to explain the surplus DNA is to suppose that it is a parasite, or at best a harmless but useless passenger, hitching a ride in the survival machines created by the other DNA.' R. Dawkins, *The Selfish Gene* (Oxford: Oxford University Press, 1989) p. 45.

4   Sophocles, *The Three Theban Plays* (Harmondsworth: Penguin, 1984, trans. by R. Fagles), p. 103.

5   Perhaps surprisingly Zarathustra directly thereafter asserts that this meaning should be 'a human meaning'! However, in the context in which this remark appears it is clear that the term 'human' is merely used to indicate that meaning is created rather than laid down by God for all time. Hence, in this context, the notion of human meaning is used to question the idea that meaning is simply a matter of immutable truth.

6   Heidegger, 'Who is Nietzsche's Zarathustra?' in *Nietzsche*, Volume Two (San Francisco: Harper and Row, 1984, trans. D.F. Krell) pp. 229–230.

7   It should be noted that Hollingdale translates the sentence such that 'impossibility' is written over the path behind Zarathustra. But literally the

last part of the sentence reads: 'and over it [*über ihm*] stands written: Impossibility.' The pronoun is ambiguous; it can be read, as I have rendered it above, as referring to Zarathustra's advancing foot.

8   'I am Zarathustra the godless' (Z 'Of the Virtue that Makes Small' 3).

Index